Tourism Imaginaries at the Disciplinary Crossroads

Imaginaries of place, destination, and travel are increasingly produced and consumed by diverse populations through expanding forms of media and opportunities for travel. Defined as the potential power of a place as a tourist destination, these spatial imaginaries are collaboratively produced and are a nexus of social practices through which individuals and groups intersect to establish a place as a credible destination. Bringing together an international team of scholars, this book provides a unique analysis of current multidisciplinary research on the complex relationships between tourism and the imaginaries of tourist destinations. Tracing the links between tourism imaginaries and their religious (heaven) and political (utopia) antecedents, the opening of the book follows the growth of the disciplines exploring this concept in tourism up to their present parallels and convergences. The substantive chapters are organised into three main thematic sections, the first explores the touristic production and consumption of place imaginaries, the second analyses the way places are practiced through imaginaries and the role imaginaries play in the tourist experience and the final section explores the way images and the media participate in the creation of tourism imaginaries.

Maria Gravari-Barbas is Professor of Geography at the University of Paris 1 Pantheon-Sorbonne. She is also in charge of the IREST (Institute of Research and Higher Studies on tourism) and EIREST (Interdisciplinary Research Group on Tourism Studies). She leads the UNESCO Chair "Culture, Tourism, Development" and coordinates the UNESCO UNITWIN network of the same name.

Nelson Graburn is Professor Emeritus of Anthropology at the University of California Berkeley. He is a founding member of the International Academy for the Study of Tourism, the Research Committee on Tourism (RC-50) of the International Sociological Association, and the Tourism Studies Working Group at U C Berkeley, and serves on the editorial board (for anthropology) of Annals of Tourism Research.

Tourism Imaginaries at the Disciplinary Crossroads

Places, Practices, Media

Edited by
Maria Gravari-Barbas
and
Nelson Graburn

LONDON AND NEW YORK

First published 2016
by Routledge
2 Park Square, Milton Park, Abingdon, Oxon OX14 4RN

and by Routledge
605 Third Avenue, New York, NY 10017

First issued in paperback 2021

Routledge is an imprint of the Taylor & Francis Group, an informa business

© 2016 Maria Gravari-Barbas and Nelson Graburn

British Library Cataloguing in Publication Data
A catalogue record for this book is available from the British Library

Library of Congress Cataloguing-in-Publication Data
A catalogue record for this book has been requested

ISBN 13: 978-1-03-224244-6 (pbk)
ISBN 13: 978-1-4724-2211-8 (hbk)
ISBN 13: 978-1-317-00946-7 (web PDF)
ISBN 13: 978-1-317-00945-0 (ePub)
ISBN 13: 978-1-317-00944-3 (mobi/kindle)

DOI: 10.4324/9781315550718

Typeset in Times New Roman
by Swales & Willis Ltd, Exeter, Devon, UK

Contents

Figures and Tables

Figures

Tables

Plates

Contributors

Saskia Cousin is a senior lecturer in anthropology at the Centre of Cultural Anthropology of Paris Descartes. She works on tourism and heritagization considered as signs of circulations of people, values, and knowledge. Her fieldwork focuses on tourists in the Loire Valley (France), tourism policies in the northern suburbs of Paris and voodoo heritage in south Benin. She also works on tourist digital footprints ("bigdata") with computer sciences researchers. Since 2005, she has led a research seminar and a broadcast network dedicated to the critical study of tourism. She serves on the editorial boards of espacestemps.net and *Mondes du Tourisme*.

Josep-Maria Garcia-Fuentes is an architect and lecturer in architecture at Newcastle University, School of Architecture, Planning and Landscape. He is also a fellow at the London School of Economics, Catalan Observatory, and was previously assistant professor and vice-dean at the School of Architecture of the Valles-Barcelona in the Universitat Politècnica de Catalunya-BarcelonaTECH, where he is an adjunct professor. He was the winner of Spain's National First Prize for University Graduates (2006) and his research has been funded by the "Caja de Arquitectos" (2005), the Universitat Politècnica de Catalunya (2006–2007), the Ministry of Science and Innovation of Spain (2007–2010), the Society of Architectural Historians and the Samuel H. Kress Foundation (2011). Josep-Maria is working on the publication of his Ph.D. dissertation on the construction of the modern Montserrat, and conducting research on architecture, preservation, museums, and heritage-making processes.

Alain Girard is a senior lecturer at the University of Perpignan Via Domitia, a teacher in the Department of Sociology and researcher at the Research Center on Mediterranean societies and environments (C.R.E.S.E.M. Team "Tourism"). A sociologist of tourism, his current research focuses on residential choices and post-touristic migrations, and the experiences of users of fair tourism products, their tourist "careers," and their civic commitment in general.

Nelson Graburn is a professor emeritus in the Department of Anthropology and Curator Emeritus of the Hearst Museum of Anthropology, at the University of California, Berkeley. He is a founding member of the International Academy for the Study of Tourism, the Research Committee on Tourism (RC-50) of the International Sociological Association, and the Tourism Studies Working Group, and serves on the editorial board of the *Annals of Tourism Research*, the *International Journal of Tourism Cities*, and the *Asian Journal of Tourism Research*.

Maria Gravari-Barbas is a professor of geography at the University of Paris 1 Pantheon-Sorbonne. She is also a director of IREST (Institute of Research and Higher Studies on Tourism) and EIREST (Interdisciplinary Research Group on Tourism Studies). She leads the UNESCO Chair "Culture, Tourism, Development" and coordinates the UNESCO UNITWIN network of the same name.

H. Hazel Hahn is a professor of history at Seattle University. She is the author of *Scenes of Parisian Modernity: Culture and Consumption in the Nineteenth Century* (2009) and a co-editor of *Architecturalized Asia: Mapping a Continent through History* (2013). Her research focuses on urban planning, urban history, and the planning of tourism in French Indochina, as well as on travel cultures examined through the popular press, travelogues, fiction, books on geography, and other cultural artifacts. She is also editing a book on cross-cultural exchange in Southeast Asia and Europe.

Julien Laverdure is a Ph.D. candidate in Sociology and Political Anthropology at IHEAL (Institute of Advanced Studies on Latin America, Paris III University—Sorbonne Nouvelle) and EHESS (School for Advanced Studies in the Social Sciences). He holds an M.A. in International Studies and Latin American Studies from IHEAL—Paris III. He conducts field research in Central America, mostly Costa Rica, focusing on the cultural entrepreneurs who construct ethnic tourism and crafts markets, and their social strategies in the context of neo-indigenism and the new economies of identity.

Iris Sheungting Lo received her Ph.D. from Hong Kong Polytechnic University and is now assistant professor in the School of Business Administration at the University of Macau. Her research interests are in the areas of tourism culture and everyday life performance. Currently she is exploring how self image shapes tourist photographic practices.

Bob McKercher has been an academic for more than 20 years and has been with the Hong Kong Polytechnic University for over 10 years. He has wide-ranging teaching and research interests. He has written two books, edited two others, and has authored or co-authored over 200 scholarly papers and reports.

Liz Montegary is assistant professor in the Department of Cultural Analysis and Theory at Stony Brook University. She is the co-editor, with Melissa Autumn White, of the collection *Mobile Desires: The Politics and Erotics of Mobility Justice* (2015), and she is currently completing a book manuscript on queer politics and family life in the United States.

Pascale Nédélec holds a Ph.D. in Geography (University of Lyon, France). As an urban geographer, she works at the crossroads of social and cultural geography. Her research focuses on innovative social and political appropriation dynamics and mobilizations in relation to the production of the city; as well as discourse analysis and urban representations, especially normative discourses on the urban experience and construction processes of urban imaginaries. Particularly interested in American cities, her dissertation demonstrated that Las Vegas is fundamentally hybrid; torn between exceptionalism—as a gaming destination— and urban banality.

Madina Regnault has a political science background and holds a Ph.D. in Social Anthropology from EHESS (Ecole des Hautes Etudes en Sciences Sociales, Paris). She was twice a Visiting Scholar at University of California, Berkeley, as part of the Tourism Studies Working Group. Employing a multidisciplinary approach, her dissertation analyzed the political and social issues of cultural tourism promotion in two French territories located in the Western Indian Ocean: Réunion Island and Mayotte Island. She is now a member of EIREST (University Paris 1—Panthéon Sorbonne).

Rita Ross is an anthropologist and folklorist who has studied the Acadians of the Canadian Maritimes and Louisiana since the 1980s. She taught for many years in the California State University system, and is recently retired from the position of Associate Director of the Canadian Studies Program at the University of California, Berkeley.

Clothilde Sabre is currently an invited researcher at the Center for Advanced Tourism Studies (Hokkaido University, Japan) and associate researcher at Clersé (University of Lille, France); she is also a member of the Contents Tourism Research Group, created in Japan (Hokkaido University). She holds a Ph.D. in Anthropology from the University of Lille 1, France. Her research focuses on tourism in Japan, understood as a consequence of Japanese pop culture's success in the West, especially in France. She is interested in exoticism, touristification, and cultural legitimization. She also teaches anthropology and sociology.

Bernard Schéou holds a Ph.D. in Economics and is a lecturer at the University of Perpignan Via Domitia, a teacher in the Institut d'Administration des Entreprises and researcher at Cresem. His current research focuses on hospitality networks such as CouchSurfing; the sense of the experience of the users of "fair tourism" products; influences on the social organization of different types of local tour operators (adventure, responsible, and mass); and the relationship of tourists to places.

Estelle Sohier received her Ph.D. in history from the University Paris 1 Panthéon-Sorbonne and the University l'Orientale of Naples. She is now a senior lecturer at the Department of Geography at the University of Geneva. Her current research focuses on the history of photography and geographical imagination between 1880 and 1930.

Raghuraman S. Trichur is a professor of cultural anthropology at Sacramento State University. Trichur has been conducting research in Goa, India since 1995 and recently published a book titled *Refiguring Goa* (2013). The book locates the development of tourism within the broader political economic transformations that inform the reproduction of the Goan society and its economy.

Luc Vacher is a senior lecturer in geography at the University of La Rochelle (France). He has published numerous articles on processes of touristification and participated with équipe MIT (Université de Paris 7) in the writing of *Tourisme 2, Moments de lieux*. His current research interests in the UMR 6250 LIENSs (Coast, Environment and Societies) CNRS-Université de La Rochelle focuses on touristic practices and the definition or redefinition of space in relation to these practices.

Philippe Viallon is a professor at the University of Strasbourg, France. With a Ph.D. in information science and communication, he was cultural attaché at the French Embassy in Berlin and a professor at the University of Geneva. He has also lectured extensively and written many articles on the image, the media, the intercultural aspect of communication, and on tourism.

Introduction

Tourism Imaginaries at the Disciplinary Crossroads

Nelson Graburn and Maria Gravari-Barbas

"When we grew up, imaginary was an adjective, not a noun!"

Those of us over fifty.

"We're going to PARIS this summer!" Paris: the Eiffel Tower, Notre Dame, cafés, perfumes, the Seine and its bridges with their love locks, French foods, wines and fashions . . . . Tourism imaginaries are the ideas that people have in their minds about places as tourist destinations. Tourism imaginaries are not the same for everyone—ideas about Paris would differ in the minds of American and German tourists, men and women, and very much so the elderly and teenagers. Tourism imaginaries would be particularly different from imaginaries of the same place in the minds of residents and local French people, and they would overlap in part and differ in some ways from those in the imaginations of visiting businessmen or government officials.

Tourism imaginaries change over time as historical events take place, and as tastes, lifestyles, and fashions change. These ideas—in our minds, as facts, fantasies, fictions, and desires—have many sources, including especially our families and friends. For famous places like Paris, tourism imaginaries are built upon what we learn as children, in history and geography lessons at school, and in books and movies, as well as through word of mouth and current news. Other more distant or more recent tourist attractions are more obviously "created," such as the Costa del Sol in Spain, the Algarve in Portugal, or Cancun in Mexico: these places have been purposely built as tourist attractions since World War II, and advertised by their developers and by regional and national governments as well as by airlines and other travel companies, using media such as newspapers and magazines, and more recently radio, television, and the Internet. These places now compete with the older tourist attractions using the same range of media, trying to become well known and to have their special characteristics and qualities find a place in peoples' minds.

Tourism imaginaries are features of modern human cultural systems that describe places that we might like to visit or worlds that we might like to inhabit. They share much with other human imaginaries, especially ideal places such as paradise or heaven. They contain features of value to prospective travelers, such as climate, adventure, relaxation, health, safety, good food and drink, cultural features such as music, dance, clothing, gardens, agriculture, architecture, style and language, and natural features such as landscape, seascapes, fauna and flora. Other human imaginaries relate to societies and communities, stressing for instance friendliness, equality, fairness, or lack of oppression or poverty, which are often features in political and even revolutionary models of society such as Plato's Republic or Moore's Utopia. This volume examines a number of different cases of tourism imaginary, as they are studied by the different modern disciplines of the social sciences. While they share some common features, the disciplines—anthropology, sociology and folklore for instance—differ from political science and cultural studies, or from history and geography in their emphases and foci. The ensemble therefore shows us a wide range of kinds of tourism imaginaries studied from a number of different angles, providing us with a multidisciplinary and complex picture.

Imaginaries of peoples, places, destinations, and travel are increasingly produced and consumed by diverse populations around the globe through expanding forms of media and opportunities for travel. As Urbain (2011) reminds us, the "desire for the World"[1] is neither spontaneous nor instinctive. For touristic systems, a range of players collaboratively produces these spatial imaginaries, defined as the potential power of place as a tourist destination (Amirou 1995). The tourist imaginary,[2] as a nexus of social practices through which individuals and groups intersect to establish a place as a credible destination, has yet to be fully defined and explored. Indeed is has been said that tourist imaginaries are as much about the mental "previews" of the travel experience as about the destination itself (Leung 2010).[3]

This volume's objective is to provide a comprehensive analysis of current disciplinary and multidisciplinary research on the multiplex relationships between tourism and the imaginaries. Close reading of the volume's chapters, each of which illustrates one or more social science approaches to the use of the imaginary, helps us to compare the conceptual development in the wide variety of disciplines contributing to the understanding and definition of tourism imaginaries: architecture, history, semantics, sociology, anthropology, folklore, geography, political science and cultural, visual, media, communication, urban, queer, literary, development and tourism studies.

Thus the book is a contribution to the "sociology of knowledge" as well as to the understanding of the construction of the fantasies and narratives, practices and policies of contemporary tourism. It teases out the convergences, the commonalities, and the remaining distinctiveness of these disciplinary analyses. This volume will be valuable not only to researchers working on different fields connected to this issue, but also to professionals of the tourism sector.

Tourism Imaginaries: A Range of Definitions

In the chapters of this book and in the extant literature on tourism, one may come across the following concepts related to the word "imaginary": abstraction, assemblage, brand, cliché, conception, creation, culture, construct, discourse, dream, ethos, fantasy, fiction, gaze, idea, identity, ideology, illusion, image, imagination, knowledge, legend, map, memories, mental life, messages, models, narratives, notions, patterns, perception, perspective, pictures, propaganda, publicity, reification, representation, schema, sentiment, stereotype, stories, symbols, visions, worldmaking, and so on.

These nouns, often in the plural, are usually qualified by one or more of the following adjectives: collective, cognitive, cosmopolitan, creative, cultural, fictional, fixed, individual, inherited, intangible, intercultural, interpretive, mental, personal, pictorial, real, representational, romantic, self-, shared, social, symbolic, unspoken, vicarious, visual, and so on. Allowing the application of just one adjective per noun would create over 1,000 terms—such as "collective memories," "shared knowledge," or "mental schemas"—though not all combinations are possible.

Why is there such a bewildering range of expressions related to our core topic? Imaginaries are intangibles, vague or specific mental concepts whose exact nature and boundaries are hard to nail down: commonly related to dreams, legends, or narratives, they are evanescent and permanent, representational and dynamic (Salazar 2010: 5–7). They are words and concepts that we don't normally have to "pin down," and in everyday speech we use them in different ways. Furthermore, imaginaries seem to connote unrealities, places that are elsewhere, that are not objectively defined or measured, key characteristics of tourism where the consumption by definition takes place "away from home" (Smith 1977; Thurot and Thurot 1983).

According to Bachelard, imaginaries represent a way of relating to space and matter that generates meaning, without strictly determining behaviors and configurations (Bachelard 1957, cited in Debarbieux 2003). They allow individuals and groups to imagine a place as a conceivable tourist destination; they create the desire, they render the place attractive, they help render travel plans concrete (by influencing both the selection of the place to be visited and the practices associated with undertaking the trip), they reduce the "distance" to the tourist destination, and they tame its exotic character (Staszak, 2008). They intervene not only when choosing the destination, but also, once there, directing, controlling, or avoiding certain practices. If they are negative, they contribute to the avoidance of certain destinations.

Tourist imaginaries thus facilitate the transition between here and elsewhere, the familiar and the exotic, the known and the unknown. They intervene decisively in travel planning. Without a tourist imaginary to select among the whole range of desirable, attractive, or challenging destinations, there can be no travel plans. The role of tourist imaginaries is thus essential, since the imaginaries allow concerned individuals to approach the tourist destination in its various dimensions, without getting physically and symbolically lost (Gravari-Barbas and Graburn 2012).

Roots and Precedents

In the core traditions of the Western world and maybe elsewhere too, one dominant imaginary was Heaven, a place we looked forward to knowing, whose characteristics and population were only "known" through cultural inheritance or supernatural visions, but a place that lacked good description because, unlike tourist destinations, people who went there were not expected to return.[4] Heaven was always imagined as an ideal and peaceful place, often conceived as a beautiful garden, a paradise—etymologically, a walled garden in the ancient Middle East (Picard 2011). Furthermore, psychologically, Heaven, like a tourist destination, was a place of escape and recuperation, a future destination promising a life bereft of the hardships and anxiety of the mundane life on Earth. Heaven also promised an "ideal" human society of equality and protection, frequently with many sensual rewards and the absence of privations.[5] The comparison between Heaven and tourism is therefore frequently found in tourism literature, both professional and academic (Matthey and Walter 2008). However, as Coëffé and Violier (2008) put it, "while most religious systems place paradise in an inaccessible 'beyond' in this world, tourism produces 'idéalités' generated by and for an earthly existence."

The Renaissance in Europe spawned a modernity which has since been both globalized and, in its spreading, differentiated. With the voyages of discovery, the advent of experimental sciences, and the Renaissance's challenge to previous world views, the intellectual classes began to focus more on the possibilities of a "heaven on earth," at least alleviation from the burdens of hunger, disease, and injustice (cf. Maffesoli 1997). An early imaginary "heaven on earth" was Sir Thomas Moore's *Utopia* (1516), an imaginary island in the Atlantic, of peace, abundance, and amity—a worthy forerunner to nineteenth- and twentieth-century Europe's island holiday destinations (Viard 2015)![6]

These idyllic, pristine, utopic, or imagined "places," that pre-existed tourism as a modern phenomenon, contributed to the creation of a globally diffused tourism imaginary of "elsewhere." Since the emergence of tourism, however, in the late eighteenth and early nineteenth centuries (Boyer 1996), tourism destinations were developed on the basis of multiple, differentiated, and segmented imaginaries that have largely transcended the "heaven" reference. What are the tourism imaginaries of the late twentieth and early twenty-first centuries? How are they produced and by whom? And how do the different disciplines approach this concept?

From Imaginary to Tourist Imaginary

In his *Modernity at Large*, Appadurai (1996) discusses the imagination as a social practice which he calls a social imaginary, essentially equated with sociologist Durkheim's "collective representations," as Cousin tells us (in this volume, see also Regnault, Sabre). Appadurai, in turn, credits his use of the concept of the imaginary to the American political scientist Benedict Anderson, who, in his book *Imagined Communities: Reflections on the Origins and Spread of Nationalism* (1983), stresses that modern political entities, such as nations and colonies, owe their imagined existence in the minds of their members to modern instruments of communication—such as newspapers, the radio, maps, censuses, widespread public education, and so on. Pre-modern communities' existence, on the other hand, was known via face-to-face encounters, word of mouth, and mythologies. This highlights a salient factor that Appadurai also invokes: contemporary social and cultural imaginaries are enhanced or even produced by modern media, especially daily and high-speed media such as daily papers, television, radio, and the Internet, much of which provides the central infrastructure for advertising, one of the main transmitters of tourist imaginaries.[7]

The association of the term "imaginary" with tourism and tourists was relatively rare until the present century (Salazar 2010: 5–15). Indeed the word does not even appear in the index of the definitive *Sage Handbook of Tourism Studies* (Jamal and Robinson 2009). Furthermore, the concept of "tourism imaginary" arrived fairly late in the social sciences. For instance, the late French sociologist Rachid Amirou wrote extensively about "*l'imaginaire touristique*" (1995; 2000) and he is often quoted as defining it as a set of ideas that allows a place to be imagined as a tourist destination (Bachimon and Dias 2012; see also Cousin, Regnault, Sabre, and Vacher, this volume).

For the contributors to this volume, tourism imaginaries are of this modern type rather than more general kinds of imaginaries such as dreams, fantasies, images, myths, narratives, stereotypes, and traditions. The construction of tourism imaginaries as part of a more general world view falls within Hollinshead's constructivist concept of "worldmaking" (2007), the ensemble of processes by which we continually experience (including learn about) and interpret the world as our lives progress (cf. Bruner 2005). Hollinshead reminds us that analysts of tourism engage in this just as much as the practitioners.

The Nature of Academic Disciplines and the Early Forms of Imaginaries

Before examining the application of different disciplinary approaches in the chapters that follow, let us briefly examine some aspects of the nature of academic disciplines and the early forms of imaginaries.

A discipline is a formal part of the intellectual infrastructure and superstructure of knowledge and education. Discipline entails being a disciple (a follower, a student of), learning in an *unequal* dyad. This implies the unquestioning following of a master (*magister*), such as the way art is taught in Japanese schools.

Academic disciplines have two aspects:

- An ordering of people (teachers, learners, administrators) in hierarchical learning institutions. These are known by their names and by their places (universities, laboratories) and their heritage, that is, founders, "ancestors," establishment in places, descendants (dyadic hierarchical pairs), national and international organizations, books and articles by name or by press/journal and associated folklore.
- Disciplines, shorn of their buildings, degrees, and books, are intellectual provinces based on the content of their knowledge, including:

  1 subject/object of study; these can be inanimate/animate, human/non-human (affects ethics of study), individual/mass, internal/micro, in time and space, archival, library, in vivo, or any combination of the above.

2   methods of study: individual cases, mass/statistical; instrumental, observational, comparative, involving inductive or deductive reasoning, inference, and aesthetics, with feedback loops (question and answer, confirmation by repetition and experiment). Many disciplines, especially the sciences, may have at any one historical period one or very few paradigms, which may be superseded (shifted) by new discoveries or understandings (Kuhn 1970). Kuhn claimed that social scientific disciplines rarely adhere to any one paradigm and witnessed constant disagreement about meanings.

Our present intellectual divisions descended from classical philosophy (the love of wisdom), the elite pursuit of knowledge about everything, natural, artificial (cultural), and spiritual or in the world. Pre-modern philosophy was based on thought, reflection, and observation, and was practiced by literati, including Christian clergy (Heilbron 1999). As universities opened in Western Europe in the eleventh century,[8] using Latin as the medium of instruction, subjects included theology, law, medicine, and the arts (skills). Modern Western disciplines grew out of these, loosened from their theological grip with events accelerating in the fourteenth century: the rediscovery of Aristotle's works and other classics, and Ptolemaic rediscoveries and Arabic sciences and medicine. Challenges to the geocentric Christian view were enlarged by the accounts of Marco Polo and Portuguese discoveries in Africa, and the North Atlantic, using a new kind of ship—the caravel—and the astrolabe.

The "discoveries" of North and South America, the Indies and Southeast Asia, and the Pacific opened the world for trade, conquests and sciences, providing revolutionary new imaginaries expressed in maps, globes, and travel narratives.

Further discoveries in archaeology and art history, joined by astronomy (Copernicus, Galileo) the Protestant reformation, nationalism and the printing press overcame static medieval and geocentric world views. This age of discovery presaged modern forms of tourism imaginaries, which involve exploration of geographical, climatic and ethnic alterities, historical interest in the past, and science fiction. In these few centuries, the imaginaries of the Western world[9] underwent irrevocable changes, setting in motion a never-ending series of inventions and innovative representations.

Most pursuits of knowledge, including the social sciences, bear the twin impulses of satisfying curiosity in apprehending and explaining phenomena, and using that knowledge to improve (parts of) the world, morally, medically, and economically. This has implications for the nature of imaginaries. Imaginaries can consist of explanatory schemes or ideas about the nature of phenomena, such as the relations between different human populations—human evolution would be one, a "natural" (God-given) order would be another—or the different climates and seasons—imagined through the tilting of the earth, and so on.

The nature of the modern disciplines, since their establishment by Renaissance intellectuals, has changed over time. We may summarize:

Natural philosophy emerged as the natural sciences (Bacon, Descartes) and split into:

a   the physical sciences: physics and chemistry became experimental while others like astronomy and geography remained observational but contributed to the imaginaries of modernity, and

b   the biological sciences and medicine, some of which became experimental. One branch became psychology—and included psychoanalysis—and contributed to the understanding of imaginaries, including tourism imaginaries. The biological sciences also gave birth to theories of evolution which in turn also contributed to the social sciences.

The core disciplines of classical philosophy continued within the social sciences. Machiavelli applied his philosophy to governance and "founded" political science, a branch of which, political economy, gave birth to economics (Adam Smith), another form of social imaginary. Sociology was founded in the same era as a positivist "science of society" (Condorcet, Comte) to both understand and hence regulate human society. Applying this economic sociology to Europe, Marx (and Engels 1884) produced a major historical (evolutionary) and ideological imaginary. Anthropology emerged as a comparative social science[10] using colonial and archaeological data; its descriptions of exotica laid the foundations for many sociocultural and touristic imaginaries. Folklore, the related comparative study of verbal and performance traditions, emerged in 1846 and contributed to imagined world views.

The arts and humanities, including theology and history, emerged as even less well defined disciplines. Fostered as central to scholarly knowledge by men of letters such as Erasmus and Montaigne, the humanities embraced philosophy, literature and languages, later comparative philology, the "high" arts[11] and art history, and architecture and architectural history. The persuasive powers of the humanities (rhetoric, literature, poetry, music, and song[12]) interact with more scientific rationales in both explaining and hence reforming the world. Many Renaissance intellectuals continued to be "multi-disciplinary" by our standards, combining, for instance, medicine, exploration, literary and political careers—and many were priests. Their persuasive powers depended on their collection of data, their imagination, their rhetorical skills, and their social and political connections and patronage.

After the original consolidation of university-based disciplines and departments in the late nineteenth century, the margins of these disciplines became more porous, and in the past three decades more research has been multidisciplinary in nature. This is because many disciplines are focusing on the same subject matter, for example tourism or imaginaries, and because some have become more "applied."

Furthermore, "qualitative methods" (cf. Denzin and Lincoln 2005) have increasingly penetrated many research disciplines, often being described as "ethnography"—in-depth, *in situ*, long-term participant observation—the key research method of socio-cultural anthropology.

Styles of argument have also shifted to more interpretive explanations—hermeneutics[13]—in many disciplines, for example in anthropology (Geertz 1973). Thus the anti-positivist disciplines encourage qualitative as opposed to quantitative methods. Hermeneutic methods are very important to the social science of the imaginaries, to semiotic approaches (Roland Barthes), the study of signs and symbols which underlies much modern linguistics, and its application to modern media by the Frankfurt School. Hermeneutic methods also underlie constructivist approaches to the study of meaning. These approaches claim that meaning depends on the context and the situated subject, as opposed to assuming there is an underlying "objective" reality independent of the observer. German sociologist Weber (1904/1949: 72–82) warned in his theory of value-relations (*wertbezeihung*) that humans are embedded in value-webs (*werturteil*) *as are social scientists* who must, however, analyze value-laden human society in a *value-free* way!

Constructivism can lead to the demonstration of "multiple realities," for example what a scientist vs. a sailor vs. a child may "think of" the rolling of a ship on a stormy sea. The constructivist approach has also been applied to socio-political analyses, for instance the Marxian view that the exploited classes are unable to see the true cause of their oppression by capitalism. They were said to be blinded by the dominant ideology which prevented them from rebelling, in the same way as feminism has claimed that (middle-class) women were "brainwashed" to see their proper place as in the home. This cultural power of the ruling class (*hegemony*, Gramsci 1971) created a world view that a people's place was natural or inevitable. Caton (2014), following Weber's *wertbezeihung* (1949), has shown that such political explanations of people's world views are constructivist: intellectuals believe that there are two sets of meanings, the hegemonic one internalized by the oppressed, which is shown to be wrong, and the analyst's interpretation which s/he believes to be correct and which could reveal the "truth" and lead to revolutionary change; in the more apolitical use of constructivism the analyst believes that there are multiple world views, but that all of them are "true" depending on the subject's sociocultural situation. We see, therefore, that constructivism is a key to understanding imaginaries and that whole industries—the media, advertising, politicking, education, religion, economic relations, the law, and so on—are in the business of constructing world views which underlie people's thoughts and actions, and that these "culture makers" often try to benefit from their actions.

Tourism as a Transdisciplinary Field of Research

In Graburn and Jafari's (1990) assessments of disciplinarity in the social science of tourism, they asked the two editors of each of 10 social science disciplines to present chapters which spelled out how their discipline entered the study of tourism and what progress had been made in which aspects of the broad field. Overall, they concluded that overlap was apparent from "adjacent" disciplines, especially when focusing on the same research topic, for instance geographers and anthropologists studying pilgrimage (cf. Echtner and Jamal 1997). As the world gets "smaller," disciplines have come to share common research targets— for instance, the isolated peoples that anthropologists used to study are now part of the global system. Originally anthropologists would study cultures and peoples using their own ethnographic methods. The study of tourism now is more like the study of, for instance, health care, where no one discipline has a priority. Graburn and Jafari (1990) found the greatest disciplinary "gap" appeared between the qualitative and quantitative social sciences, a gap which an adventurous French research team (Chareyron, Da-Rugna, Cousin and Jacquot, 2014) is attempting to bridge. Another chasm Graburn and Jafari found existed between English and non-English language researchers, where the former rarely read, cited, or used the methods of the latter, though this was not so true in reverse: most European non-English speakers knew and cited the English-language literature.[14] While these findings remain for the most part true, the current volume, organized by American and French institutions, illuminates how much progress has been made in the important field of tourist imaginaries.

In assessing the progress of interdisciplinary[15] tourism research, Graburn (2009; 2011) traced the emergence of a diminishing sense of disciplinarity in his teaching and research in the two prior decades. Having taught an undergraduate course "Anthropology of Tourism" since 1976 (Graburn 1980) and a graduate seminar "Tourism, Art and Modernity" since 1977, it was not until the early 1990s that he became aware that without conscious aim or anxiety, works and theories were discussed and read without stopping to think whether they are anthropological, sociological, psychological, or cultural studies.[16] The seminar was always attended by graduate students from many disciplines, particularly architecture, comparative literature, and ethnic studies. Commenting on this growing interdisciplinarity, Tribe has asserted (1997: 651) that it is at the inter-section of the disciplines "where tourism knowledge is created,"[17] and continues to maintain (2009) that "It is disciplines that provide well-established well-tested ways of knowing and an organized academic community for peer review of new knowledge claims."

This book aims at "the disciplinary crossroads," and as expected we find few chapters that are purely confined to one discipline. For instance, Lo and McKercher see their "Beyond Imaginary of Place: Performing, Imagining, and Deceiving Self through Online Tourist Photography" (Chapter 13) as "reflexive, dramaturgical and ethnographic," suggesting it draws on at least sociology, performance theory, and anthropology. Yet, they cite Baerenholdt, Barth, Foucault, Lacan, Larson, Leung, Robinson and Picard, Salazar and Urry, suggesting involvement with geography, cultural studies, visual studies, psychoanalysis, sociology, Asian studies, anthropology, and mobility studies, and possibly philosophy! Moreover, as Tribe (1997) would suggest, this chapter produces highly original insights about tourism. This does not, however, mean an indiscriminate mixing of eclectic theories and methods or, as Sayer (1999) put it, "promiscuous postdisciplinarity." In another context, Porfyriou (2015: 126) notes that Chio's (2014) ethnography of ethnic tourism (in China) is relevant to various "disciplinary backgrounds (anthropology, ethnography, geography, history, economics, architecture, cultural studies, heritage conser-vation, sociology, politics, etc.) to integrate the two major characteristics of tourism—which she identifies as visuality and mobility."

Disciplinary Approaches, and Imaginaries as Transdisciplinary Concepts

Cultural Studies

Cultural studies most closely continues the wide-ranging philosophical and political traditions of the pre/non-academic era. Cultural studies is an "umbrella term," covering a broad range of social sciences, concerned with popular culture in contemporary capitalist societies; as such many essays on tourism, which is a widespread modern bourgeois phenomenon, and tourism imaginaries fall within its scope. Though few authors refer to cultural studies by name, many are influenced by its aims and precepts—they are constructivist and aim for a critical political correctness in revealing cultural hegemonies or manipulation.

Cultural studies is essentially derived from a Marxian imaginary. It rests upon three related critical traditions: the twentieth-century Frankfurt School of cultural theory of Horkheimer and Adorno (1947/2002), Habermas, Benjamin, and others; the semiotics of representation (Barthes 1957/1987; Eco 1962/1968); and the ideas of hegemony—the imposed or manipulated assent of the oppressed or the governed (Gramsci 1971; see also Cousin, this volume, Chapter 1). Like Marxism it focuses on the loci and disposition of power but, unlike Marxist attention to control of the means of production in the sense of crafts and factories, it focuses on the control of the production of culture, that is, literature and modern media, including tourism imaginaries, and the disposition of these cultural productions to control the ideas and news that the mass society receives. One can see that the commercialization of leisure and the massive use of advertising in promoting tourism and destinations provides key arenas for analysis. Rather than a violent revolution as the means of redress for the imbalance of power, critical cultural theory shows that the very awareness of cultural manipulation is a remedy and that further education, strong unions, and the power of intellectuals is the path to a fairer society. One focus of Hall's work (1973) was the assertion that the cultural productions of mass media stripped creativity and imagination from their audiences in feeding them homogenized inauthentic products, much as MacCannell (1973; 1976) claimed that tourists were usually presented with staged authenticity at tourist sites.

Although cultural studies as such was not named[18] until the foundation of the famous eponymous school in Birmingham (Hall and Walton 1972), the political aims and methods of cultural studies have become widespread in many intellectual pursuits and have influenced many disciplines in the humanities or social sciences. Many of the discipline's works are directly related to tourist imaginaries even though they aim to expose more fundamental cultural-political principles. For instance Williams's *The Country and the City* (1973) exposed the long-held pastoral view of the British countryside as a "a myth functioning as a memory"; recently Lina Tegtmeyer (2016) invented the term "tourism ruinscape" in her examination of the contemporary fascination with slums and urban blight in North America.

In an evolution away from strict Marxism, cultural studies embraces modern political movements that go beyond class conflict and the control of the means of production, to work for many other human predicaments where particular socio-cultural groups are oppressed by others. These post-Marxist struggles have been called New Social Movements (Buechler 1995; Escobar and Alvarez 1992); they are often more diffuse than traditional union and political party movements and even global; but they make massive use of the Internet and social media.

These post-colonial, post-class struggles include movements involving gender and feminist studies (Butler 1990), LGBT (for example Montegary, Chapter 10, on lesbian and gay family holidays), the disabled, children's, seniors', and animals' rights, as well as environmental, peace, and anti-nuclear movements. Especially prominent in the last half century have been movements concerning the inequality of racial and ethnic groups, commonly called civil rights movements (these often involve economic redress). In the field of tourism imaginaries, this would involve empowerment by peoples wanting to control their own image (see Ross, Chapter 5, on Canadian Acadians; Regnault, Chapter 6, on non-white peoples of the French island of Mayotte in the Indian Ocean; and Trichur, Chapter 2, on post-colonial Goa. Closely related are concerns with the fair treatment of visited tribal groups (Girard and Schéou, Chapter 7, on West Africa) and the cultural authenticity of tourist arts (Graburn 1976; Laverdure, Chapter 8, on Costa Rica).

Closely related branches of cultural studies, Orientalism (Said 1978), postcolonial studies, and subaltern studies attempt to express and analyze a world view of the weak and the exploited—indeed the governed—during and after colonialism. Such disciplines are relevant because the major growth of international tourism itself took place on the heels of the retreat of imperialist colonialism.[19] Nash (1977) pointed out that tourism is "a form of imperialism" in the sense that most tourism to the Third World was advised, owned, and run by people and institutions of the former imperial power, and that the tourists, usually from former imperial countries, carried with them imaginaries based on those of the former colonizers. Cazes (1989) later also highlighted the tension between the imaginaries of Western tourists visiting the South and the lack of tourism imaginaries of their hosts. This theme of tourism as post-colonialism is common (Hall and Tucker 2004; Tucker and Akama 2009) and indeed the North-South division of the world stems from the old colonial structures and continues economic and cultural domination, even while enmeshing the dependent new nations in the global system. Anthropologist Ahmad (2011) has made a good case for the persistence of the "colonial imaginary" among contemporary tourists to Kashmir in India/Pakistan. Staszak (2008; 2012) goes further by pertinently juxtaposing the colonialist imaginary with *the exoticization and eroticization* of (tourist) places.

Visual Cultural Studies and Media Studies

Visual cultural studies and media studies—closely related sub-disciplines—examine visual production and consumption; attention in these disciplines is paid to the possible emergence of hegemony, at the national, ethnic, gender, or local levels.

One study in this realm, *Visual Culture and Tourism* (Crouch and Lübbren 2003), relates tourist imaginaries to the history and changes in arts and visual culture by drawing on postcards, paintings, museums, photography, and television, as well feedback from tourists on their experiences as consumers, and image makers.

Film tourism and its precursor literary tourism (Watson 2006; Hoppen, Brown and Fyall 2014) are powerful factors in the formation of a number of kinds of imaginaries (Beeton 2005; Connell 2012; Tzanelli 2007): "author tourism," where interest focuses on the creator of the work, can also center on directors, producers, and even actors in visual media. Two kinds of "place imaginaries" can be discerned in this branch of tourism, the first being fictional, where a society and/or a landscape is imagined by the "author" and presented in writing and/ or audio-visually, and the second, somewhat overlapping,[20] "real landscapes and communities" which are the settings for fictional or real/historical narratives. Rea (2000) has shown how young Japanese, especially women, make pilgrimages to Prince Edward Island, Canada, to find the fictional village and land of *Anne of Green Gables* (1908), which they found in the preserved and staged house of the deceased author Lucy Maud Montgomery. An *anime* (animated cartoon) TV series *Akage no An* (Red Haired Anne) (1979) boosted the numbers of young tourists. Sabre (Chapter 9) shows how Japanese animated films, embracing much of the wider field of Japanese popular culture, are a major source of imaginaries for young Europeans, in creating a semi-fictional and fantastical Japan. Ever since the 1950s the media and touristic allure of Japan's fantasy imagination has led the world (cf. Vaquer 2009).

Governments and industry everywhere have, since the nineteenth century, been conscious of the advantageous links with fiction, and increasingly film tourism or TV-series tourism (Pleven 2013). Some places, via product-placement tactics such as serving as venues for media narratives, even attempt to be seen as iconic or symbolic, often paying millions of dollars to serve as the set for a film whose story might actually take place in a foreign country! Choe (2016) describes the complicated negotiations entered into by bi- or tri-national companies, film and TV casts, fictional narratives, and intended audiences for these lucrative productions, especially in East Asia. This goes to the heart of the creation of tourist imaginaries through various forms of advertising and mass media (see, for example, Nédélec, Chapter 4, on Las Vegas; and Viallon, Chapter 14, on metropolitan city websites).

Relating our case studies to cultural studies does not exhaust our understanding of social science disciplines and research on imaginaries. Cultural studies is eclectic in the various research methods and data gathering it encompasses, using everything from searching archives, to manipulating statistics, watching television, and critiquing public debates. Cousin (Chapter 1) suggests its most specific methods are semiotic, for both verbal/textual and visual analyses (see Laverdure, Chapter 8; and Hahn, Chapter 15). Thomas (1999) claims that as cultural studies has spread globally, especially post-colonial and subaltern studies, since the demise of the original British core, authors have tended to use a formulaic framework revolving around the hegemonic and the exploited, into which they fit most power-sensitive case studies. Here, we briefly examine our cases in relation to other more "traditional" social science disciplines, with their specific research methodologies

History

Many of the contributions to this volume involve history in the sense that they study changes in communities large and small over time. Cousin (Chapter 1) asserts that it was scholars of history who legitimated the use and usefulness of the concept of imaginaries, citing particularly Anderson's (1983) "imagined communities" (see "Political Science," below). Thus the study of history can be said to produce imaginaries—indeed history itself can be considered an imaginary. Pierre Nora (1984; 1989), for example, has suggested that whereas memory was a personal, locally shared, and constantly evolving community imaginary, history was an authoritative imaginary, which strove to be "rational" and to substantiate official truths. Similarly, Said (1978) focused on the Orientalist imaginary of the Western colonial world to describe it as consisting of a set of projections of (self-) superiority versus the inferiority of "the Other," a geo-political trope which still underpins many contemporary touristic imaginaries. In this regard anthropology and history clearly intersect in colonial studies.

The historical imaginary also underpins the touristic in following diachronic trajectories such as "development" (M'bayo 2013). Trichur's account of the political and touristic history of Goa (Chapter 2) reveals the emergence of a number of imaginaries: the foreign touristic imaginary of the former Portuguese colony, the changing self-imaginaries of the different segments of the population—for example the Catholics—and India's own nationalist struggle to situate the colony it had swallowed. Ross's examination of a literary folkloric imaginary of an oppressed and displaced minority, the Arcadians of the Canadian Maritimes (Chapter 5), reveals how agents of the tourism industry and descendants of the cultural enclave have built up imaginaries both to swell tourism and to preserve their threatened ethnic identity. Montegary's history of the emergence of a "gay family" touristic identity in Provincetown (Chapter 10), Vacher's tracing of the appearance of the touristic trope of azure tropical waters following scientific advancements in color reproduction (Chapter 11), and Hahn's discussion of the turn of the twentieth-century literary trope of transportation catastrophes as illustrating France's imaginary divide between technological progress and natural and cultural risks of traveling (Chapter 15), all display aspects of forms of historical imaginaries. These case studies demonstrate the commonplace disciplinary intersections between history and anthropology (Trichur), folklore (Ross), critical gender studies—part of cultural studies—(Montegary), history of science (Vacher), and literary and visual studies (Hahn).

Another aspect of "historical" imaginaries powerfully related to tourism is "science fiction"—often situated in the past or the future—forms of "elsewhere" that are germane to the MacCannellesque "search for authenticity." Museums, for example, are venues for scientific imaginaries of all kinds, and are key nodes and tourist trajectories (Graburn 1998). Science fiction books, journals, films, and broadcast programs are also sources of imaginaries, which impel tourists to travel to geographical venues, such as the looming Devils Tower, Wyoming which appeared in Steven Spielberg's *Close Encounters of the Third Kind* (1977). Romanian historian Boia has explored a larger field of science fiction and mythology in his *Pour un histoire de l'imaginaire* (1998).

Political Science

Political science is closely related to cultural studies, with which it shares foci on social structures and power, but it is broader in scope, embracing other social formations such as feudalism and socialism, and much greater in historical depth—though it lacks a Marxist base and the direct relation of research to political action. Political imaginaries, such as Plato's *Republic*, Hobbes *Leviathan*, Machiavelli's *Prince*, Locke's *Government* or even Rousseau's *Social Contract* were all social imaginaries, based on traditional scholarship and reason, proposing a society as an improvement on the *status quo* (Baker 1990; Steger 2008).

Benedict Anderson revealed a specifically modern form of political imaginary in *Imagined Communities* (1983), showing how the concept of the nation, as a techno-bureaucratic polity rather than a feudal structure or charismatic religious sect (Weber 1922/1978) or a stateless ethnic community, was enabled by modern technical and organizational features such as maps, censuses, secular education, public museums, newspapers, magazines, and so on. It is these very instruments, plus photography, the media and the Internet, which constitute the bases for the spread of modern tourist imaginaries. In a sense today's tourists are heirs to such enabled modern imaginaries, and the ability to imagine or foresee their relationships—whether due to alterity or similarity—to members of host communities rests upon the same instruments, plus the traditional and common human "word of mouth."[21] We are all heirs to the knowledge and scholarship of the modern world, in which widespread imaginaries play a major role in tourist choices. A prime example of such modern instruments is *National Geographic*, which through travel and photography has sparked desires for travel to places selected as exotic, beautiful, and attainable (Lutz and Collins 1993); Vacher (Chapter 11) shows how *National Geographic* published the first underwater photos of fish, generating greater interest in tourism to Florida and similar destinations. In a more provocative study, Mathers (2011) shows how American foreign policy towards Africa as a continent in need of "saving" has impelled a steady stream of American tourists, travelers and Peace Corps members to feel good about themselves by helping Africans, or even "adopting" African children.

Geography

Geography is a discipline central to tourism studies; this volume's co-editor, Gravari-Barbas, and contributors Nédélec, Vacher, and Sohier are all geographers who make use of the geographical imaginary. Cousin (Chapter 1) states that this discipline invented the "spatial imaginary." Until the late twentieth century the geographical imagination was conceived as the many well-known imaginative products of the geographer's profession: maps, spheres, longitude, latitude, the equator, the Arctic, and so on. Vacher (Chapter 11) cites the geographical imaginary of "tropical waters" and, one might add, the Tropics themselves. In the past two decades geographers have begun, reflexively, to rethink the output of their imaginations, especially in terms of the moral and political implications (Proctor 1998). Others have taken the geographical imaginary as a more totalizing concept akin to and perhaps even underlying tourist imaginaries (Collignon and Staszak 2009; Hoida 2007).

Gieseking (2007) suggests that the concept of the geographical imagination developed from Mills' (1959) "sociological imagination." Coined by Harvey (1973), the geographical imagination, building on the sociological imagination, was seen as a tool to reveal similarities and differences across spaces and times in order to fight various forms of oppression. The geographical imagination had grown substantially by the time Gregory (1994) defined it as the spatialized cultural and historical knowledge that characterizes social groups. The continuing importance of the imagination in contemporary geographical research is signaled by the expansive book *Travel and Imagination* (Lean, Staiff and Waterton 2014), which illustrates the multi-faceted relationship between the imagination and travel, throughout history and in all forms of representation and the media. The authors of that study assert that the imagination, the mental link producing imaginaries, blurs the boundaries between our everyday lives and the idea of travel. Any spatialized conception represented on maps or in guides could be a form of touristic geographical imaginary, for example parks (Grenier 2012). In *L'imaginaire géographique*, Bedard, Augustin and Desnoilles have gone further to show the special relationship between place and feelings typical of tourists on vacation: "par leurs effets euphorisants, les lieux touristiques procurant ainsi, bien au-delà du sensationnel, un puissant surplus existential 'ou il me plait de l'être'" [through their euphoric effects, touristic places provide, far beyond mere sensation, a powerful existential surplus "where I like it to be."] (2012: 189).

Staszak and Debarbieux were among the first to use the concept of geographical imaginary (compared to "geographical imagination" used by Massey 2006; Harvey 2005; Gregory 2004). Staszak (2012) defines it thus:

> The geographical imaginary is formed by all the representations that make sense, separately and in system, for a group or an individual, making his world comprehensible, understandable and practicable . . . . A group can hold its existence of his geographical imaginary, particularly if it is linked to a territory. But if the geographical imaginary is involved in the construction of identity, it is necessarily, and in the same movement, in the construction of otherness—the endogroup defining itself as opposed to an *exogroup*.

The importance of this definition for tourism is obvious, a geographical imaginary is produced also in reference to others, elsewhere.

Sohier (Chapter 12) takes the concept of geographical imaginaries even further. She uses historical archival and visual cultural methods to show that for Europeans Greece has had a strong geographical and cultural imaginary for millennia, images that have changed throughout history with dramatic breaks at the exit from the Ottoman Empire and then the "divorce" from modern Turkey in 1929. She shows how Boissonnas' photography played a large part in the formation of the touristic imaginary of twentieth-century Greece and how it was used to reconstruct an aesthetically powerful image of Greece—at a time of political and economic weakness—that underlies the tourist imaginary today.

Sociology

Sociology is the prime discipline for the examination of recent and contemporary Western societies, especially class structures and urban areas (and rural areas in relation to towns and cities). It emerged from the classic treatises of pre- and early-modern social sciences to become a research-oriented social science in the service of the rational improvement of society. Like Anderson's work (1983) on the emergence of nationhood, sociology used the modern instruments of censuses, surveys, archival and textual research to examine contemporary societies, while some practitioners, such as Marx, Engels, Weber, and Durkheim, produced more synthetic ambitious works about human society in general. The political and applied aspects of tourism imaginaries are of concern not only to the inherently political cultural studies but also for many activist sociologists (and anthropologists, see below), whose analyses may point to remedial measures (Drew 2011).

Cousin (Chapter 1) shows that French philosophers Ricoeur (1984) and Castoriadis (1975) have pursued a number of important approaches to the concept of *social* imaginaries, trying to relate them in various ways to individual and collective "world views," though they had little direct effect on the conception of tourist imaginaries until the late twentieth century. This last conception, of tourist imaginaries, was more influenced by the Gilbert Durand and Julian Freund concept of imaginaries, seen as primary archetypes (Maffesoli 1997; Urbain 1991; 2011; Amirou 1995; 2000).

In another strand of sociology, Mills (1959) proposed a critique of empiricism, suggesting that "imagination" connected the self and society. He also suggested that the sociologist's imagination should be used to undertake a critique of society, as later taken up by cultural studies and critical theory (see above).

The sociological imaginary has also been applied to the way individuals see (imagine) their own society, including their tourist imaginaries and experiences (Dann and Cohen 1991). Different world cultural provinces produce different variations of social imaginaries; for instance Latin American scholars have produced a distinctive set of post-colonial imaginaries including "Turismo e imaginarios" (Sáinz and García 2014). This scholarly tradition focuses on the special nature of the growing cities of Latin America (Silva 2007) which are featured in their literature, mass media, and tourist imaginaries.[22]

One of the most important approaches to the study of tourism has been that of American sociologist MacCannell (1976) who, following the dramaturgical model of his mentor, Goffman (1959), used his imagination in likening the touristic situation to a play, with the performance on stage being constructed for the viewing audience, the tourists, as opposed to the back stage where the strings are pulled, the inventory is stored, and the infrastructural decisions are made. MacCannell posits that modern tourists are alienated from their everyday life and are in search of their imaginary of a more authentic world to be found elsewhere, in history, in nature, or in the less artificial lives of people in other cultures. He further proposes that under the "industrial" conditions of the modern tourism industry, the entrepreneurs understand this fact and present touristic experiences which pretend to be "authentic," which MacCannell called "staged authenticity."

Laverdure (Chapter 8) follows Castoriadis' view of imaginaries (1989) as "creative" in that they enable people to imagine collectivities. In examining the invention of archaic souvenir arts in Costa Rica, he sees both the touristic imaginary at work in creating a destination image and the national imaginary, in creating a compatible self-image. Girard and Schéou (Chapter 7) take a similar approach in analyzing whether the imaginary used in "fair tourism" differs from that employed in mass tourism. Other contemporary sociologists have applied the sociological imaginary to the study of the disabled as tourists (Hughes 2009) and the study of the dreams of *heimat* tourists (Pitchford 2008).

Folklore

Folklore is the source of many images and beliefs about the contemporary world, some of which are publicized and commercialized as key media icons and tourist attractions by countries such as Scotland, regions such as Lapland, companies such as Disney, or towns and villages such as Tono, Japan (Ivy 1995). In the nineteenth century, the term folklore originally comprised the "lore"—that is, beliefs, stories, myths, and characters—of the non-literate (the "folk") people of Europe—as opposed to the literate, educated classes—and of the rest of the world. Very soon it became closely associated with other "traditional" practices, such as rituals, (folk) arts and crafts, (folk) dances and other performances belonging to defined populations. By the end of the twentieth century, it was extended to the "lore" of *any* (self-)defined group in all societies, especially the oral traditions and behavior of otherwise educated peoples—for example, drinking songs, office rumors, colleges mascots and traditions, Valley girls/talk (from the San Fernando Valley of Los Angeles), Japanese beliefs about their cultural and biological uniqueness, and so on. In other words folklore is very closely identified with, and forms the basis of, stimulated imaginaries. And if any of these are put to use as identifiers or constituents of tourist destinations by word of mouth, by circulation in brochures, guides books, or on the Internet, by on and off site advertising or by plays, costumes, characters, or even copies (simulacra, see cultural studies), then they constitute tourist imaginaries.[23] Music is one of the most powerful folk expressions and carries imaginaries of places and experiences which empower and direct today's youth (Powell 1988).

Ross's chapter (Chapter 5) uncovers some of the paradoxes of the relationship between folklore and tourist imaginaries. The narrative poem *Evangeline: A Tale of Acadie* by the American poet Henry Wadsworth Longfellow (1847) is based on the real historical event of the deportation of the Acadians by the British from their Nova Scotia homeland in 1755, an event known in French as *Le Grand Dérangement*. It tells of a fictional betrothed couple, Evangeline and Gabriel, in the real Nova Scotia village of Grand-Pré, who are separated on the eve of their wedding, also the eve of the deportation (to the Southern United States). The poem begins by describing the idyllic life of the Acadians in Grand-Pré and the events leading up to the deportation. Later Evangeline searches tirelessly for her fiancé, and after many years, the pair are reunited at his deathbed.

Tourist attractions, products, and advertising based on this story are found both in Nova Scotia and in Louisiana. The expulsion, diaspora, and return of the Acadians are true but the characters are fictional. While the story is American, its characters are Francophone "peasants" (one might say "folkloric") who personify the tragedy and heroism of the group. Thus the story has become internalized as part of the culture (the folklore) of not only the Acadians but also the outsider (often Anglophone, American) tourists, and entrepreneurs—shops, travel companies, media, and regions cater to these beliefs and keep them alive. Furthermore, like "real" folklore, the stories have been modified over time and differ between places, for example in Nova Scotia and Louisiana.

The crucial links between folklore in the broadest sense and tourist imaginaries are illustrated in many of our other chapters. Anthropologist Sabre (Chapter 9) examines French tourists who visit Japan to see (the land of) characteristically Japanese folkloric creations of *manga* (cartoons) and *anime* (animated cartoons, as film or video). Rather like Longfellow's *Evangeline*, anime stories are fictional or based loosely on traditional Japanese folklore or historical characters. Architect Garcia-Fuentes (Chapter 3) shows how the folklore of the contemporary powers of Barcelona concerning the dragon figures in Gaudí's imaginative creations denies and subverts their original nature as intended by Gaudí himself. And geographer Nédélec (Chapter 4) examines the extraordinary situation whereby the commercially invented folklore concerning Las Vegas that states "What happens in Vegas stays in Vegas" has persuaded many social scientists into believing and promulgating the myths instead of the inconvenient truths.

History of Architecture

Architecture is itself an inherently creative endeavor, and one could consider architects' productions, both realized and imagined, to be among humanity's most extraordinary imaginaries. The works of Gaudí, the subject of Garcia-Fuentes contribution (Chapter 3), the presence of "follies" in the European countryside, illustrated books such as *Mondes Imaginaires* (Maizels and Von Schaewen 1999), and the cityscapes dreamed up by Frank Lloyd Wright in *The Living City* (1958) show us the enormity of architecture as cultural imaginary.[24]

The discipline of the history of architecture, to which Chapter 3 belongs, shows us the development of man's visual and spatial imagination restrained only, and barely, by technological invention, political feasibility, and financial resources. This discipline draws on the methods of visual studies and recording, archival research and sometimes fieldwork involving interviews with architects and builders, as well as the qualitative (and occasionally quantitative) studies of the publics who view and use the architecture. Garcia-Fuentes focuses on the dialectics of Catalan political and religious history, including symbolic interpretation, and is sensitive to cultural and political changes in a way that is closer to the mainstream discipline of history than to the critical underpinnings of cultural studies.

Anthropology

A plurality of the contributors to this volume were trained as anthropologists—Cousin, Graburn, Regnault, Ross, Sabre, and Trichur. However, it is only recently that anthropologists, and mainly American ones at that, have taken up the use of the concept of "imaginary," replacing perhaps, culture, cultural schemes, or collective ideologies. Strauss, in her introduction to the anthropological use of "imaginary," parallels Cousin in focusing on

> ... the key contributions of Cornelius Castoriadis, Jacques Lacan, and Benedict Anderson, as well as Charles Taylor's application of Anderson's ideas ... for Castoriadis, the imaginary is a culture's ethos; for Lacan, it is a fantasy; for Anderson and Taylor, it is a cultural model (i.e. a learned, widely shared implicit cognitive schema). (2006: 322–323)

Strauss, a cognitive psychological anthropologist, is particularly sensitive to the contentious matter of individual versus collective imaginaries.

In *The Critical Turn in Tourism Studies*, Irina Ateljevic et al. (2007) claimed their research method relied on ethnography/interpretive—and not quantitative/positivist—approaches. However, there are two kinds of ethnography: anthropological ethnography, which wants to know the "whole person," that is, their family, their home/work lives and so on, and sociological ethnography, which consists of interviewing people in a limited setting—café, pub, work, home—only knowing that part of the person. Nonetheless, either kind of ethnography allows for further questioning or following up an answer—enabling more layered or complex understandings than surveys and questionnaires if used alone.

However, because of the nature of tourism and the mobile world, even anthropologists are often forced to do "quick and dirty" (short-term) fieldwork (as explained at length in Graburn 2002), so—with limited fieldwork and a critical stance—anthropology can begin to look a little like cultural studies—as can geography and sociology. This partly explains the contemporary disciplinary convergence and "apparent" interdisciplinarity.

Anthropological and other studies of Western (European and North American) tourists' imaginaries of non-Western people and destinations have often made the same discoveries (Graburn and Gravari-Barbas 2011; see also Salazar and Graburn 2014). One common feature uncovered by these different disciplines is imagining that "the Other" is in and of "the Past," as implied or explicit evolutionary forbears, such as "Stone Age" "primitives" (Fabian 1983). Fabian has accused anthropologists of fomenting this viewpoint, but as Salazar (2009; 2010) has shown, the tourism industry, guides, guidebooks, and publicity invariably follow "old" anthropology[25] in trying to convey imaginaries which associate the "Other" with the past.[26] These imaginaries may be positive or negative, but most likely invoke familiar ambivalences: love/hate, fear/attraction, or noble/savage. For instance, Girard and Schéou (Chapter 7) recount that "fair tourism" organizations promising authentic encounters for Europeans visiting contemporary West Africa insinuate that rural African people stand outside of time and history. In regard to this phenomenon sociologist Erik Cohen has discussed (1993) the difference between ethnic peoples' touristic images as portrayed by outsiders and by themselves. One outstanding example of how the visual and cultural imaginaries of minority ethnic peoples are being constructed as the targets of today's tourism by the industry and the national majority is Chio's *A Landscape of Travel: The Work of Tourism in Rural Ethnic China* (2014).

Kalshoven's highly pertinent study (2012) of Indian hobbyists in Western and Central Europe examines the lives of urban hobbyists who spend much of their vacation time recreating the "traditional" life of Native Americans, especially Plains and Woodland (for example Iroquois) "Indians." Like many tourist imaginaries, this resembles a nostalgic search for a "noble" past, but at the same time it is an engrossing hobby (like cooking or gardening) which occupies many of these Indianists' home life during when they research their subjects (and sometimes their languages) and practice creating traditional clothes, harnesses, tipis, and so on. These hobbyists have slowly won admiration from anthropologists and Native Americans alike for their seriousness and dedication to recreating the imagined (mediated through books, journals, museums, collections) heritage of distant but admired peoples. Indigenous peoples, such as the Maori, may also hone their own tourist imaginary as encapsulating tradition and the past as they manage their own touristic presentations (Olsen 2008). More commonly, commercial organs of the tourism industry, including agents of the destination, use the same tropes of alterity and the past (Dann 1996; see also Cousin, Chapter 1) but emphasize the more negative, the exotic and primitive characteristics of the target populations, usually colonized or minority groups. In extreme cases overseas travel agencies advertise visits to the "Stone Age Cannibals" of Irian Jaya (West New Guinea), a forcibly colonized province of Indonesia,[27] stating that these "Neolithic peoples" have only recently "been discovered" and might still be practicing headhunting and cannibalism. This publicity warns of the impending demise of these exotic lifeways, exemplifying the common Western "smell of death" imaginary (Lanfant and Graburn 1992).

Anthropologists have been looking at tourism in relation to colonialism and neo- and post-colonialism. Trichur (Chapter 2), for example, explores the manner in which the discourse of tourism development has contributed to locating Goa within the imagination of the postcolonial Indian nation, and created the space for the expansion of the Indian state's hegemonic control. Colonial imaginaries only became popular for mass tourism after decades of *post*-colonialism. While the colonial imaginary of those who were involved as colonizers eventually gave way to nostalgically regretting the social and environmental changes that they and their regimes had brought about, the touristic colonial imaginary is an appeal to those who never experienced the grittiness of colonial realities to come and "play" colonialism without guilt or hope of return.

As Salazar has suggested for tourism, the anthropological imaginary "was increasingly peopled through the expansion of empire and through travelers and explorers' trails, and by the interest of the public in exotic locales . . . " (Carter 2010: 130), while the eminent anthropologist/historian Nicholas Dirks, writing of colonial India, has asserted "an anthropological imaginary dominated colonial knowledge at this time. Anthropology was no longer an administrative tool but was now an administrative episteme" (2001: 221).

Anthropologists also focused their interest on the *go-between* (see Cousin, Chapter 1, and Laverdure, Chapter 8), which represents a particularly fecund field of research. In his anthropological work on *indigenous* handcrafts, Laverdure (Chapter 8) insists precisely on the role of *cultural entrepreneurs*, who accompany the indigenous craftsmen and women, and on the production, circulation, and interpretation of these objects. He provides as evidence the political status of these "cultural brokers."

Destination Image—Branding

Increasingly the academic social science disciplines are working alongside those involved in the tourism industry and marketing. Jensen, Lindberg and Ostergaard (2015) contend that the interaction is very stimulating and can be quite revealing to academic tourist researchers.

From the applied social science or business point of view, the most important—and best defined—parallel concept to tourist imaginary is the "destination image" (Baloglu and McCleary 1999; Harrill 2009). The destination image is a commercial, sometimes political, image of a place as a destination, created to be effective in attracting tourists. The image is a simplified construction of iconic and hopefully memorable features aimed to attract the particular range or type of tourists that is desired. This important topic is studied both by marketing personnel and by academic social scientists (Pearce 2014).

This destination image is often called the tourist or destination *brand* and the construction and application of the image is called *branding* (Morgan and Pritchard 2014). The concept of branding in Western popular culture is associated with commercial brands, that is, a named line or type of object (or service) offered by a company, for example Mustang (offered by Ford) or Hennessy cognac (owned by conglomerate LVMH [Louis Vuitton Moet-Hennessy]). In modern culture a brand is a well-known name or product associated with certain qualities that makes it distinctive or even unique. Historically the brand was a distinctive or unique mark of ownership, associated with the "branding" of livestock with a symbol or letter-shaped hot iron in Europe and the Hispanic and Western Americas. Originally branding meant the mark of ownership by burning, applied to any property including slaves.[28]

For the tourism industry, including accommodation, travel, and transportation companies, as well as local and national government, the creation of a distinctive and positive imaginary—that is, a brand—is of great importance. A major goal of the industry, especially advertising, is oriented towards creating and spreading brand awareness, maintaining the brand's favorable image, and countering negative aspects that might besmirch its reputation (Campelo, Aitken, Thyne and Gnoth 2014). Politicians and business people are particularly concerned with any negative characteristics of a destination's image that may arise because of, for example, war, civil disorder, corruption, religious or racial violence, and health problems (cf. Tunbridge and Ashworth 1996 on the management of dissonant heritage).

The management of the past by calling on positively tinged concepts and images, such as "*terroir*" and "village community," and related sounds, odors, and objects, may also be linked with pleasant expectations. But, as Hunt and Johns (2013) point out, even nostalgic images must be chosen with care, since some individuals may be negatively affected by them.

The modern promotion of destination images is intimately connected with the media, which, rivaled only by general education, are the main mechanisms that "connect" the numerous members of the national, cultural and international populations. The sources of the components of images and brands are by no means "factual" or "real" in the sense of being immediately observable features of destinations. In fact, as Reijnders (2011) points out, destination images are often drawn from fiction derived from literature, mythology, plays, movies, television, and so on, which already exist in the realm of "the imagination." Thus these are "double imaginaries," fictional features or qualities which are transformed and transmitted into tourist imaginaries.[29]

This brief overview of the disciplines represented in the book also provides evidence of the disciplinary roots of the contributors. It furthermore reveals the capacity of the tourism studies field to capitalize on the different approaches and to bring together a more complex and interdisciplinary arsenal of tools and methods. Indeed, most of the young researchers that contributed to this volume hesitated to adopt a clear disciplinary position in their work, and rather employed a more transversal approach consolidated during the last 30 years in the field of tourism, heritage, gender, and cultural studies.

The Structure of the Book

This book completes a series of works published by the same team of authors since 2011 on the issue of *Tourism Imaginaries*. Previous publications include:

- an interdisciplinary special edition published in the *Journal of Tourism and Cultural Change* (Graburn and Gravari-Barbas 2011)
- a special issue of *Via@ Tourism Review* (Gravari-Barbas and Graburn 2012)
- an edited volume focused on anthropological approaches to tourism imaginaries (Salazar and Graburn 2014)

This volume is organized into three thematic parts:

- Part I explores the tourist production and consumption of place imaginaries: the influences of imaginaries in the choice of destinations; the concordance and/or dissonance between imaginaries and tourist experience; the temporalities of the imaginary and the cultural persistence of imaginaries over time; the mystification of tourist sites adhering to a strong imaginary; and the imagination of tourism's role related to the modernization process.
- Part II analyzes the way places are practiced through imaginaries and the role imaginaries play in the tourist experience: the individual resistance and modification of given cultural/institutional imaginaries; the acceptance, performance, embodiment, and *habitus*-formation of imaginaries; the temporal trajectories of narrative imaginaries as carried by travelers in relation to the micro- and macro-forces of stability and change throughout the anticipation, experience, and recollection of the tourist experience; touristic practices and performances;
- Part III explores the way images and the media participate to the creation of tourism imaginaries. The authors analyze their stability, their changes and their "instrumentalization." This part is built on the question: What is left to the imagination beyond all the stories, pictures, and brochures?

The interdisciplinary approach of this book intends to shine a new light on the complex issue of imaginaries. We hope that it will be useful not only to scholars and academics but also to tourism practitioners.

Notes

1 "L'envie du Monde."
2 Leite (2014) suggests a difference between *tourism* imaginaries, as those parts of our general cultural imaginaries of the world which may be applicable to tourist destinations or situations, and *tourist* imaginaries which are specific images about tourist destinations and experiences, as in guide books, brochures, media, word of mouth narratives, photographs, souvenirs, and so on.
3 In her perceptive study of Chinese "donkey friend" (independent, middle-class youth) tourism, Leung explained (2010: 55) "For these blogging middle class tourists, value in travel is not only about the physical travel experience itself, but also about how one (re)presents themselves through the travel narrative in these blogs. These travelers, by blogging, are simultaneously (re)creating the tourist imaginary about place and experience, and at the same time these representations become part of the process in how they construct value and differentiate their own status within the rapidly shifting terrain of consumable experiences. As the donkey friend website tries to explain, 'Actually, travel is the norm of life. Our entire life is one long journey.'"

4 Until the twentieth century it was often said that "partir, c'est un peu mourir" (to depart is to die a little) with some likelihood of not returning alive. Indeed this may have been true before modern medicines and forms of transportation (Graburn 1983; 2012). Even today, dying while on vacation is not always felt to be a catastrophe. One man dying of a heart attack during his vacation in the Inuit village of Povungnituk, Hudson Bay, said that this was a place (the Arctic) he'd always dreamed of visiting, and if he had to die this was a good place for it (personal experience 1967). This parallels the elderly German tourist on the tropical island of La Réunion who, motivated by the saying "See the Antilles and then die" (Picard 2011: 15–17) wondered how the (former East German socialist) government could have denied him this experience for most of his life. Lucky for him, after the fall of the Berlin Wall, and reunification with West Germany, he was allowed to travel to the tropical isle, completing one of the items on his "bucket list."

5 It is therefore understandable that Club Med Villages are inspired by Heaven's imaginary and promise an egalitarian "Antidote to Civilization" (Réau 2011; Thurot and Thurot 1983).

6 Moore's Utopia was perhaps inspired by Plato's political imaginary, the Republic. Like many imagined perfect vacation spots, Utopia meant "No Place," that is, unlike England or any known country at that time. As a schoolboy scholar of ancient Greek, Graburn always considered it would be much more appropriately "Eutopia," a "Good Place"!

7 Strauss points out (2006) that two well-known American anthropologists, Marilyn Ivy (1995) and George Marcus (1995), made significant use of the concept "the imaginary" and yet are rarely cited.

8 Alongside or as an outgrowth of monastery-related schools found everywhere in Christendom. University-like institutions were also found in the Muslim Mediterranean, India and China, though they contributed less to modern disciplinary schemes.

9 Of course, the imaginaries of other peoples were also irrevocably changed by their own discoveries, for example, by the Arabs, the Chinese and the Japanese, and their contacts, colonization, and conversion by Western agencies.

10 It combined with biological data in framing a comprehensive evolutionary theory.

11 *Ars*, *artis* (Latin) originally meant a skill, but after the Norman Conquest of England and especially the decentering of the Church in the Reformation, the more secular "*beaux arts*" were elevated and separated from lower-class and women's crafts—craft is a word based on the Germanic word for skill, *kraft* (Graburn 2015).

12 See, especially, Bloch (1974), who argues for the power of the arts based on cadence, repetition, symbolic illusions, archaism, and syntactic and lexical restrictions.

13 Originally applied to the interpretation (exegesis), the attempt to understand the meaning of (religious) texts, and more recently studying anything "cultural" as text.

14 Dann and Parrinello (2009) focused on non-English European contributions in order to reverse this bias.

15 We use "interdisciplinary" in the general sense of researchers citing the findings and using the methods of more than one discipline; "multidisciplinary" refers more to one or more researchers consciously using the methods of two or more disciplines, and "transdisciplinary" to problems and works which knowingly extend across disciplinary boundaries. For further consideration of disciplines in tourism research, see Tribe (1997).

16 This stemmed in part from contact with two visiting graduate students, William Mazzarella from Cambridge, England and Peter Phipps from Melbourne, Australia, who introduced many topics into cultural studies and subaltern theory.

17 The Statement of Purpose of Berkeley's Tourism Studies Working Group, founded 2003 says "The Tourism Studies Working Group provides a forum in which faculty and graduate students from a wide range of disciplines can exchange ideas, circulate and/or informally present works in progress, hear from visiting scholars, and receive feedback

on their research. Rather than a discipline in its own right, we see tourism studies as a node at which numerous disciplines intersect and cross-fertilize." (www.tourism-studies.org, accessed July 3, 2014). The same interdisciplinary approach characterizes EIREST (Equipe Interdisciplinaire de Recherche Sur le Tourisme), founded in 2008 at Paris 1 University. The first and only research team in France to specifically focus on tourism, it brings together researchers from 12 different disciplines.

18 By Richard Hoggart at the founding of the Birmingham Centre for Contemporary Cultural Studies (CCCS) in 1964.

19 As opposed to the "internal colonialism" of minority groups who find themselves inexorably encapsulated within modern nation states (Graburn 1976).

20 Even in non-fictional portrayals, authors and directors are of course "creative"—that is, selective and nuanced in their depiction of places and people—and it is their views which shape tourist imaginaries.

21 The importance of this original political science model is indicated by the citation of Anderson's work in Chapters 2, 5, 6, 8, 11, 12, and 13. However, only one contributor, Regnault, claims to have a background in political science.

22 Kindly brought to our attention by Edna Rozo of Bogota, Colombia.

23 Ultimately, we distinguish between the materials studied, folklore, and the study of folklore, folkloristics. In scholarly usage, *folkloristics* represents an emphasis on the contemporary, social aspects of expressive culture, in contrast to the more literary or historical study of cultural texts (Dundes 2005).

24 For a thorough historical example of an integrated house and garden imaginary, see Harney (2013).

25 Fabian's work was part of the "writing culture" reflexive critique of anthropology which pointed out that ethnographers commonly stood apart from and "objectified" the people studied rather than seeing their own actions as part of the social context being studied (see Clifford and Marcus 1986; Marcus and Fischer 1986).

26 This is consistent with MacCannell's assertion (1976) that tourism is driven by alienation from modern life, and is a search for authenticity which is thought only to be found "elsewhere" either in the past, in alterity or in nature.

27 See, for example, www.papuatrekking.com (accessed July 3, 2014).

28 The word "brand" is a linguistic cognate of "burnt," that is, wood or skin "branded" by a hot iron.

29 Of course, the connections may be multiple, with the fictional places borrowing from other historical, travel, or tourist imaginaries.

Bibliography

Ahmad, Rafiq (2011) "Orientalist imaginaries of travels in Kashmir: Western representations of the place and people." *Journal of Tourism and Cultural Change* 9(3): 159–174.

Amirou, Rachid (1995) *Imaginaire touristique et sociabilités du voyage*. Paris: Presses Universitaires de France.

—— (2000) *Imaginaire du tourisme culturel*. Paris: Presses Universitaires de France.

Anderson, Benedict (1983) *Imagined Communities: Reflections on the Origins and Spread of Nationalism*. London: Verso.

Appadurai, Arjun (1996) *Modernity at Large: Cultural Dimensions of Globalization*. Minneapolis, MN: University of Minnesota Press.

Ateljevic, I., A. Pritchard and N. Morgan (eds) (2007) *The Critical Turn in Tourism Studies: Innovative Research Methodologies*. Oxford; Amsterdam: Elsevier.

Bachimon, Philippe and Francisco Dias (2012) "In memory of Rachid Amirou." *Via@, Tourism Review*, 1. [Online] March 16, 2012. http://viatourismreview.com/2015/06/in-memory-of-rachid-amirou/.

Baker, Keith M. (1990) *Inventing the French Revolution: Essays on French Political Culture in the Eighteenth Century*. Cambridge: Cambridge University Press.

Baloglu, S. and K.W. McCleary (1999) "A model of destination image formation." *Annals of Tourism Research* 26(4): 868–897.

Barthes, Roland (1957) *Mythologies*. New York: Hill & Wang (trans. 1987).

Bedard, Mario, Jean-Pierre Augustin and Richard Desnoilles (eds) (2012) *L'imaginaire géographique: perspectives, pratiques et devenues*. Quebec: Les Presses Unversitaires de Quebec.

Beeton, Sue (2005) *Film-induced Tourism*. Clevedon; Buffalo, NY: Channel View.

Bloch, Maurice (1974) "Symbols, song, dance and features of articulation: is religion an extreme form of traditional authority?" *European Journal of Sociology* 15: 55–81.

Boia, Lucian (1998) *Pour une histoire de l'imaginaire*. Paris: Les Belles Lettres.

Boyer, Marc (1996) *L'invention du tourisme*. Paris: Gallimard-Découvertes.

Bruner, Edward M. (2005) *Culture on Tour: Ethnographies of Travel*. Chicago, IL: University of Chicago Press.

Buechler, Steven M. (1995) "New social movement theories." *Sociological Quarterly* 36(3): 441–464.

Butler, Judith (1990) *Gender Trouble: Feminism and the Subversion of Identity*. New York: Routledge.

Campelo, Adriana, Robert Aitken, Maree Thyne and Jeurgen Gnoth (2014) "Sense of place: the importance of destination branding." *Journal of Travel Research* 53(2): 154–166.

Carter, Donald M. (2010) *Navigating the African Diaspora: The Anthropology of Invisibility*. Minneapolis, MN: University of Minnesota Press.

Castoriadis, Cornelius (1975) *L'Institution imaginaire de la société*. Paris: Seuil.

—— (1989) *Les carrefours du labyrinthe*, vol. 4. Paris: Seuil.

—— (2014) "Between you and me: making messes with constructivism and critical theory." *Tourism, Culture and Communication* 13: 127–137.

Cazes, Georges (1989) *Les nouvelles colonies de vacances? Le tourisme international à la conquête du Tiers-Monde*. Paris: L'Harmattan.

Chareyron, Gaël, Jérôme Da-Rugna, Saskia Cousin and Sébastien Jacquot (2014) "Étudier TripAdvisor. Ou comment Trip-patouiller les cartes de nos vacances." *EspacesTemps. net*. [Online] August 29 2014. http://www.espacestemps.net/articles/etudier-tripadvisor-ou-comment-trip-patouiller-les-cartes-de-nos-vacances/.

Chio, Jenny (2014) *A Landscape of Travel: The Work of Tourism in Rural Ethnic China*. Seattle, WA: University of Washington Press.

Choe, Youngmin (2016) *Tourist Distractions: Traveling and Feeling Hallyu Cinema*. Durham, NC: Duke University Press.

Clifford, James and George E. Marcus (eds) (1986) *Writing Culture: The Poetics and Politics of Ethnography*. Berkeley, CA: University of California Press.

Coëffé, Vincent and Philippe Violier (2008) "Les lieux du tourisme: de quel(s) paradis parle-t-on? Variations sur le thème de l'urbanité touristique." *Articulo*, 4.

Cohen, Erik (1993) "The study of touristic images of ethnic individual peoples: mitigating the stereotype of a stereotype," in Douglas Pearce and Richard Butler (eds) *Tourism Research: Critiques and Challenges*. New York: Routledge, pp. 36–69.

Collignon, B. and J.-F. Staszak (2009) "Des imaginaires géographiques aux imaginaires touristiques: une approche par la geographie culturale." Paper given at the conference "Industrie patrimoniale et imaginaires touristique," Paris, 11 June.

Connell, Joanne (2012) "Film tourism: evolution, progress and prospects." *Tourism Management* 33: 1007–1029.

Crouch, David and Nina Lübbren (2003) *Visual Culture and Tourism*. Oxford: Berg.

Dann, Graham (1996) "The people of tourist brochures," in T. Selwyn (ed.) *The Tourist Image: Myths and Myth Making in Tourism*. Chichester: Wiley, pp. 61–81.

Dann, Graham and Erik Cohen (1991) "Sociology and tourism." *Annals of Tourism Research* 18: 155–169.

Dann, Graham and Giuli Liebman Parrinello (eds) (2009) *The Sociology of Tourism: European Origins and Developments*. Bingley: Emerald.

Debarbieux, Bernard (2003) "Imaginaire géographique," in J. Lévy and M. Lussault, *Dictionnaire de géographie*. Paris: Belin, p. 489.

Denzin, N.K and Y.S. Lincoln (eds) (2005) *The Sage Handbook of Qualitative Research*. Thousand Oaks, CA: Sage.

Dirks, Nicholas B. (2001) *Castes of Mind: Colonialism and the Making of Modern India*. Princeton, NJ: Princeton University Press.

Drew, Emily M. (2011) "Strategies for antiracist representation: ethnic tourism guides in Chicago." *Journal of Tourism and Cultural Change* 9(2): 55–69.

Dundes, Alan (2005) "Century." *The Journal of American Folklore* 118(470): 385–408.

Echtner, Charlotte and T. Jamal (1997) "The disciplinary dilemma of tourism studies." *Annals of Tourism Research* 24(4): 868–883.

Eco, Umberto (1962) *La structure assented: la ricers semiotic e il method structural*. Milan: Bimini [trans. as the *Absent Structure* (1968)].

Engels, Freidrich (1884) *The Origin of the Family, Private Property, and the State: in the light of the researches of Lewis H. Morgan* (*Der Ursprang der Family, des Privateigenthums und des Staats*). Zurich.

Escobar, Arturo and Sonia Alvarez (eds) (1992) *The Making of Social Movements in Latin America: Identity, Strategy, and Democracy*. Boulder, CO: Westview Press.

Fabian, Johannes (1983) *Time and the Other: How Anthropology Makes Its Object*. New York: Columbia University Press.

Geertz, Clifford (1973) *The Interpretation of Cultures*. New York: Basic Books.

Gieseking, Jen J. (2007) "Understanding the geographical imagination." *jgieseking.org*. [Online] September 15.

Goffman, Erving (1959) *The Presentation of Self in Everyday Life*. New York: Anchor.

Graburn, Nelson (ed.) (1976) *Ethnic and Tourist Arts: Cultural Expressions from the Fourth World*. Berkeley, CA: University of California Press.

—— (1980) "Teaching the anthropology of tourism." *International Social Science Journal* (UNESCO) 32(1): 56–68 (also in French and Spanish).

—— (1983) "The anthropology of tourism," in Nelson Graburn (ed.) Special Issue of *Annals of Tourism Research* 10(1): 9–33.

—— (1998) "A quest for identity." *Museum International* (UNESCO) 59(4): 13–18.

—— (2002) "The ethnographic tourist," in Graham Dann (ed.) *The Tourist as a Metaphor of the Social World*. Wallingford: CAB International, pp. 19–39.

—— (2009) "Existe uma antropológia do turismo? Tendências contemporâneas," in Nelson Graburn, Margarita Barretto, Carlos Alberto Steil, Rodrigo de Azeredo Grünewald and Rafael José dos Santos (eds) *Turismo e antropologia: novas abordagens*. Campinas: Papirus.

—— (2011) "The pleasures of interdisciplinarity?" Paper given at the conference "Advancing the Social Science of Tourism," organized by John Tribe, University of Surrey, Guildford, June 28 to July 1.

—— (2012) "The dark is on the inside: the *honne* of Japanese exploratory tourists," in David Picard and Mike Robinson (eds) *Emotion in Motion: Tourism, Affect and Transformation*. Farnham; Burlington, VT: Ashgate, pp. 49–71.

—— (2015) "Art, anthropological aspects," in James D. Wright (ed.) *International Encyclopedia of the Social and Behavioral Sciences*, 2nd edition, vol. 2. Oxford: Elsevier, pp. 15–20.

Graburn, Nelson and Maria Gravari-Barbas (eds) (2011) *Imagined Landscapes of Tourism.* Special issue of *Journal of Tourism and Cultural Change* 9(3).

Graburn, Nelson and Jafar Jafari (1990) "Tourism social sciences: introduction." *Tourism Social Sciences*. Special issue of *Annals of Tourism Research* 19(1): 1–11.

Gramsci, Antonio (1971) *Selections from the Prison Notebooks*. New York: International Publishers.

Gravari-Barbas, Maria and Nelson Graburn (2012) Editorial, "Tourism imaginaries / imaginaires touristiques." *Via@ Tourism Revue* 1. [Online] March 16, 2012. http:// viatourismreview.com/2015/06/tourist-imaginaries-3/.

Gregory, Derek (1994/2004) *Geographical Imaginations*. Oxford; Cambridge, MA: Blackwell.

Grenier, Alain A. (2012) "Parcs du Nunavik." *Téoros. Revue de recherche en tourisme* 31(1): 92–102.

Hall, C. Michael and Hazel Tucker (eds) (2004) *Tourism and Postcolonialism: Contested Discourses, Identities and Representations*. London: Routledge.

Hall, Stuart (1973) *Encoding and Decoding in the Television Discourse*. Birmingham: Centre for Contemporary Cultural Studies.

Hall, Stuart and P. Walton (1972) *Situating Marx: Evaluations and Departures*. London: Human Context Books.

Harney, Marion (2013) *Place-making for the Imagination: Horace Walpole and Strawberry Hill*. Farnham: Ashgate.

Harrill, Rich (2009) "Destination management: new challenges, new needs," in Tazim Jamal and Mike Robinson (eds) *The Sage Handbook of Tourism Studies*. London: Sage, pp. 449–463.

Harvey, David (1973) *Social Justice and the City*. Baltimore, MD: Johns Hopkins University Press.

—— (2005) "The sociological and geographical imaginations." *International Journal of Politics, Culture, and Society* 18(3/4): 211–255.

Heilbron, John L. (1999) *The Sun in the Church: Cathedrals as Solar Observatories*. Cambridge, MA: Harvard University Press.

Hoida, Bridget (2007) "Plotting the geographic imaginary: the nostalgic impulse in the California novel and so L.A." PhD dissertation. Los Angeles: University of Southern California.

Hollinshead, Keith (2007) "'Worldmaking' and the transformation of place and culture: the enlargement of Meethan's analysis of tourism and global change," in I. Ateljevic, A. Pritchard and N. Morgan (eds) *The Critical Turn in Tourism Studies: Innovative Research Methodologies*. Oxford; Amsterdam: Elsevier, pp. 165–193.

Hoppen, Anne, Lorraine Brown and Alan Fyall (2014) "Literary tourism: opportunities and challenges for the marketing and branding of destinations?" *Journal of Destination Marketing and Management* 3(1): 37–47.

Horkheimer, M. and T.W. Adorno (1947) *Dialectic of Enlightenment: Philosophical Fragments*, ed. G.S. Noerr, trans. E. Jephcott (2002). Stanford, CA: Stanford University Press.

Hughes, B. (2009) "Wounded/monstrous/abject: a critique of the disabled body in the sociological imaginary." *Disability & Society* 24(4): 399–410.

Hunt, Louise and Nick Johns (2013) "Image, place and nostalgia in hospitality branding and marketing." *Worldwide Hospitality and Tourism Themes* 5(1): 14–26.

Ivy, Marilyn (1995) *Discourses of the Vanishing: Modernity, Phantasm, Japan*. Chicago, IL: University of Chicago Press.

Jamal, Tazim and Mike Robinson (eds) (2009) *The Sage Handbook of Tourism Studies*. London: Sage.

Jensen, Øystein; Lindberg, Frank; Østergaard, Per (2015). "How Can Consumer Research Contribute to Increased Understanding of Tourist Experiences? A Conceptual Review." *Scandinavian Journal of Hospitality and Tourism* 15: 9–27.

Kalshoven, Petra T. (2012) *Crafting the "Indian": Knowledge, Desire, and Play in Indianist Reenactment*. London: Berghahn.

Kuhn, Thomas (1970) *The Structure of Scientific Revolutions*. Chicago, IL: University of Chicago Press.

Lanfant, Marie-Francoise and Nelson Graburn (1992) "International tourism reconsidered: the principle of the alternative," in Valene L. Smith and William R. Eadington (eds) *Tourism Alternatives: Potentials and Problems in the Development of Tourism*. Philadelphia, PA: University of Pennsylvania Press, pp. 88–112.

Lean, Garth, Russell Staiff and Emma Waterton (eds) (2014) *Travel and Imagination*. Farnham: Ashgate.

Leite, Naomi (2014) "Afterword: locating imaginaries in the anthropology of tourism," in Noel Salazar and Nelson Graburn (eds) *Tourism Imaginaries: Anthropological Approaches*. New York: Berghahn, pp. 260–278.

Leung, Jenny (2010) "Changing consciousness of work and leisure in Chinese tourists." MA Thesis Berkeley, CA: University of California.

Lutz, Catherine A. and Jane L. Collins (1993) *Reading National Geographic*. Chicago, IL: University of Chicago Press.

M'bayo, Tamba (2013) "Africa's past, present and future underdevelopment: dependency in the context of globalization," in Alain Laurent Aboa, Hilaire de Prince Pokam, Adama Sadio and Aboubakr Tandia (eds) *Démocratie et développement en Afrique: perspectives des jeunes chercheurs Africains*, vol. 2: *Imaginaires et practiques du développement à l'épreuve de la politique international*. Paris: L'Harmattan, pp. 23–50.

MacCannell, Dean (1973) "Staged authenticity: arrangements of social space in tourist settings." *American Journal of Sociology* 79: 589–603.

—— (1976) *The Tourist: A New Theory of the Leisure Class*. New York: Schocken.

Maffesoli, Michel (1997) *Du nomadisme. Vagabondages initiatiques*. Paris: Le Livre de Poche.

Maizels, John and Deidi Von Schaewen (1999) *Mondes Imaginaires—Fantasy Worlds*. Cologne: Taschen.

Marcus, George E. (ed.) (1995) *Technoscientific Imaginaries: Conversations, Profiles, and Memoirs*. Chicago, IL: University of Chicago Press.

Marcus, George E. and Michael Fisher (1986) *Anthropology as Cultural Critique: An Experimental Moment on the Human Sciences*. Chicago, IL: University of Chicago Press.

Massey, Doreen (2006) "The geographical mind," in D. Balderston (ed.) *Secondary Geography Handbook*. Sheffield: Geographical Association, pp. 46–52.

Mathers, Kathryn (2011) *Travel, Humanitarianism, and Becoming American in Africa*. New York: Palgrave Macmillan.

Matthey, Laurent and Olivier Walther (2008) "Introduction, 'Le Paradis sur Terre'? Une géographie culturelle et politique du tourisme." *Articulo*, 4.

Mills, C. Wright (1959 [reprinted 2000]) *The Sociological Imagination*. Oxford: Oxford University Press.

Morgan, Nigel and Annette Pritchard (eds) (2014) *Destination Branding*. Special issue of *Journal of Destination and Marketing Management* 3(1).

Nash, Dennison (1977) "Tourism as a form of imperialism," in Valene L. Smith (ed.) *Hosts and Guests: The Anthropology of Tourism*. Philadelphia, PA: University of Pennsylvania Press, pp. 33–47.

Nora, Pierre (ed.) (1984) *Les lieux de mémoires*. Paris: Gallimard.

—— (1989) "Between memory and history: Les lieux de mémoires." *Representations* 26: 7–25.

Olsen, Kjell (2008) "The Maori of tourist brochures: representing indigenousness." *Journal of Tourism and Cultural Change* 6(3): 161–184.

Pearce, Douglas G. (2014) "Towards an integrative conceptual framework of destinations." *Journal of Travel Research* 53(2): 141–163.

Picard, David (2011) *Tourism, Magic and Modernity: Cultivating the Human Garden*. New York: Berghahn.

Pitchford, Susan (2008) *Identity Tourism: Imaging and Imagining*. Bingley: Emerald.

Pleven, Bertrand (2013) "Paris cinématographique, métropole touristique hyper-réelle," in Maria Gravari-Barbas and Edith Fagnoni (eds) *Métropolisation et tourisme. Comment le tourisme redessine Paris*. Paris: Belin.

Porfyriou, Heleni (2015) "Review of Chio, Jenny (2014) *A Landscape of Travel: The Work of Tourism in Rural Ethnic China*. Seattle, WA: University of Washington Press." *Journal of Cultural Heritage* 16: 126.

Powell, Alison (1988) "Like a rolling stone: notions of youth travel in pop music." *Kroeber Anthropological Society Papers* 67–68: 28–34.

Proctor, James D. (1998) "Ethics in geography: giving moral form to the geographical imagination." *Area* 30(1): 8–18.

Rea, Michael (2000) "A *furusato* away from home." *Annals of Tourism Research* 27(3): 638–660.

Réau, Bertrand (2011) *Les Français et les vacances: sociologie des pratiques et offres de loisirs*. Paris: Editions CNRS.

Reijnders, Stijn (2011) *Places of the Imagination: Media, Tourism, Culture*. Farnham: Ashgate.

Ricoeur, Paul (1984) "L'idéologie et l'utopie: deux expressions de l'imaginaire social." *Autre temps* 2(2): 53–64.

Said, Edward (1978) *Orientalism*. New York: Pantheon.

Sáinz, E.M., and M. García (2014) *Turismo e imaginarios*. Hermosillo, México: El Colegio de Sonora.

Salazar, Noel (2009) "Recycling 'old' anthropology and archaeology in 'new' tourism." Paper given in session PO2: "Imagineering the past: the (mis)uses of anthropology and archaeology in tourism," at the ASA09 meetings. Bristol, April 6–9.

—— (2010) *Envisioning Eden: Mobilizing Imaginaries in Tourism and Beyond*. New York: Berghahn.

Salazar, Noel and Nelson Graburn (eds) (2014) *Tourism Imaginaries: Anthropological Approaches*. London: Berghahn.

Sayer, A. (1999) "Long live postdisciplinary studies: sociology and the curse of disciplinary parochialism/imperialism." Lancaster University. [Online] webpage last revised December 5, 2003. http://www.lancaster.ac.uk/fass/resources/sociology-online-papers/papers/sayer-long-live-postdisciplinary-studies.pdf.

Silva, A. (2007). *Imaginarios urbanos en América Latina: urbanismos ciudadanos*. Barcelona: Edición de la Fundación Antonio Tápies.

Smith, Valene (ed.) (1977) *Hosts and Guests: The Anthropology of Tourism*. Philadelphia, PA: University of Pennsylvania Press.

Staszak, Jean-François (2008) "Danse exotique, danse érotique. Perspectives géographiques sur la mise en scène du corps de l'Autre (XVIIIe–XXIe siècles)." *Annales de géographie*, 660–661 (mai–juin): 129–158.

—— (2012) "La construction de l'imaginaire occidental de l'Ailleurs et la fabrication des exotica—le cas des toi moko maoris," in D. Herniaux and A. Lidon (eds) *Geografía de los imaginerarios*. Barcelona: Anthropos / Mexico: Universidad Autónoma Metropolitana Iztapalapa, pp. 179–210.

Steger, Manfred B. (2008) *The Rise of the Global Imaginary: Political Ideologies from the French Revolution to the Global War on Terror*. New York: Oxford University Press.

Strauss, Claudia (2006) "The imaginary." *Anthropological Theory* 6(3): 322–344.

Tegtmeyer, Lina L (2016) *Branding the Crisis: Aesthetics of failure between urban wasteland and Detroit's touristic ruinscape. Re-contextualizing visual representations of urban decay in US culture*. Berlin: Doctoral dissertation, John-F.-Kennedy-Institut für Nordamerikastudienm, Freien Universität Berlin.

Thomas, Nicholas (1999) "Becoming undisciplined: anthropology and cultural studies," in Henrietta L. Moore (ed.) *Anthropological Theory Today*. Cambridge: Polity Press, pp. 263–279.

Thurot, Jean-Maurice and Gaétane Thurot (1983) "The ideology of class and tourism: facing the discourses of advertising." *Annals of Tourism Research* 10(1): 173–189.

Tribe, John (1997) "The indiscipline of tourism." *Annals of Tourism Research* 24(3): 638–657.

—— (2009) *Philosophical Issues in Tourism*. Bristol: Channel View.

Tucker, Hazel and John Akama (2009) "Tourism as postcolonialism," in Tazim Jamal and Mike Robinson (eds) *The Sage Handbook of Tourism Studies*. Thousand Oaks, CA: Sage, pp. 504–520.

Tunbridge, J.E. and Gregory J. Ashworth (1996) *Dissonant Heritage: The Management of the Past as a Resource in Conflict*. Chichester; New York: J. Wiley.

Tzanelli, Rodanthi (2007) *The Cinemaic Tourist: Explorations in Globalization, Culture and Resistance*. London: Routledge.

Urbain, Jean-Didier (1991) *L'idiot du voyage*. Paris: Payot.

—— (2011) *L'envie du monde*. Paris: Bréal.

Vaquer, Armand (2009) *The Monster Movie Fan's Guide to Japan*. Los Angeles, CA: Compress.

Viard, Jean (2015) *Le triomphe d'une utopie: vacances, loisirs, voyages: la révolution des temps libres*. La Tour d'Aigues: Editions de l'Aube.

Watson, Nicola J. (2006) *The Literary Tourist: Readers and Places in Romantic and Victorian Britain*. Basingstoke and New York: Palgrave Macmillan.

Weber, Max (1904/1949) *The Methodology of the Social Sciences*. New York: Free Press.

—— (1922/1978) *Economy and Society*. Berkeley, CA: University of California Press.

Williams, Raymond (1973) *The Country and the City*. London: Chatto and Windus.

Part I

Producing / Consuming Place Imaginaries

Madina Regnault

The focus of the first part of the volume is on the commodification of tourism and its impacts on touristic places. The contributors question the dichotomous approaches of the production and consumption of tourism. Irena Ateljevic (2000) uses the neo-Gramscian concept of hegemony as a key theoretical framework that lays a foundation to overpass such binary logic. From this perspective, it is not relevant to study production or consumption *per se*, but the interest must be on the interface between these processes. Tourism has to be conceptualized as a "nexus of circuits operating within production-consumption dialectics enabled by the processes of negotiated (re)production" (Ateljevic 2000: 371).

Studying the interface between the production and consumption of imaginaries leads us to the tourism industry. Intrinsically, tourism imaginary has the power to summarize the complexity of a place in only one or a few clichés. As a consequence, tourism stakeholders have to deal with it, make the most of it, or try to change it with the building of a new imaginary. But previous imaginaries of a place are difficult to erase from people's minds, they are more like "palimpsests" because of the multitude of present and past discursive and physical layers that are used by people to interpret places such as cities or regions (Sizemore 1984; Lutz 2004; Mitin 2007). This work stresses the layers of imaginaries of places made by tourists and tourism.

As Salazar and Graburn argue, one further aspect of the temporality of imaginaries is their stability or instability over time. We can make typologies of places regarding the temporality of their imaginary. In fact, "many imaginaries, especially those clinging to historically important places, are slower to change" (Salazar and Graburn 2014: 10). The tourism industry plays a central role in the production or consumption of imaginaries in mystifying sites. "Tourism destinations are often reconstructed or even erected as 'museums of themselves'" (Salazar and Graburn 2014: 13). Paradoxically, tourism imaginaries also try to capture the essence of one place as if it was something immutable, whereas places are constantly changing. We can go further in this multi-level analysis on the temporality of places and temporalities of place imaginaries. Whereas it might seem to be historically objective to situate places as old or modern, we can see that because tourism imaginaries are socioeconomic constructions, the way tourists actually consume travel as a product is a subjective process. The concept of tourism imaginaries involves mapping representations linked to almost every place in the world. From (cultural) anthro-pology to (cultural) geography, the interconnected work of social sciences in the first part of the volume is achieved through Gramscian theory. Critical theorists within cultural studies maintain that by creating a neo-Gramscian terrain based on negotiation between the production and consumption processes, both can be examined together, as they are interconnected through reproduction.

Bibliography

Ateljevic, Irena (2000) "Circuits of tourism: stepping beyond the 'production/consumption' dichotomy." *Tourism Geographies* 2(4): 369–388.

Lutz, Hartmut (2004) "Race or place? The palimpsest of space in Canadian Prairie fiction, from Salverson to Cariou." *Textual Studies in Canada* 17: 171–185.

Mitin, Ivan (2007) "Mythogeography: region as a palimpsest of identities," in L. Elenius and C. Karlsson (eds) *Cross-cultural Communication and Ethnic Identities: Proceedings from the Conference Regional Northern Identity*. Luleå: Luleå Tekniska Universitet, pp. 215–225.

Salazar, Noel and Graburn, Nelson (2014) *Tourism Imaginaries: Anthropological Approaches*. Oxford: Berghahn Books.

Sizemore, Christine (1984) "Reading the city as palimpsest: the experiential perception of a city in Doris Lessing's *The Four Gated City*," in S. Squier (ed.) *Women Writers and the City*. Knoxville, TE: University of Tennessee Press, pp. 176–190.

1 Images, Imaginaries, and Imaginations: French Notes

Saskia Cousin

Introduction

Sartre, Bachelard, Caillois, Ricoeur, Durand, Deleuze, Derrida, Lyotard, Castoriadis, Jung, Lacan, ... Philosophy, semiotics, linguistics, psychoanalysis, literature . . . . With the notable exception of sociology and anthropology, where the term has been persistently denied any scientific value, French thought has been very interested in questions of the imaginary. We intend to offer a brief review of some of the more well known French approaches—Bachelard, Lacan, Castoriadis, Ricoeur—before examining how, after decades of being excluded by academics, the very exile of the imaginary has allowed this notion to find favor. We will then consider the ideas provoked by the introduction of the imaginary into ethnographic research, for this work and, more generally, for the anthropology of tourism. Finally, we suggest some avenues for further research.

Approaching the Imaginary: The View from France

Relatively recent, the interest of French philosophy in the term "imaginary" originates, in particular, from a disaffection with the notion of imagination, which, up to the mid-twentieth century, indicated the faculty of producing and using images. Such an approach could not resist the rational-scientific study of the properties and effects of images and, from the mid-twentieth century, there was a movement away from the study of the psychological formation of images—difficult to substantiate—towards the study of their effects, particularly collective ones. Such interest remained essentially philosophical, psychoanalytical, even esoteric until the early twenty-first century.

The Swiss psychiatrist Carl Gustav Jung (1875–1961) influenced the psychoanalytic branch of work on the imaginary: Mircea Eliade, Gilbert Durand, and Gaston Bachelard. For Jung, personal imaginary depended on a collective unconscious structured by archetypes, that is to say a finite number of themes (the dragon, paradise lost, and so on) encountered in dreams, myths, fairy tales, and legends, which constitute the grammar, the matrix of the imaginary. Largely known in France for his work on the epistemology of science, his contemporary Gaston Bachelard (1884–1962) spent his whole life working on the relationship between the imaginary and rationality, out of which emerged work influenced at the same time by psychoanalysis (Freud, Jung), French epistemology (Comte, Bergson, Koyré), and German idealism (Kant, Hegel, Nietzsche). For Bachelard, the imaginary was not opposed to the real; on the contrary, the imaginary, even in the form of poetic dreaming, is in sympathy (*sympathie*) with the real, while science is bound to distance the real: for Bachelard, science must therefore be antipathetic to the real. Bachelard's richest contribution to anthropology is doubt-less the manner in which he conceptualizes the relationships between images, imagination, and the imaginary.

For the psychoanalyst Jacques Lacan, the imaginary stands in opposition to the symbolic, not to the real. The imaginary is rooted in the ego (me and mother) and must be surpassed by the symbolic (the father's word) to realize the subject and society. Such an approach is without doubt not excluded from the contempt in which the question of the imaginary is held by the social sciences, something to which we will return.

More relevant to us is the work of Cornelius Castoriadis. He deploys the con-cept of "social imaginary" to forge what he calls the "project of autonomy," a societal project whose aim is an autonomy at the same time both individual and collective. This concept of social imaginary allows him to oppose historical deter-minism as much as the structuralism of Lévi-Strauss. Castoriadis maintains that societies auto-create themselves and that their institutions cannot be reduced to functionalist explanations. Effectively, for him, the social imaginary,

> . . . which creates language, which creates institutions, which creates the very form of the institution—something which makes no sense seen from the perspective of the individual psyche, . . . [is] the creative capacity of an anonymous collective coming into being each time humans are assembled, and which institutes itself each time in a particular form, in order to exist. (Castoriadis 1989: 113)

In his work *The Imaginary Institution of Society* (1987), Cornelius Castoriadis dis-tinguishes an *instituting* social imaginary (creative activity), from the *instituted* social imaginary (the result of that activity: norms, languages, ways of being). The instituting social imaginary is close to what Bachelard, Ricoeur, or Appadurai would call imagination, understood as a *social practice* and distinguished from the imaginary which would be the *product*, and images, the *support and base*. Philosopher of language, literary works, and of their reception and interpretation, Paul Ricoeur is at the heart of a hermeneutic current which developed in opposition to the determinist structuralism of the 1960s. For him, reception is an interpreta-tion, hence an action, thanks to the imagination which constructs both collective sense and agency. Ricoeur shows that collective stories are not or at least not only the product of a given society, but the means of producing collective identities. In the field of historical studies, the first Annales School also worked on the notion of imaginaries, to the point that we might even term historians like Duby, Nicole Loraux, Jacques Le Goff, or even Vidal-Naquet "historians of the imaginary."

The Imaginary, Social Science, and the Anthropological Taboo

Before considering the reflexions of anthropologists of the imaginary, it is timely to mention the controversial work of Gilbert Durand, author of numerous works on the question, including *Anthropological Structures of the Imaginary* (1999). If Durand is not considered legitimate by the scientific community, due to a character more esoteric than scientific, in France he is well known by a wider public, and his ideas employed by techniques such as marketing.

Following the example of Jung and considering that a finite number of imaginaries existed, Durand sought to identify unchanging plans and structures (which he termed "schemes"). He drew on a classical Freudian schema: firstly what he terms the anthropological id (*ça anthropologique*), purely mythic, immutable, the collective unconscious of Jung (at the level of "archetypal images"). At the other extreme he placed the imaginary superego (*surmoi imaginaire*), that is to say the set of rules, codes, laws, precedences, of a society at the moment it is the subject of consideration. Finally, in the middle, the social ego (*moi social*), the instance through which each individual cobbles together (*bricole*) their behavior and comes to terms with the two poles by constructing a social role. According to Durand, it is at this level that the imaginary exists and that important changes of the dominant myth of a society can take place, for example—Durand cites the changes in France in 1789.

If we strip this proposition of its psychoanalytical clothing, and of its (con) fusion between the individual and the collective, we rediscover the distinction between imaginary, image/symbolic/image and imagination favored by Ricoeur, Bachelard, or Appadurai.

Subsequently, with his work on ancient imaginaries, Joël Thomas (1998) reintroduced a more scientific method for identifying where imaginaries were active. It remains the case that practically all work on the imaginary applies to stories, fairy tales, fictions, art work, in short mythologies and literary/artistic productions, not practices or more ordinary social norms, nor elements less constituted. This is linked to the discipline—mainly philosophy and literature—of the authors but, no doubt equally the difficulty of apprehending complex and fluid social realities using this notion. Mention should be made here of Roland Barthes, whose *Mythologies* (1972) can be read as a decoding of certain contemporary imaginaries.

Due to a historical taste for rationalism and the lengthy hegemony of structuralism and materialism, the notion of the imaginary has barely infused French social science, even if we can find similar reflexions in the historical domain: for example in the history of mentalities of the Annales School, Dumézil's study of mythologies and ideologies (Dumézil 1968; Littleton 1973), or the analysis of fiction (literature, cinema, and so on) and its inscription into a social and cultural context.

Cultural geography also developed notions of "spatial imaginary" or "geographical imaginary," to designate representations of the world and of place without, however, the distinction between images and imaginaries being the subject of a specific analysis. The imaginary remained until recently beyond the pale for French anthropology. This is explained in part by reference to the point of view expressed by Claude Lévi-Strauss in his introduction to the works of Marcel Mauss (1968; 1987). Lévi-Strauss states that symbolic practices are essentially a social reality, that there is a primacy of the symbolic over the imaginary and the real. This assertion, reflecting less the position of Mauss than Lévi-Strauss's own research agenda, was clearly a determining factor in the relegation of the imaginary and its corollaries within French anthropology. This despite the fact that, paradoxically, the relegation was accepted in the name of an epistemology placing Bachelard at the center of its Pantheon—the Bachelard of *Nouvel esprit scientifique* (1934), of the epistemological rupture, and of the struggle against "primary illusions" of course, not the Bachelard of *Psychanalyse du feu* (1949). Furthermore, this notion of imaginary fitted only awkwardly with historical materialism and questions of social class: Marxism didn't know what to do with the imaginary, which constituted a rather troublesome superstructure.

Finally, the contempt of the "master" Lévi-Strauss, problems of method and the uniclassist character of the notion, the grip exerted over the concept by Gilbert Durand, and, above all, of his student, the highly mediatized and very controversial sociologist Michel Maffesoli, rendered its serious consideration, even its use, suicidal from an academic point of view for several generations of anthropologists.[1]

The Journey to America and a Return to Favor

However, over the last 15 years, thanks notably to detours via the United States, it has become possible to discuss certain authors and ideas. This is the case for Foucault and historians, Derrida for philosophers, and the imaginary for anthropologists. The legitimization of the concept of the imaginary/imagined came mainly via the discipline of history, thanks to historians mentioned above and, above all, the flourishing of ideas around the "national imaginary," a concept introduced by Benedict Anderson. His concept of the "imagined community" was, on the other hand, little used in a France where fear of communitarianism meant a dislike for the notion of community. Anderson allowed a focus on the production, reproduction, and circulation of stories, clichés or images forming a narrative model which did not emerge solely from History with a capital H or the "real arts": folklore, fashion, tourism, songs. The historian Anne-Marie Thiesse was concerned with the production and circulation of stories founding European national identities in the eighteenth and nineteenth centuries in which tourism played an important part (1999). Other historians sought to identify which scheme or "elementary archetype" constituted, for example, these European nationalisms (Bruhns and Burguière 2003).

The relation between images, imaginaries, and imagination worked on by Bachelard was invigorated by the work of Arjun Appadurai in his *Modernity at Large* (1996), even if Ricoeur's work and his interest in the imagination is just as important for understanding its return to favor—both being drawn on by different currents in French anthropology.

The world we live in today is characterized by a new role for the imagination in social life. To grasp this new role, we need to bring together the old idea of images, especially mechanically produced images (in the Frankfurt School sense); the idea of the imagined community (in Anderson's sense) and the French idea of the imaginary (*imaginaire*), as a constructed landscape of collective aspirations, which is no more and no less real than the collective representation of Emile Durkheim, now mediated through the complex prism of modern media. The image, the imagined, the imaginary—these are all terms that direct us to something critical and new in global processes: *the imagination as a social practice.* (Appadurai 1996: 31)

Appadurai turns to the term imaginary several times, generally in expressions such as "imaginary landscapes" (p. 31) "postnational imaginary" (p. 177), "spatial imaginary" (p. 16), "national imaginary" (p. 19), and "mass mediated imaginary" (p. 6). Fortunately Appadurai is not burdened by institutional tensions, epistemological taboos, or French ideologists. Mingling influences and schools, using imaginary (*imaginaire*) as a synonym for the collective representations of Emile Durkheim, Appadurai in fact uses the term imaginary (*imaginaire*) with restraint and does not focus his analysis on the term, preferring questions around images and imaginations, in the manner of Bachelard and Ricoeur: "Modernity at Large shows how the imagination works as a social force in today's world, providing new resources for identity and energies for creating alternatives to the nation-state."

Thanks to Ricoeur and Appadurai we have rediscovered the work of Bachelard before his memory was compromised.

Nevertheless, if the notion of the imaginary is today used by nearly all Anglophone anthropologists, notably those working in tourism (including D. MacCannell, Barbara Kirshenblatt-Gimblett, G.D Boorstin, A. Appadurai, and others), the situation is not the same in France, due to the power of certain taboos, but equally because until very recently there were practically no anthropologists working on tourism.

Of these only two had any particular use for the notion of the imaginary: Jean-Didier Urbain, anthropologist, semiologist and professor of linguistics, very well known in the Francophone world, elaborated throughout his works a generalized anthropology of tourism imaginaries. He mixes work on the imaginary together with the mythologies of Thomas, Durand, Lévi-Strauss, Barthes, the semiotics of Greimas (inventor of the semiotic square), the contribution of an historian of mentalities like Philippe Ariès, or again Georges Dumézil's theses on the relations between mythology and ideology. Rachid Amirou, who completed a thesis under the supervision of Jean-Didier Urbain, published two works that dealt with the relations between the imaginary and tourism.

Imaginaries, the Symbolic, and Collective Representations

How can we work on imaginaries today? An important matter—more methodological than epistemological—consists, in our opinion, in drawing a distinction, even provisionally, between the imaginary as an object of study and the imaginary as an analytical concept. Are we studying imaginaries, or is it that this notion allows us, without really making it explicit, to identify (to imagine?) certain practices, or certain meanings given to practices? With the tourism imaginary we often find ourselves in the same dead end as we do with culturalism: the notion of culture is invoked to explain a social practice for example, whereas culture doesn't explain anything, it is that which remains to be explained. Similarly, the tourism imaginary is invoked to explain the seduction wrought by tourism imaginaries as they are applied to exotic imagery: tourism imagery would thus echo occidental exotic imaginaries.

Such tautologies do not encourage any sort of explanation for the structuring of particular sets of relations to others considered specifically occidental (a specificity which appears somewhat doubtful in the context of work on the course of world history). This specificity is termed exoticism and tautology does not clarify in any satisfactory manner the lure and the transmission of certain forms and representations more than others.

However, it is clear that taking the imaginary seriously as an object of study is not simple, in particular for anthropologists, although it would be false to claim that anthropology does not acknowledge that mental categories exist (ideas, shared values, and so on). But, in France at least, the discipline considers these from the perspective of notions of the symbolic and representation, reserving the imaginary world for individuals and their psyches, placing it outside the field of study appropriate to the discipline. This can be explained most notably by the normative (hence prescriptive) position taken by the "master" Lévi-Strauss. He laid particular emphasis on the pre-eminence and anteriority of the symbolic over the imaginary. Anthropologists thus preferred to focus on "representations," defined as the ensemble of ideas and values which permit the understanding of how a society or a community makes sense of the world. For example, according to Descola, one of the heirs to Lévi-Strauss, the Achuar maintained social relations with non-humans because their representations, their elementary categories of social life, authorized them to represent their relations with non-humans as if they were relations between people. On the contrary, still according to Descola (2005), occidental people are "naturalists," that is for them, it is the categories of the division between humans and non-humans (humanity/non-humanity) which organizes these relations.

Such a hypothesis allowed Descola to propose a typology of relations of continuity/discontinuity between humans and non-humans, based notably on Greimas' semiotic square (used by politicians and marketing experts as well as authors considering how social life might be structured by the imaginary). Descola himself does not employ the term imaginary and uses the semiotic square without even explaining what it is. This may be explained by a hierarchy of legitimacies at the heart of the discipline: the concepts of the imaginary and the semiotic square are at the bottom of the pile! For all that, can we seriously suggest that the elemental categories of social life have nothing to do with collective imaginaries?

Doesn't work on the imaginary pose questions about relations between real and reality, imaginaries, myths, representations, images, the symbolic, a whole range of notions which seek to say something about how people make sense of the world, or at least, of their world? How to articulate such notions and draw advantage from their nuances and complexity? Relations between the imaginary, representations and the symbolic are not really discussed in this volume any more than they generally are elsewhere. Thus, for Arjun Appadurai, imaginaries are the same thing as collective representations—in this he explicitly references Emile Durkheim.

Equally, there is often confusion between the imaginary and imagery, notably so in the field of tourism. For example, work on touristic images does not allow us to infer conclusions about tourist imaginaries. For those researchers who ask questions about the imaginary and are not content to consider it simply a synonym for imagery, the debate often centers on whether images produce imaginaries or if the latter, finite in number, and in some sense archetypal—elementary structures of the imaginary—could be at the origin of multiple images, that is to say of myths, legends, ancient and modern stories. For structuralists, humans and their imagination are in the last resort unimportant: myths and stories originate and find fulfilment in their own rationale and it is in this context that they should be studied. With such attitudes it is easy to understand the limited interest evinced in individual and collective imaginaries.

There is, however, perhaps some intellectual profit to be drawn from these distinctions—images/imaginaries, representations/imaginaries, symbolic/collective imaginaries—by allowing them to distance us from such oppositional forms as real/imaginary, from the Lacanian opposition imaginary/symbolic, and from the Lévi-Straussian pre-eminence of the symbolic over the imaginary.

In this way, Maurice Godelier distinguishes himself from Lévi-Strauss by affirming that "the symbolic is nothing without the imaginary which gives it meaning. Thus, if there is a primacy, it is that of the imaginary over the symbolic, of thought over language" (Godelier 2001–2002). Godelier reclaims the distinction between imaginary, symbolic, and the real by ridding them of their psychoanalytic connotations and considering the symbolic to be a codification of the imaginary.

> Its concrete form and its staging. Imaginary representations are 'idealites,' which is to say mental realities. Symbols, gestures, symbolic practices set the stage for them. Translated into rituals, they permeate the body, structure space and time, build obligatory behaviours. Without access to this imaginary, rites and symbolic practices have no sense. They are like mathematical symbols written in a book for non-mathematicians. (Godelier 2001–2002).

In the field of tourism, the distinction made by Godelier appears the most fruitful for studying relations between the real, the imaginary, and the symbolic. Effectively, tourism can be understood to combine collective and individual imaginaries, standard products and practices that emerge from the symbolic, the real or rather reality; this by the fact that imagery, imaginaries, and so on produce social relations, of power or otherwise, whatever the artificial character of the imageries that have provoked the practices.

Some Tracks to the Future or the Return of the Imagination

Mobility, such an important value for our world, can be considered as constitutive of an imaginary of modernity. Similarly, if tourist practices are nourished by images, ideas, and narratives, we can address ourselves to the way in which tourism itself could be constituted as imaginary, as an object of desire, of value, of expectation. This idea applies to several surveys of inhabitants, elected representatives, and local actors responsible for welcoming tourists or promoting a given territory, a town, or a site in Europe, Africa, and South America. The common theme in all these surveys is that they were all localized in areas marginal to major tourist sites yet the local political and economic powers worked energetically, at least in a discursive sense, to develop tourism. Encouraged by doctrines and international cooperation, these authorities represented tourism as a simple solution to often complex socio-economic problems, an industry requiring low-level investment with tourists inevitably seduced by the assets on offer.

Because it is invested with positive images, tourism can equally allow the emergence of urban transformations or a conservation politics otherwise unacceptable to the local populations. Starting with preconceptions, stereotypes, past images, and experiences, the host populations imagine what are the desires and expectations of largely occidental tourists (what they're looking for): "good" organization of tours or a short break, adequate comfort, and so on. As with a pleasure trip, tourism is equally the object of numerous projections for those who cannot travel, for whatever reasons. In short, if tourism and tourists are repulsive to a small number of cultivated travelers, for numerous populations they constitute a field of expectation whose representations are yet to be adequately researched.

Such an imaginary of tourism and mobility is currently complicating if not challenging the great modernist narrative founded with and on the nation state. There could be a triad of symbolic, imaginary, reality, where the symbolic could help us think about the rupture between tourist imaginaries (fantasy) and realities of place and practices. In this case the rupture would be explained most notably by a deficit in the symbolic, not to say imaginative alterity, despite shared imaginaries.

As Marc Augé noted, "The crisis of modernity, where some see a crisis of identity, could be attributed to the fact that one of two languages (that of identity) is winning today against the other (that of alterity). It would be better described as a crisis of alterity" (Augé 1994: 87).

Although, from the perspective of the host communities, and specifically their civic authorities, the desire for tourism, the desire for flow—for fluidity—can be understood as a desire for the desire of the other. I hypothesize this to be first and foremost a desire for self. Tourism, as an emergent value for politics and identity depends on economic and institutional categories, "tourism," "tourists," "demand," the examination of which reveals that they are screens, mirrors whose end is to permit each person to recognize themselves in the form of the projected images. As Pierre Legendre notes in *Dieu au miroir* (1994), discovering himself in the water's reflection, Narcissus believes he loves another, but his desire is for himself. In consequence there are unforeseen elements in the exchange and a deficit of alterity: the politics of identity and identification are self-referential, identifying images congeal its historical, territorial and cultural characteristics. Various people's images are different or differentiating, according to their position and role in the staging which represents the symbolic. This does not mean that the hosts and tourists do not share a common "national imaginary" for example (the collective imaginary) or perhaps an "anthropological imaginary" of Paradise Lost, of Nature or of Modernity.

Academic studies of the circulation of images and imaginaries in the field of tourism constitute an innovative research track. In particular raising the question of the connections between anthropological imaginaries and tourism imaginaries, but also the identification of intermediaries and the question of popularization.

Indeed, whereas many works deride the travesties of academic research as presented to tourists, we could also write that the legitimacy of tourism is derived as much from the aristocratic Grand Tour as from the ethnographic field study. This means that we could examine the heuristic foundations of tourism imaginaries, understanding tourism as an encyclopedic practice for the popularization and appropriation of an imaginary of Otherness built by knowledge. When studying tourism the ethnographer is confronted with essentialist descriptions produced by his or her predecessors, the geographer comes up against exotic images as propagated by geographical societies, and the historian has to deal with sanitized representations of the past. Tourism is taken here to be a social field in which, since its invention in the nineteenth century, there can be observed a process of knowledge transfer (popularization, appropriation, commercialization), produced by the social and human sciences with the purpose of imparting knowledge of the Other—be it a social, a spatial or a cultural Other. I use the term popularization in the dual sense in which it is employed in the history of values attributed to the diffusion of scientific knowledge, that is to refer both to the actual transmission of knowledge (scientific mediation and culture) and also to the disdain frequently displayed by scholars and academics for the circulators and receptors of "popularized" knowledge.

This implies the broader question of circulation and intermediaries. We shall examine the role and diversity of the intermediaries, who from the very beginnings of leisure mobility have appropriated, embodied, transposed, and/or translated the location, the peoples, the ways of life, the systems of education and belief sought out by tourists—have produced imaginaries thanks to their imagination. These intermediaries can be people (guides, scholars, new inhabitants, and others), mechanisms (networks, transport systems, guidebook collections, and so on), or representations (paintings, photographs, literature, travel accounts, social science works). These intermediaries, these "go-betweens" can be analyzed as a chain, from those advertising the "authentic and traditional" to the "local" guides, from small-time cultural entrepreneurs to fully-fledged anthropologists, attempting to identify social characteristics and the contexts that allow them to emerge. Situated on the fringes of mass tourism, the spaces chosen and their intermediaries could appear to have value as models for understanding the role of tourism in the globalization and circulation of knowledge and imaginaries of otherness. The hypothesis is that recurrent factors exist in the secular appropriation of knowledge, but that these recurrent factors cannot be reduced to a mere phenomenon of global imperialism or post-modernist globalization. The "other's Other" is locally and globally produced.

How is this other's Other produced and how do we study its production? In response to such questions it is perhaps useful to return to Gaston Bachelard and to the central role he gives to the imagination.

For him, imagination is the power to change, combine images, thanks to imaginaries. Imaginaries are much more than images. Indeed, Bachelard writes that imagination is a movement while images are forms and the problem is that we focused on forms, forgetting the power of movement.

> As in so many other domains, there is opposition in the reign of the imagination between constitution and mobility. And as a description of forms is easier than a description of movements, we tell ourselves that psychology takes primary care of the former. It is, however, the latter which is the more important. The imagination, in a total psychology, is, above all, a type of spiritual mobility, the greatest, liveliest, living type of spiritual mobility. We must therefore always include in the study of an image the study of its mobility, its fertility, its life.[2] (Bachelard 1943: 7–8)

For Bachelard, the imagined world exists *prior to* the represented world, the imaginary before the represented, the image: "the world is imagined before being represented, the world is beautiful before being true. The world is admired before being tested" (Bachelard 1943: 192). In brief, imagination is not a power to create images but liberation from them, power to deform them, change them. This has methodological consequences: we cannot infer shifting imaginaries from collective representations and congealed images (the catalogue). Moreover, such imagination no longer designates a psychological process, but rather capacities of appropriation, the agency of poaching or making do (*bricolage*), in short a capacity for action.

What to do? We need to focus on the modalities of production, of reproduction but also of misuse of certain images, concentrating on the meanings—shared or divergent—given to the images by producers, receivers, and intermediaries. What transformations can we observe given historical and socio-cultural circumstances? All in all, we must no longer be content simply to study the structure of images, but allow the producers and receivers to speak and manage to extract ourselves from the repetition of the couplet image/gaze. We need to act like the nymph Echo who attempts to distract Narcissus from his mirror (Legendre 1994).

Looking Like a Conclusion: From the Particular to the General and Back

Seen like this the discussion has yet to approach a crucial problem: the distinction between the individual and the collective, even the social, imaginary. Most of us affirm and reaffirm that it is a serious error to believe that ontogeny summarizes phylogenesis, that the particular can ever account for the collective. This theory of summation is certainly scientifically untenable, but we must admit that our reasoning around touristic imaginaries (imaginaries that are *a priori* collective) is constantly produced by what we infer from individual imaginaries (our own, for example). How do we escape such an aporia?

The first thing to do is to bring, to think together the disdain for the imaginary, the constant use of summation and its denial. Disdain, use, and denial tell us something about those who expound and denounce in these terms.[3]

In order to study the imaginary, the use of analogy appears more productive than facile generalization or simple denial. For example, on the condition that the sexual assignment of the symbolic and the imaginary is avoided, the distinction symbolic/imaginary could prove itself fertile for the proposition of certain hypotheses concerning impulses behind a desire for tourism. In fact, from the perspective of the producers of tourism images as well as tourists, the touristic imaginary is born of narcissism, a desire for the self and identity, characterized, as discussed above, by a deficit of alterity, an alterity which according to Lacan, depends on the symbolic. It is not about explaining the general by the particular, but of provoking the right questions.

Such an analogical approach can also open us up to a more precise consideration of the connections between, on one hand, memory and individual imagination, and on the other, the temporal, spatial and social context, where these memories, histories, and images are recounted, displayed, and exchanged. The most recent research in neuroscience reveals that memory and imagination is located in the same zone of the brain. This allows us to wonder about the relationship between memory, history, narrative, and the constitution of collective imaginaries. Confident, following his experiences in Madagascar, the anthropologist Maurice Bloch affirmed that "the memory a subject conserves of what he lived during his life—his autobiographical memory—is not by nature that different from the knowledge that he has of historical events more distant and which he cannot in any case have experienced" (Bloch 1996: 61).

Thus individual memory would be also collective: no need to have lived an event in order to feel it, to repeat it, to relive it. Following Maurice Halbwachs who was interested in the relations between individual memory, collective memory, and the spatial dimension (Halbwachs 1997), Maurice Bloch shows equally that this individualized collective memory is rendered possible by the context and the landscape within which the narrative takes place. Could we not say the same of imagination? Our personal imagination, for example the way in which we imagine, project but also recount, recognize the other, the stranger we have encountered—host or tourist—is it not always shared? The form and the movement of our imaginary of alterity are not different to the form and movement of our collective imaginary of alterity. Take the example of exoticism—is this common to a whole group, is it social or cultural?

If at the level of our brain, our memory and our imagination combine, images of alterity—notably exotic touristic imagery—are integrated within our narration and shared as if they were experiences that end up constituting the context.

In the manner of scientific imagination, touristic imagination is only possible in a certain context, a specific époque, where particular connections are permitted. We are left with analogy not being causality. Research must continue.

Notes

1 With the exception of the notion of the "national imaginary" taken from Benedict Anderson, articles which dealt with questions of the imaginary were nearly all published in journals edited by M. Maffesoli, *Sociétés* et *Les Cahiers européens de l'imaginaire*.
2 My translation.
3 In an ironic mode: we might note that French anthropologists despise the notion of the imaginary because they think about it from the perspective of the Lacanian vision distinguishing between the individual imaginary (me, identity, the mother, the domestic) and the symbolic (the father, alterity, society, the outside). Whether imaginary or collective, the imaginary leaves no space for the father and thus to males who make up the vast majority of anthropologists.

Bibliography

AMIROU, Rachid (1995) *Imaginaire touristique et sociabilités du voyage*. Paris: Presses Universitaires de France.
—— (2000) *Imaginaire du tourisme culturel*. Paris: Presses Universitaires de France.
ANDERSON, Benedict R. (1991) *Imagined Communities: Reflections on the Origin and Spread of Nationalism* (2nd edn). New York: Verso.
APPADURAI, Arjun (1996) *Modernity at Large: Cultural Dimensions of Globalization*. Minneapolis, MN: University of Minnesota Press.
AUGE, Marc (1994) *Pour une anthropologie des mondes contemporains*. Paris: Aubier.
BACHELARD, Gaston (1934) *Le Nouvel esprit scientifique*. Paris: Alcan.
—— (1943) *L'Air et les songes*. Paris: Corti / (2011) *Air and Dreams: An Essay on the Imagination of Movement*, trans. E. and F. Farrell. Dallas: Dallas Institute of Humanities and Culture (Bachelard Translation Series).
—— (1949) *La psychanalyse du feu*. Paris: Gallimard.
BARTHES, Roland (1972) *Mythologies*, trans. A. Lavers. New York: Hill and Wang.
BLOCH, Maurice (1996) "Mémoire autobiographique et mémoire historique du passé éloigné." *Enquêtes* 2 (Tradition et écriture): 59–76.
BOORSTIN, D.J. (1992/1962) *The Image: A Guide to Pseudo-events in America*. New York: Vintage.
BRUHNS, H. and BURGUIERE, A. (eds) (2003) "Imaginaires nationaux. Origines, usages, figures." *Annales. Histoire, Sciences Sociales* (58)1: 37–39.
CASTORIADIS, C. (1987) *The Imaginary Institution of Society*, trans. K. Blamey. Cambridge, MA: MIT Press.
—— (1989) *Les carrefours du labyrinthe*, vol. 4. Paris: Le Seuil.
CERTEAU, M. de (1980) *L'invention du quotidien 1 / Arts de faire*. Paris: coll. 10–18.
DESCOLA, P. (2005) *Par delà nature et culture*. Paris: Gallimard.
DUMEZIL, Georges (1968) *Mythes et epopéees*. Paris: Gallimard.
DURAND, G. (1999) *The Anthropological Structures of the Imaginary*, trans. M. Sankey and J. Hatten. Brisbane: Boombana Publications.
GODELIER, M. (2001–2002) "L'imaginaire, le symbolique et le réel." *Revue Sciences humaines, hors série: Les sciences de la cognition* 35: 20–22.

HALBWACHS, M. (1997) *La Mémoire collective*. Paris: Albin Michel.

KIRSHENBLATT-GIMBLETT, B. (1998) *Destination Culture: Tourism, Museums, and Heritage*. Berkeley, CA: University of California Press.

LACAN, J. (1977) "The mirror stage as formative of the function of the I," trans. A. Sheridan, in J. Lacan (ed.), *Écrits: A Selection*. New York: W.W. Norton, pp. 1–7.

LEGENDRE, P. (1994) *Leçons III. Dieu au miroir. Etude sur l'institution des images*. Paris: Fayard.

LEVI-STRAUSS, C. (1968) "Introduction à l'œuvre de Marcel Mauss," in M. Mauss, *Sociologie et anthropologie* (4th edn). Paris: Presses universitaires de France. [Online] Available at: http://classiques.uqac.ca/classiques/mauss_marcel/socio_et_anthropo/0_introduction/intro_socio_et_anthropo.pdf (accessed 2013).

—— (1987) *Introduction to the Work of Marcel Mauss*, trans Felicity Baker. London: Routledge and Kegan Paul.

LITTLETON, Scott F. (1973) *The New Comparative Mythology: An Anthropological Assessment of the Theories of Georges Dumezil*. Berkeley, CA: University of California Press.

MACCANNELL, Dean (1976/1999). *The Tourist: A New Theory of the Leisure Class*. Berkeley, CA: University of California Press.

RICOEUR, Paul (1985) *Temps et récit*, vol. 3: *Le Temps raconté*. Paris: Seuil.

—— (1986) *Du texte à l'action. Essais d'herméneutique II*. Paris: Seuil.

—— (1990) *Soi-même comme un autre*. Paris: Seuil.

—— (1994) "Imagination in discourse and in action," in G. Robinson and J.F. Rundell (eds), *Rethinking Imagination: Culture and Creativity*. London: Routledge, pp. 87–117.

THIESSE, Anne Marie (1999) *La création des identités nationales*. Paris: Seuil.

THOMAS, Joel (1998) *Introduction aux méthodologies de l'imaginaire*. Paris: Ellipses.

URBAIN, Jean-Didier (1994) *L'idiot du voyage: histoires de touristes*. Paris: Éditions Payot & Rivages.

—— (1998) *Secrets de voyage: menteurs, imposteurs et autres voyageurs invisibles*. Paris: Éditions Payot & Rivages.

2 Imagining Goa
Tourism Development and State Formation in Postcolonial Goa

Raghuraman S. Trichur

Introduction

It is common knowledge that social, political and economic transformations in the twentieth century, especially since the end of World War II and the beginning of the era of decolonization, have challenged and indeed destabilized anthropology's assumptions of culture. At the same time, various attempts have been made to replace and/or dress culture with alternate discourses. The proliferation of "the imaginary" in recent times could be attributed to this disciplinary dilemma. This situation helps us better understand Claudia Strauss's claim that "cultural anthropology's use of imaginary has . . . a tendency towards cultural abstraction, reification and homogenization" (2006: 322). Furthermore, anthropological writings that do use the idea of imaginary focus on the process of cultural subject formation. While this is important, it is possible to use the idea of imaginary creatively to talk about other broader social processes. Following the insights provided by Lacan (1977), Anderson (1983) and Taylor (2002), it is possible to approach imaginaries as strategies critical, dovetailing ideology (Althusser 1971), to the on-going processes of state formation within a society. These strategies are shaped by the historically defined conflicts and contradictions that inform the process of class and state formation in society. Approaching from this perspective, this chapter is an attempt to explore the manner in which the state uses its ability to imagine and create the space for the expansion and implementation of its hegemonic control over the society.

Discussions of tourism in recent years have stressed the meaning of space, and the interplay between space, as place and region, and social structures, experiences, and identity (Urry 1990; Shields 1991; Rojek 1993; Ashworth and Dietvorst 1995). Such a notion is particularly relevant for the conceptualization of destinations as places of tourism, for as Urry (1995: 1) contends, "[a]lmost all the major social and cultural theories bear upon the explanation of place." In order to understand the political economic significance of the tourism destination, it is important to recognize the role of space and the instructional and cultural practices which construct it. Dominant theories of tourism destination pay attention to the quantifiable aspects of the tourism destination while simultaneously ignoring its historical and social nature. As a result the conceptual power of the destination is treated in a cavalier fashion by theoretical constructs, which tie it to neither space nor history (see Harvey 1989; 1993).

The development of a tourism destination is a process of producing spaces, constructed by historically contingent institutional practices and cultural discourse (Shields 1991). The tourism destination is both a representation of space and space for representation. It is a space saturated by power and in the words of Henri Lefebvre, "a stake, the locus of projects and actions deployed as specific strategies, and hence the object of wagers on the future" (Lefebvre 1995: 142–143). Approached from this perspective, a close reading of the tourism destination and its associated discourses could provide a commentary on the developments within the society in which it is located (see Harvey 1989; 1993). This chapter firstly analyzes the political and economic developments that unfolded in postliberation Goa. Secondly, it explores the manner in which the discourse of tourism development has contributed to locating Goa within the imagination of the postcolonial Indian nation, and created the space for the expansion of the Indian state's hegemonic control[1] (see Crehan 2002) over Goan society (see Franklin 2003).[2]

The Days before Liberation

The relation between the newly formed postcolonial Indian state and the colonial Goan society between 1947 and 1961 was determined, on the one hand, by the position occupied by India as a member of the fledging postcolonial international community, a founding member of the Non-Allied Movement, and a promoter of non-violent and peaceful means of conflict resolution.

As soon as the independent Indian nation state was established, the Indian government under the leadership of the Indian National Congress (henceforth INC) was forced by its membership within the international community to view Portuguese colonialism in Goa through the lens of its foreign policy. This contributed to ambiguities in the political rhetoric of the Indian government which had real consequences for Goa's freedom struggle that also drew membership from Goans settled outside Goa, especially in Bombay. For example, with respect to the support sought by Goan freedom fighters for a *satyagraha* (civil resistance) they had planned in 1954, Prime Minister Jawaharlal Nehru said:

> "during the last seven years we have restrained our people. Normally speaking I do not want non-Goans to go to Goa. But I am not going to stop Goans from functioning." (quoted in Gaitonde 1987: 98)

According to Nehru, *satyagraha* was a strategy which could be employed by people only to bring pressure on their own government and that the use of this strategy in any other situation would be inappropriate (Nehru 1968: 383–384). In other words the involvement of Indians in a *satyagraha* directed at the Portuguese colonial administrators in Goa was meaningless. While in this situation there was an implicit distinction drawn between India and Goa, on another occasion, Nehru in a speech he delivered on August 21, 1955, said:

> "Opposed as we are to colonialism everywhere, it is impossible for us to tolerate the continuation of colonial rule in a small part of India. It is not that we covet Goa. That little bit of territory makes no difference to this great country. But even a small enclave under foreign rule does make a difference, and it is a constant reproach to the self-respect and national interest of India." (quoted in Palmer 1958: 294)

The inconsistencies in the position of the Indian government strained the relationship between the Indian government and the anti-colonial forces in Goa. Until August 1961, Nehru had adopted a wait and watch approach to the whole Goan situation. In fact, Nehru's plea for a peaceful resolution was well received by the advanced capitalist countries, especially the United States. On the other hand, it was viewed by anti-colonial leaders in Africa as a sign of weakness on the part of India (Rubinoff 1997: 63–69). They equated India's unwillingness to take action against the Portuguese in Goa to abetting Portuguese repression in Africa (ibid.). Eventually, on December 20, 1961, the Indian Army occupied Goa, removing the last vestiges of European colonialism in the South Asian subcontinent. This was a simultaneous response to these international pressures as well as the electoral pressures that resonated from within the Congress Party (Palmer 1963).[3]

The Days after Liberation

The integration of Goan society within the Indian nation state and its incorporation into the Indian state's sphere of hegemonic influence proved problematic. The Indian state approached Goan society as a distinct product of Portuguese colonial rule. Considering the apprehensions among Goa's Catholic population voiced within and outside Goa, the integration of Catholic communities was viewed as being of primary importance—a test of India's credential as a secular nation. This increasing emphasis on the distinctive characteristics of the Goan society and its colonial legacy contradicted the manner in which the Indian nation imagined and linked its own history to the pre-colonial past. This emphasis on the part of the Indian state was received with caution by Goa's Hindu majority, especially those members of the anti-colonial campaign in Goa who had forged close links with key political outfits in neighboring Maharashtra.

The Congress Party lacked any kind of organic link with the freedom struggle waged in Goa (Esteves 1986). The links that existed were established through the predominantly Brahmin petty bourgeois Hindu and Catholic Goans who had migrated to British India but were not viewed favorably by the majority of the Goan population—the non-Brahmin rural laboring class. However, despite these internal conflicts, Congress, given its track record of success in elections since 1947, considered itself to have the best chance of winning the first ever election to be conducted in post-liberation Goa, in 1962. The Congress Party fielded a list of

28 candidates. Of these 28, 24 were Brahmins, including members of Goa's mercantile elite, who were viewed as part of the problem by the majority. This elicited strong response from non-Brahmin party factions within the Congress Party who broke away to form the Maharashtrawadi Gomantak Party (henceforth referred to as MGP).[4] The MGP, an aggregate of mutually antagonistic economic classes that came together guided only by the dual objective to eliminate Brahmin domination and the marginalization of Catholic influence in Goa, won the election in 1962 and remained in power till 1979. The overnight emergence and success of the MGP had a critical impact on the postcolonial Goan economy.

The Stagnant Post-liberation Goan Economy (1961–1979)

The liberation of Goa from Portuguese colonial rule unsettled the position occupied by the predominantly Brahmin Goan mercantile bourgeoisie and subjected them to the scrutiny of the Goan masses. During the colonial period, the administration had safeguarded the interests of this class. However, the opportunity for the Goan majority, the non-Brahmin, rural laboring class, was provided by the first free election to be conducted in liberated Goa. In the face of the threats to their position of dominance, and sensing the influence of the MGP, the Goan mercantile elite where forced to maintain a low profile. In addition, the Goan mercantile elite faced the threat of possible competition from the well-established Indian bourgeoisie. This fear was not realized during the tenure of the MGP.

The popularity of MGP and its policies were also the party's limitations. The MGP's overarching concern to merge with Maharashtra was accompanied by disinterest in the economic conditions in Goa. Other than populist agrarian measures, the MGP did not significantly alter the economic conditions prevailing in Goa. This, combined with the private ownership of mines, unwittingly reproduced the dominance of the mercantile bourgeoisie over the Goan economy. The MGP's lackadaisical approach to the economy by default obstructed the entry of Indian capital into the Goan economy, while select factions from within the Goan mercantile elite made inroads into the Indian economy. At the same time, the Goan mercantile bourgeoisie devised strategies to gain acceptance and soften the skeptical gaze of the masses in postcolonial Goan society. They financed the establishment of educational institutions[5] and assumed control over the print media.[6] The mercantile elite used their financial influence to shape public opinion through the newspapers and educational institutions that they had established. Through the control of the media, the Goan bourgeoisie managed to divert and dodge any criticism about their links with the erstwhile Portuguese colonial administration.

By late 1970s, the top Goan business houses which had interests in trading and owned mining operations in Goa had grown in value and were considered the fastest growing business groups in India. The growth of these business groups had a telling effect on the Goan environment. The successes of these businesses were solely responsible for the ravaging of Goa's environment in the mining belt, the pollution of Goa's rivers, and the reduced life-span of Goan miners (Alvares 1979). The Goan bourgeoisie that emerged in the last phase of the colonial period had safeguarded and indeed reinforced their position in post-liberation Goa by exploiting the fragile situation determined by communal politics.

The development of the mining sector and its ancillaries were restricted to the interior of Goa, the Hindu-dominated, erstwhile New Conquest areas of colonial Goa. Open strip mining and scant regard for the environment contributed to further accentuate the difference between the New Conquest and the Old Conquest areas of Goa. However, the development of mining in the former did have a significant economic and social impact on the latter. The expansion of capitalist relations of production found its way into fishing which along with agriculture was the mainstay of the coastal communities of Goa. The Indian government, focusing on increased production, encouraged the mechanization of fishing and financed the operation of fishing trawlers. The trawlers were purchased by petty capitalists who were well connected with politicians and were financed by the mercantile elite. By 1978 there were approximately 400 trawlers which were allowed to operate, most of them "owned by 'moneyed unwanted elements' and not by traditional fishermen" (Kagal 1979). Amidst the confusion in the post-liberation Goan economy, Goa's mercantile elite were able to weather the shock, relocating themselves from a colonial society to postcolonial society, and retain their hold over the economy.

The on-going changes in Goan society, coupled with land tenure legislation soon after liberation, contributed to the destruction of agriculture and the decline in the already low level of agricultural production. The impact of these events was felt more in the Catholic-dominated Old Conquest areas of Goa than in the Hindu-dominated New Conquest areas. Many families that controlled land in the Old Conquest areas had migrated after having contracted with *mundkars*, whereas in the New Conquest areas, the families that controlled land were in residence. The land-controlling families in the New Conquest areas were able to take precautionary steps, legal and illegal, in order to disqualify *mundkars* from claiming any rights of ownership. In the case of the Old Conquest areas, due to the long history of migration, a significant number of families having settled outside Goa could do nothing to retain control. The *mundkars*, on paying an amount predetermined by the state to the *bhatkar*, became the legal owners of the plots of land that they cultivated and a similar agreement was made for the plots of land on which their residences stood. The situation contributed to a significant increase in petty commodity production especially in the Old Conquest areas.

This is evident in the emergence of tourism and the involvement of peasant families in it. The populist measures undertaken by the MGP contributed to the increasing presence of the Goan peasantry that emerged from the ruins of colonial Goa. On the other hand, the MGP, through its policies, successfully restricted the entry of capitalist forces from outside into Goa. While on the one hand, this secured the position of the mercantile elite in a society which was witnessing the increasing presence of petty commodity producers, on the other, declining agricultural productivity forced the peasant households to add other economic activities to their existing repertoire of activities for survival, most important being their involvement in the tourism industry.

Tourism as a Strategy for Survival

Among the people most affected by the developments in postcolonial Goa were the Catholic *kharvis* (fisherman), who also held tenancy rights on plots controlled by the *gaunkari*. The *kharvis* belonged to the lowest rung of the Catholic community in Goa. The *kharvi* families, due to abject marginalization and poverty, could not take advantage of the opportunities provided to the newly converted Catholic population during the colonial era, or of the benefits from the tenancy reforms legislated in the postcolonial period. They did not have the means to exercise their right to assume ownership over the plots they cultivated. Secondly, the increase in commercial fishing due to the involvement of the merchants in these activities (mentioned above) saw a decline in their already meagre incomes.

The position of the *kharvis* was further marginalized by the increased supply of money in the Goan economy fueled by mining and remittances from migrant Goans, which increased the cost of living. The lack of alternatives encouraged members of the *kharvi* community to become involved in non-traditional economic activities. While a few became involved in illegal activities such as smuggling foreign goods and precious metals like gold bound for markets within India, others involved themselves in the provision of boarding and lodging facilities to incoming tourists (Siquiera 1991). This participation of the Catholic *kharvi* community in tourism has such broad ranging significance that it cannot be viewed as a decision made purely on the basis of economics of survival. The decision could also have been instigated by the centuries-long social marginalization of the *kharvis* within Goa's Catholic community.[7]

Kharvi involvement in tourism-related services effectively started in 1966 with the arrival of the first wave of hippies from Nepal who were either driven out of there, or had become tired of the place which was viewed as an esoteric refuge (Institute of Social Sciences 1989: 21–22). In a matter of two or three years, Goa emerged as an important node in the hippie world circuit which spanned the islands in southern Europe, the high altitudes in Nepal, and the beaches of South East Asia (Odzer 1995; Teas 1988).

Kharvi households took advantage of their proximity to the beach and the increasing demand for lodging among the hippies visiting Goa, in order to earn extra money. In the initial stages, these families allowed the hippies to stay within their residences, in exchange for rent paid in cash. The rent received was nominal and was used to finance household expenses. However, the main occupation of the families remained either fishing or cultivation. It was not long before families went to the extent of renting their whole houses to hippies, temporarily relocating to makeshift thatched-roof shelters constructed in their backyards. Many families also cooked for and served food to the hippies and other visitors to the beaches in temporarily constructed structures referred to as shacks.

Based on information gathered through interviews, it is reasonable to state that the flexibility and tolerance of the hippies enabled even families with minimal residential space to be active participants in the expanding tourism trade—the new economic activity which was beyond the control of local institutions or the rural elite. There were no intermediaries, nor were any laws in existence regulating the practice of hosting guests. The hippies paid their rent for accommodation and other services in cash. The esoteric lifestyle of the hippies had always encouraged them to live among the "natives," which helped them distance themselves from the "tourists" who lived in hotels and had minimal interaction with most members of the local society (Siquiera 1991). Hippies, unlike "tourists," stayed longer in Goa. Some even stayed the whole tourism season which extended for six months; others stayed for a shorter period of time. Many hippies viewed their lifestyle in Goa as a statement of resistance to the increasing commoditization of everyday life in their home countries.

The *kharvis* were aware that the hippies viewed them as poor and primitive but interacted with their hosts as individuals and not as members of a lower caste. Considering their marginalized position within the wider Goan community, the *kharvis* preferred to articulate this image of the simple primitive within the hippie-centered space in order to earn money. At the same time, interaction with the tourism-dominated space enabled the *kharvis* to distance themselves from the social position they occupied within the society at large (Afonso 1989). This had far-reaching economic and social significance. Tourism enabled them to enjoy a better standard of living. The affluence generated by the money earned was exhibited in the local markets and various public gatherings. Thus, hosting hippies was also viewed by the *kharvis* as a status-enhancing mechanism. It enabled them to imitate the lifestyle of the landed elite of the colonial period who frequently played hosts to colonial administrators and other foreign visitors. It must also be noted here that renting rooms to foreigners was considered more prestigious than renting rooms to Indian tourists, as Indians were looked down upon; they were considered rude and uncivilized.[8]

The most significant impact of hosting tourists was that the womenfolk of the *kharvi* families withdrew from the workforce within the local communities. This can be viewed as another strategy for aping the lifestyles of elite households where the women were restricted to the domestic sphere and to select public spaces such as the church and community festivals. The women of the *kharvi* families, instead of expending their labor power outside the household, stayed home and took care of the needs of the tourists.

Involvement in tourism had its own advantages for the members of the coastal households when compared to opportunities offered by the mining industry in Goa. Employment in the mining industry required an individual to leave his household and relocate to a new place, leave his family behind and face physical hardships in return for wages, which were anyway measly. Tourism did not impose any such demands on the households. There were few new skills to be learnt and there was little need for capital investment. The space for tourists was created from the existing arrangements.

According to informants, members of the younger generation among the *kharvis*, especially men, are clear about their goals as far as tourism trade is concerned—make money any which way and improve one's financial status. Involvement in tourism, as far as the families interacting with it were concerned, was a strategy to move away from physically demanding and labor intensive activities which were the hallmark of a *kharvis'* social existence. It was a step towards upward mobility within the Goan society.

The tourism season lasts six to seven months in a year, starting in October and peaking towards December. It starts to fade in the second week of March. By the end of May the shacks are dismantled in anticipation of the monsoon season. In the initial stages, there was no competition among the resident families with regard to the location of their shacks. Once an individual or a family occupied a particular location, that location belonged to that person or family for years to come. However, families living closer to the beach have an advantage over the others. These families could temporarily convert their front porches into sitting areas to serve food and drinks to the customers, further reducing the need for investment. In the initial period, families depended exclusively on members within the household to provide the required labor to service the needs of the hippies. The female members of the family cooked the food and the male members interacted with the customers. Other than bottled alcoholic and non-alcoholic beverages, a majority of the items served in the shacks were produced in the temporary kitchens set up alongside the shacks. Initially, the shack operators restricted their operations to the few tables and chairs that they could accommodate within the confines of the shacks and the immediate surrounding areas. However, the increasing competition among shack operators forced them to develop new strategies for reaching out to more people on the beaches. One common strategy, besides increasing the number of tables served, is the employment of people, on a commission basis, to walk up and down the beaches selling bottled drinks. Following channels other than the standard travel agents and tour operators, the peasant families in coastal Old Conquest areas had created their own networks to sell their services to the "tourists." All members of the local community involved in tourism trade, in addition to the money they earn providing their respective services, also from time to time earn commissions for introducing clients to fellow participants in tourism trade.

By the early 1970s, the hippies were spending an average of Rs. 1,000,000/- per season (six months, between October and March), in the communities located between Calangute and Anjuna beaches alone (Institute of Social Sciences 1989).[9] Thus tourism contributed to an increase in the incomes of the heretofore most marginalized sections of the coastal communities in the Old Conquest areas. More importantly, the gradual increase in the arrival of hippies attracted more families to the tourism trade. It was not long before the landowning *bhatkars* also became involved by constructing rooms either in their own residences or separately, with the intent to rent.

In the first two decades after liberation in 1961, Goa's tourism trade expanded at its own pace. Over this period, more peasant households became involved in it. While some modified their existing living arrangements to accommodate tourists, others took advantage of the financing schemes and loans provided by the state government. On reassessing the situation, the tenancy laws passed by the MGP government after liberation cleared the first hurdles for the involvement of peasant families in the tourism trade. The law bestowed the *mundkars* with absolute ownership rights, giving them the right to use their household as they wished. Though not ratified with the intention of developing tourism, the Tenancy and the Mundkar Acts cleared the way for interactions between peasant families and the tourism trade in the coastal areas of Goa. Families with requisite documents were able to claim clear title to the plot of land they cultivated, and on which their house was constructed. Using the property as collateral, the families concerned availed of subsidized loans provided by the government and used them either to construct rooms that could be rented to tourists or to buy vehicles that could be operated as taxis (based on personal interview).

The MGP government had not instituted a clearly defined tourism development policy, but did not discourage the expansion of tourism trade in Goa. Some elements of the national bourgeoisie, however, did take notice of these developments in coastal Goa. The first capital intensive beach resort to operate in Goa, the Fort Aguada Beach Resort, is a property of the Indian Hotels Co. Ltd., a national chain of hotels operating in India. It was constructed in the early 1970s (Institute of Social Sciences 1989: 21), and remained the only nationally reputed capital intensive beach resort in Goa till the early 1980s. Coincidentally, the steady increase in the number of tourists coming into Goa continued, which aided the increasing involvement of peasant families in tourism in various capacities. The specific manner in which the peasant families interacted with tourism trade was determined by the location of their residences with respect to the beach. By the end of MGPs tenure as ruling party in 1979, tourism trade had witnessed healthy growth. From a few thousand in 1960, Goa received more than 350,000 tourists in 1979, 8 per cent of whom constituted foreign tourists.

The Tourism Destination in Goa

The cultural space constructed within the tourism destination in Goa is centered on the reproduction of *Goa Duarado* (Golden Goa), a colonial construction, and *sossegaddo* (meaning relaxed, idyllic, and leisurely), the lifestyle of the colonial catholic landed gentry. It was reproduced amidst on-going caste/class conflicts between landowning Catholic Brahmin[10] *bhatkars* (landlords), non-Brahmin *mundkars* (tenants), and landless laboring communities. *Goa Duarada*, which during the colonial period was a class signifier within the Catholic community, was, much to the dismay of the landed elite, rapidly transformed into a Catholic community signifier during the postcolonial period.

This Portuguese colonial socio-cultural image of Goa constitutes the very foundation on which the tourism destination in Goa is constructed. This is evident in the cultural forms and events highlighted by the touristic performances and discourses, or simply in the assumed passivity and tolerance of the Goan people. The idea of *sossegado* is redefined in the context of the tourism discourse to mean peaceful demeanor, contented nature, friendliness, and hospitality. The trickling in of hippies into Goa during the 1960s and 1970s led to their integration into the exoticized image of Goa. The hippies became an integral part of the Indian tourist's experience of Goa, an object of the Indian gaze. The dominance of Goan Catholics within the emerging tourism destination space, their interactions with the predominantly white international tourist population, and the touristic rituals of the latter together confirmed the distinctiveness of Goan society to Indian tourists.

The Congress Party, which had heretofore struggled to secure a foothold in Goan politics, became an attractive platform for individuals in the MGP and the UGP whose class interests were constrained by the political ideology of these political parties. An assortment of individuals sharing similar class interests joined the Congress Party and ensured that it came to power in Goa for the first time since liberation. Soon after the Congress Party assumed control over the state government of Goa in 1980, plans were drawn up for the development of tourism along the lines of capital–wage relations. To set the ball rolling Goa was chosen as the venue for the retreat after world leaders attended the 1983 Commonwealth Heads of Government Meeting in New Delhi.[11] Soon after this event, authorized by the Congress Party-dominated Central Government of India, a Master Plan for the development of tourism was formulated in 1987 (Newman 1984).[12] Tourism in Goa was perceived as heralding the new progressive and regulatory mechanism through which everyone would benefit. The promotion of tourism and the marketing of the specific manner in which the tourism destination was constructed were viewed as the only means of creating environmentally friendly and culturally sensitive strategies for the modernization of Goan society.

The Congress Party-controlled state government in Goa, playing upon the fears of rising unemployment, pushed forward the agenda of tourism development. Slowly but steadily the tourism destination became the dominant space for interaction between Goa and the wider world. Moreover, the tourism destination in Goa soon emerged as the space representing Goa. An individual's/group's class and/or communal affiliation could now be identified from the manner in which they interacted with and within the tourism destination and voiced their concerns about on-going developments related to tourism in Goa.

The social spaces created along the coast by interactions between tourists and members of the local community become markers within the Goan social landscape, which were ascribed symbolic values and historicized. The globalization of the social space occupied by the tourism destination, thanks to the steady increase in the number of incoming tourists, both Indian and non-Indian and the intensity of capital–wage relations contributed to the emergence of the tourism destination in Goa as the representative of the larger Goan society.

The establishment and reproduction of the tourism destination reconfigured power relations and redefined class relations within the Goan society in many ways. The inflow of Indian capital, if not completely at least to a significant extent, eroded the dominance of the mercantile elite. The ascendance of the tourism destination as the representative social space within Goa and the expansion of capital-wage relations that resulted destabilized and marginalized the ideological content of the MGP and those segments of the Goan population that had earlier championed the erasure of the Goan society's historical specificity through the merger of Goa with Maharashtra. Their reactionary anti-Catholic rhetoric was now trained at the cultural construction of the tourism destination. Many refer to tourism as a new form of cultural colonialism. They often would point to the demonstration effect of tourism on the local population. Needless to say, the venom of the MGP's communally charged politics was significantly eroded.

The postcolonial reproduction of *Goa Duarada*, a cultural space that was the preserve of the catholic elite, within the confines of the tourism destination by the non-elite, redefined elite apprehensions about their future as subjects of postcolonial India. The postcolonial tourism destination emerged as a more immediate threat to their self-definition as Goans and their imagination of the Goan society. This encouraged the Catholic elite and their institutions to criticize and resist the emerging spatial configuration of the tourism destination and the impact of its associated performances on social and cultural values. This is evident in the increasing participation of Catholic Goans, including nuns, priests, and teachers, in some of the anti-tourism rallies in Goa. The report prepared by the Sub-Committee of the Diocesan Pastoral Council (DPC) of Goa in 1988 is a perfect example. The DPC report is presented well within the framework of *Goa Duarada*. It reproduces the images that constitute the tourism destination in Goa. Among other things it refers to the "natural and scenic beauty" of Goa (p. 8) and the "normally uninterfering . . . docile nature" and "easy going manners" (p. 8) of the Goan people. The report further laments the loss of traditional occupations of fishermen and toddy-tappers and ridicules opportunities for wage-labor offered by the capital-intensive hotels and resorts. While condemning the development of tourism, the report at the same time reflects the Catholic elite's nostalgia for the golden Goa of the colonial period. This process worked to the advantage of the Indian state.

In response to the resistance to the expansion of tourism, the Indian state unleashed the development apparatuses at its disposal. It sought assistance from international agencies such as the UNDP to study the potential for tourism development in Goa, hired marketing consultants, and used the print media—the most effective medium of communication in Goa—to erode the legitimacy of the criticism levied against tourism. This is evident in a series of articles written by travel writers Hugh Gantzer and Colleen Gantzer and published in the *Navhind Times*, a local newspaper (Gantzer and Gantzer 1991). The Gantzers validated and supported the Indian state's attempt to promote tourism development in Goa. The Gantzers employed the scientific temper of modernization to suggest that all the criticisms that had been directed at the existing policies of tourism development in India conclusively and deliberately sought to prevent the emergence of a modern, more humane, scientific, progressive and democratic order in postcolonial Goa.

In order to provide a sense of "scientific objectivity," the Gantzers documented the views emerging from both sides of the debate: the pro-tourism and the anti-tourism lobbies. However, their bias becomes evident in the manner in which they provide a rationale for the fears of the pro-tourism lobby while considering the allegations of the anti-tourism lobby as absurd and exaggerated. The articles alleged that the anti-tourism rhetoric was an elitist response rooted in the frustration felt by the traditional Catholic elite's loss of power and prestige in the post-liberation Goan society. According to the Gantzers, by opposing tourism, both the ambitious priests of the Church and the scions of the socially diminished landowning class had found a single agitationary path to regain their erstwhile position of power and prestige. The Gantzers further suggested that by pinpointing the so-called "evils" of tourism development, the traditional elite were creating a "wounded psyche" vote bank which would at the same stroke distance them from the political burden of their colonial past while projecting them as the new saviors of Goa. According to them the "only way that this unholy brew (anti-tourism agitation) can be 'destroyed is by the truth' which can only be realized if Goa's own tourism industry is united" (Gantzer and Gantzer 1991) and further effectively developed.

This kind of writing reflects the approval of the Indian state's development regime by independent observers. Adopting a confrontational style of writing, the Gantzers stopped short of accusing all critics of tourism as anti-progress, anti-democratic, anti-development, and anti-India. Their report elevated the tourism debate from a terrain of political, social and economic considerations to a moral consideration between development and stagnation. The Gantzers had clubbed all criticisms of tourism development in Goa together as elitist and anti-development, and anti-national. In other words, pro-tourism also implicitly meant pro-India, anti-tourism by default meant anti-India. This was essentially a strategy to streamline voices of dissent that had emerged within Goa. Some legitimate concerns were glossed over, while others concerns like the exploitation of miners in the hinterland were rendered invisible. Tourism became the discursive framework within which this interaction within Goan society and between Goan society and the Indian nation state was legitimized.

As Alito Sequiera notes, in his essay entitled "Tourism and the Drama of Goan Ethnicity" (1991), there is a case for which to argue that suggests that specific elements of the Goan elite have indeed sought to oppose tourism development in Goa for reasons which do not genuinely seek to address the concerns of Goan society as a whole. It was more an attempt by a segment of the society to reconfigure its position within the emerging tourism centered economy in post-liberation Goa.

State Formation in Postcolonial Goa

State formation[13] is not the history of rational management, for the sake of social progress and prosperity, but a tense and contingent way of producing and reproducing class relations. The state might act on behalf of the dominant class, but its interest cannot be reduced simply to the interests of the former. The exigencies of social control require that the state concerns itself with reproduction of class relations as a whole. Thus, state formation in other words is a multi-pronged process. Firstly, it involves the absorption or subordination of peoples with differing traditions and levels of socioeconomic integrations into an over-arching economic structure and ideological apparatus that seeks to legitimate class relations. Secondly, it involves the insertion of the state as the arbitrator of conflicts between various segments of the society.

As evidenced earlier in this chapter, the incorporation of postcolonial Goa into the Indian nation was particularly difficult. Firstly, Goa was never viewed as integral to the imagination of postcolonial India. Secondly, the Indian state, though responsible for the liberation of Goa from Portuguese colonial rule, was not able to effectively articulate with/within the Goan society. The politics that emerged in Goa soon after liberation, which was more an attempt to settle colo-nial accounts, exposed the limitations and the resulting powerlessness of the Indian state.[14] The shape and form of postcolonial India is largely defined by its history of British colonialism. And, for this very reason, Goa never figured in this imagination of independent India. The difference represented by Goan society and its colonial history was something that could not be rationalized and accommodated.[15] In this situation, a definition of India or an Indian that would accommodate this gap between Goan society and the rest of India was difficult to formulate. Needless to say, the politics that unfolded in Goa immediately after liberation made sure that it was impossible. However, in order to legiti-mize its position, the Indian nation state had to articulate and accommodate Goa's historical specificity and its difference.

It is precisely in such situations that one could appreciate the power of tour-ism and its related discourses. Students of tourism have recently argued that "the language of nationalism enables tourists to navigate other places and find significance" (Franklin 2003: 44). While this is true it also limits our ability to appreciate the role tourism can play in the process of nation-building as demon-strated in this chapter. Tourism development contributed to Goa's integration with India—something even liberation could not achieve. The very issue of historical difference that impeded the integration of Goa with India was suc-cessfully articulated as the cultural foundation of the tourism destination in Goa. This new form of commoditization propelled the tourism destination, the space that accommodated the process, as *the* representative space of the Goan society, validating the Indian and foreign imagination of Goa as a part of India with a "difference."

The development of commoditized experience mediated by the Indian state reconfigured the relationship between the Goan, the Indian and the global economy. Tourism discourse has inscribed certain characteristics on to the Goans and mapped them into specific coordinates of control, transforming their subject position as the object of the touristic gaze (Urry 1990: 23–28) and inserted Goa into the develop-ment regime (Ludden 1991) of the Indian state. The continued expansion of tourism and the requirements for its reproduction disciplines Goans and normalizes the tour-ist gaze as the very condition of their existence. As critical constituents of the tourism destination—the Indian-ness of Goan society and individual Goans is rooted in and routed through their ability to perform/engage with "difference" and thus be part of the tourism destination.

Notes

1 I approach Gramsci's concept of hegemony as a way of thinking about how consent and coercion are intertwined with one another (see Gramsci 1971: 12, 159–160, and 261). For a detailed analysis see Crehan (2002).
2 In the recent past, it has been argued that the process of globalization has eroded the significance of the nation. Contrary to this belief, in this chapter I argue that tourism, a poster boy of the process of globalization, is contributing to the consolidation of the nation state (see Franklin 2003).
3 The third general elections for the Lok Sabha in India were scheduled for January 1962. A majority of the parties had the Goan question on their agenda and all were more militant than the position assumed by Congress. This was detrimental to the election of then Defense Minister Krishna Menon who was contesting in a district which was heavily populated by people of Goan descent (see Palmer 1963).
4 The MGP had its organizational roots in the National Congress (Goa) which had been in existence since 1946 and had support from political parties in India such as the Jan Sangh and Hindu Mahashaba, both of whom were right-of-center Hindu communal organizations which did not necessarily subscribe to the secular position of the Indian state.
5 The leading business houses had contributed to the establishment of educational institutions in Goa, for instance, Chowgules funded the Arts and Science College in Margao, the Salgaonkars founded the law college, and Dempos funded the Dempe College at Miramar.
6 Chowgules own the newspapers *Gomantak Times* and *Uzvadd*, the Salgaonkars own the *Navhind Times* and *Navprabha*.
7 The economic emergence of the *kharvis* within the Catholic community through their involvement in the tourism trade can be viewed as parallel to the political emergence of the non-Brahmin Hindus in the form of MGP and its reaction to Brahmin dominance within the Goan Hindu community.
8 This situation arose as a result of the manner in which Goans and other Indians perceive each other. The image of Goans as easy going and carefree has been central to the Indian imagination of Goa. On the same plane, the Goan image of Indians as rude and uncivilized is the product of a colonial elitist construction.
9 In terms of US dollars the approximate prevailing rate then was Rs. 12.30 per US dollar, which amounts to $81,300. The State Bank of India branch in Calangute was at one time the top rural branch in terms of volume of foreign exchange remittance and handling.
10 The caste system was integral to the reproduction of both Hindu and Catholic agrarian communities in Goa. Conversion to Catholicism did not erode this social reality, with occasional intermarriage between religions but within caste.
11 This is strange considering Goa was not even part of the British Commonwealth.
12 This was preceded by the granting of statehood to Goa and the recognition of Konkani as Goa's official state language. Robert Newman (1984) has suggested that these events were the final steps in the integration of Goa with India. I view these events as the necessary preliminary steps in the deployment of the Indian state's development regime in Goa.
13 In his widely cited publication, Newman (1988) has argued that Goan society's integration with India has been achieved through recognition of the primordial unity it shares with India. This, according to Newman, is exemplified by the granting of statehood to Goa and the recognition of Konkani as the official language of Goa in 1987. These events, though important, are not sufficient in and of themselves to integrate Goa with India. These events, at best, serve as necessary preconditions as they establish the societal framework of Goa, the target of the Indian state's development regime.
14 One should be careful not to equate the MGP's demand for the merger of Goa with Maharashtra and the integration of Goa into the Indian nation state as one and the same. Goa's merger with Maharashtra would have meant the erasure of Goa's historical specificity.

15 Indian-ness meant radically different things to Indians and Goans. This was crystallized during the last decade of colonial rule in Goa which roughly coincided with the first decade of postcolonial India's existence. The colonial Goan economy thrived as a result of Portuguese neutrality during World War II and the policies of economic liberalization formulated by the colonial administration. In comparison, the Indian economy was in the doldrums. In fact many Goans, particularly those from the most visible segment, the petty bourgeoisie who were employed by the colonial administration, distanced themselves from India and Indians.

Bibliography

AFONSO, Ave Cleto, "Impact of tourism in Goa," in *Tourism in Goa: Socio Economic Impact*, manuscript report published by Institute of Social Sciences, New Delhi, 1989.

ALTHUSSER, Louis, "Ideology and ideological state apparatuses (notes towards and investigation)," in Louis Althusser, *Lenin and Philosophy and other Essays*, translated by B. Brewster (New York: Monthly Review Press, 1971), pp. 121–176.

ALVARES, Claude, *Homo Faber: Technology and Culture in India, China and the West: 1500 to the Present Day* (New Delhi: Allied Publishers, 1979).

ANDERSON, Benedict, *Imagined Communities: Reflections on the Origin and Spread of Nationalism* (London: Verso, 1983).

ASHWORTH, G.J. and DIETVORST, A.G.J., *Tourism and Spatial Transformations* (Wallingford: CAB International, 1995).

CREHAN, Kate, *Gramsci, Culture and Anthropology* (Berkeley, CA: University of California Press, 2002).

ESTEVES, Sarto, *Politics and Political Leadership in Goa* (New Delhi: Sterling Publishers, 1986).

FRANKLIN, Adrian, *Tourism: An Introduction* (London: Sage Publications, 2003).

GAITONDE, Pundalik D., *The Liberation of Goa* (New York: St. Martin's Press, 1987).

GANTZER, Hugh and GANTZER, Colleen, "Tourism development," *Navhind Times*, April 14, 21 and 28, 1991.

GRAMSCI, Antonio, *Selections from the Prison Notebooks* (New York: International Publishers, 1971).

HARVEY, David, *The Conditions of Postmodernity* (Oxford: Blackwell, 1989).

——, "From space to place and back again," in John Bird, Barry Curtis, Tim Putnam and Lisa Tickner (eds), *Mapping the Futures: Local Cultures, Global Change* (New York: Routledge, 1993), pp. 2–28.

INSTITUTE OF SOCIAL SCIENCES, *Socio-Economic Impact of Tourism in Goa* (New Delhi: Institute of Social Sciences, 1989).

KAGAL, Ayesha, "Matsyanyaya: big fish eat small fish," *Illustrated Weekly of India*, April 8, 1979, p. 28.

LACAN, Jacques, *Écrits: A Selection*, translated by Alan Sheridan (New York: W.W. Norton, 1977).

LEFEBVRE, Henri, *The Production of Space*, translated by Donald Nicholson-Smith (Cambridge: Blackwell, 1995).

LUDDEN, David, "India's development regime," in Nicholas B. Dirks (ed.), *Colonialism and Culture* (Ann Arbor, MI: University of Michigan Press, 1991), pp. 247–288.

NEHRU, Jawaharlal, *Speeches, March 1963–May 1964* (New Delhi: Ministry of Information and Broadcasting, Government of India, 1968).

NEWMAN, Robert, "Goa: the transformation of an Indian region," *Pacific Affairs* 57(3) (1984): 429–449.

——, "Konkani Mai ascends the throne: the cultural basis of Goan statehood," *South Asia*, New Series, 11(1) (1988): 1–24.

ODZER, Cleo, *Goa Freaks: My Hippie Years in India* (New York: Quality Paperback Book Club, 1995).

PALMER, Norman D., "Indian attitude towards colonialism," in Robert Strausz-Hupe and Harry W. Hazard (eds), *The Idea of Colonialism* (New York: Fredrick A. Praeger, 1958), pp. 271–310.

——, "The 1962 election in North Bombay," *Pacific Affairs* 36(2) (Summer 1963): 120–137.

ROJEK, C., *Ways of Escape* (London: Macmillan, 1993).

RUBINOFF, Arthur G., *The Construction of a Political Community: Integration and Identity in Goa* (New Delhi: Sage Publications, 1997).

SHIELDS, Rob, *Places on the Margin: Alternative Geographies of Modernity* (New York: Routledge, 1991).

SIQUIERA, Alito, "Tourism and the drama of Goan ethnicity," paper presented at All India Consultation: The Human Cost in Modern Tourism: A Challenge to All Religions. Conference organized by the Ecumenical Coalition on Third World Tourism, November 4–9, 1991, Vasco, Goa.

STRAUSS, Claudia, "The Imaginary," *Anthropological Theory* 6(3) (2006): 322–344.

SUB-COMMITTEE OF THE DIOCESAN PASTORAL COUNCIL, "Tourism in Goa: its implications," *Renovacao* (August 1988).

TAYLOR, Charles, "Modern Social Imaginaries," *Public Culture* 14 (2002): 91–124.

TEAS, Jane, "I'm studying monkeys—what do you do? Youth travelers in Nepal," *Kroeber Anthropological Society Papers* 67/68 (1988 [1974]): 35–41.

URRY, John, *The Tourist Gaze* (London: Sage Publications, 1990).

——, *Consuming Places* (London: Routledge, 1995).

3 Reinventing and Reshaping Gaudí

From Nation and Religion to Tourism. Architecture, Conflict and Change in Barcelona's Tourist Imaginary[1]

Josep-Maria Garcia-Fuentes

Introduction

Architecture solves functional, constructive and structural problems posed by human needs but also involves memory, imagination, and the relationship between them. This derives from two main factors: firstly, architecture is also expected to meet the need to represent the ideas and thoughts of the persons commissioning it and, by so doing, it often fixes their memories as well. Indeed, architecture then becomes a powerful device for building and spreading memories in addition to creating imaginaries. Secondly, a factor of no less importance is that architecture is directly related to memory and imagination because the creative work of architects is a referential activity establishing relationships with earlier architectural works and memories as they are interpreted at the time of the building process, that is to say, according to the contemporary imaginary of the times and the way in which such earlier works and memories were then conceived.

Imaginaries in the field of architecture are important for these two reasons, revealing how an architectural work is understood by the people who commission it and those who build it, while providing a better understanding of the political and social tensions and polemics to which they give rise. Likewise, imaginaries are valuable for their use as a creative element in architects' design processes. The study of imaginaries is thus essential to a better understanding of any architectural work and its processual changing nature: changes in imaginaries reshape, often in pervasive ways, not only the understanding of their object but also the object itself. This is a very significant aspect of architecture since, together with the imaginary, tastes are constantly changing, consciously or unconsciously, defining in this way a new appreciation of the object and, consequently, a new criterion for handling it, including its preservation, restoration, and alteration, and by so doing they also define new creative approaches.

It is this relationship between the imaginary, creativity, and architecture that will be explored in this chapter To do so, we will make use of two case studies of Antoni Gaudí's architecture, originally built around the end of the nineteenth century and the first two decades of the twentieth according to a fervent national and religious imaginary that was progressively replaced between the mid-twentieth century and the present to fit in with a kind, friendly imaginary of Barcelona and

Catalonia at large. Before going any deeper into Gaudí, however, it would be well to reconsider a previous digression on architecture and heritage as processes since Gaudí's works are listed as heritage sites in Catalonia and Spain and some of them are World Heritage Sites.

Heritage, Architecture, and Tourist Sites as Processes

It is widely accepted, as Gregory J. Ashworth (1997; 2008) clearly explains, that heritage should not be defined as an object but "as a process . . . that uses sites, objects, and human traits and patterns of behaviour as vehicles for the transmission of ideas in order to satisfy various contemporary needs." Heritage can therefore be described as "a medium of communication, a means of transmission of ideas and values and a knowledge that includes the material, the intangible and the virtual" (Graham 2002). This definition of heritage can also be applied to both architectural and tourist sites as they are often one and the same, sharing common narrations. It is not necessary to insist on how architecture is often used to represent, foster, and spread the postulates of those who commission, control, exploit, or maintain it: one need only consider, for example, corporate headquarters, shops, or institutional buildings of all types.

However, while architecture, heritage, and tourist sites may be defined as processes linked directly to the social construction of places (Halbwachs 1968; Nora 1986), they should not be confused with either identity or place (Ashworth 2008). Monuments, sacred places, *lieux de mémoire*, and tourist sites are social and cultural constructions conveying intangible meanings. Focusing on the case of monuments and heritage sites, it is easy to realize how a narration—which regards a social group and is not necessarily historical—is associated with concrete material objects such as monuments and sites, which are in turn linked to society by the same or other narrations. The ideological and political implications of these site-making processes are obvious (Ashworth 2008). Nevertheless, it is also important to emphasize that this narrative, which is socially and culturally constructed and associated with heritage and tourist sites, is not the same as history. Whereas history is essentially a "text"—a continuous narration—that seeks to "establish a more objective record of the past" on the basis of dated, contextualized documents that may be properly authenticated, heritage, like architecture and tourist sites,

> is rather curated and conserved, possessed and performed. Heritage is artefactual more than textual; it is realized with material objects such as art or craft works, tools and buildings, sites, special places and even whole landscapes, or else it is performed in speech or dress, in ritual, ceremony, dance or song. (Cosgrove 2003: 114–115)

This understanding of heritage and tourist sites as processes gives rise to policies that are more active and dialogical and generates an understanding of contested flexible identities (Cosgrove 2003: 103).

Hence, if heritage, architecture, and tourist sites are processes related to the inner dynamics of society, they—the site itself, for example, and its imaginary—should be as mutable as both the society and the people who create, preserve, modify, or visit them. Once we appreciate that understanding heritage and tourist sites is something dynamic, any changes in this understanding and imaginary should reshape the site itself since any novel understanding will establish a new appreciation of it and, consequently, produce changes in the criterion used to handle it and interact with it. Gaudí and his work provide a clear example of this understanding of architecture, heritage, and tourist sites as processes in constant change, while reflecting the relationship between changes in a site's imaginary and its material reshaping.

On Gaudí's Architecture: From Nation and Religion to Tourism

The process of inventing the imaginary of Antoni Gaudí's architecture is a little-known example with which to illustrate and study in depth the concepts of change and reshaping in heritage and tourist site-making processes. To begin with it should be said that Gaudí's imaginary derives in turn from the highly complex development process of Barcelona's modern tourist imaginary. It involves an invention process that is closely related to the city's modernization and to the definition of modern Catalonia's identity, which was shaped by an accretion of diverse layers of imaginaries and power relations that produced dissonances and conflicts, beginning in the mid-nineteenth century with national and religious postulates and imaginaries relating to the cultural and political ambitions of the local elites, and subsequently evolving towards tourism (see, for example, Lahuerta 1999 or Resina 2008). Moreover, it is not only a process that has reshaped Gaudí's imaginary on several occasions but one that has also reshaped and transformed Gaudí's architecture itself, as we shall see.

By analyzing the various reinventions of Gaudí's architecture, this chapter seeks to assess the conflicts involved and the changes in its imaginary, focusing on how they reshape this architecture as the imaginary's object. To this end we may consider postcards, both old and new, guidebooks, "official" texts, and some key studies on Gaudí, as well as the debates on the restoration of his buildings and the ongoing works of the Sagrada Família church, while commenting on the tourist operation of Gaudí's present-day imaginary. The ultimate aim is to take Gaudí's architecture as a basis for a reflection on the major influence wielded by tourism imaginaries in reshaping, often in far-reaching ways, not only the understanding of their object but also the object itself according to its contemporary idealization.

The Original Imaginary of Gaudí and His Architecture

Antoni Gaudí's architecture was built in the late nineteenth and early twentieth centuries as an expression of the cultural and political ambitions of Barcelona's Catholic haute bourgeoisie and, later, of those of the Catalan Catholic Church. Accordingly, Gaudí's architecture sought to reflect the status of the families who commissioned the architect's work (Lahuerta 1999) as well as their ideals, which were closely linked to Catalan nationalism and the Catholic Church. During those years, Spain and Catalonia were involved in the process of defining the modern structure of the Spanish state and the tensions between Spain and Catalan society, which proclaimed its wish to form a Catalan state—Catalonia—within an Iberian or Spanish federation, were increasing year by year in response to cultural and linguistic postulates, as well as for economic and financial reasons.[2] This aspect was of special importance for the wealthy families who commissioned Gaudí and other prominent architects of the times to represent their own particular ideas.

In this context, Gaudí's buildings became the favorite architecture for representing the postulates of the Catalan haute bourgeoisie because of its richly complex symbolism and structure, full of mythical and historical references that quite often contained diverse meanings at one and the same time. Gaudí's architecture also found favor because of its strange, singular, formal and aesthetic character. This attractiveness was intensified by Gaudí's strong personality as a very religious, fervently Catalan nationalist and as a person of great humility—indeed, he lived as a poor man throughout his life despite his renown and his important clients and connections. It is not surprising, for these reasons, that Gaudí and his architecture soon became the perfect medium for the Catalan Catholic Church's ideas and was finally used to represent Catalan nationalism as a whole.

Before proceeding any further, however, it would be well to clarify the difference between *Modernisme*, that is to say, the Catalan *Modernista* architecture produced by Gaudí, and other contemporary architectural forms designated by the terms Art Nouveau or Jugendstil, among others (depending on the geographical area involved), with which *Modernisme* is often confused or which it is frequently considered to resemble, as may be seen in many of the guidebooks on Barcelona. This is a misconception. Whereas Art Nouveau was a 14-year fashion that was quick to age, Gaudí's architecture continued to be built for over 40 years and sought to be transcendental, attempting to situate itself beyond time. This endeavor to avoid fashion, to move beyond time and to transcend was a consequence of Gaudí's firm Catholic faith combined with his Catalan nationalist ideals, his two almost obsessive concerns as previously mentioned. This significant difference between Gaudí's Catalan *Modernista* style and Art Nouveau and similar movements can also be seen in the contrasting techniques used by the respective groups of architects. For instance, the leitmotiv of Art Nouveau or Jugendstil architects was "a long and sinuous movement," according to Robert Schmutzler (1962), which means that they designed their structures with connected curved lines in continuous twists, with tangencies and continuities, in an unbroken way. Their obsession was to merge and fuse materials and elements as well as the personal aesthetics of the artists and craftsmen involved in the construction process (see for example Crane 1900). Gaudí's architecture, on the other hand, was based on discontinuous forms that were always broken and interrupted: nothing in it fits perfectly or is precisely suitable. The celebrated handmade *trencadís* mosaic is perhaps the technique that best represents Gaudí's way of designing. It comprises two opposite steps: the first one is based on breaking and destroying, while the second involves adhering and rejoining. Moreover, its result is not a continuous surface but a broken one that highlights and exaggerates the discontinuous and broken form. It is a technique that is closer to those of collage and the avant-gardes than to Art Nouveau. Thus, *trencadís* was not only a constructive technique but was also very carefully conceived to celebrate the act of creating from destruction, with all the religious and non-religious metaphors that this understanding entails. It is not surprising, then, that *trencadís* was used in the main representative elements of each building for religious, national, or mythical references, often with distinct sophisticated meanings, as may be seen in Gaudí's works (see, for example, Marfany 1975; Lahuerta 1999).

Gaudí always worked by adding a multiplicity of highly complex symbolic meanings to the structure as a whole and its details for the purpose of conveying religious and national messages (Lahuerta 1999: 7–61). This led to very powerful seductive works that were at once dreamlike, monstrous, sinister, and mysterious. For instance, the constant presence of a fierce aggressive dragon in all his works, as for example in the entrance to the Finca Güell, on the stairway at Parc Güell or in the Casa Batlló, should be understood as a direct reference to the legend of Saint George, the protector of the Catalan nation (see, for example, Lahuerta 1999: 39–41). But its presence is often enriched by overlapping meanings that "forcibly reinforce" its symbolism, as may be clearly seen in the dragon at Parc Güell, which will be the first of our two case studies.

Parc Güell began to be designed and built by Gaudí in 1900 when Count Eusebi Güell asked him to build a luxury housing estate along the lines of the English Garden City on one of the hills of Barcelona that was then situated on the outskirts of the city. Although this undertaking eventually proved to be commercially unsuccessful, the project centered Güell's efforts and ambitions to promote and represent his vision of Catalonia. The urban development of the high hill where it stands was organized not only according to a natural functional plan, that is to say, as a Garden City, but also in keeping with an ambitious symbolic and mythical plan. Güell and Gaudí defined a very sophisticated concept, using references and symbolism from classical architecture, picturesque approaches, and many other techniques, mixing and combining them to better represent their ideas and dreams on the origin and future of Catalonia. It is beyond the scope of this chapter to go any further in these general ideas about the park, but it would be worthwhile to deal in a certain detail with the dragon and its symbolism as conceived by Gaudí. Here, the inescapable Catalan symbolism of Saint George and the dragon overlaps with references to Delphi and Greek mythology—one of the fields of reference used openly at that time to build the Catalan imaginary by poets like Jacint Verdaguer and architects like Gaudí. So, as Lahuerta (1999: 39) so brilliantly and sophisticatedly states in his description of Parc Güell's entrance, where the dragon is positioned on the stairway:

> The cavern, situated under the columns of the Doric temple, pours water from its interior lake [the tank located under the columns] through the dragon's mouth; the Earth emerges in its most fantastic shapes from the depths

of the discontinuous recess that splits the white order of the two sections of the stairway, expelling the damp breath of the cavern; the ring set over the spring where the tripod stands . . . what are these if not images of the sanctuary of Delphi, of its myths and ritual instruments? In effect, at Apollo's Doric temple, placed in the centre of the holy walled enclosure at the end of the Sacred Way, stood the *opisthodomos*—an open fissure between two rocks from which sprang Kastalia's fountain, interpreted as the mouth of Gea, the Earth Mother. From it was born the snake Python, which Apollo stole from the oracle. Above this fissure was a steel tripod . . . on which the Pythia or Pythoness pronounced the oracles. Lastly, a conical marble stone, considered the *omphalos* or *umbilicum terrae*, was kept inside the *cella* of the temple . . . The way in which everything matches the elements on Parc Güell's stairway is too precise to ascribe it to mere coincidence: could someone like Eusebi Güell, who was so interested in Delphi . . ., ignore all these aspects of the Delphic rituals, of the myths contained in them, of their elements and instruments for the cult? (Lahuerta 1999: 163)

This is a compelling representative example of the sophisticated symbolism that Gaudí used to create his architecture, highlighting and underlining it by means of the constructive techniques and complex design details used to create the final materiality of his works. Accordingly, if one looks carefully at the set of dragons he designed, one finds that they all bear an aggressive expression, just as could be expected of a beast that, according to the popular legend, wages a struggle to the death with Saint George. The dragon at Parc Güell is not an exception. Nevertheless, while Gaudí's dragons were usually made of steel, a strong hard material that is well suited to represent and singularize a dragon, the one at Parc Güell was built by the *trencadís* technique, probably due to its overlapping symbolism and in order to lend prominence to its importance through the use of colored ceramic tiles. The dragon's expression was, of course, an aggressive one, as is shown by the big sharp claws and teeth to be seen in old photographs from the time of its creation by the architect.

Another example of Gaudí's singular way of working and of the many highly complex symbolic meanings used to define the structure as a whole and its details, can be found in our second case study: the Sagrada Família. This celebrated church should be conceptualized, just like the other churches built by Gaudí and his followers, as a key element within the patriotic-religious campaign unfolded by a group of people belonging to the Catalan Catholic Church of the times, called the "Vic group." The various patriotic-religious campaigns organized by this group of clerics between 1880 and the early twentieth century sought to foster and reinvent the associations between the Catholic religion, the land of Catalonia, and their cultural, social and political objectives (see, for example, Junyent 1990; Lahuerta 1999: 254–269; Garcia-Fuentes 2009: 239–260). Of course, the final aim of these campaigns was to promote the Church's political, social, religious and cultural influence, and to achieve this goal the Vic group appropriated the writer, politician and freemason Victor Balaguer's earlier attempt to create a new symbolic network in connection with the Catalan monasteries and, more specifically, the mountain of Montserrat and the monastery-sanctuary that stands on it. This appropriation was highly contested at the time by non-religious groups (see Ganau 1997; Garcia-Fuentes 2009; 2012), giving rise to a rivalry and struggle between the various social and cultural groups that wished to capitalize on the strange mountain's symbolism. In this context, in opposition to the popular reproductions of Montserrat that were built in parks and gardens for leisure, Gaudí defined an understanding of the mountain itself as a temple and used its shape in the design of his religious buildings. This identification between his churches and Montserrat reached its most sophisticated expression in the Sagrada Família project, where the mountain is also viewed as a temple in ruins expressing a mythic religious time. The complexity of its symbolism, together with the definition of its materiality, led Gaudí to envisage with great care every single detail, symbolism, and constructive technique—like the previously considered *trencadís*—and even to plan the construction process as a metaphor of these ideas about time and the Catalan nation (for a study of these ideas in greater depth, see Lahuerta 1999; Garcia-Fuentes 2012).

Thanks to this complexity and to the capacity of Gaudí's architecture to generate different narrations and symbolisms, the Sagrada Família was appropriated by the Catalan Church as a key element in its "campaigns," and soon after even by the whole Catalan nationalist movement. This led to both popular and intellectual reactions that were as diverse as they were intense, with some sectors of society adopting a position that was completely opposed to his architecture (for a further consideration of this aspect of the Sagrada Família, see, among others, Rohrer 1990: 191–212, and especially Lahuerta 1999: 254–315).

However, for the matter at hand it is not necessary to deal any further with the context, ideas, and imaginary of Gaudí's architecture at the time of its building. Parc Güell and its dragon together with the Sagrada Família are good examples of the complexity of Gaudí's architecture as he and his contemporaries conceived it. Indeed, these examples illustrate the essential importance of the integration of the complex symbolism and the constructive techniques in his works, seeking to define a very carefully planned atmosphere and expression while creating a highly sophisticated architectural work. All this highlights the immense importance of every single detail and choice of material.

From Nation and Religion to Tourism

After the architect's death and the Spanish Civil War, the imaginaries related to Gaudí's architecture changed considerably, while internationally the architect and his works fell into oblivion. In Catalonia, experts started to study Gaudí's work in new ways in the 1940s, contextualizing him as a genius and a forerunner of Modern architecture and even of many avant-garde artists (Lahuerta 1999: 316–332; Garnica 2010: 397–406), as well as a visionary of techniques and structures (Collins 1960; Martinell 1967). During this period, which was totally conditioned by the Franco dictatorship, all the initial political and national resonances of Gaudí's work seemed to be forgotten.

However, a representative turning point within the progressive definition of a new imaginary around Gaudí's work can be found in the year 1950, when the prestigious Italian architecture historian Bruno Zevi visited Barcelona, marking the international rediscovery of Gaudí's architecture and the beginning of its present-day appreciation. Zevi (1950) found Gaudí to be an excellent reference for the new organic architecture that he was seeking in order to move beyond the "overly simplified" Modern architectural concepts. From that moment on, Gaudí became a visionary genius of architecture and a new approach to his works was consequently launched, the focus of interest being "the comprehensive reintegration of the walls, the use of splendid colour, [and] the spatial consciousness of Gaudí" as "sources of inspiration for organic architects" (Garnica 2010: 400). This reveals a more rational approach that does not consider the associated symbolic and mythical narrations. The same symbolism that was inseparable from the materiality, constructive details, and techniques, and any other more rational aspects of Gaudí's works when they were built and conceived by the architect now became irrelevant to these works' value. The change of understanding and interpretation of his architecture in the wake of this renewed interest is evident. From this moment on, Gaudí's architecture became progressively linked to rational values and especially to gentler, more optimistic attitudes, shedding in this way all reference to the "big crisis" (Cirlot 1954: 13) that it once represented, that is to say, its intense and sophisticated national and religious symbolism.

From the 1950s on, an immense number of publications, guidebooks, and tourist guides in addition to diverse academic papers began to appear, changing the way in which Gaudí's architecture was considered, researched, conceptualized, and valued according to this new understanding focused on its technical and structural aspects while undervaluing and even forgetting the transcendental aspect of its original mythical, national and religious postulates. A new imaginary of Gaudí's architecture has been created in this way, shaping the manner in which it is now understood. Today the architect's works have become one of the foremost, if not the foremost of all the attractions for people visiting Barcelona from abroad in ever-increasing numbers. Indeed, the countless publications that emphasize and spread this new outlook and conceptualization beyond the original serious national and religious symbolism, have marked a veritable turning point in the consolidation of the modern imaginary of Gaudí's architecture because all these guides and academic papers have been manuals for the *artialisation* of Gaudí, to use Alain Roger's expression (Roger 1997). They have made it possible for individuals and society at large to interact with the reinvented Gaudí and with this new narration of Gaudí as a genius and a technical and structural visionary, forming an imaginary which is more seductive and understandable for foreigners than its complex creational national or religious ambitions and thus better suited to attract all sorts of tourists. Of course, references to these original aspirations are almost always avoided, except in a few relatively recent and quite brilliant papers (see especially the scholarly work by Lahuerta 1999).

It is important to note another point regarding the maintenance and quality of the materiality of Gaudí's work. Many of the materials and techniques used by the architect, like his celebrated *trencadís*, are materials and constructive details of scant durability in contrast to other types of materials and structures. For example, when *trencadís* is located outdoors and exposed to the elements, it undergoes a rapid degradation process compared to other architectural materials because of its poor quality, inasmuch as it consists of broken ceramic tiles with no protection and thus absolutely unable to withstand major oscillations of temperature, sun, rain, and the effects of frost. This caused a quick degradation of many of the façades and exteriors of Gaudí's buildings as well as of some of his interiors, making it necessary to restore them soon after their construction in often less-than-well-documented interventions, as is revealed by any careful study.

Thus, the combination of this change in Gaudí's imaginary and the necessary intervention to maintain and preserve his buildings enables us to examine the transformations that they underwent from the 1950s to the present, and to understand more clearly how the new imaginary of the architect's work has reshaped not only the way it is understood but even its materiality. Any small change in the way a specific architecture or building is understood, leads to a new and different appreciation of it and its value, and consequently to a new way of dealing with it when working on its maintenance—consciously or unconsciously. The case studies presented above—the Sagrada Família and the Parc Güell dragon—show how Gaudí's architecture was created and understood at the time of its building and provide excellent examples in this respect.

The debate on the ongoing works of the Sagrada Família began after Gaudí's death, reaching its peak in the 1960s and 1970s. The architect did not come to finish the church and he never completed the drawings for the project as a whole. Moreover, a number of his documents were destroyed in the Spanish Civil War. The question was whether it made sense to continue the works under these circumstances and, if the answer was "yes," what type of architecture was to be used? Was it possible to build it as if it were built by Gaudí? For these reasons, the ongoing works of the Sagrada Família have been vehemently challenged by numerous architects and historians since at least 1965, when a group of experts together with UNESCO (despite the fact that the part which had been built by Gaudí himself was not yet listed as a World Heritage Site) demanded a halt in the works.

Aside from the basic questions at issue in this polemic, however, the debate on the works reveals how the change of the imaginary has reshaped the ongoing works and the understanding of the project. This may be seen on taking a quick look at the newly built parts and comparing them to the old ones or to other structures. On the basis of Gaudí's earlier works (such as the crypt of the church at the Colònia Güell), his drawings, and the part of the Sagrada Família (including the façade) that was built in his lifetime, as well as the references to the mountain of Montserrat we pointed out above, one would expect a dreamlike, monstrous, sinister and mysterious building, a sort of immense handmade collage, with important pieces of *trencadís*. This is not what we see today, however, in the new parts of the church, which are perfect, straight, rational, and technological, because the architects who currently direct the project understand Gaudí's conception in a different way, prioritizing the technical ideas behind his architecture (see, for example, Collins 1960; Gómez 1996; Giralt Miracle 2002).

Indeed, this is why the new parts of the Sagrada Família, the materials used to build them, and their technical materiality stand closer to some spectacular contemporary hi-tech architecture (see, for example, the architecture of Santiago Calatrava) than to Gaudí's other works. In these new parts, the architecture adopts perfectly clean lines and one clearly perceives that they have little to do with Gaudí's concepts. Probably because of this similarity to certain works of contemporary architecture, one of the leading architects who demanded a halt in the works made a provocative ironic collage in 2002, showing the Sagrada Família transformed into Barcelona's central train station (Galí 2002: 16–17). This collage also shows that the debate on the Sagrada Família has come down to the present, highlighting the way in which the evolution of Gaudí's imaginary and the changes in the building may be studied in greater detail through this polemic that has extended from the 1950s to the present.

Not only were the ongoing works of the Sagrada Família reshaped by this change in Gaudí's imaginary, which was aimed to make his architecture fit better into a touristically broader, more modern and friendlier concept, causing it to lose its original mysterious and sinister appearance in this way. It is a progressive change that unfolds in parallel to the touristic exploitation of Gaudí's architecture. Indeed, many of Gaudí's finished works underwent significant alterations in the course of their restoration or preservation before their listing as World Heritage Sites in 1984 and even after this date, as will be seen.

An illustrative example is the second case study, the little-known restoration work on the Parc Güell dragon discussed above: while the dragon as designed by Gaudí presented a fierce, aggressive expression, as was reflected by its big, sharp claws and teeth, after the restoration works both claws and teeth were made smaller and the dragon's expression became "gentler," totally changing its appearance (Figure 3.1).

Figure 3.1 On the left, detail of the Parc Güell dragon as built by Gaudí (from an old postcard from 1907) and, on the right, as it is today (2011) following modern restoration works (the last in 2007)

The restorations that changed the dragon's expression are undocumented but probably took place between the 1950s and 1987, when the first modern restoration was begun after the listing of Parc Güell in its entirety as a World Heritage Site. In 1987, the well-known architects in charge of the restoration works, Elias Torres and José Antonio Martínez Lapeña, were fully aware of the "great significance" of Gaudí and his work in the tourist imaginary of Barcelona, as well as of the complexity of Gaudí's architecture (Torres and Lapeña 1987). Accordingly, the restoration was understood by Torre and Lapeña as a task of "extreme importance," basing it on a criterion of

> . . . remaining faithful, not only in preserving the image of the monument in all its details, but also in intervening to rebuild its structure. Its elements have been remade to favour their stability exactly the same as in the original construction, using, of course, tools and materials available in today's building industry that provide greater quality and assurance.

The restoration of 1987 was thus fully respectful of the original and based on a thorough historical and constructive study. The architects observed the previous undocumented restoration works and warned about how aggressive they were to the monument (Torres and Lapeña 1987). However, they did not observe the change of the dragon's expression between the time of its creation and the present.

Quite probably, however, the earlier interventions had sought to restore the *trencadis*, the material and constructive technique with the least durability of the whole structure, as pointed out above, and thus the one requiring the most care and restoration. This is what led to the remaking of the dragon in 1987 and the unconscious change in its expression in the preceding years. It is also interesting to compare the Parc Güell dragon, the most popular of all Gaudí's dragons among tourists, to other such beasts designed by the architect, such as the one at the Pavelló Güell, also in the city of Barcelona. The dragon at the Pavelló Güell has not been changed and maintains its aggressive appearance, perhaps because it is not as popular as the one at Parc Güell and not as emblematic, but most probably because it is built of steel, making it much more durable.

However, no one noticed the big change in the Parc Güell dragon's expression and it became as friendly as Barcelona's tourist imaginary itself. It should be pointed out in this respect that the representations of Gaudí's work, together with guidebooks and studies, play an important role in raising the awareness of this new and "gentler" tourist attraction aimed to seduce visitors and to spread the new imaginary. In tourist shops, for example, one finds an amazing number of Parc Güell dragons in the form of soft toys, pin badges, keyrings, T-shirts, children's books, and even a poker game based on Gaudí, showing the "friendly" dragon of Parc Güell on one of its cards, among many other articles that repeat time and time again this new gentle reshaped and reinvented expression.

One last episode in the life of the Parc Güell dragon shows just how great the reshaping of Gaudí's architecture and imaginary has been. In 2007, the dragon was attacked by a group of young Catalan boys who totally destroyed its mouth by bashing it with a steel rod. The attack on the dragon was not an action to demand or represent anything but only a stupid prank by problematic youth. Newspaper articles condemned this act of vandalism by "young thugs" who destroyed—as was stated by Francesc-Marc Álvaro, a cultivated writer who is quite well known in Catalonia—the park's "kindly tolerant dragon on the stairway." It was also stated that the dragon had become a "symbol of the most admired and well-mannered Barcelona" (Álvaro 2007: 15). What is most surprising, however, is how the dragon was restored after the destruction of its mouth, comparing the restoration to the remarks and statements about it in the newspapers. The selfsame mayor of Barcelona stated just after the attack that the reconstruction works to recover this "jewel" and "symbol of the city" (Peirón 2007: 2), would start immediately. It could be expected, of course, that the restoration works in 2007 would follow a documented scientific approach, basing the process on a historical study before proceeding to repair the dragon. The restoration did not rebuild the dragon's mouth as Gaudí had made it, however: the dragon was rebuilt just as it had been before the attack, that is to say, as a "gentler," "kindly and tolerant" dragon and not as an aggressive one. The works did not restore the original dragon's big sharp claws and teeth, even though a simple historical investigation would have revealed evidence of them. In any case, a restoration such as this would make no sense. The comments in the newspapers and the letters to the editor showed, just as has been explained, that the new imaginary linked to the dragon was so powerful and so widespread that any other restoration would appear strange and even false.

Indeed, the current imaginary of the dragon is so strong that in the summer of 2012 a new debate arose in the newspapers when some companies producing souvenirs tried to patent the Parc Güell dragon and even the *trencadís* technique (Sesé 2012: 13–14). The attempt to patent them was widely criticized and led to the drafting of a manifesto signed by a number of prominent cultural personalities of the city and society at large. The manifesto (manifestgaudi.blogspot.com. es) condemns the appropriation for commercial purposes of what does not belong to anyone, but it is also a call to save and preserve Gaudí's works. The manifesto reveals no awareness, however, of the dragon's transformation from the time of its creation, nor of the radically different architecture that is being used to complete the Sagrada Família, for example. This is because the new imaginary of Gaudí cannot be separated from the transformed architecture of his works which, just as has been shown, have not as much to do with the original works as one might think.

Conclusion

These few selected examples of Gaudí's architecture reveal how the imaginary of his architecture has changed between the time of its construction and the present, and how these changes in the imaginary have finally come to reshape the architecture itself. Just as has been said, the original mythical symbolism of Gaudí's architecture, related to Catalan nationalism and its symbolic universe, has been gradually transformed into a more technical, universal and gentler symbolism that fits in better with the modern friendly imaginary of the city of Barcelona, in a process that began in the 1950s and has been gaining impetus in recent decades. This is a change in the imaginary relating to Gaudí and his work that has progressively changed the way this work is understood as well as the materiality of the architect's buildings.

Gaudí's case is not an isolated one, however, because processes of the same type may be observed in many other heritage and touristic sites. For instance, a similar reshaping took place on the face in the entrance to Sydney's Luna Park (Marshall 1995), as well as in Barcelona's Gothic Quarter (Ganau 2006; 2008), in the Spanish monasteries (Garcia-Fuentes 2010), and in Venice (Fortini Brown 1997; Cosgrove 2003). In all these instances, changes in the imaginaries reshape, often in far-reaching ways, not only the understanding of their object but also the object itself. This is because tastes are constantly changing, consciously or unconsciously, together with the imaginary, defining in this way a new appreciation of the object and, consequently, a new criterion for its handling, including its preservation, restoration, and alteration, and in this way they also define new creative approaches to architecture.

Notes

1 This chapter has been possible thanks to the support of the Universitat Politècnica de Catalunya (UPC) and the Ministry of Science and Innovation (MICINN) of the Government of Spain.
2 An immense body of historical and interdisciplinary studies exists on the origins of Catalan nationalism and the social and political tensions of the late nineteenth and twentieth centuries in Catalonia and Spain at large. For a well documented and compelling study that deals with this subject both in depth and at length, see Ucelay-da Cal (2003).

Bibliography

ÁLVARO Francesc-Marc, "Bestias contra dragones," *La Vanguardia—revista*, p. 15, February 11, 2007.
ASHWORTH Gregory J., "Conservation as preservation or as heritage: two paradigms and two answers," *Built Environment* 23(2): 92–102, 1997.
——, "Heritage: definitions, delusions and dissonances," in ALMOÊDA Rogério et al. (eds), *Heritage 2008: World Heritage and Sustainable Development*, Lisbon, Green Lines Institute for Sustainable Development, pp. 3–9, 2008.
BONET Joana, "El arte herido," *La Vanguardia*, p. 31, October 10, 2007.
CIRLOT Juan Eduardo, *El Arte de Gaudí*, Barcelona, Ediciones Omega, 1954.
COLLINS George R., *Antonio Gaudí*, New York, George Braziller, 1960.
COSGROVE Denis, "Heritage and history: a venetian geography lesson," in SHANNAN PECKHAM Robert (ed.), *Rethinking Heritage: Culture and Politics in Europe*, London, I.B. Tauris, pp. 113–123, 2003.
CRANE Walter, *Line & Form*, London, G. Bell & Sons, 1900.
FORTINI BROWN Patricia, *Venice and Antiquity: The Venetian Sense of the Past*, New Haven, CT, Yale University Press, 1997.

GALÍ Beth, "La Sagrada Família," *La Vanguardia*, pp. 16–17, December 18, 2002.

GANAU, Joan, *Els inicis del pensament conservacionista en l'urbanisme català, 1844–1931*, Barcelona, Publicacions de l'Abadia de Montserrat, 1997.

——, "Invention and authenticity in Barcelona's 'Barri Gotic'," *Future Anterior* 3(2): 11–23, 2006.

——, "Reinventing memories: the origin and development of Barcelona's Barri Gòtic, 1880–1950," *Journal of Urban History* 34: 795–832, 2008.

GARCIA-FUENTES Josep-Maria, "La construcció del Montserrat modern. I. Els inicis 1848–1885," Master's dissertation, Barcelona, Universitat Politècnica de Catalunya, 2007.

——, "Dissecting Montserrat: on the cultural, religious, touristic and identity-related construction of the modern Montserrat," in TRONO Ana (ed.), *Tourism, Religion and Culture: Regional Development through Meaningful Tourism Experiences*, Lecce, Mario Congedo Publisher, pp. 239–260, 2009.

——, "Recycling heritage: on a Catalan-Spanish process," in *Heritage 2010: 2nd International Conference on Heritage and Sustainable Development*, Évora, Greenlines Institut, pp. 1315–1323, 2010.

——, "La construcció del Montserrat modern / The construction of modern Montserrat," Ph.D. dissertation, Barcelona, Universitat Politècnica de Catalunya, 2012.

GARCÍA GUILLEN Luis, "Un trabajo de artesanía," [Online] Available at: http://www.gaudiclub.com/esp/e_links/rest4.htm [accessed October 14, 2012], 1987.

GARNICA Julio Fidel, "1950, Souvenir: Gaudí," in *VII Congreso Internacional Historia de la Arquitectura Moderna Española. Viajes en la transición de la arquitectura española hacia la modernidad*, Pamplona, T6 Ediciones, pp. 397–406, 2010.

GIMENO Albert, "La cabeza del dragon," *La Vanguardia—Vivir*, p. 7, February 11, 2007.

GIRALT-MIRACLE Daniel (ed.), *Gaudí. La búsqueda de la forma. Espacio, geometría, estructura y construcción*, Barcelona, Lunwerg, 2002.

GÓMEZ Josep et al., *La Sagrada Familia. De Gaudí al CAD*, Barcelona, Edicions Universitat Politècnica de Catalunya, 1996.

GRAHAM B.J., "Heritage as knowledge, capital or culture," *Urban Studies* 39: 1003–1017, 2002.

HALBWACHS Maurice, *La mémoire collective*, Paris, Presses Universitaires de France, 1968.

HOBSBAWM Eric and RANGER Terence (eds), *The Invention of Tradition*, Cambridge, Cambridge University Press, 1983.

JUNYENT Josep, *Jaume Collell i Bancells: les campanyes patriotic-religioses: 1878–1888*, Vic, Patronat d'Estudis Ausonencs, 1990.

LAHUERTA Juan José, *Antoni Gaudí (1852–1926) Arquitectura, ideología y política*, Madrid, Electa, 1999.

LOWENTHAL David, *The Past Is a Foreign Country*, Cambridge, Cambridge University Press, 1985.

——, *Possessed by the Past: The Heritage Crusade and the Spoils of History*, New York, The Free Press, 1996.

MARFANY, Joan Lluis, *Aspectes del modernisme*, Barcelona, Curial, 1975.

MARSHALL Sam, *Luna Park Just for Fun*, Sydney, Luna Park Reserve Trust, 1995.

MARTINELL César, *Gaudí: su vida, su teoría, su obra*, Barcelona, COACB, 1967.

NORA Pierre (ed.), *Les lieux de mémoire*, Paris, Gallimard, 1986.

PEIRÓN Francesc, "Un drac petaner," *La Vanguardia—Vivir*, p. 2, February 9, 2007.

PERMANYER Lluís, "Se veía venir: el Park Güell estaba en peligro," *La Vanguardia—Vivir*, p. 7, February 10, 2007.

RESINA Joan Ramon, *Barcelona's Vocation of Modernity, Rise and Decline of an Urban Image*, Stanford, CA, Stanford University Press, 2008.

ROGER Alain, *Court traité du paysage*, Paris, Gallimard, 1997.

ROHRER Judith, "Una visió apropiada: el temple de la Sagrada Família de Gaudí i la política arquitectónica de la Lliga Regionalista," in LAHUERTA Juan José (ed.), *Gaudí i el seu temps*, Barcelona, Barcanova, pp. 191–212, 1990.

SABATÉ Joan and AUMEDES/PEÑA, "Criterios de la intervención," [Online] Available at: http://www.gaudiclub.com/esp/e_links/rest2.htm [accessed October 14, 2012], 1987.

SCHMUTZLER Robert, *Art Nouveau*, New York, Abrams, 1962.

SESÉ Teresa, "¿De quién es el DRAC?," *La Vanguardia*, pp. 34–35, July 13, 2012.

TORRES Elias and LAPEÑA José Antonio, "Ilusión y respeto," [Online] Available at: http://www.gaudiclub.com/esp/e_links/rest3.htm [accessed October 14, 2012], 1987.

TUNBRIDGE John E. and ASHWORTH Gregory J., *Dissonant Heritage: The Management of the Past as a Resource in Conflict*, Chichester, Wiley, 1996.

UCELAY-DA CAL, Enric, *El imperialismo catalán. Prat de la Riba, Cambó, D'Ors y la conquista moral de España*, Barcelona, Edhasa, 2003.

ZEVI Bruno, *Storia dell'architettura moderna dalle origini al 1950*, Turin, Einaudi, 1950.

4 "What Happens in Vegas Doesn't Stay in Vegas"

When Tourism Imaginaries Fashion the Scientific Discourse

Pascale Nédélec

Introduction

Las Vegas stands out in the American psyche, even in the mental landscape of non-Americans worldwide. "Sin City," city of vice and perdition, Las Vegas embodies a free-wheeling, anything-goes place where almost everything is allowed. That image has been built via tourist practices that in turn influenced the cultural world of the American nation. As a true icon, Las Vegas is omnipresent in American cultural references, whether it is movies, TV shows, or even idiomatic expressions like "What happens in Vegas stays in Vegas" or "Only in Vegas."

To study Las Vegas is to study the relationship between city and tourism (Gravari-Barbas 2001), but even more between a tourist discourse and an academic discourse. In the case of Las Vegas, those discourses are so similar, despite the duality commonly postulated between them, that one can question the influence of tourism imaginaries on academic production.

This chapter argues that the Las Vegas tourism imaginaries, its stereotypes and its clichés, are found in scientific discourses. The city is studied from a double perspective: using a bottom-up approach, highlighting perceptions and representations produced by tourism, but also from a top-down point of view, examining academic theorizations of Las Vegas. This being so, three levels of interpretation are interrelated: the production of urban images by tourists and the tourism industry; the reception of those images by researchers; and finally the scientific production on this topic. My analysis focuses on material produced and spread in the United States, since Las Vegas is essentially a domestic destination.[1] The scientific discourse is to be comprehended through a bibliographic review in English encompassing books and papers by scholars from social and human sciences dealing with Las Vegas.

Thus, Las Vegas offers an ideal case study on the relations between production and reception of tourism imaginaries within a specific social group that is the researchers in human and social sciences. More broadly, this chapter questions the production and position of academic knowledge within the circulation of ideas, and more precisely the role of the academic institution as a culturally productive and usually authoritative social group.

With the above in mind, this chapter first addresses the issue of defining the concept of "tourism imaginaries" and how they apply to Las Vegas. The second part shows how those tourism imaginaries have seemingly taken-over the scientific production on "the Entertainment Capital of the World."

Tourism Imaginaries and Las Vegas

Defining Tourism Imaginaries

Imaginary is one of those notions that are easier to recognize empirically than to define theoretically. In its literal definition, imaginary describes something "existing only in imagination or fancy" (*Oxford English Dictionary* online: http://oxforddictionaries.com/definition/english/imaginary). The use of the word in informal language in its plural form transforms somewhat that first definition to conjure up a collection of representations, of fantasies differing from reality. The connection or disconnect between imaginaries and reality lie at the core of the definition issue: the building of imaginaries mixes tangible and demonstrable with perceptions and senses of reality, producing an intermediate level of knowledge between reality and sensibility. Working on the idea of "tourism imaginaries" is thus especially interesting.

For the sake of this chapter, "tourism imaginaries" are defined as a collection of images and representations initially produced and used within the tourism sphere and then spread to the rest of society. As such, tourism imaginaries crystallize values with places. They are fixed images associated with specific places or type of spaces. They are transcending images and mediating perceptions expected and looked for during one's travel. For example, a white sand beach with coconut trees is usually viewed as a dream destination, a paradise on earth associated with exoticism and escape. Likewise, the Manhattan skyline, the Great Wall, or a landscape of serene grassy hills encapsulate tourism destinations such as New York City, China, and rural England. It would be wrong though to consider tourism imaginaries as immutable: they arise in a specific historical time and cultural space. Those meanings of place gradually change in patterns of use, of social codes, or in general behavior which may also create and give birth to "new meanings of place" (Zukin et al. 1998). Today, most would consider lying on a sunny beach, getting a tan on the French Riviera as an epitome of vacations. On the contrary, until the beginning of the twentieth century, French turned away from beaches on the Mediterranean Sea since they were associated with diseases (malaria) and embodied the dangers of the sea. Tourism imaginaries are neither eternal nor immanent: they do come from someone and from somewhere. Two broad categories of tourism imaginaries' producers can be identified: on one side, the tourism industry, driven by economic and marketing objectives, and on the other side the individuals that are confronted with tourism that is, in our increasingly globalized world, almost everyone. Meanings attached to specific places result from deliberate image creation in the case of place marketing or from a more subtle individual consolidation of significance. The complex production of tourism imaginaries can thus be simplified and visualized with the image of a circle of actors and processes around a tourist destination (Figure 4.1).

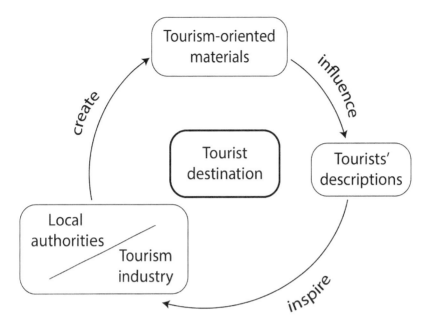

Figure 4.1 Tourism imaginaries circle: production and diffusion of tourism imaginaries

Studying tourism imaginaries raises methodological questions on how to deline-ate a corpus and how to single out the source of production. Travel guides, travel agencies' brochures, and their pictures, ad campaigns in the media stand out as private and institutional materials. Grasping the individuals' imaginaries, in their diversity and individuality, is more complicated. It is difficult to establish the dis-tinction between personal and original tourism imaginaries created by an individual (Vietnam is exotic because it reminds me of my grand-mother's bed-time stories) and marketed tourism imaginaries thought to optimize attractiveness for potential visitors (Vietnam is an up-and-coming destination where you will enjoy great value for your money). As marketing tools, tourism imaginaries' first goal is to attract tourists. Gradually, what used to be mere branding materials are appropriated and internalized by the public opinion as social constructs and valued representations. Thus, tourism imaginaries must be understood as an element of a larger "social imaginary" (Zukin et al. 1998: 629). Underlying this is the difficulty to measure the (un)conscious appropriation of those imaginaries by individuals, by groups (locals, politicians, researchers, and so on), and by society as a whole. One way to face this challenge is to analyze material where individuals express their opin-ions about places and tourist destinations such as travel diaries, travel journals, or travel blogs. Numerous tools can also be examined to grasp the vernacular culture reproducing and diffusing tourism imaginaries: language, media in their diversity (movies, books, television shows, songs, theater plays, newspaper articles, post-cards, commercials, and so on). Nevertheless there is an intrinsic complexity in comprehending sensibilities and perceptions, and most of all in generalizing from individuals' opinions to public opinion.

The tourism imaginaries, following Zukin et al.'s work on "urban imaginary," can be defined as a "mythologized set of cultural meanings" expressing "social power exercised by cultural symbols." As such, tourism imaginaries are symbolic but yet "materialized and [they] become real in all sorts of spatial and social practices" (Zukin et al. 1998: 628). This is precisely the impact of Las Vegas tourism imaginaries on the social practices of researchers that I intend to examine in this chapter.

Las Vegas-specific Tourism Imaginaries

How and why does Las Vegas stand out so much in the American culture? Over the years, three main elements fashioned the Las Vegas tourism imaginaries: gambling, the Mafia, and entertainment.

The first reason why Las Vegas appears so special is to be found in the practice of gambling. The gaming industry has profoundly structured the entire Las Vegas Valley. In addition to the hotels-casinos that have made the reputation of the Strip and Fremont Street, gambling is everywhere in the valley, especially in the form of slot machines. Numbering 135,781 in Clark County[2] slot machines are the crown of casinos' jewels but are also scattered at the McCarran Airport, in supermarkets, in gas stations, and even at the old bus stop terminal. Officially and definitively legalized in 1931, gambling has made Nevada stand out for 47 years as the only state in the US were money games were legal (until gambling legalization in New Jersey in 1978[3]). Raento (2003) explains the early institutionalization of gambling in Nevada by economic, cultural and historical motivations.

> Gambling has long roots in Nevada's nineteenth-century mining and railroad towns, characterized by liberal attitudes toward drinking, gambling, and prostitution. . . . The state's demographic and cultural profile also played a role: A high proportion of males in the overall population, low church membership, and the strong individualism, materialism, and transient lifestyle of miners and ranchers created a specific society that could be open to legal experimentation with social forms outlawed elsewhere. (Raento 2003: 229)

Las Vegas embodied the wild side of the Wild West: light morals, a profusion of saloons, card games, prostitution, and a very weak will to enforce the Prohibition laws. Of note, Nevada's history as a "frontier" state promoted a renegade spirit that is still present in contemporary Las Vegas tourism imaginaries. The City of Las Vegas took advantage of that momentum in the 1930s and 1940s to market itself as the "Last Frontier Town" (Gragg 2007). Las Vegas built its reputation on gambling which became by far the urban area's first industry and its most profitable one. Even without its original monopoly, Las Vegas maintained its status of premium gambling destination, with a "reputation as the ultimate frontier in the eyes of thrill-seeking postindustrial middle-class Americans" (Raento 2003: 245).

The second element which shaped the image of Las Vegas is the Mafia. Until the 1970s gambling was largely the domain of the Mob, since few other investors would risk being associated with such a morally despised activity in the American post-war puritan society. Even if the Mafia did not own all the properties, hotels-casinos, first on Fremont Street in downtown City of Las Vegas and then along what was to become the Strip, were often a combination of dirty money laundering (especially the Teamster Union money), booze, girls, and cash (Schwartz 2003; Moehring 2000). Even if the mobsters' reign is long gone, the Mob still generates interest and revenues: the "Mob Experience" at the Tropicana and "The Mob Museum" (a.k.a. National Museum of Organized Crime and Law Enforcement) newly opened in the downtown City of Las Vegas count on the everlasting fascination for gangsters' stories to revitalize visitor traffic.

In the 1970s, the Mob gave way to the world of capitalism and shareholders. Incidentally, Las Vegas went corporate and reinvented itself once again to be billed "the Entertainment Capital of the World." From then on, Las Vegas was about a global experience of entertainment, whether it is gambling, shopping, eating, or even admiring buildings. Not specific to Las Vegas, the growing synergy between entertainment and more "traditional" activities has been coined by the retail industry as "shopertainment, eatertainement and edutainmnent" (Hannigan 1998: 89). Going one step further is the increasing popularity of architainment, unequalled outside Las Vegas. The different hotels-casinos along the Strip are attractions in their own right, a true architectural spectacle. The New York-New York Hotel & Casino reproduces the skyline of New York with its own Statue of Liberty, its own Brooklyn Bridge and its own Chrysler Building. Likewise, the Bellagio stages a supposedly Italian village on the bank of an 8-acre Como Lake.

Thus, Las Vegas today is intrinsically associated with entertainment. The city is famous for its numerous nicknames, one of the best known being "Sin City." To talk about Las Vegas is to postulate a free-wheeling, anything-goes place, representing access to "forbidden pleasures" (Fuat Firat 2001: 105). Among them, sex is undeniably emphasized. Much of Las Vegas tourism interest relies on the marketing of women's bodies and sexuality, ranging from the cabaret tradition to its more recent by-products, mixing TV shows, so-called celebrities, and striptease. The key element to activate the sense of total freedom at the heart of the Las Vegas tourism imaginaries is the notion of escape: escape from social conventions, from legal restrictions (gaming, drinking in the street, and near-by prostitution[4]), from an ordinary environment and daily routine. Las Vegas is often seen as a place where everything is possible, where anyone can arrive a nobody and leave a millionaire.

The Spreading and Diffusion of Las Vegas Imaginaries

To understand the production and diffusion of Las Vegas imaginaries, attention has to be drawn to its supports. Three main vehicles should be emphasized: advertising, lexicon, and TV shows. Advertising has played a fundamental role in the production of Las Vegas tourism imaginaries. A succession of advertising campaigns highlights marketing efforts by the local tourism industry and city boosters. The advertising firm R&R Partners has been especially influential for the past decade in promoting Las Vegas' "up-front marketing of vice and adult entertainment" (Borchard 2003: 194). R&R Partners came up with the from now on incontrovertible slogans "What happens here, stays here" and "Only in Vegas." Those slogans became part of the vernacular and the best-selling argument for Las Vegas. Working for the Las Vegas Convention and Visitors Authority (LVCVA) since the early 2000s, R&R Partners has turned Las Vegas into a national—if not worldwide—brand. The "What happens here, stays here" campaign has coursed its way into the popular lexicon in a way few advertising slogans ever do: a *USA Today* survey named the campaign the "most effective" of 2003, and the trade publication *Advertising Age* termed it "a cultural phenomenon" (Friess 2004). As an ultimate accolade, in 2011 "What happens here" joined the prestigious Madison Avenue Walk of Fame in New York City, passing at the finishing line competitors such as Nike's "Just Do It" or Capital One's "What's in Your Wallet." The advertisement's success lies in suggesting what Las Vegas is about rather than in making it explicit. As Jeff Candido, one of the main authors of this campaign, stated: "We knew we couldn't show a lot of what people do in Las Vegas on prime-time TV, so the slogan lets them guess" (Friess 2004).

Las Vegas tourism imaginaries have thus reached a unique status in the American psyche. And to better grasp how Las Vegas is perceived in American pop culture, we here turn to language and expression and the changing nature of speech. Some websites provide an opportunity to see the processes of language in the making and provide the researcher with some solid ground. UrbanDictionary.com, "A veritable cornucopia of streetwise lingo, posted and defined by its readers" (UrbanDictionary.com) is one of those resourceful websites. Studying only this one website may not be sufficient to draw definite conclusions; nonetheless UrbanDictionary.com's quality and breadth allows us to see how Las Vegas stands out in vernacular popular speech. Table 4.1 sums up its Las Vegas utterances.[5]

Table 4.1 Las Vegas streetwise lingo, according to UrbanDictionary.com

Number of utterances	"Las Vegas": 48 definitions "Vegas": 9 definitions "What happens in Vegas": 1 "What happens in Vegas stays in Vegas": 2 "Las Vegas Syndrome": 2
Examples of some of the 23 compound expressions with "Las Vegas"	"Las Vegas breakfast," "Las Vegas Eiffel Tower," "Las Vegas facelift," "Las Vegas lunchbox," "Las Vegas penguins," "Las Vegas cocktail," "Las Vegas wake-up" . . . (Most of the expressions have a sexual connotation).

Some definitions are deemed especially representative of the Las Vegas aura in pop culture. For example, the word "Vegas" by itself is defined as:

'A modifier that's tacked on to the end of a town or city, usually replacing the term "ville" that the denizens sarcastically use to give their village the appearance of being hip and/or happening.' A quote illustrates this definition: Joe: 'Where you headed this weekend?' Schmoe: 'Non-stop excitement. I'm off to Nashvegas or Knoxvegas.'

Another definition for "Vegas" adds an almost philosophical dimension:

'Vegas, A Sisyphusean struggle to reach utopia.' Illustrated by the sentence 'Vegas Baby, Vegas.'

As part of the American mythology, Las Vegas holds a special place in the media, especially in movies and TV shows. One can observe a virtual circle of production and consumption of the Las Vegas imaginaries in media such as music, movies, TV shows, advertising, and the like. The listing of all the books, movies, TV shows, or even songs that take place in or relate to Las Vegas is a life project on its own (Eumann 2005). Indeed, almost every TV shows has a "Vegas" episode. Looking at some of the most popular American TV shows provides some examples of Las Vegas' omnipresence in mainstream television. Throughout the 22 seasons of *The Simpsons*, three episodes took place in Las Vegas.[6] The episode "Viva Ned Flanders"[7] ranked tenth in the "Best Episodes Ever" ranking at Amazon.com. Its plot speaks for itself: "Homer and of all people Ned Flanders enjoy a bender in Vegas." In the same vein, it is in Las Vegas that *Friends* characters Ross and Rachel got accidentally married (at the Little White Chapel) after a night of heavy drinking.[8] These two examples, among many other possible, illustrate the general trends of storylines one would see in programs and movies dealing with Las Vegas.

Las Vegas imaginaries have evolved since the foundation of the city in 1905. However, in the cultural landscape of the United States, Las Vegas is almost always associated with its tourist characteristics. Throughout the years one element imposed itself: there is no place like Las Vegas and nowhere else is it possible to have the true Las Vegas experience, summarized as "gambling, booze and all-night-partying" (Lasker 2011). This sense of uniqueness is reinforced by the pale attempts to reproduce the Las Vegas feel in places like Atlantic City or Macao which gives a particularly strong cultural specificity to the city.

The Las Vegas tourism imaginaries were built around tourism and tourist corridors. Thus, the Strip has become the synecdoche where the part has absorbed the whole, that is the other economic activities and a metropolitan area of almost 2 million people. As a consequence, the tourism imaginaries and the city imaginaries have merged to become one at the expense of the "regular" metropolitan area. That the tourism industry should emphasize the experience offered by the hotels-casinos on the Strip makes complete sense. It should therefore fall to researchers and academics to reveal the discrepancy between the relatively small tourist districts and the rest of the urban area; and to parse the tourism imaginaries to better grasp the beyond the scenes "reality" of Las Vegas.

Tourism Imaginaries versus Scientific Discourse: A Difficult Reassessment?

Two Supposedly Different Discourses

One would expect scientific discourse to be different from tourist and popular culture discourses. Here it is necessary to establish the specific characteristics of an academic or scientific discourse. According to Berthelot (2003: 16), a scientific discourse can be identified thanks to three criteria: it expresses an intention of knowledge, it is recognized by a learned society aspiring to this intention, and it is published within a specific context. Moreover, a scientific discourse speaks to a limited public. A scientific discourse is also supposed to be as neutral and objective as possible based on facts and thorough investigation, constituting an argued demonstration. Thus a scientific discourse offers a mediation of a reality into an analytical framework. In comparison, a non-scientific text is more of a story, which is a narration, a feeling of a situation. Hence, there are supposedly two very separate ways of apprehending information and grasping reality whether you are an academic or a mere individual like a tourist.

It is true that it would be naïve to think that a scientific text is an exclusively rhetorical construction or a pure reflection of an exterior reality. Therefore, in the end what is interesting is less the scientific text by itself than the semantic (reality vs. code) and epistemological (description of reality vs. theoretical construction) status of the contents conveyed therein (Berthelot 2003: 7).

> [what is] important doesn't lie in the text as such but in the work that is at its origin, and in the fabric of interactions at the heart of which it takes part; rhetorical work of composition and persuasion, implemented in an intention of seduction, of conformation to a 'reader-response,' of inscription in an argumentative polyphony. (Berthelot 2003: 6)[9]

The Permeability of Scientific Discourse

The scientific discourses' supposed ideals of neutrality and detachment from biased perceptions stand at odds with writings on Las Vegas. Indeed in the case of Las Vegas it seems that tourism imaginaries have spread into the minds of academics, especially within the human and social sciences. A thorough bibliographic review reveals common characteristics in works about Las Vegas. My goal here is not to go through a comprehensive review of everything that has ever been written on Las Vegas. My corpus will focus on scholarly books and papers in social and human sciences dedicated to Las Vegas. The numerous works of journalists, what I call "journalistic novels" about Las Vegas, will not be taken into consideration since their authors are less inclined to adopt a neutral stance when researching a topic. Among the references identified, some are more used than others. Thus, *Zeropolis* by the French philosopher and academic Bruce Bégout (2003) will be especially quoted in this chapter: its ornate prose is exemplary of the rhetorical excess often sparked off by Las Vegas. Moreover, it figures prominently in bibliographies on the city. Two recent special issues on Las Vegas lay also at the heart of my demonstration (*M@n@gement*, 2001 and *Human Geography*, 2009). Those two publications allow one to see how postmodernists are very fond of Las Vegas, used within the framework of a postmodern paradigm to embody the poster child for the excesses of our contemporary society.

Following the characteristics of scientific production mentioned above, one would expect to find references on the tourism industry but also on the metropolitan area of the greater Las Vegas. Indeed, despite the unquestionable influence of tourism on Las Vegas' identity, the Las Vegas Valley urban area counts 1,945,149 inhabitants as of August, 2012[10] and the tourist districts hardly cover 1 per cent[11] of the entire agglomeration. However, the great majority of texts focuses exclusively on the Strip and the tourism industry at the expense of the metropolitan area. One cannot reproach scholars in tourism studies for researching tourist spaces. Notwithstanding choosing a research topic on Las Vegas almost always comes down to its tourist dimension along with the concealment of the rest of the urban area, including its relationship with tourism. Most of the time, the agglomeration as a whole and the locals behind the tourist scene are not even mentioned. These one-sided stories give the impression that the Strip *is* Las Vegas and that there is nothing else in the valley but hotels-casinos and tourists. Failing to mention the rest of the urban area comes to the denial of Las Vegas urbanity. *Zeropolis* is based on the negation of Las Vegas's entirety as revealed by the explanation of its title: "to locate the very essence of the urbanity of the future being developed in Las Vegas: in nothingness as a number" (Bégout 2003: 121, endnote 1). Other authors embrace the same analysis about the city:

> this is precisely the Las Vegas utopia of having us believe that it is a city. (Bégout 2003: 104)

> Is there anything to learn from Las Vegas? It was, after all, considered to be not a 'real' place, but a city of 'sin,' not to live in, but to escape to in order to satisfy the dark side of human desires. In the middle of a desert, contradicting all the natural environment, it was built as a place to visit, and then to leave. (Fuat Firat 2001: 101)

> the city itself was originally conceived as an absence. (Bier 2009: 86)

By appropriating the *topoi* promoted by the tourism industry, the scientific literature validates them, gives them credibility and takes part in their diffusion within academic circles. The authoritative nature of researchers and academics amplifies the phenomenon. As a consequence, the tourism imaginaries and the city imaginaries merge to become one at the expense of the "regular" metropolitan area.

Second, writings on Las Vegas seem to call for hyperbolic prose. Categorical affirmations with lack of nuance, exaggerations, word plays, and puns are legion. In some cases it feels like a bid for the most outrageous title. This quest for grandiloquence and escalation in the scientific discourse seems to follow the same pattern as the proliferation of superlatives in contemporary urban studies (Beauregard 2003). One can wonder about the seeming spectacularization of research, a phenomenon that could be explained by the growing need to attract attention in the field of paper production. As Beauregard notes, the excess of metaphors and superlatives constitutes a slippery slope that can lead to "blur[ring] the distinction between theory and publicity" (2003: 184). Some recurrent themes are especially popular among Las Vegas commentators: the omnipresence of consumption and entertainment.

> The city itself is nothing but a gigantic non-stop spectacle. The postcard has absorbed the whole reality and spat it back out pretty quickly in the form of thinly processed psychedelic icons for the middle classes. (Bégout 2003: 51)

> Las Vegas is the ultimate spectacle of production and consumption in a deconstructing world. (Boje 2001: 80)

> Las Vegas casino-hotel as the paradigmatic cathedral of consumption. (Ritzer and Stillman 2001: 83)

> This analysis reveals Las Vegas to be a city remade for visual consumption where the streetscape becomes a fantascape and the arts that are on display are amusement goods—patterned and predigested products for consumption. (Carr 2001: 121)

> What makes Las Vegas unique is not its disgustingly amenitized landscape, or its overabundance of trashy commodities, but rather, it magically transforms emotions—joy, sorrow, ecstasy—into commodities. (Van Dyke 2009: 99)

> It requires minimal critical or intellectual acuity to detect the sleight-of-hand which makes the city appealing to so many people the frenzied neon signage inviting you to participate in gluttonous consumption, the busy street flooded with anonymous people drifting from hotel to hotel in search of something indefinable yet promised to them. (Van Dyke 2009: 96)

> There is no other world where hedonism, consumer intoxication and the impassioned fabric of individualistic values devoted to narcissism, such as they animate liberalism, are as dominating and bewitching. (Arrault 2010: 43)[12]

By engaging in what I call the "Sin City rhetoric," academics play the game of Las Vegas. It is interesting to note also the great liberty taken by different authors in describing Las Vegas, to the point of issuing numerous disputable statements or even untruths. Thus, for Arrault, the Strip is "the principal artery (and quasi unique one)" of the city (2010: 45). Likewise, Bégout dreams slot machines "even in the toilets of McCarran Airport" (2003: 38). It seems that the scientific requirement of accuracy is not as necessary when one is writing about Las Vegas. At the same time Las Vegas apparently doesn't need to be investigated, since most "already know" everything there is to know about it.

> It strikes me that I would be not very far from the truth if I were to answer anyone who happened to ask me what I had learned in Las Vegas with the perfectly simple reply: 'Nothing.' I would mean by this not only that the town itself resembles nothing; pure urban chaos, but I would also be saying that I saw nothing there that I didn't already know. (Bégout 2003: 11)

Final characteristics—most of the writings on Las Vegas contain some kind of moral condemnation and devaluation of the experience offered by tourism. Such moralizing approaches are expressed in the following quotes:

> The image of Las Vegas was, then, one of gambling, entertainment, mobs, glitter, hollow dreams. It had, overall, an image of the sleazy side of American culture. (Fuat Firat 2001: 101)

> . . . visitors . . . as lost souls who are just conned into a dream world, who are less than adequate in thinking for themselves. (Fuat Firat 2001: 116)

> Maybe deconstructing Las Vegas is an impossibly easy task. Easy because it requires minimal critical or intellectual acuity to detect the sleight-of-hand which makes the city appealing to so many people—the frenzied neon signage inviting you to participate in gluttonous consumption, the busy streets flooded with anonymous people drifting from hotel to hotel in search of something indefinable yet promised to them, prompting them to continue walking aimlessly out in the enclosed open, and possibility. Capitalism, for many, becomes a spectacle here. Bitter people who feel tired, exhausted, and used up, alarmingly retreat to this spot in the hope of easily winning the improvement they've been sold as their entitlement. And yet the visual, dizzying, and cacophonic displays of capitalism is impossible to deconstruct all the same when you have to confront this endless searching, when you walk through the casinos, or up and down the strip, by day or night, but especially at night when the saturnine grimaces shine through more clearly on the faces of people who are already helplessly broken, who have sought reprieve from their troubles in this place, and who are convinced a few days of rampant, unthinking consumption, gambling, and the joys of dislocation provide an easy remedy. (Van Dyke 2009: 96)

As a result, the main characteristic shared by numerous writings on Las Vegas is a biased vision, that contrasts with the quest for balanced analyses. Hence, a paradoxical situation: the success of Las Vegas's tourism imaginaries lead to the denial of the city as an interest-worthy scientific topic. By interest-worthy I mean a topic whose examination can enrich any intellectual thinking and contribute to the fabric of knowledge. Scientific discourse on the city ends up consuming the Las Vegas tourist imaginaries instead of producing a more neutral analytical discourse.

A Reign of Moral and Social Condemnation

More than the texts themselves their semantic status is interesting: the reality that they describe relies on moralizing codes denouncing Las Vegas. Therefore their reality is deeply shaped by a rhetorical construction that tends to supplant more empirical and analytical elements. More broadly, studying geographical writing allows us to identify the modalities of knowledge production and to question the fabric of sciences and scientific knowledge. To understand this seeming paradox, one must not lose sight of the social context of the production of scientific discourse and its status as "social constructs" (Latour 1979). Academic knowledge doesn't evolve in a closed world, protected from non-scientific influences. Scientific works on Las Vegas are produced within intellectual circles which highly value culture, and claim distance from mass-culture. Bégout is especially explicit in his assessment of Las Vegas' cultural value:

> . . . cultural, social and aesthetic poverty. (Bégout 2003: 13)

> . . . a theology of profoundest mediocrity. (Bégout 2003: 23)

> Las Vegas has long since left behind the stage of good taste, or more precisely of culture in general. By virtue of its incapacity for universal appeal, it has absorbed every artistic, cultural and social value (for example its parodic recuperation of the institution of marriage) into the bottomless pit of its excess, and has made it all in a certain way innocent and puerile, dull and indifferent. Las Vegas is a pretend city, a city without pretensions. (Bégout 2003: 84)

> *Leaving Las Vegas*—that sums up the only way of salvation. (Bégout 2003: 117)

But Bégout is not the only one to complain about the lack of culture in Las Vegas; arts critics are particularly vocal in their contempt for Las Vegas:

> Built to be exactly what it is, this [Las Vegas] is the real, real fake at the highest, loudest and most authentically inauthentic level of illusion and invention. (Huxtable 1997)

> In a town where 'Art' is normally the name of someone's limo driver . . . In a city of such overripe simulacra, whose most characteristic museum is dedicated to the memory of Liberace, what room is there for the clean, piercing, complex presence of real works of art? (Hughes 1998)

> For several years now, there has been talk about whether Las Vegas could handle what in any other city might be referred to as real architecture. . . . But whether Las Vegas wants to be rescued from kitsch remains to be seen. (Goldberger 2010)

Most of the authors quoted in this chapter would claim to be representative of a social group characterized by cultural expectations and a longing for intellectual enrichment. Those authors tend to conform, knowingly or not, to an expected and socially demanded vision of Las Vegas: that is no one with the slightest education can nor must like Las Vegas. After all Las Vegas is for most writers not much more than a "middle-American freak show" (Rothman and Davis 2002: 5). Academic circles and scientific spheres feel a need to differentiate themselves from what is considered basic, even vulgar aspirations such as partying and getting loose. Rothman and Davis confirm this apparently compulsory figure:

> The other preoccupation of Vegas writing is with the bizarre extremism of the average Middle Americans who blunder their way, like herds of dazed, overfed cattle, through the fleshpots of the Strip. Mom and Dad from Sioux Falls—she's in her new wig, he smokes a cigar—have never been stranger, or more normal: 'casino zombies' in the words of one writer. Las Vegas has become the favorite setting for hip anthropologists to mock the distended appetites of the majority; in the process, they tell us more about their own faux elitism than they do about the people they are observing. (Rothman and Davis 2002: 5)

Wolfe (1965), admittedly more of an ironical popular writer than a serious academic, goes one step further by linking the general disdain towards Las Vegas to its status of a "prole" destination:

> The usual thing has happened, of course. Because [Las Vegas] is prole, its gets ignored, except on the most sensational level. (Wolfe 1965: xv–xvi)

A quote from the opening address of the 2009 annual meeting of the American Association of Geographers (AAG), held that year in Las Vegas, confirms this demand of differentiation from the masses and claim for "high culture." Apparently, the choice of Las Vegas wasn't an easy pick, and the AAG's president had to explain why on earth geographers would meet in such an unusual place:

> The decision to locate the 2009 AAG Annual Meeting in Las Vegas, Nevada has not met with universal acclaim. Some people complain that Las Vegas is not a 'real' city and that it lacks the high culture we should demand of our convention sites. It is seen as the ultimate 'fake' city built on fantasies that recycle the real character of other places as presumably 'cheap' (but not inexpensive!) imitations. (AAG 2009: 3)

This quote expresses the aura surrounding Las Vegas: a gambling Mecca, luring lower-class Americans, built on simulacra and merchandisable entertainment. But it also exemplifies the social condemnation and moral judgment influencing Las Vegas's perception within the scientific discourse: a place of vice and perdition, where there is no culture, where gambling is seen as a "threat to the moral axioms of the state" (Scriven 1995); a destination far away from the high intellectual spheres of New England and the "enlightened" West Coast that could be reduced to a "déclassé" destination. As a result, Las Vegas is not deemed interest-worthy as an academic topic by many; and the denunciation of Las Vegas, most of the time disguised as a postmodernist "deconstruction," becomes a figure of speech, a stylistic effect destined to be repeated with small variations.

Thus, Las Vegas is criticized from a double perspective: either by critics of extreme liberalism, of a hyper individualistic society that lost sight of common good; or by partisans of a moral discourse that takes roots in puritan values, bemoaning the loss of community and the founding principles of American society. Las Vegas is used by both extremes of the political spectrum to illustrate their respective positions. Likewise it is noteworthy to see how radical thinkers deal with Las Vegas when it comes to class conflict. The general valorization of workers in a working context seems to disappear and strive for contempt when the same individuals look for entertainment and recreation among the middle-class.

One article stands alone, very interestingly questioning the issue of the knowledge fabric. Chatterjee (2009) reads between the lines of class struggle and analyzes the "deconstruction" of Las Vegas as a potential "class project." She underlines the opposition between an "intellectual class" and a "common class" embodying the clash between Las Vegas lovers and haters. She asks her reader:

> Why did many geographers find Vegas 'cosmetic and superficial' when it appeals to millions of tourists every year? Are we intellectuals? Being intellectuals are we engaged in symbolic struggle with those 'common' others, whose garish tastes we do not share? Is deconstructing Vegas a class project, embarked on by those who do not lead a banal existence, whose habituses are stimulated by the intellectual and the authentic, violated by the fake? By engaging in such a project are we legitimizing our scheme of classification? (Chatterjee 2009: 84)

Conclusion

> Without the least uncertainty, Las Vegas has set its just measure in excess, its happy medium in extremes. Nothing in the city can be promoted unless it is susceptible to infinite exaggeration. (Bégout 2003: 76)

Bégout couldn't be more right about how Las Vegas attracts the extremes, even and maybe especially in his own writing.

It is obvious to most that Las Vegas has developed a very special place in the American pop culture: those overpowering tourism imaginaries seem to have vanquished the scientific discourse, thanks partly to feeble resistance from academics themselves. The responsibility of European thinkers is here to be underlined since their critical interpretation of the United States, Eco's fakery (1985) and Baudrillard's simulacra (1994) in the lead, has been so influential on many Americans intellectuals. In the case of Las Vegas, tourism imaginaries and scientific discourse intersect to diffuse the tourist(y) image of the city. It is interesting to note the overall defeat of the scientific discourse in the tourism staging of a city, and its appropriation within the context of knowledge production. Las Vegas appears as a perfect study case of the intertwined knowledge production networks linking scientific and secular.

Las Vegas reveals the worst side of intellectual and academics: by putting on the appearance of Las Vegas's imaginaries, researchers have an excuse to promote some moral hypocrisy and scientific prejudices. However, it would be false to think that what is written about Las Vegas stays in Las Vegas!

On the other hand, the goal is not to embrace the other extreme that would be an iron-clad promotion of Las Vegas, denying the reality of the Strip and its possible excesses. But a more balanced apprehension and reading of the city must be advocated. To study Las Vegas is at the same time enriching and challenging. The weight of the city's imaginaries tends to smudge its analysis and spread cookie-cutter reasoning but should not cover the intrinsic value of Las Vegas for intellectual questioning. Fortunately, some authors recognized the scientific value of Las Vegas. Venturi, Scott Brown and Izenour are a notable exception, preaching an "open-minded and nonjudgmental investigation" (1972: ix). For them, "Learning from popular culture does not remove the architect from his or her status in high culture. But it may alter high culture to make it more sympathetic to current needs and issues" (1977: 161). Venturi and Scott Brown were interested in the city, not as it should be or as the researcher wished it to be, but in what it actually is. Like it or not, Las Vegas is more than a world-renowned tourist destination. It has been the fastest growing metropolis in the United States for the past 20 years (US Census Bureau), and may embody the future of urban America (Dear and Flusty 1998: 66). Las Vegas should be taken seriously as a "real" city worthy of scientific interest questioning the very trends of urbanization in the United States (Gravari-Barbas 2001). Unfortunately, in the long run Venturi's recommendation hasn't been crowned with success. It is about time to put aside prejudices and learn to learn from Las Vegas.

Notes

1 According to the Las Vegas Convention and Visitors Authority, in 2012 83 per cent of visitors to Las Vegas were Americans (*2012 Las Vegas Visitor Profile*, p. 81).
2 Nevada Gaming Commission, Quarterly Statistical Report, March 2013: http://gaming.nv.gov/modules/showdocument.aspx?documentid=7862, p. 8 (retrieved July 29, 2013).
3 Today only two states forbid any kind or form of gambling: Utah and Hawaii.
4 Under Nevada state law, any county with a population under 400,000 is allowed to license brothels if it so chooses (NRS 244.345). Therefore, prostitution is illegal in Las Vegas, Clark County population being 1.94 million in 2012 (Clark County population estimates, Demographics Department).
5 UrbanDictionary.com (retrieved April 20, 2011).
6 *The Simpsons*: "Homer at the Bat" (season 3, ep. 17—Originally aired on Fox, February 20, 1992), "$pringfield (Or, How I Learned to Stop Worrying and Love Legalized Gambling)" (season 5, ep. 10—Originally aired on Fox, December 16, 1993), "Homie the Clown" (season 6, ep. 15—Originally aired on Fox, February 12, 1995). See also French DVD "Simpsons Classics. In Las Vegas" (Amazon.fr).

7 Originally aired on Fox, January 10, 1999.
8 *Friends*: "The One in Vegas" parts 1 and 2 (season 5, eps 23 and 24—Originally aired on NBC, May 20, 1999).
9 Translation by the author.
10 Clark County, 2012, http://www.clarkcountynv.gov/Depts/comprehensive_planning/ demographics/Documents/PlacePopulation.pdf (retrieved July 29, 2013).
11 Estimates by the author, after Google Earth and ArcGIS Softwares.
12 Translations by the author.

Bibliography

AAG Newsletter, 44(2), February 2009.
ARRAULT Valérie, *L'Empire du kitsch*, Paris, Klincksieck, 2010.
BAUDRILLARD Jean, *Simulacra and Simulation* [translation], Ann Arbor, MI, University of Michigan Press, 1994.
BEAUREGARD Robert, "City of superlatives," *City & Community*, 2(3): 183–199, September 2003.
BÉGOUT Bruce, *Zeropolis: The Experience of Las Vegas* [translation], London, Reaktion Books, 2003.
BERTHELOT Jean-Michel (ed.), *Figures du texte scientifique*, Paris, Presses universitaires de France, 2003.
BIER Jess, "Self-de(con)structing Vegas," *Human Geography*, 2(2): 86–90, 2009.
BOJE David, "Introduction to deconstructing Las Vegas," *M@n@gement*, 4(3): 79–82, 2001.
BORCHARD Kurt, "From *flanerie* to pseudo-*flanerie*: the postmodern tourist in Las Vegas," *Studies in Symbolic Interaction*, 26: 191–213, 2003.
CARR Adrian, "Understanding the 'imago' Las Vegas: taking our lead from Homer's parable of the oarsmen," *M@n@gement*, 4(3): 121–140, 2001.
CHATTERJEE Ipsita, "Deconstructing Vegas: class project?," *Human Geography*, 2(2): 83–85, 2009.
DEAR Michael and FLUSTY Steven, "Postmodern urbanism," *Annals of the Association of American Geographers*, 88(1): 50–72, 1998.
ECO Umberto, *La Guerre du faux*, Paris, Livre de Poche, Grasset, 1985.
EUMANN Ingrid, *The Outer Edge of the Wave: American Frontiers in Las Vegas*, Frankfurt, Peter Lang, 2005.
FRIESS Steve, "A firm hits jackpot on Las Vegas ads: campaign phrase enters the lexicon," *Boston Globe*, March 28, 2004.
FUAT FIRAT A., "The meanings and messages of Las Vegas: the present of our future," *M@n@gement*, 4(3): 101–120, 2001.
GOLBERGER Paul, "What Happens in Vegas: can you bring architectural virtue to Sin City?," *The New Yorker*, October 4, 2010.
GRAGG Larry Dale, "From "Sodom and Gomorrah" to the "Last Frontier Town": the changing perceptions of Las Vegas in American popular culture, 1929–1941," *Studies in Popular Culture*, 29(2): 43–62, April 2007.
GRAVARI-BARBAS Maria, "La leçon de Las Vegas, le tourisme dans la ville festive," *Géocarrefour*, *Le tourisme et la ville*, 76(2): 159–165, 2001.
HANNIGAN John, *Fantasy City: Pleasure and Profit in the Postmodern Metropolis*, London, Routledge, 1998.
HUGHES Robert, "Las Vegas over the top: Wynn win?," *Time Magazine*, October 26, 1998.
Human Geography, special issue on Las Vegas, 2(2), 2009.

HUXTABLE Ada Louise, "Living with the fake, and liking it," *The New York Times*, March 30, 1997.

LASKER Adam, "Welcome to unfabulous Macau," *Las Vegas Weekly*, February 3–9, pp. 20–21, 2011.

LATOUR Bruno, *Laboratory Life: the Construction of Scientific Facts*, Beverly Hills, CA, Sage Publications, 1979.

M@n@gement, special issue: "Deconstructing Las Vegas," 4(3), 2001.

MOEHRING Eugene, *Resort City in the Sun Belt: Las Vegas 1930–2000*, Reno, NV, University of Nevada Press, 2000.

RAENTO Pauliina, "The return of the one-armed bandit: gambling and the West," in HAUSLADEN Gary (ed.), *Western Places, American Myths: How We Think about the West*, pp. 225–252, Reno, NV, University of Nevada Press, 2003.

RAENTO Pauliina and DOUGLASS William, "The tradition of invention: conceiving Las Vegas," *Annals of Tourism Research*, 1: 7–23, 2004.

RITZER George and STILLMAN Todd, "The modern Las Vegas casino-hotel: the para-digmatic new means of consumptions," *M@n@gement*, 4(3): 83–99, 2001.

ROTHMAN Hal and DAVIS Mike (eds), *The Grit beneath the Glitter: Tales from the Real Las Vegas*, Berkeley, CA, University of California Press, 2002.

SCHWARTZ David, *Suburban Xanadu: The Casino Resort on the Las Vegas Strip and Beyond*, New York, Routledge, 2003.

SCRIVEN Michael, "The philosophical foundations of Las Vegas," *Journal of Gambling Studies*, 11(1) (Spring): 61–75, 1995.

VAN DYKE Chris, "Losing my Dasein in the penny slots: an impressionistic deconstruc-tion of Las Vegas," *Human Geography*, 2(2): 96–100, 2009.

VENTURI Robert, SCOTT BROWN Denise and IZENOUR Steven, *Learning from Las Vegas*, Cambridge, MA, MIT Press, 1972 (revised edition, 1977).

WOLFE Tom, *The Kandy-Kolored Tangerine-Flake Streamline Baby* (3rd edition), New York, Farrar, Straus and Giroux, 1965.

ZUKIN Sharon et al., "From Coney Island to Las Vegas in the urban imaginary: discursive practices of growth and decline," *Urban Affairs Review*, 33(5): 627–654, May 1998.

5 Evangeline, Acadians, and Tourism Imaginaries

Rita Ross

Introduction

In an oft-quoted statement about the concept of "social imaginary," the Canadian sociologist Charles Taylor says:

> I want to speak of social imaginary here, rather than social theory, because there are important—and multiple—differences between the two. I speak of imaginary because I'm talking about the way ordinary people "imagine" their social surroundings, and this is often not expressed in theoretical terms; it is carried in images, stories, and legends. (Taylor 2002: 106)

In his emphasis upon ordinary people and their store of images, stories, and legends, he highlights two important areas of cultural and social life that are chief concerns for folklorists: ordinary people are the *folk*, and their stories and other shared artistic forms are the *lore*. In the early days of folkloristics the "folk" were often equated with peasants, but it is now understood that a "folk" may be any group of people that share some important characteristic. Thus one may encounter the folklore of college professors or of computer scientists—or, no doubt, of tourist guides. "Lore" is considered to be the artistic creations of groups of people, including the stories and legends mentioned by Taylor, as well as myths, jokes, and many other genres. The birth of the academic field of folkloristics in the nineteenth century coincided with growing interest in nationalism, and many of the original uses of folklore are still in operation today; see, for example, the article "Colonizing the National Imaginary: Folklore, Anthropology, and the Making of the Modern State" (Linke 1997).

As summarized by Alberta Arthurs, the social imaginary is concerned with "how people of our time collectively invent and administer the systems that surround and maintain them" (Arthurs 2003: 579). If one leaves out the phrase "of our time" and thinks of the past as well as the present, the folklore of a people may be thought of as one of the ways to represent and maintain social or cultural imaginaries. Folklorists as well as several other related researchers such as anthropologists and sociologists have for some time been describing and interpreting various constructs that are now being gathered under the umbrella of the term imaginary—cultural patterns, models, ethos, and other such over-arching concepts—all referring in some way to widespread, shared and largely unconscious sets of understandings about the world. As the folklorist Alan Dundes has argued, "folklore, consisting as it does of native documents or autobiographical ethnography, is prime data for investigation of cognitive patterning" (Dundes 1968: 404). In other words, folklore may give voice to underlying beliefs and patterns that are neither consciously held by the people themselves, nor easily discoverable by outside ethnographers, and yet are powerful contributors to imaginaries.

For folklorists the term imaginary is often used without being defined, in much the same way as terms like culture or worldview or indeed folklore itself. The article "Fairy Tale Activists: Narrative Imaginaries along a German Tourist Route" (Bendix and Hemme 2004) is one example that assumes familiarity with the term. But whether overtly or covertly expressed, the concerns of folklorists are intimately concerned with the construction, transmission, and influence of imaginaries.

This chapter looks at the cultural imaginary that brings together the story of Evangeline, the heroine of Longfellow's poem (1847) and the realm of tourism. In the Canadian Maritimes, and to a lesser extent in Louisiana, one is surrounded by Evangeline's name and image. In Nova Scotia one could until recently drive on the Evangeline Trail and one can still shop at the Evangeline Mall in Digby; in Prince Edward Island one finds the Evangeline Credit Union and even the Evangeline Funeral Home. The park at Grand-Pré in Nova Scotia, with its statues of Evangeline and Longfellow, is paralleled in Louisiana by the park and statue at St. Martinville. Although her status today is problematic, Evangeline has served, and in some ways still does, as a model for Acadian identity within the group, as a symbolic link between Acadians and Cajuns, and as a representation of the group to outsiders, especially tourists.

How did a fictional character, the protagonist of an English-language poem written by an American, come to have such a powerful hold on the imagination of Acadians and non-Acadians alike? This chapter explores the genesis and development of what may be called the "Evangeline imaginary," a phenomenon that still persists in the Acadian region today and in the minds of tourists who visit there. (A good discussion of "the imaginary" as used in tourism research is Salazar 2010: 5–13. See also Taylor 2002 and Strauss 2006.) Attitudes towards Evangeline herself have changed—from near worship at one time to frequent dismissal and even scorn more recently, but for good or ill Evangeline remains a potent cultural symbol, one that is intimately connected with tourism. This chapter draws upon insights from the burgeoning field of tourism studies. For important anthropological contributions see Smith (1977; 1989), Smith and Brent (2001), Graburn (1977; 1983; 2010), Selwyn (1996), Nash (1981; 1996,) Urry (1998), Badone and Roseman (2004), and Gmelch (2010). The work of sociologist Dean MacCannell (1976) has also been influential. Smith, MacLeod, and Robertson (2010) provide a useful brief overview of concepts.

Background

The long narrative poem *Evangeline A Tale of Acadie* was published in 1847, written in English by the eminent American poet Henry Wadsworth Longfellow, who had never set foot in Acadia. It was wildly popular among Longfellow's readers around the world and was eventually translated into more than 130 languages (Wagenknecht 1986: 85–86; among the voluminous literature on Longfellow and his poem the most relevant here are Samuel Longfellow 1891 and Hawthorne and Dana 1947).

The poem's backdrop is the real historical event of the Deportation, or Expulsion, of the Acadians by the British from their homeland in 1755. This defining event in Acadian history is known in French as *le Grand Dérangement*. It tells of a fictional betrothed couple, Evangeline and Gabriel, in the real Nova Scotia village of Grand-Pré, who are separated on the eve of the Deportation, which Longfellow also makes the eve of their wedding. Part I of the poem tells of the idyllic life of the Acadians in Grand-Pre and the events leading up to the Deportation and the couple's separation. In Part II, after the Deportation, Evangeline searches tirelessly for her fiancé, and finally, after many years, the pair are reunited at his deathbed.

The Deportation certainly happened. For a comprehensive introduction see the edited volume by Jean Daigle, *L'Acadie des Maritimes: études thématiques des débuts à nos jours* (1993) and its subsequent English version, *Acadia of the Maritimes: Thematic Studies* (1995), and the work of Bona Arsenault (1978), Naomi Griffiths (1969; 1973; 1992) Jean-Claude Dupont (1977), and Thomas Barnes (1988). The Acadians were removed in ships, their lands burned and their cattle killed. Some were deposited among the British colonies of the American seaboard, and some were sent to the West Indies or to France. Some fled into the forests of New Brunswick and even to Quebec to escape deportation. Although the goal of English policy, according to Griffiths, was "not for the physical extermination of those who were Acadian, but for the eradication of the idea of an Acadian community" (1992: 63), in the actual carrying out of the dispersion many Acadians suffered greatly. And, although it was not British policy to deliberately separate nuclear families, the conditions of the deportations and of life in their places of exile made it inevitable that such separations did occur. Separations between betrothed couples such as Longfellow's fictional Evangeline and Gabriel were probably not uncommon. After several years of suffering in exile, the dispersed Acadians were allowed to return to Nova Scotia beginning in 1763, and many did.

By the mid 1800s, almost a century since they had been allowed to return, they were a virtually forgotten people. By then their rich farmlands had been usurped by New England "planters," and the Acadians were forced to the margins of society, living in small, isolated groups on the fringes of a dominant Anglophone majority culture that had taken their lands, and who considered them backward peasants and the descendants of traitors. In many of their original settlements, including Grand-Pré, no Acadians remained. Many of them had now settled elsewhere in Nova Scotia around Digby, and in present-day New Brunswick, and their livelihood turned to fishing and lumbering. Their culture survived, but with French schools and newspapers prohibited it was largely an oral one. It is safe to say that during these long dark years no *imaginaire* of the Acadians existed in the minds of outsiders.

Evangeline and the Acadian Renaissance

For good or ill, the Deportation, known in French as *le Grand Dérangement*, has become the defining moment in Acadian history. It is precisely because Longfellow's *Evangeline* is set against the background of this tragic episode that the figure of his heroine has been so intimately connected with the growth of Acadian cultural consciousness. The poem's publication in 1847 coincided with the very beginnings of a search by a small Acadian elite for a new vision of *acadienité* (Richard 1986: 74–77). This quest for identity launched the cumulative changes in attitude, consciousness, and institutions collectively known as the "Acadian Renaissance." This period in Acadian history, generally dated from 1867 to 1914, had a profound impact on Acadian society, especially on the development of its public, official face. The Renaissance leaders fostered an Acadian ethnic identity based heavily on language, religion, and a particular view of the Acadians' unique history.

Evangeline had been widely circulated in written form (in a French translation by the Québécois Pamphile Lemay which appeared in various versions beginning in 1855), and apparently from person to person in oral form as well (Rumilly 1955: 715). It was known and cherished by the early leaders of the Acadian Renaissance, who in the latter part of the nineteenth century were consciously searching for ways to embody what they considered the unique Acadian spirit and soul, the essence of *acadienité*. They turned to Evangeline as the perfect representation of all that was good and pure in the Acadian national character. Several scholars have traced the evolution of Evangeline's connection with the Renaissance; see Martin's *L'Evangéline de Longfellow et la suite merveilleuse d'un poème* (1936) as well as Griffiths (1982) and Ross (1993).

Acadian identity, especially in New Brunswick, is stronger than the term "ethnic group" usually implies. It may be more illuminating to think of the Acadians as what Edward H. Spicer has called a "persistent people" (Spicer 1980; see also Castille 1981). In his book on the Yaquis, Spicer argues that the survival of persistent peoples is not dependent upon the factors often associated with ethnicity, such as racial ties, an unchanging homeland, a language, or a unique way of life (1980: 339–346). Although all these factors are important, he says, a "sense of common identity" expressed through a set of symbols is even more so:

> It is our contention that we find in every case of an enduring people common understandings concerning the meaning of a set of symbols . . . . The kind of symbols involved are those which have associations with the unique

experience of a people throughout their history. Every people has a historical experience which no other people has undergone . . . . The experiences
are associated with specific places, with specific persons, with triumphs
and defeats, with sufferings, with friendly alliances, with persecutions and
betrayals . . . . It is the symbols which a people develops, together with their
meanings, concerning their experiences as a people, that constitute their collective identity. (Spicer 1980: 347)

Apparently believing in the need for powerful symbols, the leaders of the
Renaissance consciously constructed what the anthropologist David Kertzer calls
a "symbol system" (Kertzer 1988: 4). After considering and then rejecting over-
tures to share in Quebec's flag and national holiday, the Acadian leaders devised
their own flag, patron saint, national holiday, and national song, all closely tied
to the Virgin Mary (Griffiths 1973; Richard 1986; Biddiscombe 1990). From
the beginning Evangeline became intimately entwined in this particular brand
of nationalism, heavily intermixed with the Catholic religion. It is no coincidence that the character of the meek, mild, and long-suffering Evangeline has
much in common with the Virgin Mary, the Acadians' patron saint. Longfellow's
poem offered, ready-made it seemed, an appealing national heroine and a stirring
national story, and they were embraced passionately. It is difficult to overstate the
depth of emotion evoked by Evangeline in that and several subsequent generations of Acadians. In fact Evangeline illustrates what the anthropologist Sherry
Ortner calls a "key symbol" (1993), one that encapsulates multiple meanings and
resonates with all the other symbols of *acadienité* discovered or invented in the
nineteenth century.

Besides becoming a paramount symbol for Acadians themselves, the poem's
popularity in the English-speaking world also turned Evangeline into a symbol of
Acadia to outsiders. Although I have argued elsewhere that Longfellow had no
more intention of setting up Evangeline as an Acadian cultural symbol than he did
of providing Hiawatha as a model for the Iroquois (Ross 1993), both Acadians
and others insisted on interpreting the story as one championing the purity and
steadfastness of the Acadian spirit and condemning the cruelty of the British.
Though Acadia had been a virtual blank space in the consciousness of outsiders
for more than a century, through Longfellow's story and especially through the
figure of Evangeline, an imaginary of Acadia began to take root. And tourists
followed.

Tourism and Tourism Imaginaries

By the 1920s the popularity of the poem had already stimulated tourism to Nova
Scotia. The first tourists to Grand-Pré were lovers of Longfellow's poem and
seekers of a connection with its heroine. The phenomenon of literary tourism
has been widely discussed; many people want to visit the sites described in a
well-loved book (Buzard 1993; Robinson 2002; Robinson and Andersen 2002;
Gmelch 2010; Smith, MacLeod, and Robertson 2010). To name but two of many

possible examples, think of Beatrix Potter tourism to England's Lake Country (Squires 1994), and the crowds, including large numbers of Japanese tourists, who flock to the Prince Edward Island home of the author of Anne of Green Gables (Herbert 2001; Cormac and Fawcett 2002). As Sharon Ingalls says, "Nineteenth century love of sentimental narrative, and pastoral scenery peopled by rustic, but virtuous peasants was embodied in Evangeline and reflected in the landscape and people of Nova Scotia" (Ingalls 1989: 27). Unfortunately, early tourists to Grand-Pré were disappointed in their quest to find Evangeline there, for the pre-Deportation village had been completely destroyed and the area taken over by newcomers from New England. One of the few locals with an Acadian background, John Frederic Herbin, bought some of the property surrounding the site of the pre-Deportation Acadian church in 1907 (Herbin 1915; 1921; Varennes 1987: 15–21). Although he was forced to sell before realizing his dream of creating an Acadian memorial park, fortunately the new owners, the Dominion Atlantic Railway (DAR), became interested in the commercial and tourist possibilities of the Evangeline connection. From almost the earliest stages, then, the phenomenon of Evangeline tourism included a commercial component. The DAR commissioned the now famous statue, which Deborah Robichaud says has been the model for twentieth-century artistic representations of Evangeline (Robichaud 1993: 5). Created by a father-son team of Acadian descent, it was unveiled at the park in 1920. Ironically, the guests at this dedication included no Acadians; as Achard says, "Il n'y eut pas une voix française pour faire retentir l'antique parler qui résonnait jadis sur ces champs" (Achard 1946: II, 122). Still, local Acadians were inspired to begin raising funds for a new memorial church at the site, and after some years of negotiation were deeded the area by the DAR. In an article about Nova Scotia's tourism cultivation efforts beginning in the 1930s, Ian McKay notes the earlier success of the DAR:

> The most impressive attempt to exploit history in the interests of tourism was the Dominion Atlantic Railway's 'Evangeline' promotion, in which American tourists were enticed to the Annapolis Valley with images of Longfellow's imaginary heroine (commemorated in a park after 1917), and by the quintessentially antimodern appeal of an unspoiled region of romance. (McKay 1993: 106)

Now a Canadian National Historic Park since 1961, the Grand-Pré National Historic Site, with its statue of Evangeline and memorial church, remains an important cultural and tourist destination. It offers in plenty what Valene Smith calls the "4 H's of tourism - habitat, history, heritage, and handicrafts" (Smith, 1995, p. 112). Since 2012 it has been listed as a UNESCO World Heritage Site. (For more on cultural tourism in Acadia and Canada, see Jones and Ells 2009, and MacDonald and Jolliffe 2003.) To tourism of the literary variety, or the sort of general visits to historic or picturesque sites that "take place between lunch and dinner" (Bergman 1997: 18) must be added the complex and intertwined elements of pilgrimage, as well as heritage, ethnic, and roots tourism (Herbert 2001;

Boyd and Timothy 2002; Pitchford 2007). As Nelson Graburn (1977) and others (Badone and Roseman 2004; Ebron 1999) have suggested, for some tourists the journey includes elements of pilgrimage and the expectation, or at least the possibility, of entering into a liminoid state from which one will emerge profoundly altered. In this sense Grand-Pré may be called a secular sacred site for some Acadians at least, and the word "pilgrimage" is explicitly used again and again when discussing it. As one Acadian writer forcefully states, visits there are "plus que le tourisme culturel, mais plutôt des pèlerinages comme pour les Musulmans lorsqu'ils font le voyage jusqu'à La Mecque" (Léger 1990: 6). For Acadians and non-Acadians both, Grand-Pré with its associated story of the Deportation, exemplified by Evangeline, became what Pierre Nora calls a *lieu de mémoire*, "codifying, condensing, [and] anchoring national memory" (Nora 1989: 12).

For other Acadians Grand-Pré seems to function more as a locus of Acadianness, and in that way more a representation of group identity, where one may find a place, a heroine, and a story that represent the history and uniqueness of the Acadians as a people. One Acadian father, visiting the park with his family, is quoted as saying, "It helps teach kids their identity. I want them to be proud of their ancestors" (Bergman 1997: 18). And all this is despite changing attitudes towards Evangeline, which I have discussed elsewhere (Ross 1993) and will refer to briefly below.

At the same time as it drew, and continues to draw, Acadians from near and far, the park more than fulfilled the original hopes of the Dominion Atlantic Railway, becoming a big draw for non-Acadian tourists as well (Bergman 1997; Le Blanc 2011; Rudin 2009: 185–187). Most of the 100,000 or so people who make their way to Grand-Pré each year are not Acadians. Although many are Canadians, many more are Americans, who were targeted as potential tourists from the beginning, and others come from all over the world. Once again Evangeline, in her original role as central symbol in the Grand-Pré complex, serves as a representation of Acadianness to both Acadians themselves and to outsiders.

And, of course, Evangeline has a prominent place in the gift shop. From the beginning Evangeline maintained her high profile partly through her physical image and through items of material culture such as small statues. Although the original edition of Longfellow's poem was not illustrated, images of Evangeline appeared soon afterwards and quickly crossed over into popular and commercial art, appearing widely in illustrations, souvenirs, postcards, and advertisements. Chocolates manufactured by the Ganong company featured her picture on the box and were marketed as exhibiting the same "purity, excellence, constancy, romance, and sweetness" as Evangeline herself (Rudin 2009: 22). Eventually several films of *Evangeline* were made, the most famous of which, starring Dolores del Rio, appeared in 1929. There are even several operas (Potvin 2012). Statues, books, and other tourist memorabilia are still produced and still eagerly consumed (Le Blanc 2011). Thus the Evangeline souvenir industry and Evangeline tourism are significant economically. It is clear that Evangeline in her many manifestations, literary, ethnic, and economic, is a powerful and persistent key symbol lying at the center of the Acadian *imaginaire*, for both Acadians and non-Acadians.

The Cajun Evangeline

Evangeline's high profile in Nova Scotia is paralleled to some extent in the Cajun country of southwest Louisiana, where Evangeline's name is almost as common as it is in the Maritimes: there is an Evangeline Parish, Evangeline Highway, Evangeline Museum, Evangeline Downs racetrack—there was once even an Evangeline Hot Sauce. Louisiana, like Nova Scotia, has been called "The Land of Evangeline" in countless books and tourist brochures, and has its own statue of her as well. The Cajun Evangeline, like the Nova Scotia one, is deeply intertwined with a longing for representations of identity, which satisfy a need among the locals while at the same time providing the foundations of a tourism imaginary for visitors. Yet there are interesting differences as well.

The origin of the Cajuns lies in the Acadian Deportation of 1755. Some deportees eventually made their way to the French settlements of Louisiana, and their descendants have become known as Cajuns (an Anglophone corruption of *'Cadiens*). Useful background information on the Cajuns may be found in Brasseaux (1987; 1991) and Cormier (1986), while treatments of Evangeline's story in particular are Ancelet (1982) and Brasseaux (1988). The Cajun connection grows out of a brief incident in Part II of Longfellow's poem, which chronicles his heroine's wanderings around the United States in search of her fiancé Gabriel. In one episode Evangeline travels by boat down the Mississippi towards Louisiana, having heard that Gabriel is there. The very night before her party reaches its destination, however (in one of the coincidences that is either poignant or maddening, depending upon one's literary tastes), she and Gabriel, going in opposite directions, miss each other in the dark. Upon arrival at the Acadian settlement she learns that he has just left. In Longfellow's poem, then, she spends barely a day in Louisiana before starting out once again on her quest.

Since such a scenario leaves much to be desired from the point of view of the Louisiana Acadians, it is not surprising that another tradition has grown up in which the Louisiana locale plays a bigger part. The Louisiana version of the Evangeline story raises the issue of authenticity to a much greater extent than the Maritime version, or indeed Longfellow's version. The folklorist Richard Dorson (1969; 1976) coined the term "fakelore" to designate a fictional story claiming its origin in a true oral tradition. A Louisiana fakelore version of Evangeline's story was invented and nurtured by Felix Voorhies, whose book *Acadian Reminiscences: The True Story of Evangeline* (Voorhies 1907) features a pair of lovers called Emmeline and Louis. This story ends quite differently from Longfellow's, for Emmeline is not old when her lover returns. He has not been as steadfast as she, however, and during a reunion scene under a large oak tree, she learns that Louis is betrothed to another. She goes mad, dies in her grandmother's arms, and is buried under the oak.

The Voorhies version, despite its subtitle, is a deliberate fiction, as has been clearly demonstrated by Brasseaux (1988). But it long fulfilled a need for Cajuns who were looking for a representation of their own local version of *acadienité*.

As the folklorist Alan Dundes has said, the need for a national story is so strong, that if an authentic tradition is not available it is sometimes invented:

> Fakelore apparently fills a national, psychic need: namely, to assert one's national identity, especially in times of crisis, and to instill pride in that identity . . . . It may be true that ideally folklore serves the cause of national identity cravings, but where folklore is deemed lacking or insufficient, individual creative writers imbued with nationalistic zeal have felt free to fill in that void. They do so by creating a national epic or national 'folk' hero *ex nihilo* if necessary. (Dundes 1989: 50)

The Louisiana Evangeline wasn't created exactly *ex nihilo*, since Longfellow's poem already existed, but many details were changed or added to make the story more locally relevant. Today in Louisiana it is explained that "Longfellow got the story wrong." To satisfy the desire for sites/sights associated with Evangeline, a visitor to St. Martinville is shown the Evangeline Oak (which is not present in the poem). Moreover, according to Carl Brasseaux (1988: 32) the Evangeline Oak is the latest of three! Of course Louisiana's own statue of Evangeline is also there. Most surprisingly, so is her gravesite, although in Longfellow's poem Evangeline dies in Philadelphia. Through their adoption of Evangeline the Cajuns have fulfilled their desire for a unique group identity, strengthened their bonds with their Canadian cousins through their shared appropriation of Evangeline (Cormier 1986; Ross 1991), and not surprisingly, have taken care that when tourists come looking for the "other" Evangeline (see Urry's *The Tourist Gaze*, 2002) they have something to see.

The Second Acadian Renaissance: Rethinking Evangeline

For both tourists and pilgrims, according to Badone and Roseman, travel is often motivated by a desire to experience or recover an idea of "imagined communities that outlast the lifetimes of their individual members" (Badone and Roseman 2004: 184). These desires have also motivated people searching for heritage, authenticity, and national symbols in both the past and present (Hobsbawm 1983; Hobsbawm and Ranger 1983; Anderson 1991; Bendix 1997; Kirschenblatt-Gimblett 1998 among others). In Canada and Louisiana Evangeline certainly refers back to an imaginary of a past Acadian Golden Age as first presented in Longfellow's poem. As Tom Selwyn, following MacCannell (1976), suggests, modern (or post-modern) tourists are seeking "to recover—mythologically—those senses of wholeness and structure that are missing from modern life" (Selwyn 1996: 2). Although Evangeline's story is often referred to as a founding myth and the yearning for such myths is understandable, the issue of authenticity arises when one considers the issue of whose myths are being presented to tourists.

The "myths" of Evangeline and an Acadian Golden Age that began with Longfellow operate on several levels among the Acadians, and have been problematic for some time. Starting in the second half of the twentieth century, Acadian scholars, concerned with present and future meanings of *acadienité*, began to challenge the traditional view of their past. This reexamination of Acadian history and culture among elites is now referred to as "the Second Acadian Renaissance." Many people are now critical of the blatant romanticism and idealization of the Acadian past that they claim Evangeline represents. Because the figure of Evangeline is intimately connected with both the Deportation and the first Acadian Renaissance, it is not surprising that she has become, once again, a symbol—but this time, a symbol of false consciousness (Forest 1969; Roy 1978; 1981). The celebrated Acadian writer Antonine Maillet has rather scornfully referred to the whole complex constructed by the nineteenth-century elite—"un mélange d'Assomption, de tricolore étoileé, de loyalisme envers la langue, la religion et la terre des aïeux"—as *évangélinisme* (Maillet 1971: 13). "Evangelinism" is now often seen as an appeal to a past, but to a romanticized and idealized past that never was. While in the nineteenth century Evangeline was a positive factor in the growth of Acadian cultural consciousness, in recent years she has fulfilled almost the opposite function—she now provides a model of what many of the current intellectual elite would like to leave behind.

The situation is more complex than a simple argument between idealization and reality, however, or between differing visions of the Acadian past and future. One needs first to acknowledge that Acadians are, in Valene Smith's terminology (Smith 1989), both "hosts" and "guests," that is, they act as hosts to outsiders, for instance in local fairs and at the National Historic Park at Grand-Pré, while at the same time both local and diasporic Acadians are guests, or visitors, at these same sites. Another complicating factor, which I have discussed elsewhere (Ross 1993) is the different cultural levels on which the figure and story of Evangeline are transmitted and received—elite, folk, and popular. Rejection of Evangeline by elites does not necessarily carry over into folk and popular ideas about her.

Nor are the Acadians incapable of well-judged responses to these philosophical difficulties, and some of these responses are enacted in the realm of tourism. Although Selwyn states that tourism "is about the production and consumption of myths and staged inauthenticities" (Selwyn 1996: 28), it seems that Acadians have become more consciously concerned about the staging of their past. The tourist information center at Grand-Pré, recently revamped and expanded, now covers the entire history of the Acadians, with considerable attention given to the Deportation, an event that was relatively underplayed in Canada only a few decades ago (Le Blanc 2003; 2011). Evangeline and her story are still there, but are no longer the central part of the exhibit, as they were when the site comprised mainly the statue and the church. A recent study of the "multivocality of identity at Grand-Pré" (Arseneau n.d.) posits that there are three important strands in the current story of the Acadians displayed there, and although Evangeline is one of them, increasing attention is also being paid to the other two: historical documents and archaeological remains found at the site. Moreover, says Arseneau, based on her interviews with employees at the site, Evangeline's preeminence is now downplayed:

The guides and employees do not discuss her. They refer tourists to the exhibit and the statue, but try not to facilitate the romanticized imagery that has emerged as a result of the poem. Mr. Tétrault explained that at the site tourists are drawn to visit because of Evangéline but once they arrive the site presents the reality of the Acadian story. (Arseneau n.d.: 42)

To put it in other words, the imaginary of Evangeline still exists at the Grand-Pré site, and still draws visitors (and consumers), but once they arrive at the site they are deliberately presented with what many Acadians now feel is a more authentic version of their history.

Conclusion

All these developments have added layers to the original story told by Longfellow in 1847. Evangeline now exists in an imaginary cultural realm created from a complex mixture of literature, folklore, history, economics, and nationalistic yearnings. Tourism plays into all these dimensions, both responding to and stimulating them. It is impossible to say that Evangeline exists just for the Acadians these days, as she has evoked powerful responses from outsiders practically since the beginning. On the other hand, it is equally indefensible to dismiss her as "merely" a tourist phenomenon, as she still holds a cherished, though diminishing, place in the hearts of many Acadians. As a recent researcher has argued, Evangeline "still holds significance in contemporary performances of Acadian identity and Acadians are not passive victims of the tourist industry, misusing Evangeline to capitalize on their culture" (Pidacks 2005: 18)—a conclusion with which I agree. Acadian responses to Evangeline are multiple and varied, and have changed over time. The unfolding of Evangeline's story reminds us that tourism is rarely "merely" or "just" about tourism, but in fact is constantly imagined and reimagined as part of a complex cultural web.

Bibliography

ACHARD Eugène, *La touchante odysée d'Evangéline*, vol. I: *En Acadie*, vol. II: *Sur les routes de l'exil*, Montréal, Librairie générale canadienne, 1946.
ANCELET Barry Jean, "Elements of folklore, history and literature in Longfellow's Evangeline," *Revue de Louisiane/Louisiana Review* 11: 118–125, 1982.
ANDERSON Benedict, *Imagined Communities: Reflections on the Origins and Spread of Nationalism*, revised edition, London, Verso, 1991.
ARSENAULT Bona, *Histoire et généalogie des Acadiens*, 6 vols, Montreal, Leméac, 1978.
ARSENEAU Jennifer, "The many voices of 'Acadianness': the multivocality of identity at Grand Pré," Thesis, St. Francis Xavier University, n.d. (2009?).
ARTHURS Alberta, "Snapshot: social imaginaries and global realities," *Public Cultures* 15(3): 579–586, 2003.
BADONE Ellen and ROSEMAN Sharon R. (eds), *Intersecting Journeys: The Anthropology of Pilgrimage and Tourism*, Urbana and Chicago, IL, University of Illinois Press, 2004.
BARNES Thomas G., "Historiography of the Acadians' Grand Dérangement, 1755," *Québec Studies* 7: 74–86, 1988.

BENDIX Regina, *In Search of Authenticity: The Formation of Folklore Studies*, Madison, WI, University of Wisconsin Press, 1997.
BENDIX Regina and HEMME Dorothée, "Fairy tale activists: narrative imaginaries along a German tourist route," *Folkloreostika svetur* 21: 187–197, 2004.
BERGMAN Brian, "Sad land of broken dreams," *Maclean's* 110(32): 18, 1997.
BIDDISCOMBE Perry, "Le tricolore et l'étoile: the origin of the Acadian national flag, 1867–1912," *Acadiensis* 20(1): 120–147, 1990.
BOYD Stephen and TIMOTHY Dallen, *Heritage Tourism*, London, Prentice-Hall, 2002.
BRASSEAUX Carl A., *The Founding of New Acadia: The Beginnings of Acadian life in Louisiana 1765–1803*, Baton Rouge, LA, Louisiana State University Press, 1987.
——, *In Search of Evangeline: Birth and Evolution of the Evangeline Myth*, Thibodaux, LA, Blue Heron Press, 1988.
——, *"Scattered to the Wind": Dispersal and Wanderings of the Acadians, 1755–1809*, Lafayette, LA, University of Southern Louisiana, 1991.
BUZARD James, *The Beaten Track: European Tourism, Literature, and the Ways to Culture, 1800–1918*, Oxford, Oxford University Press, 1993.
CASTILLE George Pierre (ed.), *Persistent Peoples: Cultural Enclaves in Perspective*, Tucson, AZ, University of Arizona Press, 1981.
CORMAC Patricia and FAWCETT Clare, "Cultural gatekeepers in the L.M. Montgomery tourist industry," in ROBINSON Mike and ANDERSEN Hans Christian (eds), *Literature and Tourism*, pp. 171–190, London, Continuum, 2002.
CORMIER Clement, "Les Acadiens de la Louisiane et nous," *Société historique acadienne* 17: 11–13, 1986.
DAIGLE Jean (ed.), *L'Acadie des Maritimes: études thématiques des débuts à nos jours*, Moncton, Chaire d'études acadiennes, Université de Moncton, 1993.
—— (ed.), *Acadia of the Maritimes: Thematic Studies*, revised edition, Moncton, Chaire d'études acadiennes, Université de Moncton, 1995.
DORSON Richard M., "Fakelore," *Zeitschrift für Volkskunde* 65: 55–64, 1969.
——, *Folklore and Fakelore: Essays toward a Discipline of Folk Studies*, Cambridge, MA, Harvard University Press, 1976.
DUNDES Alan (ed.), *Every Man His Way: Readings in Cultural Anthropology*, Englewood Cliffs, NJ, Prentice-Hall, 1968.
——, "The fabrication of fakelore," in DUNDES Alan, *Folklore Matters*, pp. 40–56, Knoxville, TN, University of Tennessee Press, 1989.
DUPONT Jean-Claude, *Héritage d'Acadie*, Montreal, Leméac, 1977.
EBRON Paulla A., "Tourists as pilgrims: commercial fashioning of transatlantic politics," *American Ethnologist* 26(4): 910–932, 1999.
FOREST Léonard, "Evangéline, qui es-tu," *Liberté* 11(5): 135–143, 1969.
GMELCH Sharon, "Why tourism matters," in GMELCH Sharon (ed.), *Tourists and Tourism: A Reader*, pp. 3–24, Long Grove, IL, Waveland Press, 2010.
GRABURN Nelson H., "Tourism: the sacred journey," in SMITH Valene (ed.), *Hosts and Guests: The Anthropology of Tourism*, pp. 17–32, Philadelphia, PA, University of Pennsylvania Press, 1977.
——, "The anthropology of tourism," Introduction to special issue on the "Anthropology of Tourism," *Annals of Tourism Research* 10(1): 9–33, 1983.
——, "Secular ritual: a general theory of tourism," in GMELCH Sharon (ed.), *Tourists and Tourism: A Reader*, pp. 25–36, Long Grove, IL, Waveland Press, 2010.
GRIFFITHS N[aomi].E.S., *The Acadian Deportation: Deliberate Perfidy or Cruel Necessity?* [Issues in Canadian History], Toronto, Copp Clark, 1969.

——, *The Acadians: Creation of a People* [Frontenac Library, 6], Toronto, McGraw-Hill Ryerson, 1973.

——, "Longfellow's Evangeline: the birth and acceptance of a legend," *Acadiensis* 11(2): 28–41, 1982.

——, *The Contexts of Acadian History, 1686–1784*, Montreal and Kingston, ON, McGill-Queen's University Press, 1992.

HAWTHORNE Manning and DANA Henry Wadsworth Longfellow, "The origin of Longfellow's Evangeline," *Papers of the Bibliographic Society of America* 41: 165–203. Also published as *The Origin and Development of Longfellow's "Evangeline,"* Portland, ME, Anthoesen Press, 1947.

HERBERT David, "Literary places, tourism and the heritage experience," *Annals of Tourism Research* 28(2): 312–333, 2001.

HERBIN John Frederic, *The History of Grand-Pré, the Home of Longfellow's "Evangeline,"* 5th edition, Saint John, NB, Barnes & Co., 1915.

——, *The Land of Evangeline: The Authentic Story of Her Country and Her People*, Toronto, Musson, 1921.

HOBSBAWM Eric, "Mass-producing traditions: Europe, 1870–1914," in HOBSBAWM Eric and RANGER Terence (eds), *The Invention of Tradition*, pp. 263–307, Cambridge, Cambridge University Press, 1983.

HOBSBAWM Eric and RANGER Terence (eds), *The Invention of Tradition*, Cambridge, Cambridge University Press, 1983.

INGALLS Sharon, "Mad about Acadians," *The Beaver: Exploring Canada's History* 69 (June–July): 21–27, 1989.

JONES Ginger and ELLS Kevin, "Almost indigenous: cultural tourism in Acadia and Acadiana," *Journal of Enterprising Communities: People and Place in the Global Economy* 3(2): 193–204, 2009.

KERTZER David I., *Ritual, Politics, and Power*, New Haven, CT, Yale University Press, 1988.

KIRSCHENBLATT-GIMBLETT Barbara, *Destination Culture: Tourism, Museums, and Heritage*, Berkeley, CA, University of California Press, 1998.

LE BLANC Barbara, *Postcards from Acadie: Grand Pré: Evangeline and the Acadian Identity*, Kentville, NS, Gaspereau Press, 2003.

——, "Grand-Pré in Acadie," *Encyclopedia of French Cultural Heritage in North America*. [Online] http://www.ameriquefrancaise.org/fr/article-271/Grand-Pr%C3%A9_en_Acadie. html (accessed February 2, 2011).

LE MAY Pamphile, *Essais poétiques*, Quebec, G.E. Desbarats [includes first edition of his translation of *Evangeline*, 1855], 1865.

LÉGER Maurice, "L'importance du caractère épique et mythique d'Evangéline pour le développement du tourisme culturel en Atlantique," Paper presented at Folklore Studies Association of Canada annual meeting, Moncton, June 1990.

LINKE Uli, "Colonizing the national imaginary: folklore, anthropology, and the making of the modern state," in HUMPHREYS S.C. (ed.), *Cultures of Scholarship*, pp. 97–138, Ann Arbor, MI, University of Michigan Press, 1997.

LONGFELLOW Henry Wadsworth, *Evangeline, a Tale of Acadie*, Halifax, Nimbus, [1847] 1951.

LONGFELLOW Samuel, *Life of Henry Wadsworth Longfellow, with Extracts from His Journals and Correspondence*, 3 vols, Boston, MA, Houghton Mifflin, 1891.

MACCANNEL Dean, *The Tourist: A New Theory of the Leisure Class*, London, Macmillan, 1976.

MACDONALD Roberta and JOLLIFFE Lee, "Cultural rural tourism: evidence from Canada," *Annals of Tourism Research* 30(2): 307–322, 2003.

MAILLET Antonine, *Rabelais et les traditions populaires en Acadie*, Québec, Presses de l'Université Laval, 1971.

MARTIN Ernest, *L'Evangéline de Longfellow et la suite merveilleuse d'un poème*, Paris, Hachette, 1936.

MCKAY Ian, "History and the tourist gaze: the politics of commemoration in Nova Scotia, 1935–1964," *Acadiensis* 22: 102–138, 1993.

NASH Dennison, "Tourism as an anthropological subject" [and comments and reply], *Current Anthropology* 22(5): 461–481, 1981.

——, *Anthropology of Tourism*, Tarrytown, NY, Pergamon, 1996.

NORA Pierre, "Between memory and history: les lieux de mémoire," *Representations* 26: 7–25, 1989.

ORTNER Sherry B., "On key symbols," *American Anthropologist* 75(5): 1338–1346, 1993.

PIDACKS Adrienne Marie, "Following the Evangeline trail: Acadian identity performance across borders," Thesis, University of Maine, 2005.

PITCHFORD Susan, *Identity Tourism: Imaging and Imagining the Nation*, Oxford, Elsevier, 2007.

POTVIN Gilles, "Evangeline," *Canadian Encyclopedia: The Encyclopedia of Music in Canada*. [Online] http://www.thecanadianencyclopedia.com/articles/emc/evangeline (accessed November 29, 2012).

RICHARD Camille-Antoine, "Le discours idéologique des conventions nationales et les origines du nationalisme acadien: réflexions sur la question nationale," *Société historique acadienne* 17: 73–87, 1986.

ROBICHAUD Deborah, "Images of Evangeline: continuity of the iconographic tradition," Paper presented at the Annual Conference of the Southwest Association for Canadian Studies, Lafayette, Louisiana, February 1993.

ROBINSON Mike, "Between and beyond the pages: literature-tourism relationships," in ROBINSON Mike and ANDERSEN Hans Christian (eds), *Literature and Tourism*, pp. 39–79, London, Continuum, 2002.

ROBINSON Mike and ANDERSEN Hans Christian (eds), *Literature and Tourism*, London, Continuum, 2002.

ROSS Rita, "Evangeline in Louisiana: the Acadian-Cajun connection," *Canadian folklore canadien* 13(2): 11–23, 1991.

——, "Evangeline: An Acadian heroine in elite, popular and folk culture," dissertation, University of California, Berkeley, CA, 1993.

ROY Michel, *L'Acadie perdue*, Montreal, Editions Québec-Amérique, 1978.

——, *L'Acadie, des origines â nos jours: essai de synthèse historique*, Montreal, Editions Québec-Amérique, 1981.

RUDIN Ronald, *Remembering and Forgetting in Acadie: A Historian's Journey through Public Memory*, Toronto, University of Toronto Press, 2009.

RUMILLY Robert, *Histoire des Acadiens*, 2 vols, Montréal, Fides, 1955.

SALAZAR Noel B., *Envisioning Eden: Mobilizing Imaginaries in Tourism and Beyond*, New York, Berghahn Books, 2010.

SELWYN Tom, "Introduction," in SELWYN Tom (ed.), *The Tourist Image: Myths and Myth Making in Tourism*, Chichester, John Wiley & Sons, 1996.

SMITH Melanie, MACLEOD Nicola and ROBERTSON Margaret Hart, "Literary Tourism," in SMITH Melanie, MACLEOD Nicola and ROBERTSON Margaret Hart, *Key Concepts in Tourist Studies*, pp. 108–111, London, Sage, 2010a.

——, *Key Concepts in Tourist Studies*, London, Sage, 2010b.

SMITH Valene L. (ed.), *Hosts and Guests: The Anthropology of Tourism*, Oxford, Blackwell, 1977.

—— (ed.), *Hosts and Guests: The Anthropology of Tourism*, revised edition, Philadelphia, PA, University of Pennsylvania Press, 1989.

——, "Tourism changes and impacts," in SMITH Valene L. and BRENT Maryann (eds), *Hosts and Guests Revisited: Tourism Issues of the 21st Century*, pp. 107–121, Elmsford, NY, Cognizant Communication, 2001.

SMITH Valene L. and BRENT Maryann (eds), *Hosts and Guests Revisited: Tourism Issues of the 21st Century*, Elmsford, NY, Cogizant Communication, 2001.

SPICER Edward H., *The Yaquis: A Cultural History*, Tucson, AZ, University of Arizona Press, 1980.

SQUIRES Shelagh, "The cultural values of literary tourism," *Annals of Tourism Research* 21: 103–120, 1994.

STRAUSS Claudia, "The imaginary," *Anthropological Theory* 6: 322–344, 2006.

TAYLOR Charles, "Modern social imaginaries," *Public Culture* 14(1): 91–124, 2002.

URRY John, *The Tourist Gaze: Leisure and Travel in Contemporary Societies*, London, Sage, 1998, revised 2002.

VARENNES Fernand de, *Lieux et monuments historiques de l'Acadie*, Moncton, Editions d'Acadie, 1987.

VOORHIES Felix, *Acadian Reminiscences: The True Story of Evangeline*, Lafayette, LA, [1907] 1977.

WAGENKNECHT Edward, *Henry Wadsworth Longfellow: His Poetry and Prose*, New York, Ungar, 1986.

Part II

Tourism Practices and the Imaginary

Madina Regnault

The second part of the book is not only focused on Tourism Imaginaries but on its interconnection with Touris*t* Imaginaries (Leite 2014)[1]. In this part, we are getting closer to tourists *praxis* but also to their hopes, their expectations, their *habitus* that involve them on certain practices in order to make their journey the more accurately follow how they imagined it *ex-ante*. Through their wishes and deepest needs, tourists are emotionalising the places they visit.

In a desire to differentiate their experience from dominant, homogeneous, common and superficial mass-tourism practices, these *post-tourists* (Urry 2002)[2] create niches of alternative ways of travel and alternative imaginaries to represent it. Many contributions emphasize the differences between on the one hand, local and alternative tourist imaginaries and, on the other hand national and dominant tourism imaginaries. Whereas all the authors conducted fieldwork and analysed very different cases studies, we can see that all these chapters situate those micro-practices in macro- or national contexts, mainly related to political issues of power. We are not just witnessing the construction or deconstruction of tourism imaginaries but also the clashes of imaginaries that produce contemporaneous unexpected ways of thinking touristic practices. All these phenomena reflect the mutations of Tourism itself and the power of local communities that are being more and more involved in tourism. What were formerly margins are now multiple micro-centers of tourism in a world where the 'unusual' is becoming the norm. Because of these new forms of social forces, the neo-Gramscian theory arises again and this second part of the book is clearly counterbalancing this approach with the concept of Hegemony.

In sum, this part focuses on the practices that link hosts and guests and the tourism imaginaries that are made from both tourists' and hosts' practices. Actually, the distinction between "hosts and guests" is not that clear. In French, there is one word to describe both: "l'hôte". The "hôte" is both the person received and the person who receives. This linguistic peculiarity symbolized the fact that what is important is the whole process of the encounter is the exchange. And this exchange is narrated, transformed and performed in tourism imaginaries.

Notes

1 Leite, Naomi (2014) "Afterword: Locating Imaginaries in the Anthropology of Tourism." *In* Noel Salazar ad Nelson Graburn (eds.) *Tourism Imaginaries: Anthropological Approaches*. New York: Berghahn, Pp. 260–78.
2 Urry, John (2002), The *Tourist Gaze*. London: Sage Publications

6 Tourism Imaginaries and Political Discourses of Mayotte Island[1]

Madina Regnault

Introduction

Referring to the notion of "imaginaries" immediately leads scholars in political science to think about Anderson's conception of "imagined communities" (Anderson 1991). His founding work legitimated the use of the concept of "imaginary" and gave it a scientific dimension. His theories and his background make him one of the first scholars to be, *de facto*, interdisciplinary. No wonder that his work is nowadays overwhelmingly used in anthropology, history, and ethnic studies. Nevertheless, it seems that scholars in political science also consider him to be one of their own. After all, he studied politics his whole life.

Let us come back to the expression that is always linked to Anderson's name: "imagined communities." As Chivallon (2007) reminds us, the notion is overused. She explains that the phenomenon, far from only being of concern to political science, is spreading to the other disciplines of social sciences. What is powerful about Anderson is how he uses his constructivist approach to demonstrate the mechanisms by which imaginaries are socially built.

Starting from this postulate, this chapter uses this constructivist perspective in explaining the making of some specific "*imaginaires de lieux*" (imaginaries of places). Images powerfully shape these "*imaginaires de lieux*" that we all immediately have about any particular destination. This is what makes us think about the Eiffel Tower, wine, cheese, bread when we speak about "Paris." Similarly images of Tiananmen Square, Mao, and the Great Wall fill our heads when someone mentions China. Thus the sounds of samba, the colors of Carnival, the figure of the Corcovado, and the wildness of Amazonia come to our minds when someone says she just returned from Brazil. And what is striking about these imaginaries we have is that they are the same as those of someone living on the opposite side of the planet. This is how I define the *tourism imaginary*: a shared representation of touristic places based on images, story-telling, and, most of all, powerful *clichés*.

But *clichés* only work for established touristic destinations. What about a place like Mayotte Island? When you hear the name Mayotte Island, what do *you* think? What is your imaginary of this place?

Mayotte does not exist on the international market of tourist destinations. Furthermore, it seems that even the French do not consider it a tourist destination. Most of France's inhabitants have no image or mental representation of Mayotte, and most of them don't even know where it is located. Yet, the island has been French since 1841, and a French Département since March 2011. Certainly, its size (374 km^2) and population (200,000) mark the island as somewhat insignificant at the world level; however, other small islands nearby successfully manage to draw on the *imaginary of place*: Mauritius, the Seychelles, Zanzibar, and others.

Rachid Amirou (2000) states, "the [tourist] imaginary transforms a neutral space into a touristic destination." Does this mean "nothing" precedes the social construction of an imaginary?

Taking the example of Mayotte Island, in the Indian Ocean, this chapter demonstrates that a place that is neither touristified nor built on a precise imaginary is not "neutral." The fieldwork I carried out in 2007, 2008, and 2010 revealed that even if Mayotte has no clear, specific tourist imaginary structured by the tourist industry, *fragments of an imaginary*, when put together, make up a vague and fluctuating picture of this destination. Travelers themselves are the main actors in the construction of the imaginary. The bearers of the intermediary visual and narrative images, who were initially receivers, are transformed during their stay into powerful imaginary-makers. Here, under our gaze, appears the imaginary of the 101st French Département.

The first part of this chapter describes the expansion of the tourism sector of Mayotte Island. The second part focuses on the agents of this social process by defining the effective "imaginary makers" of Mayotte. The third part puts together the pieces of the puzzle preceding the genesis of this tourism imaginary.

Imagining Tourism in Mayotte Island

Mayotte: Forgotten or Spared?

Marie-Francoise Lanfant (1980) has shown how tourism is an ingenious and pervasive global phenomenon, while at the same time, the parts of the world that escape this "industrial machine" are particularly rare. Furthermore, in order to sell the more exotic and pleasant destinations, the professionals of the tourism industry deploy a considerable range of assets.

Although it is rich in natural and cultural resources that could easily stamp it as "exotic" according to Western standards, Mayotte seems to be a forgotten place, outside the global tourism gaze. Tourism in Mayotte is more a "perpetual project" than a social or, even less, economic reality. Are there ways in which various elements can be put together in order to give the island the status of a "tourist destination"? To consider the question requires first qualification of the concept in relation to Mayotte.

First, we note the absence of a *touristic culture* in relation to Mayotte. A touristic culture prepares people for places they are about to visit. In one sense, as highlighted by Franklin and Crang (2001: 10), culture shapes the imaginary of tourist attractions:

> Touristic culture is more than the physical travel, it is the preparation of people to see that other places are objects of tourism, and the preparation of those people and places to be seen . . . the touristic gaze and imaginary shape and mediate our knowledge of and desires about the rest of the planet.

Thus touristic culture demonstrates that the journey actually begins before it physically occurs. Imagination is the first step in the touristic experience.

Second, located at the north end of the Mozambique Channel, Mayotte as a destination, is not easy to reach. Indeed, there are still no direct flights to Mayotte from the French mainland. The most common way to reach Mayotte from France is to change flights at Réunion Island, having passed, paradoxically, over the Mozambique Channel *en route*. After nearly nine hours of flying, passengers traveling to Mayotte can see on the monitor showing their flight path that they are flying over Mayotte, yet they still have another two hours of flying before they reach Réunion, where they must transfer to a second flight and finally fly back in the direction they just came.

Tourism in Mayotte today appears more as a migratory phenomenon than as something that has been thought out or imagined. Statistics (INSEE) indicate that the number of tourists increased from 8,695 in 1995 to 23,000 in 2000. Since 2010, approximately 50,000 tourists per year have visited the island; the goal of policy-makers is to increase that figure to 150,000 by 2020 in accordance with the recommendations of the Development Plan and Tourism Planning of Mayotte.[2] Nevertheless, the tourism industry, as a structured sector, is still a fiction. Despite the tourist boom—in terms of flow—we can still only speak of the "balbutiements du tourisme Mahorais" (the beginnings of tourism in Mayotte), the expression used by J.-C. Gay (1999) when he analyzed the first faltering steps of Mayotte tourism. According to Gay, tourism was the "providential solution to develop Mayotte" and to save it from a "dead end," that is, its economic dependence on the outside. Since then the number of foreign tourists has been increasing and yet the tourism industry is still in its infancy.

In 2001 a report published by the IEDOM[3] was clear about the fact that the island was struggling to promote its image. According to the report, this could be explained by several interconnected factors such as the cost of air travel and the competition of neighboring destinations. Thus positioning the island on the regional or international market appears to be a challenge. Furthermore, while the destination seems naturally oriented towards tourism and especially "green" tourism, ultimately Mayotte suffers from a chronic lack of capacity, qualifications and training among the local workforce.

As a destination Mayotte remains selective. Although local policy-makers have placed tourism high on the agenda, and between 2005 and 2011, €3.8 million were awarded in the form of grants to the tourism sector and €10 million to the CDTM (Comité Départemental du Tourisme de Mayotte [Departmental Committee of Mayotte Tourism]), in a speech made in February 2012 by Daniel Zaïdani, President of the Conseil Général de Mayotte, he explained: "We have chosen to exclude mass tourism but we do not preclude luxury tourism."[4]

The Politicization of the Touristic Scenery

Mayotte, the forgotten island, is still looking for its own market segment in the tourism industry arena. This desire is not characterized by a unique strategy but by a variety of different orientations that have marked the discourse attached to the image of Mayotte. This inconsistency in strategy is the central reason for the deficiency in terms of imaginary. However, beyond the differences that mark the "selling arguments" experienced by the island since it opened to tourism, one regular feature appears: the island's political situation.

The traveler who wants to learn about Mayotte will likely refer to the website of the Comité Départemental du Tourisme de Mayotte, which is the official office in charge of promoting the island. Its website clearly displays the island's political condition: a slogan trumpets at the top of every web page: "Mayotte, the Treasure Island of France." The emphasis on exoticism is certainly noteworthy but it is coupled to a reassuring speech:

> Mayotte fait partie de ces privilégiées . . . seule des « îles de la lune » à avoir choisi d'être française, tout en conservant vivaces ses racines africaines, son environnement exceptionnel . . . fait de cette île un endroit idéal pour un dépaysement garanti.
>
> (Mayotte is one of those privileged . . . the only one of the 'islands of the moon' which chose to be French, while maintaining its perennial African heritage, its unique environment . . . making the island an ideal place for a change of scenery.)

Once in Mayotte, the traveler will assuredly admire the view in the small dining room upstairs in Mayotte's minuscule airport situated in Dzaoudzi (in "Petite Terre," a small island of 10.95 km^2). He or she will then see a poster produced by the Tourism Committee of Mayotte. This poster is one of the few visual productions made to promote tourism that can be found on the island. Time has passed but the poster remains. Affixed to a wall close to windows that afford passengers a view of the runway tarmac surrounded by a bright, intense blue lagoon, the poster (see Figure. 6.1) provides a representation of the same lagoon. Proudly overhanging the runway floats a huge French Tricolore. In yellow type, the poster bears the following words: "Mayotte, the Other France of the Indian Ocean."

Among others, these concrete examples show how Mayotte's political affiliation is constantly put on display. The primary goal is not to establish Mayotte on the international tourism scene, but within a circle of national "overseas" destinations. Yet, by focusing on the French imaginaries, the island is still not integrated into the representations of former "overseas territories," as are Martinique, Guadeloupe, and Réunion. This last island, often considered Mayotte's "Older Sister" (not at a cultural level but at the institutional level, as in some sectors Réunion is considered the guardian of Mayotte), is central to the range of tourist facilities in the western Indian Ocean. It seems difficult, therefore, for Mayotte to live in Réunion's shadow. However, the *Guide du Routard*—a reference for

Figure 6.1 Old poster hanging in Mayotte's airport

every French traveler—compared Mayotte to Réunion by extolling the virtues of the smaller island, which, unlike Réunion, is not too modernized, too developed, or too Westernized yet: "Un petit coin de paradis où les routards seraient bien inspirés de faire un tour avant que Mayotte ne rattrape sa grande sœur réunionnaise" (A little corner of paradise which travelers should be inspired to visit before it becomes like its big sister Réunion).

In a system where every tourist destination tries to stand out from every other destination, Mayotte's exoticism is immediately supplemented by a reference to its belonging to France. While this creates a reassuring psychological point of reference—as Graburn notes (1995: 174): " . . . Much of the homogenization and familiarity of which we are well aware, instead of preventing people from travelling makes it easier for them to overcome cultural and linguistic barriers"— the text conveys the image of an island that exists specifically in relation to its Frenchness. Couldn't it exist by and for itself?

On the Ambiguity of the Political Orientation

The Call for Papers for the "Tourism Imaginaries" Conference (2010) defined the "tourist imaginary" as "a nexus of social practices through which individuals and groups intersect to establish a place as a credible destination." The tourist imaginary of a destination will generally be made by the "tourism stakeholders" and the "tourism system." In Mayotte, the cornerstone of the tourism system is the one and only institutional structure in charge of tourism: the Tourism Committee of Mayotte, which in theory has a monopoly on the making of the island's imaginary. What are the approaches it has used to promote desire for this destination?

Examining the images used to promote the island, we notice a change in the approach employed by the Tourism Committee of Mayotte in trying to shape the imaginary of the place. The discourse differs between the one seen in the poster in Figure 6.1, and the one created in the middle of the 2000s (see the poster in Figure 6.2). "Mayotte, the Other France of the Indian Ocean," becomes the more neutral: "Mayotte, the new destination of the Indian Ocean."

If the first approach is no longer used, it is *not* because locally a post-colonial interpretation could be applied in which tourism is seen as a form of imperialism (Nash 1977). The link with France is a source of pride for Mahoran's, the result of a long-term fight to remain French. In any case, the new touristic formulation seems to have removed completely the political dimension of the formula. The intention to distinguish Mayotte from Réunion, however, remains, but is expanded to distance Mayotte not only from a bilateral relationship with its "older sister," but also from all touristified and marketed destinations including Réunion (cf. Picard 2011), Mauritius, and the Seychelles (strongly associated with the imaginary of luxury tourism). Far from that imaginary, Mayotte positions itself in the marketable niche of the "imaginary of discovery."

Echoing the foundational work of Marie-Françoise Lanfant (1980), mentioned above, David Picard and Mike Robinson (2006: 37) point out how competition in tourism has the effect of promoting differentiation of the product, each destination deploying its ingenuity to affirm the uniqueness and variety of its cultural assets. If at the global level, the protagonists involved in tourism policies and tourism management suggest that the key to success is the specific delineation of a destination, the same can be applied in the case of Mayotte. However, we see constant and self-contained behavior that expresses itself via the difficulty of valuing what constitutes the uniqueness of the Mahoran people. Mahoran singer Bo Houss expressed to me:

> "And if there is a cultural orientation to adopt, it would be to save all assets, whether linguistic or all other dimensions anyway. Because there is nothing yet! We do not exist as Mayotte. We do not exist as a culture with a history or a particular wealth!
>
> Take the example of La Réunion, which is known for many things. Recently, they have been included on the UNESCO World Heritage list! And what about us? We don't exist! This is not because we don't have enough resources; it is because nobody wants to work in that direction. No one cares, that's it!" (interview, August 22, 2010)

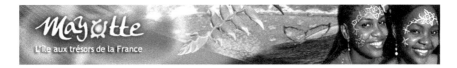

Figure 6.2 "Mayotte, France's Treasure Island"

These virulent remarks made by a Mahoran artist are based on social experience and a proven political situation. The comparison with Réunion is relevant because it demonstrates how a heritage exists only when it is presented as such. Indeed, "heritagization" ("*patrimonialisation*" in French) is made possible only when the cultural-historical heritage is appropriated by the local communities, though establishing a political continuum of such popular appropriation is also essential. However, a cultural difference exists in the understanding of the notion of "heritage." Even if the traditional Western vision of "heritage" has clearly evolved to include the institutional recognition of intangible forms by UNESCO, in reality the gap still exists in Western representations. As stated by the Tourism Committee, and repeated by other sources, it appears that "[because it is] based on an oral tradition, the heritage of Mayotte is not visible" ("basé sur une tradition orale, le patrimoine mahorais n'est pas visible").[5]

From Tourist Imaginaries to Tourism Imaginaries

Travelers/Tourists/"Mzoungous"

Jean-Didier Urbain (2002) was interested in "stories of tourists." We will focus here on "stories of *Mzoungous*."

As soon as he places his foot on Mayotte land, the Westerner learns the term. *He* is the *Mzoungou*. In Shimaore (the local Swahili dialect), the word means, in general, "white." It could refer to the classic tourist who comes to visit the island for a short period but most of the time it refers particularly to French state employees who came to Mayotte for two to four years: teachers, police officers, nurses, doctors, and so on. *Mzoungous* constitute a separate group, with their habits, their networks and their abilities to coalesce and to stay together.

In Mayotte, the official producer of the imaginary (the Tourism Committee) has been supplanted by the travelers themselves (including those we can call "local tourists"). These bearers of images provide the elements that form a fluctuating imaginary. Roles are not categorically defined. Marc Augé (1997) argues that tourists are constantly looking for a "*voyage de découverte*" (journey of discovery), secretly dreaming of being the first to experience something. However, this journey of discovery is no longer possible, as, according to Augé, there are no places left to discover. Putting Augé's statement in perspective, some places are more "mysterious," more "wild," or more "scenic" than others. Even if they have already been discovered by other Westerners, an illusion of discovery persists. The unique sensation sought by the traveler, that spark of novelty is cherished by the few "sellers of dreams" on the island, the tourism professionals who know how to attract a potential customer. On the home page of its website, the Tourism Committee of Mayotte presented the place in these words: "The traveler that you are, looking for authentic experiences, new islands to conquer, will be surprised to discover that in the twenty-first century, there is still a destination at the other end of the world, that has preserved intact its lifestyle, its ancient traditions and its environment."[6]

Nostalgic about the time when it was still possible to discover unknown lands and exotic communities, the tourist is still trying to reach this emotional state. Even if she does not reach it, she likes to believe that she can realize this dream, at least in part. But she appreciates even more the ability to make her peers believe it (Thurot and Thurot 1983). Visual and narrative images are receptacles of this quest for discovery, and become the discovery's "evidence." Today's traveler is making tomorrow's tourist dream.

Travelers as Imagination Consumers, Purveyors of Images and Imaginary Makers

Among the tourists/*Mzoungous* I met in Mayotte, almost half of them had their own webpage or website (usually in the form of blogs) in which they were expounding, day after day, on their stay in Mayotte.[7] Thus, increasingly among the *Mzoungou* community "expatriated" in Mayotte,[8] these means of communication are having a significant impact on the creation of an imaginary that was initially absent. Filling in the missing narrative, the importance of these blogs also reflects the fact that Mayotte is seen as a mysterious land, which deserves to be narrated. Through this information and communication technology, tourists, shaped into real imaginary makers, are bequeathing to uninitiated future travelers the key to understanding Mayotte. Eventually, the beginnings of a new tourism imaginary appear online before the tourism industry itself is created on the island. Jean-Didier Urbain (2002) describes how the traveler is a key player in this phenomenon:

> Le voyageur qui met un point d'honneur à se distinguer du touriste en faisant de lui son antithèse est aujourd'hui le premier moteur du tourisme. Créant des routes et des manières nouvelles de voyager. C'est maintenant pour le tourisme que le voyageur travaille. Chaque itinéraire qu'il trace est un nouveau circuit. Jadis avant-gardiste d'une civilisation, le voyageur n'est plus que l'avant-garde d'une industrie.

Urbain points out that the traveler who strongly distinguishes himself from the tourist is paradoxically not becoming part of the tourism system but is creating the system itself.

In the case of Mayotte, stories carried by tourists and/or travelers themselves are more powerful than the institutional discourse. In addition, they are highly appreciated by the soon-to-be travelers who, as they can identify themselves with narrators, give them more credibility and attention than they have for promotional, marketing discourse. The illusion of the genuine aspect of these narratives is also relevant for post-tourists who "know that tourism is a game or a series of games with multiple texts and no single, authentic tourist experience" (Urry 1990: 100).

The Ethnoscape as an Imagined Place of Refuge

By bringing together the discourses collected during fieldwork (interviews) and on the Web (that is, blogs), I note that once they arrived in Mayotte, *Mzoungous* faced a major cultural gap for which they were not really prepared. The blogs and official discourses promoting the islands help to prepare the traveler but the actual experience *in situ* is overwhelming. This cultural shock pushes them to cling to reassuring elements, allowing them to stay connected to the world they left behind. They took refuge in what Appadurai (2001) has conceptualized under the notion of *ethnoscape*. This imaginary space provides a bridge between here (Mayotte) and there (the mainland). For some foreigners, the *ethnoscape* is sometimes so strong that it becomes impossible for them to detach from it. The bridge then becomes a wall. The encounter with the Other (the local people) is impossible.

Challenging an Emerging Imaginary: Opposing Discourses

From the Traveler's Point of View: The Founding Triad of the "Imaginaire de Lieu"

Focusing on the case of Mayotte Island, I would like to explain why I do not agree with Rachid Amirou's theory (2000) that a place that is not built toward a strong imaginary is "neutral" ("*neutre*"). I prefer Dean MacCannell's theory (1976), in which the tourism imaginary can be seen as the way an unknown place becomes known. Even if Mayotte is not clearly "known," it is not "neutral." We cannot say that there is no imaginary at all.

In Mayotte, there are three types of imaginary, each bonded to the others. While demonstrating how these three referents mingle, and situating the phenomenon in a temporality to better analyze it, we are witnessing the construction of a fluctuating tourist imaginary, which precedes the invention of a tourist image (understood as a precise brand, shaped by tourism professionals). Ultimately, this issue can be put into a political perspective by wondering to what extent the departmentalization of Mayotte is accelerating the creation of the image and imaginary of Mayotte. While institutions are also purveyors of representations—in particular public institutions—another powerful catalyst intervenes in this creative process: the media. Even when it is producing a discourse that is not part of the tourist discourse, it is still influencing and shaping the imaginary of the place. However, a deep gap exists between the personal stories of travelers themselves (on the Web, in particular) and the discourses found in the media. On one side of the process is thus the narrative of the tourists and/or foreigners.

The first component of the tourism imaginary is the imaginary of the "island." Since the beginning of a literature of insularity—in which islands were seen as Eden-like, in the works of Thomas More or Daniel Defoe, for example—tropical islands have always fascinated the traveler (Marimoutou and Racault 1995). Mayotte is first and foremost, seen and then shown as a "typical" image of a "tropical island" with all the required ingredients: beaches, sun, sand, coconut trees, and so on. In reality, this immediate representation of Mayotte Island is absolutely not specific to Mayotte! This promotion of the island makes the place look like a static image, a postcard. Furthermore, the desire to reproduce representations of insularity results in the island being presented as a single entity, as if nothing else were around; but the island is not an isolated place—it is strongly connected with the other territories/islands in the area. It is as if the geostrategic tensions resulting from the context are erased in order to draw a simplistic picture of a territory that should exist *per se*.

According to my interviews, the fantasy of Africa is the second imaginary and maybe the main marker between the three imaginaries being emphasized here. "Rien à voir avec les autres territoires français. On est avant tout en terre noire, ici. Dépaysement garanti." This is how this island is described in *Le Routard*: as a place that is "nothing like the other French territories," that is above all a "black land" which guarantees a "change of scenery." The imaginary attached to Africa—in its stereotypical version (that is to say wild and mystic)—is present before, during, and after the encounter with the Other. At a conference on social anthropology in the South West Indian Ocean, I had an exchange with a young French anthropologist (whose identity will remain anonymous) whose work focused on rites of possession in Mayotte. I told her about the study I led on the phenomenon of *Mzoungous'* "intrusion" in ritual arenas. She told me that during her field research, she gained so much trust and respect from her guests, that they ended up calling her "*fundi*" ("master"). She confided to me that on one occasion, a guest introduced her to a *Mzoungou* who wanted to attend the possession ritual. As the only "white" initiated to the ritual, this researcher said that her host asked her to handle the *Mzoungou* presence and to explain to the *Mzoungou* what she was about to see. The anthropologist said that if the *Mzoungou* needed the practices to be explained during the ritual, there was also work to do before-hand regarding the confrontation with the Other. The anthropologist explained: "I told her [the *Mzoungou*], do not worry, it would be spectacular. Yes, you're going to have blood and everything!" Ultimately, this story shows us how the researcher's role can also be altered due to the lack of official intermediaries/local go-betweens. The anthropologist or ethnographer is not only an observer; she becomes an agent of the object under study. Nevertheless, if the fantasy of Africanness prevails, it turns out that it is much more appreciated by foreigners as long as it remains a fantasy—in other words, as long as it remains intangible, imaged, or enjoyed in small doses (as in the aforementioned experience) while maintaining a distance from the local. The fieldwork thus reveals that the relationship to the Other is sometimes appreciable only when the exchange remains incomplete, in order to avoid any confrontation with an Other that is perceived as so different that it causes misunderstanding at best, or fear at worst. The case is overwhelming regarding expatriate civil servants in Mayotte. During the work which was part of the Reflection Group on the Institutional Future of Mayotte (1996–1997), Jean Fasquel had already raised the issue by warning:

> Une évolution équilibrée dépend beaucoup de l'engagement des fonction-naires, bien au-delà de leurs obligations de base, dans la vie culturelle locale, dans les démarches de prévention, dans l'entretien des échanges. . . . Cela exige des fonctionnaires français qui arrivent dans l'île non seulement de la compétence mais aussi de la sympathie, l'acceptation de mêler vraiment un pan de leur vie personnelle à celle de leurs hôtes. (Boisadam 2009: 334–335)

He explained that fair development heavily depends on the commitment of the public staff well beyond their basic obligations. They have to get involved in local cultural life while agreeing to "actually mix their personal lives with that of their hosts."

When I asked tourists what their first impression was when they arrived, they all said: "C'est l'Afrique ici!" ("It's Africa here!"). In their blogs, foreigners I met convey this image of "Africanity" with both their narration and their pictures. Regarding narration, a recurrent habit is to perpetuate the imaginary of a welcoming people as a standard of "African tradition." The foreigner also performs mostly as an anthropologist, since many of the blogs maintain an informative tone, while referring to the history and the culture of Mayotte's inhabitants. By explaining how they "succeed" in bonding with local people, providing one or two examples as evidence (commonly their invitation to attend a traditional wedding), they are at the same time perpetuating the *cliché* of African warmth but also their own accomplishment in having a "real" experience with the Other. The tone is very much the same from one blog to another: it reveals a wish to transmit to friends/family what they have learned about "these people." The encounter with the Other is hardly analyzed and the difference of culture or tradition is mostly "explained," not argued. Sometimes these foreigners have difficulty finding the right words to describe their "encounters." Sometimes, it is easier to use other people's words to describe representations ante and post encounter. Such was the case of a French teacher who preferred to explain in his blog how his four children perceived this change of scenery. We learn that "Gustave was not happy to come to Mayotte. He said to his nanny that he doesn't like black people (he was only four). During the first two years, he exclusively had *mzungu* friends."

The third component of the imaginary of this place is the Muslim aspect. *The Routard* uses a reassuring tone regarding this Muslim destination: "L'islam pratiqué à Mayotte est tolérant. La polygamie y est interdite depuis 2003. Chez les femmes, le foulard se porte surtout par coquetterie": ("The kind of Islam practiced in Mayotte is a tolerant one. Polygamy has been banned since 2003. For women, wearing the veil is first of all an act of coquetry.") The religious component is predominant and recurrent in the imaginary of the place. Spirituality is so pervasive in everyday life that it becomes commonplace in touristic discourse. Religion is part of the landscape. In one striking example the *Guide du Routard* encourages travelers to go to a traditional Muslim "Big Wedding," in the same way as it invites us to see the "whales" or "lemurs": "Prenez le temps pour découvrir les îlots de sable blanc, faire quelques brasses dans le lagon avec les tortues géantes, aller observer les baleines et leurs petits, assister à un « grand mariage » ou nourrir les makis, friands de bananes . . . " (*Routard* guide, page on Mayotte). My previous fieldwork—especially during the summers of 2007, 2009, and 2010—led me to observe the increasing number of Westerners who attended these "traditional weddings" (called "Arusi" in the local language) where most of the time they didn't even know the bride and groom. My study revealed that the intrusion of foreigners in the circle of friends and family is always motivated by a deeper desire for exotic encounters, but it also reflects a vacuum in terms of tourism opportunities. This lack is the reason why *Mzoungous* search elsewhere for an experiment that is not provided by a tourism industry. Local people also endorse the role of intermediary and tourist go-between, and do so without monetary consideration. I call this process *"rite de partage"* (Regnault 2011a; 2011b) in reference to Van Gennep's (1909) notion of "rite of passage."

The imaginary makers emphasize the fact that Mayotte is an island where 97 per cent of the population is Muslim, because it sounds "unique" for a French territory, which makes it all the more interesting. Blog writers very often mention two facts about the Islam practiced in Mayotte that make it specific to the island. The first is that it is a very tolerant form of Islam. Many of my interviewees explained that as soon as they learned that Mayotte's inhabitants were Muslim, their families were worried about the fact that they moved there. In a context where Islam is increasingly seen as a threat to Occidentals, the interviewees felt obliged to assert that the local people are nothing like radical Muslims. The second fact given regarding the atypical nature of Islam practiced in Mayotte is its syncretic links with animist rituals (from East Africa and Madagascar). A lot of blogs mention one cultural-religious practice in particular: the "Arusi." If the Muslim world has an Arabic origin, this Comorosian ritual is imbued with mixed traditions.

It is interesting to note that these *"Mzoungous'* stories" perpetuate an imaginary of discovery, of a cultural isolate, of "traditional" authenticity frozen in time, while it does not match with the experience of a local social environment that is undergoing major mutations. Highlighting the way in which long-stay tourists "analyze" the local people demonstrates that the local is consistently marked by protean cultural interactions.

The Sociopolitical Construction of Media Discourses

On the other side of the process is the media discourse. In parallel with the statutory evolution of the island, the national print and broadcast media (on the French mainland) are sparing in divulging information about the island.

While tirelessly searching for catchy topics, the media value the most disturbing or controversial elements they can find. For example, in the case of Mayotte, one specific aspect among many others as been heavily reported: illegal immigration from the Comoros Islands, from Anjouan in particular. In mainland France, a significant portion of the population now associates Mayotte Island with the issue of "illegal immigration." The imaginary of the place is therefore becoming closely associated with geostrategic and political issues. Illegal migrants constitute almost a third of the population of the island. Outside of the island, in mainland France, Mayotte is unfortunately becoming known because of the recurring headlines specifying that "another" *kwassa kwassa* (small boat) capsized during the crossing between Anjouan (Comoros Islands) and Mayotte. In conclusion, this insular aspect of the territory is essential for understanding local social and political events.

A second topic was presented through the media, but it was only temporarily in the "news." On March 28, 2008, an anti-white riot shook up Mayotte's fragile social balance. The media did not clearly explain the origins of the conflict, neither were they accurate about the identities of the demonstrators. In reality, the origin of the riot was not local but resulted from the political situation in the nearby Comoros island of Anjouan. This tense period was punctuated by several incidents of military incursions on Anjouan starting in the beginning of March, with notable events including an abortive Comoron raid on Domoni in the south of the island, the seizure of two Anjouan soldiers on the coast close to Sima, and the crash of a French military helicopter also near Sima. In the early hours of March 25, Anjouan was invaded by a combined Comoros and African Union force. The island's capital, airport, seaport, and second city were all overrun by dawn to scenes of jubilation among the local population. Reports indicated that the local leader, Mohamed Bacar, had fled the island incognito, seeking exile in Mayotte. Soon afterwards, the French government confirmed that Bacar had fled to Mayotte and had requested that France grant him political asylum. As soon as it emerged that the French government was considering the request, the large population of Comorans living in Mayotte expressed dissatisfaction with Bacar who was no longer recognized as a leader by its people. The Comoran government had issued an international arrest warrant for Bacar and asked France to hand him over so that it could put him on trial. Subsequently, the French moved Bacar to Réunion Island on the night of March 27–28, along with 23 of his supporters who had accompanied him when he escaped to Mayotte. It was thought that he would be charged on Réunion with weapons possession and illegal entry due to his arrival on Mayotte by speedboat. Comoran President Ahmed Abdallah Sambi said that if the French objected to extraditing Bacar to Comoros, where the death penalty is allowed, then it could send him to the International Criminal Court in The Hague for trial. Thousands of Comorans participated in a protest on March 28 to demand that Bacar be extradited. It was widely believed in Comoros that France secretly worked to protect him. In its extradition request, the Comoran government accused Bacar of the "embezzlement of public funds, homicide, rape, torture and other abuses against the people of Anjouan." The situation quickly degenerated in Mayotte, especially with violent attacks against white people that were widely circulated in newspapers, on radio and television.

In contrast, the steps preceding the transition of Mayotte to French departmental status were not heavily broadcast in the national media. However, all major newspapers addressed the issue at the time the referendum took place. Media on both sides of the political spectrum stressed one particular element: Mayotte is a French Département, but is 97 per cent Muslim. The information was presented as a paradox, if not a problem, or at worst, a scandalous inconsistency. The media presentation was biased and simplistic.

To summarize, using Salazar's expression, we face a "clash of imaginaries" (2010: 167).

Conclusion

Having introduced this chapter with reference to Anderson's theory of the imaginary, I must admit that this is not the most challenging approach, despite its perfect relevance to the topic.

More original than Anderson, French sociologist Michel Maffesoli based almost all his research since the mid-1970s on the issue of "imaginary." However, while Anderson finds perfect consensus with peers beyond his discipline, this is not the case with Maffesoli who was highly criticized by researchers within his own discipline. Strongly influenced by political anthropology, the new theory he has tried to establish was originally presented in *Logique de la domination* (1976). The major concepts of Maffesoli's approach are: ideologies, utopias, and imaginary. The "Maffesolienne" approach—or can we say ideology?—became even more obvious in his *La Conquête du present* (1979). His epistemological switch consisted in putting at the center of the analysis concepts that were not previously found in the field of sociological studies. The imaginary has since become the Maffesoli's workhorse. Even in Maffesoli's works, which often offer theories that appear—in the original sense of the term—disconnected from reality, the notion of imaginary remains firmly rooted in the social and economic contexts, but also, more than anything, in the political context. Indeed, relations between imaginary and power are at the center of his theories on *post-modern* societies.

The lack of a tourism imaginary of Mayotte raises questions at a time when the island is trying to find its place in the Republic. It is interesting to note that the intervention "Mayotte, the Island without (any) Tourism Imaginary?" (Regnault, Tourism Imaginaries Conference, University of California, Berkeley, February 2011) was quoted in *Mayotte Hebdo*, the island's official journal, in early March 2011. Barely two months later, the magazine *Eco Austral*[9] published in its issue 253 of May 2011 an article whose title strangely echoes that formulation: "Mayotte, une destination encore en quête d'image" ("Mayotte, a destination still in search of its own image"). In the article, we read: "Mayotte a donc au moins conscience qu'elle doit construire et vendre à l'extérieur une image d'elle-même qui la démarque des autres îles de la région. Pas si facile ! Comment promouvoir en France l'image d'une île française si peu francophone ?" ("Mayotte is at least aware that it needs to build and sell abroad an image of itself which differs from other islands in the area. Not so easy! How to promote in France its image as a

French island with so few French-speakers?"). While the media should be more informed about local developments, it seems they are perpetuating representations that are no longer based on accurate social background data. It is simply wrong to pretend, in 2011, that most of Mayotte's inhabitants do not speak French!

However, the "*imaginaire de lieu*" should blossom beyond institutional shackles. But the more the image is built up, the more the institutional influences (from political and media arenas) put pressure on an imaginary that is disorientated even before it has had time to make its mark in the tumultuous sector of the tourism industry. Narrative imaginaries are carried by travelers in relation to the micro- and macro-forces of the building process, more precisely at the meeting place of political agendas, tourist experiences, and media discourses. Ultimately, the changes that mark the "*imaginaire de lieu*" highlight the question of the relationship between imagination and truth. The tourism imaginary could thus be this moving in-between, this variable and malleable distance between our representations and truth.

Notes

1 I would like to express my sincere gratitude to Prof. Nelson Graburn for the immeasurable support and guidance he has provided in the editing of this work.
2 Compte—Rendu de la 2ème édition des Assises du Tourisme de Mayotte du 23 février 2012 (Summary of the second edition of Assizes on Mayotte Tourism of February 23, 2012).
3 L'Institut d'Emission des Départements d'Outre-Mer.
4 Summary of the second edition of Assizes on Mayotte Tourism of February 23, 2012.
5 http://www.mayotte-tourisme.com/2010040846/actualites/editorial/editorial.html and http://www.lerochers.com/portail/population_mayotte.htm (Travel guide on the Indian Ocean) (both accessed September 22, 2012).
6 http://www.mayotte-tourisme.com/2010040846/actualites/editorial/editorial.html (accessed September 22, 2012).
7 Between 2007 and 2011, I met 35 tourists and 72 *Mzoungous* working there as agents of the state. I conducted interviews with each of them but I also chose to stay in touch with them and met them when they were back in France (for the tourists) and when I came back to conduct fieldwork in Mayotte (for the state employees living there for a couple of years or more). I mostly analyzed how those *Mzoungous* were presenting their experience, especially on their blogs or personal web pages, since among a panel of 72 interviewed, 32 were also relating their "journey" on the web. The way they shared their memories on the web was not the same as the way they presented them during the interviews.
8 See http://www.expat-blog.com/fr/annuaire/afrique/mayotte/ (accessed September 27, 2012): a list of blogs written by *Mzoungous* living in Mayotte.
9 Established in December 1993 in La Réunion, the monthly magazine *Eco Austral* is written for economic actors in the Southwest Indian Ocean.

Bibliography

AMIROU, Rachid, *Imaginaire du tourisme culturel*, Paris, Presses Universitaires de France, 2000.
ANDERSON, Benedict, *Imagined Communities: Reflections on the Origin and Spread of Nationalism*, London, Verso, 1991.

APPADURAI, Arjun, *Après le colonialisme. Les conséquences culturelles de la mondialisation*, Paris, Payot, 2001.

AUGE, Marc, *L'impossible voyage: le tourisme et ses images*, Paris, Rivages poche / Petite Bibliothèque, 1997.

BOISADAM, Philippe, *Mais que faire de Mayotte? Chronologie commentée d'une "affaire aussi dérisoire," 1841–2000*, Paris, Editions l'Harmattan, 2009.

CHIVALLON, Christine, "Retour sur la 'communauté imaginée' d'Anderson. Essai de clarification théorique d'une notion restée floue." *Raisons politiques*, 27: 131–172, August 2007.

COMITE DEPARTEMENTAL DU TOURISME DE MAYOTTE, official site: www.mayotte-tourisme.com/ (accessed September 22, 2012).

COMPTE—RENDU de la 2ème édition des Assises du Tourisme de Mayotte du 23 février 2012.

FRANKLIN, Adrian and CRANG, Michael, "The trouble with tourism and travel theory?" *Tourist Studies* 1(1): 5–22, 2001.

GAY, Jean-Christophe, "Les balbutiements du tourisme mahorais." *Travaux et Documents* (Faculté des Lettres et des Sciences humaines, Université de La Réunion), 11: 137–152, 1999.

GRABURN, Nelson, "Tourism, modernity and nostalgia," in AHMED, Akbar S. and SHORE, Cris (eds), *The Future of Anthropology: Its Relevance to the Contemporary World*, pp. 158–177, London, Athlone Press, 1995.

LANFANT, Marie-Françoise, "Introduction. Le tourisme dans le processus d'internationalisation." *Revue internationale des sciences sociales* (UNESCO), 32(1): 14–45, 1980.

MACCANNELL, Dean, *The Tourist: A New Theory of the Leisure Class*, New York, Schocken, 1976.

MAFFESOLI, Michel, *Logique de la domination*, Paris, Presses universitaires de France, 1976.

——, *La Conquête du présent. Pour une sociologie de la vie quotidienne*, Paris, Presses universitaires de France, 1979.

MARIMOUTOU, Jean-Claude and RACAULT, Jean-Michel, *L'Insularité, thématique et représentations*, Actes du colloque international de Saint-Denis de la Réunion (April 1992), Paris, L'Harmattan, 1995.

NASH, Dennison, "Tourism as a form of imperialism," in SMITH, Valene (ed.), *Hosts and Guests: The Anthropology of Tourism*, pp. 33–47, Philadelphia, PA, University of Pennsylvania Press, 1977.

PICARD, David, *Tourism, Magic and Modernity: Cultivating the Human Garden*, London, Berghahn, 2011.

PICARD, David and ROBINSON, Mike, *Tourisme, culture et développement durable*, UNESCO Division de la Culture, 2006.

REGNAULT, Madina, "Mise en scène des patrimoines musicaux à La Réunion et à Mayotte," in DESROCHES, Monique, PICHETTE, Marie-Hélène, DAUPHIN, Claude and SMITH, Gordon (eds), *Territoires musicaux mis en scène*, pp. 93–95, Montréal, Presses de l'Université de Montréal, 2011a.

——, "Converting (or not) cultural wealth into tourism profits: case studies of Reunion Island and Mayotte," in BANDELJ, Nina and WHERRY, Frederick (eds), *The Cultural Wealth of Nations*, pp. 156–174, Stanford, CA, Stanford University Press, 2011b.

ROUTARD (Le), page on Mayotte: http://www.routard.com/guide/code_dest/mayotte.htm (accessed September 28, 2012).

SALAZAR, Noel B., *Envisioning Eden: Mobilizing Imaginaries in Tourism and Beyond*, New York, Berghahn Books, 2010.

THUROT, Gaétane and THUROT, Jean-Maurice, "The ideology of class and tourism: facing the discourses of advertising." *Annals of Tourism Research* 10(1): 173–189, 1983.

URBAIN, Jean-Didier, *L'Idiot du voyage: histoires de touristes*, Paris, Payot, 2002.

URRY, John, *The Tourist Gaze*, London, Sage, 1990.

VAN GENNEP, Arnold, *Les rites de passage: étude systématique des rites de la porte et du seuil, de l'hospitalité, de l'adoption, de la grossesse et de l'accouchement, de la naissance, de l'enfance, de la puberté, de l'initiation, de l'ordination, du couronnement, des fiançailles et du mariage, des funérailles, des saisons, etc.*, Paris, É. Nourrie, 1909.

7 Fair Tourism and the "Authentic" Encounter

Realization of a Rite of Recognition in the Context of the Myth of Authenticity

Alain Girard and Bernard Schéou

Introduction

Consequent to our research project on the experiences of tourists who travelled with French Fair tour-operators,[1] we present our initial hypothesis, built at the crossroads of our conceptual ex-ante constructions and the analysis of 10 qualitative interviews conducted on an exploratory basis between late 2010 and early 2011 (we collected, for about an hour in each case, stories and comments about the trips which were made and/or planned). The tourists we interviewed travelled with two associations (in France, non-profit associations can organize and sell leisure travel). The first offers stays in rural villages of West African countries and the second organizes tours in India and Central Asia. We will illustrate our discussion by using data mainly from the tourism conducted by the first operator, with whom we are better acquainted.

It is common to place in opposition fair tourism and mass tourism, in other words, tourism of true/genuine encounters with alien cultures versus superficial tourism without any true/genuine encounters. Based on our preliminary results, we first hypothesize that fair tourism experiences mainly take place under a ritual structure that is no more conducive to experience strangeness than what is called mass tourism. Secondly, we hypothesize that behind any ideological opposition between mass tourism and fair tourism, there is the same tourist imaginary,[2] which is the "authenticity code" that structures the experience and relationship with "the Other" in both these forms of tourism.

This authenticity code is based on a *culturalist illusion*. By culturalist illusion, we refer to the conjunction of at least a couple of beliefs that lead people first, to act as if the cultures were homogenous and well-limited realities—like islands— and secondly, to act as if all individuals could be related to a specific culture such that their behavior could be explained simply as the expression of their culture, or otherwise as deviance (Augé 1992: 57–68). In most cases the culturalist illusion led directly to the "myth of authenticity"—that is, seeing and celebrating these island-cultures as traditions disconnected from history, whose authenticity is threatened by modernization; modernization is seen in this regard as a homogenizing force for progress that imposes uniform commercial and industrial standards and that snatches people from "belonging to a culture" (in which each individual acts according to his or her cultural values) and directs them towards individualism that leads all of us to be animated solely by the satisfaction of our personal interests (Girard and Schéou 2012). The tourist desire that rules over the ideal encounter consists in finding one's own lost authenticity among Others (MacCannell 1976; Selwyn 1996; Beck 2000).

Once the limits generating the culturalist illusion are clarified regarding the intercultural encounter projected by fair operators, the question of the practical consequences that can be drawn from the distancing of the code of authenticity remains.

Is our analysis just a product of academic knowledge, that cannot be reused in the field of action and is even contradictory to it? If this were the case, it seems to us that the very validity of the knowledge produced would be questionable, because it would not lead to the empowerment of the stakeholders. Indeed, we argue that one cannot settle for critical knowledge, for merely being bound to revealing illusions. This would contradict the aim of emancipation at the foundation of critical sociology.

The Encounter Projected in Fair Tourism and Appreciated by Most Tourists

The fair tourism operators' encounter project does appear to be elaborated in opposition to mass tourism. Thus, it is a "genuine meeting" which is offered, in opposition to the non-encounter or to the fake encounter in mass tourism.[3] Besides the fairness aspect of the proposed experiment (a fair price that enables locals to pursue development through their own choices), it is its authenticity which is here addressed: one resides in the heart of a living cultural community where one will be able to share that community's daily life. This sharing of the typical daily life of a traditional culture is conducted through a framework that integrates the tourist activity into the territory rather than damaging it through tourism. Such tourist attendance does not impose a new use of the territory—for example, reorganizing a territory according to a recreational tourist use such as swimming, water sports, hiking, and so on. The traditional use of land is simply shared with the tourists during their stay. To achieve this, attendance is reduced in size and limited to a few periods of the year. Profits are used to fund projects improving the well-being of the locals, such as the construction of public amenities. Since this activity does not entail any redeployment towards tourism but actually strengthens traditional activities, it is conceived as allowing visitors to come into contact with the real life of a cultural community and not merely that community being scenery for the tourists.

In this context, where tourism neither deconstructs nor reorders the life of the local community, visitors can get to know an authentic culture. They enter into the everyday life of a village without distorting it and by sharing concretely in some of their activities, allowing them access to the real life of a village community. Hence, one expects that the hosts, villages or families feel valued thanks to the interest granted to their culture and that they benefit from the conversion of this interest into economic resources, which then allow them to develop their community according to their own lifestyle. The community will therefore be more likely to host fair tourists with warmth and to exercise a form of sociability susceptible of enhancing mutual knowledge.

Thus, the type of relationship proposed by fair tourism contrasts with the distance experienced in the relationships built on self-interest observed in mass tourism: the moments of sociability, shared daily activities, and interest in the culture of the Other make possible a true encounter between visitors and visited and lead to a better mutual understanding.

Even though our collection of vacation stories reveals a few drawbacks, all the tourists we interviewed were rather enchanted by their stay. This general enchantment suggests that the encounter takes place as desired—according to the projected model of the genuine intercultural encounter.

In the following sections, we would like to revisit the meanings that can be attributed to this general enchantment and also to consider the ambiguities which tend to be buried in this interpretation of the encounter.

An Encounter that Performs a Ritual of Recognition through the Myth of Authenticity Instead of Producing Mutual Knowledge

We have identified some discrepancies between the projected encounter which we just depicted and the actual intercultural encounters induced by the tours and stays.

An Authentic Encounter?

Before undertaking any study of real encounters, one might ask if there is any paradoxical shift between the project of authentic encounter and the chosen means, and more precisely how an organized encounter could claim to be based on the spontaneity of the protagonists? The characteristics of a genuine encounter would rather be: (1) contingency, a meeting due to chance or luck, to something unexpected, which arises in circumstances not orchestrated by the actors, (2) singularity, the emergence of a singular event, not reproducible, which depends both on people and circumstances, (3) gratuitousness that cannot be the subject of a commercial transaction even though it is guaranteed fair.

The project of authentic encounter organized within the framework of fair tourism seems to contradict the characteristics of the authentic encounter because it is organized, repeatable, and is the subject of a trade transaction, even if it is fair. However, if this is true when the encounter is considered as a whole, the provided framework does not prohibit singular and gratis moments. Indeed, people are not a totality; they are not all involved in tourism or in the commercial transaction that results.

Moreover, this paradox of a spontaneous organized encounter is well considered by the concerned tour operator who has above all made the choice of respect, whose programming is a guarantee, rather than something spontaneous.[4] If there is a genuine encounter in another sense, therefore, it remains to be elucidated.

An Encounter Which Produces Knowledge of Otherness?

Can we say, then, that a "true" encounter takes place when the conditions are met to allow a mutual exchange of knowledge? By sharing the daily life of a traditional community, do the tourists gain the knowledge of another culture? And do the villagers, in return, learn the culture of the other by interacting with the visitors?

Without claiming to provide evidence, at this stage of the study, the stories do not really appear to fit this dynamic. The actual encounters tend to be limited to the possibility of the tourists recognizing in the other the manifestation of a typical culture and of feeling an enchantment in that recognition.

Here, we distinguish between the verbs to *know* and to *recognize*, which have the same root in French. Acquiring knowledge (to know) means forming a representation which did not pre-exist the experience of contact and which makes it possible to understand something that one did not understand before. Recognizing is seeing, appreciating something that our categories of representation predisposed us to see: I recognize the Great Wall of China; I recognize an authentic culture in such a manifestation of the village life. In knowledge, there is some enrichment or redesign of the actor's representation categories. But in recognition, there is an enrichment of the emotions and memories within a system or category of representations which is preliminary to the contact and which is strengthened by the recognition. The knowledge of another culture produces an experience of strangeness which will not necessarily generate an enchantment; the recognition of a "genuine culture" must necessarily produce an enchantment.

The experience of strangeness corresponds to a moment of subversion of the frame leading to a transformation of our gaze patterns. An experience of strangeness consists in experiencing a meaning or a meaning system that was unknown to us before. In return, this understanding of a different meaning reveals to us the strangeness of part of our original systems of representation. This results in the "denaturalization" of a system made of assumptions, a system within which we were locked without knowing it! It is by entering a different system of meanings that this system appears in its singularity and in its strangeness. This involves being forced to stop applying only our own cultural patterns to the alien, abandoning ethnocentrism, and seizing at least partially some of the other's cultural patterns. This partial understanding of the other leads us to seize the singularity and the non-naturalness of our own cultural patterns. The experience of strangeness is something that destabilizes our assumptions, that bothers us in a stimulating way and helps us to transform ourselves. We cannot really be the same after having experienced strangeness: "the experience of strangeness is what, by apprehending different possibilities, destabilizes the set of the possible which had solidified in us, making a natural and necessary universe" (Girard 2000: 224–225). Todorov summarizes Segalen on this point: "In our daily existence, the automatisms of life blind us: we take for natural what is only conventional . . ." (Todorov 1989: 381). The detour caused by the understanding of another everyday life allows me to seize the specificity of my daily life and its set of limited possibilities. I can see in me what habits had made invisible.

The stories we gathered tend to demonstrate that the encounter accomplished through this form of sharing the everyday life is above all an experience of the enchanted *recognition* of the authenticity of a form of typical life. And that it only causes very few experiences of strangeness. This latter is highly channeled, though not exclusively, by the opposition between "the absence of authenticity in modern life / the authenticity of traditional culture."

If the intercultural encounter proposed is not spontaneous and does not result in the production of reciprocal *knowledge*, one is led to wonder whether something different from the expected encounter is happening.

The Analytical Framework Proposed by MacCannell

The encounter organized by associations of fair tourism consists in the following transaction: asking people to provide visitors with a service of "true meeting" as a counterpart of the development enabled by the revenue received from tourist visits, that is to say, in fact, providing a welcoming ritual, more or less collective, and showing and sharing some activities. This transaction could be interpreted in the framework proposed by MacCannell in the 1970s, which identified the tourist as a modern man in search of authenticity. The inauthenticity and alienation peculiar to modernity push tourists to look elsewhere for authentic experiences (MacCannell 1976). By reusing the distinction made by Goffman between the front stage and the back stage (Goffman 1959), MacCannell places the tourist experience within a symbolic universe made up of layers varying according to the degree of authenticity and the degree of opening to the tourists. The front stage constitutes the tourist façade, a social space to which the tourists are confined, that motivates them to go and see what is behind it. The back stage, on the other hand, is the setting of people's true life, which is not staged for the tourists, to which one prohibits access. In between, MacCannell distinguishes various intermediate levels: "a touristic front region that has been decorated to appear, in some of its particulars like a back region"; "a front region that is totally organized to look like a back region"; "a back region that is open to outsiders"; "a back region that may be cleaned up or altered a bit because tourists are permitted an occasional glimpse in" (MacCannell 1973: 598).

With regard to the relationship between tourists and locals, this universe can be translated in terms of the oppositions "staying away or being left remotely / having real contact with people"; "being in a commercial relationship market / being in a free relationship." Tourists evaluate, with various degrees of intensity, the moments of leaving the front stage and entering people's true life. In response to this expectation held by the tourists, we can see the installation, through various initiatives, of scenic devices built to give the impression to tourists that they access this back stage authenticity. This gives rise to a range of performances of authenticity, more or less played. Thus, tourists are more or less satisfied in their quest and, at the same time, more or less misled since these scenes were manufactured to look like real life. So, by pretending to give a tourist the privilege of not being regarded as a *tourist* but as the first *traveler*, the tourist is deluded but the illusion makes it possible to produce an enchantment. Faced with this duplicity, which could be just as badly intentioned (benefiting from making a fool of the tourist) as well intentioned (the desire to give pleasure to the tourist), and is probably most of the time well intentioned, the tourists can adopt a plurality of positions. Thus, if one follows MacCannell's analysis, they can be totally deluded and remain in an unproblematic enchantment. Quite often, however, they are not fooled. Ultimately, though, many do not take offence as they know it is a setting made to look like a backstage area—for them this does not make the stage absolutely fictive but allows them pleasant access to a substitute authenticity, at least tacitly perceived as such. Others are aware that the authenticity is always more or less manufactured and does not exist as an absolute form. If this makes possible the production of a feeling of authenticity, an enchantment,[5] then one can be satisfied, especially as one knows that access to something truly authentic would require an implication of oneself that one is rarely willing to implement. Furthermore, this feeling of authenticity also makes it possible to acquire a symbolic appreciation within the home society, a distinctive value given for having travelled without being a simple tourist. Finally, only some will be scandalized by being misled in their search for authenticity and will denounce the illusion and will direct themselves towards experiences that would be "not tourist."

A Projected Encounter Which Follows the Pattern Outlined by MacCannell

The pattern outlined by MacCannell seems to apply to the system of authentic encounter we have analyzed. One can find in the villages where our interviewees stayed the same ambiguities regarding the reception conditions as those Chabloz highlights about a host village in Burkina Faso, responding to the same project of encounter. Chabloz evokes the reception of the tourists as presented in the tour operator's brochure distributed to tourists before departure: a "party atmosphere when we arrived. As if we were the first travelers to spend a few days in this village" (Chabloz 2008: 42). This welcome refers accurately to a meeting which is intended to give the tourists the feeling that they arrive, unexpectedly, as new travelers. And indeed, this seems to work, at least with some: "the reception of the village when we arrived, you can't find that every day, and that seems so spontaneous. There's always something authentic, something not-prepared" (Chabloz 2008: 42).

This echoes the phrases by which one of our interviewees began his story: "the way in which this man accommodated us, immediately had something important for me, that touched me greatly . . . it is a very strong impression which carried me throughout the voyage, the impression that something new was at stake, something humane, speaking of a relational point of view." While the tourists tend to get the feeling of being welcomed in a spontaneous, authentic way, the device of the reception is the subject of preparation and is not free from any game of interests. In the case of the village in Burkina Faso, the villagers profit from an amount of money for a drink in exchange for staging the welcoming ceremony. Thus, the tourists believe they have been welcomed in a spontaneous and unselfish way whereas it is a prepared and remunerated performance. Despite the villagers' lassitude they manage to keep up appearances, in most cases (as at the village in Burkina Faso), though sometimes they do not, as happened during one of our interviewees' stays. The interviewee relates that the group of tourists complained about the absence of a welcoming ceremony and that, even if they were delighted by the cultural evening, they all knew that it was pre-organized "because one had given the villagers a dressing down."

Even if it is staged, at least to some degree, the effect of authenticity produced on the arriving public is what is essential. As noted, the visitor can even be quite conscious of the construction. If this was not the case for the tourist quoted by Chabloz, our "fair tourist" was conscious of the system, even if she qualified the welcoming ceremony as the highlight of her stay, relating that it gave her access to a sense of "common humanity": "I said to myself, we are humans." Here we experience the various attitudes vis-à-vis the system of manufacturing authenticity about which MacCannell wrote: tourists can be misled for their greater pleasure (the illusion facilitates the enchantment) but may also be aware of the fiction without being too disturbed by it. Let us note that the third figure, of the scandalized tourist, is much rarer (even if Chabloz finishes her article with an account of one, we have thus far not met any in our investigation). The fact that the device also serves a community development project prevents the tourists from calling into question either the sincerity of the organizers or the needs of the villagers, and undoubtedly discourages disappointed tourists from reporting it.

How is it possible to think that a tourist can access "pure everyday life," without any transformation, by sharing the daily lives of villagers? As one interviewee noted: "I thought we would be closer, I thought we would have a homestay . . . we did not stay with a host, we were still relatively protected." Even if the information about the accommodation is clearly announced ("in huts built separately but according to the local architecture"), the promise of sharing the daily life of a village community could have involved homestay accommodation. This disappointment expresses the fact that sharing the villagers' daily life cannot be limited to a presentation of activities of daily work or even punctually taking part in it. The sharing of everyday life was for this tourist being invited into the families. This option is not offered by the relevant tour operator—on the one hand because the operator made the choice to privilege collective development so as not to exacerbate inequality by favoring those whose social position might allow them to receive tourists, and on the other hand because the tourists might not tolerate the discomfort and potential problems of food hygiene. This choice was validated by what our interviewee said afterwards: "at the same time I said to myself, but what would happen if we stay with a local resident?" Can you share everyday life without sharing meals? By eating side by side, each according to their own standards? The arrangement of an encounter thus proposes compromises such as serving the local cuisine (or at least preparing local food) but guaranteeing a level of hygiene. Let us also observe that by taking into account precisely the cultural differences and the possibility of an experience of strangeness, this problem can be translated differently: wanting homestay accommodation corresponds to a cultural code of hospitality that differs from that of the villagers with no perceived difference. Hospitality, welcoming someone within their village, does not mean the villagers must invite visitors into their personal homes. In West Africa, the tradition of hospitality consists in accommodating foreign visitors, who make the request to the chief of the village, in accommodation which is assigned to this function (among others). So, if being hosted in a specific tourist area appears to the people interviewed a bit contradictory with the idea of being welcomed among villagers and signifies for them a certain distance or being kept apart, the same practice does not have this meaning for the villagers. Offering the experience of strangeness can precisely consist in handing the tourists over to the hospitality tradition of the culture of the other—the locals—rather than asking the host society to adjust to the tourists' code of hospitality. This is achieved here by the tour operator[6] without being explained to the other protagonists. This would require informing the tourists about the hosts' code of hospitality and reciprocally sharing with the hosts the rules of hospitality which are spontaneously expected by the French tourists.

However, it is generally inevitable that the everyday represented and even shared with tourists will have a different meaning, at least partially, and is not something ordinary. The presented daily routine is unusual, practiced under quite specific circumstances because of the touristic encounter. In this regard, we can talk about a "touristic everyday life." We might even think that nothing is more likely to prevent the tourists from dealing with the villagers' authentic daily life than to turn it into a form of tourist attraction. This does not condemn the practice on the grounds of facticity, that is, superficiality and deception, but making the people's everyday life into an object of the tourist experience inevitably brings effects of reinvention and selection to meet the expectations of the tourist other.

It should be noted here that although we have talked about inhabitants, local people, or villagers as if they constituted a whole, the attitudes of the inhabitants to the tourists, and their participation in the tourist staging of the backstage, are highly variable among individuals, according to their involvement in tourism. The African rural villages with which the first tour operator is a partner are relatively spread out, geographically speaking, and it is rare that the habitat is concentrated like the French villages of the tourists. The villages can number several thousand inhabitants. Moreover, most of the population is in no way concerned with the tourist activity, does not care for tourists, and continues their everyday activities as usual, without participating in any manner whatsoever in the staging described above. Some take part in the larger collective moments organized for the tourists (welcoming ceremony, cultural evenings, and so on); others are concerned, on every occasion, with the visiting group of tourists (village chiefs, craftsmen, teachers, and so on) and are expected to play a social role. Finally, only a handful of employees working for the tourist project are in daily contact with tourists or engaged in permanent relations. These play the role of stage directors for the spectacle by working out the program of activities and by selecting the people with whom the tourists will meet. Furthermore, the tourists do not remain in the village but radiate out from it to discover the surroundings. Thus the reality is that it is not really the everyday life of the villagers that is staged but a number of well selected moments of the everyday lives of some of the village's key people.

The Encounter as a Rite of Recognition

These considerations provide nuances to MacCannell's formula without invalidating the conclusions we have made about what effectively happens in the encounter. Thus, one may redefine the reality of the effective encounter as a rite of *recognition* of a typical culture. This rite is achieved in the framework of the myth of authenticity. The conditions that precipitate the fair tourists' enchantment tend to be grounded in a positive maintenance or strengthening of the culturalist illusion, in its version of the myth of authenticity. Thus, one has to experience contact with warm people who are "like specimens of a genuine culture." In the setting of the transaction that is being conducted—that is, the performance of an authentic encounter in exchange for development aid—it is in everyone's interest that the system of "authentic encounter" be recognized as working well, and that it produces the enchantment sought by the tourists. Consequently, some villagers have to adjust themselves to the code of authenticity, which requires signs of a warm welcome and allowing tourists a certain degree of access to their typical everyday life, for example through craft activities and so on. As one interviewee said, "they were playing the game by showing us what they were making in the villages, ironworking, pottery, cooking, ..."

In the scene of the authentic encounter, the hosts' interest lies in being able to continue taking advantage of the economic resources generated by tourism. The tourists' interest lies in experiencing the pleasure of enchantment via the feeling of a genuine encounter. Finally, the fair tourism operators' interest lies in ensuring that the action in which they invested shows signs of meeting expectations on all counts.

The celebration of the myth of authenticity maintained by the rite slows down the emergence of any experience of strangeness, whereas a true intercultural encounter would generate such an experience. And if this celebration allows *recognition* of the typical person by the tourists, it can be seen as an obstacle to the formation of mutual *knowledge*. We can say that the aim of mutual knowledge is thus supplanted by the goal of tourist enchantment. Moreover, the recognition process itself is fragile because it is partly based on a conflicting quest for authenticity. The valorization of a typical culture only works if one stays within the bounds of what the authenticity norm dictates and authorizes. By leaving this framework, enchantment may give way to disenchantment and to radical disillusionment, which would lead to the overthrow of the positive stereotype that allowed the recognition of the authenticity in its opposite: if the Other is not genuine then he is corrupt. This recognition within the code of authenticity carries with it this ambivalence and is somehow the price that has to be paid, as long as the experience of strangeness does not challenge the stereotypes and as long as the actors approach the others with positive or negative stereotypes in mind.

Relationship Problems Buried within the Rite of Recognition of an Authentic Culture

In the villages we studied, the encounter is founded on a denied asymmetry: while it is an aim for the tourists, it is a means for the villagers. What establishes symmetry or equality in the economic exchange (the presence of tourists contributes to the development of the community devoid of predatory behavior) is what creates an asymmetry of roles in the symbolic exchange: there are those who help and those who are helped. In this exchange ratio, the locals are not interested in the encounter itself but in the help it brings. While for the tourists, the encounter itself is the aim of the stay.

This organized framework makes the intercultural encounter an end for some and a means for the others.[7] This may explain why the relationships that are forged have an instrumental purpose for some of the locals: one seeks to establish a special relationship with the friendliest tourists in order to ask their assistance for a personal project, in addition to the projects funded by the profits of tourism, which are determined by the Village Council.

Moreover, the nature of the transaction in which the ritual of recognition takes place, results in the fact that the counterpart of the authenticity performance is the development aid given to the villagers. But "development" often does not have the same signification as it does for the tourism association: among the villagers, there is not necessarily a true "religion of development," so the concept is then reduced to the concreteness of a contribution in cash or resources.

For the association, development refers to something somewhat idealized that transcends individual interests and the simple fact of directly earning money, while for the hosts, development is generally associated with collecting money not necessarily for community projects. Thus the boundary between development aid and charity-help that is well defined by fair tourism associations does not necessarily make sense to all the villagers. From this standpoint, some villagers also expect parallel aid in return for their gift of sociability and of typical authenticity: interviews with tourists reveal the importance of solicitations which find echoes (and encouragement) in many tourists' willingness to be charitable. Consequently, the encounter between hosts and visitors tends to be polluted with parallel aid requests.[8] If the villagers do not really disturb the fair tourists, it is because they fit, consciously or otherwise, within the relationship "helpers/helped," "rich/poor." One of them speaks "*to give alms.*"

Though some contamination of the reality of actual encounters between visitors and visited by suppressed market logic no doubt exists, it is primarily a consequence of this misunderstanding of "development" and the nature of the fair commercial transaction. Paying the "fair" price for a tourist stay does not erase all the asymmetry, which is, as a result, still present in the interface of the encounter and could possibly pollute it.

Getting Away from the Myth of Authenticity: What Are the Implications for the Project of Intercultural Encounter?

One might conclude, as Chabloz does, that in this fair tourism experience, the "encounter is an illusion." For her, the tourism association is obliged to lie by omission, to ignore anything that contradicts the promise of an authentic encounter because it needs to sell its tourism product to continue to exist. For us, although the intercultural encounter does not match certain criteria which appear to be associated with an authentic encounter (freedom, respect on one hand and the formation of a mutual understanding through the experience of strangeness on the other), the encounter succeeds in producing enchantment through the recognition of the authenticity of the life of village communities.

So, what practical implications can we draw from this elucidation of the nature of the real encounter, which corresponds instead to a rite of recognition as part of the celebration of the myth of authenticity? This rite is weak in terms of its leading to mutual knowledge. It is also based on an asymmetry between those who help and those who are helped in a transaction where the tourists win the opportunity to be enchanted by a typical and warm culture as a counterpart of their community development "penny." The villagers, for their part, earn development aid in exchange for efforts to provide the tourists an opportunity of recognition of a typical and cordial culture.

We propose three options:

- Knowingly maintain the culturalist illusion and the implementation of the rite of recognition of a typical culture.
- Stop linking fair tourism to the fiction of a "genuine encounter" and thus stop using it as the main promotional argument and the purpose of the journey.
- Redirect the aim of the genuine intercultural encounter towards a framework that tries to produce an experience of strangeness instead of a rite of recognition.

Knowingly Maintain the Culturalist Illusion and the Implementation of the Rite of Recognition of a Typical Culture

The culturalist illusion helps to ensure a functional *méconnaissance* that results in both the enchantment of tourists and the creation of economic resources for the villagers. If the main purpose of the system is development and if the myth of authenticity can achieve it by providing economic resources to the locals, why not be satisfied? Especially as it would jeopardize tourist attendance, already low, to provide an experience that would disturb the tourism imaginary and threaten the conditions of the enchantment or the "pleasure" of the tourist?

Moreover, although the framework of the proposed encounter is not organized in order to provide an experience of strangeness, some visitors and some hosts may yet experience it as an unexpected event. If the set of positive stereotypes is an obstacle to the experience of strangeness, it is also what allows visitors and hosts to meet each other under favorable conditions. Moreover, it is during this rite of recognition of authenticity that people can still experience the strangeness as if by accident. Note here that it is probably rather the asymmetry "helpers/helped" than the myth of authenticity that reduces the chances of the emergence of the experience of strangeness, which is also a paradoxical way to experience common humanity.

More generally, the manufacture for tourists of authenticity or tradition can be seen as a process of construction of culture that is no more authentic or fake than any other construction process, especially if we just consider that every culture is always a multiple construction. One might therefore consider the tourist reinvention of traditions not in a critical way but see in such tourism the formation of a sort of post-modern compromise. Traditions valued by tourism have little to do with traditions that would have existed before modernity but are inventions by the selection and reclassification of certain elements drawn from a story to multiple scales, but often much less extensive in time than we think. Fair tourism does here nothing but participate in broader post-modern processes of a selective reinvention of traditions for primarily aesthetic modern uses. For this reason, what we have called the myth of authenticity is not so much a collective illusion than a representation matrix which inspires multiple novel devices.

Stop Linking Fair Tourism to the Fiction of a "Genuine Encounter" and thus Stop Using It as the Main Promotional Argument and the Purpose of the Journey

We could stick to the requirement of a respectful encounter, applicable to all forms of tourism, and offer more classical tourist attractions but ones less ambiguous than the authentic encounter. After all, why should we try to associate fair tourism (including the idea of a fair economic transaction) with an authentic encounter? Why not consider fair trade transactions without claiming to make of them an occasion of authentic encounter? This redefined fair tourism, then, would be limited to the provision of visiting services or of more classic tourist experiences (bathing, walking, visiting monuments, and so on). To rephrase it by using the distinction between front and back: it would no longer be a promise of going backstage, but would simply propose access to a front that meets the criteria of a fair commercial transaction.

Redirect the Aim of the Genuine Intercultural Encounter towards a Framework that Tries to Produce an Experience of Strangeness Instead of a Rite of Recognition

If we want to keep central the goal of an intercultural encounter that contributes to the formation of mutual knowledge and try to better achieve this goal, then we should probably frame the encounter in a more constraining way. In order to have an intercultural encounter other than the realization of a tourist enchantment under the myth of authenticity, there must be either no organized framework, or a very stringent framework that engages the aspects of a cross-cultural training session firmly oriented towards the production of an experience of strangeness. For example, how to claim reciprocal cultural knowledge when the only language used is French and when the interaction's intensity depends on the use of French by the hosts. As such, seeking the experience of strangeness might lead to proposing sessions to introduce the language of the other. This would have the advantage of positioning the villager as someone with skills to transmit (we know, for example, that behind the scenes some craftsmen sometimes express a certain dissatisfaction with having to provide unpaid services, which introduces an ambiguity into the nature of the interactions established). Placed in the clear role of trainers, villagers may also receive clear compensation for their teaching. Regarding crafts, training sessions for tourists could also be introduced rather than just visits to the craftsmen and sharing a pseudo-informal moment of practice. Finally, cultural exchange sessions could also be considered. Such sessions could be based on the expertise of experienced organizations: work on stereotypes, work on misunderstandings about notions like "development," "community" or "aid," for example.

However, let us also observe that by refocusing on the objective of living an experience of strangeness, and getting away from culturalist illusion and the authenticity myth, fair tourism no longer needs to intervene primarily or exclusively in rural communities (rural being associated with authenticity, and the city marked as the seal of corruption or disintegration of cultures in Africa). Fair tourism may also invest in cities. Moreover, in consideration of the disintegration of cultures, if we want to privilege the intercultural encounter in a world where cultures are always moving, where people from different cultures are mixed in urban areas, should we not start by encouraging intercultural encounters in these places?

The Same Imaginary for Fair and Mass Tourism

We could have asked ourselves whether this promise of a true meeting proposed by fair tourism operators were not in line with the actual experiences of the tourists. Not because the expectation of a "true meeting" would not have been shared by the "fair tourists," but because the reality of the encounter would have led them to experience, in a negative or a positive way, something different than what they expected. On the contrary, in the interviews, people repeatedly expressed the feeling of having experienced an authentic encounter, in accordance with the contract, to some extent.

So although fair tourism operators struggle to guide a collection of customers to the height of their expectations, this difficulty cannot be linked to some tourists' disappointment regarding the nature of the encounter. Almost without exception, the tourists return delighted by their fair tourism trip.

Our initial assumption was the existence of a discrepancy between the model of the true encounter and the actual experience of tourists, which was in no way incompatible with the enchantment of the fair tourists. It rather proposed a different argued interpretation of this enchantment. That the opposition between tourism of the true encounter and mass tourism of the false encounter happens within the sharing of a common tourist imaginary. On this level, far from being opposed to mass tourism, the model of the authentic encounter takes place within the same system of representations. And one of the common characteristics of this tourist imaginary is to guide the tourists towards an experience of the recognition of the other as projected by the tourist imaginary, rather than towards the formation of knowledge of the cultural otherness. Thus, to assess the experiences of fair tourism in terms of the acquisition of a knowledge of cultural differences, which we might be entitled to make, given the fact that the "genuine encounter" tends to arise—such as access to a knowledge of the other prohibited by mass tourism—one could support the idea that the cognitive output hardly differs from that constituted by mass tourism. This does not lead to the devaluation of fair tourism but to a reconsideration on this point of the links between different forms of tourism as well as those between tourist experience and knowledge of cultural otherness.

One manifestation of this common tourist imaginary is the way in which the opposition between true encounter and mass tourism arises, every time, as something new. In May 2007, in a *Newsweek* issue entitled "Why Moving Less and Seeing More Is the New Mantra for Today's Traveler," an expert on the topic pointed out: "rather than zip through 20 countries in 20 days, they are more interested in hanging out in a remote corner of one, interacting with locals and sampling new customs. Quality and depth of experience matter far more than crossing hot spots off a checklist." The expectations attributed to these new trends opposing mass tourism, however, had been well developed in interviews as the base of an article published by Burgelin in 1967. In the article, the author shows how a critical discourse on sightseeing, supported by essayists in the field of sociology, can be found in the tourists' interviews. Scholarly criticism of sightseeing had raised against practitioners of tourism the critique that the tourist is blind to the real world and remains on the surface of things by seeing only pre-built images of places and cultures.

Not only was this critique of sightseeing—as "the systematic inspection, at a frenzied pace, of monuments, museums or sites with the help of a Baedeker or a Blue Guide" (Burgelin 1967: 87)—found among the tourists Burgelin interviewed (members of the upper middle class), but moreover, these tourists referred to alternatives to mass tourism they practice or wish for: "other modes of knowledge or contact with reality: impregnation, adventure, discovery, deepening intellectual, sensual contact" (p. 89). Thus, impregnation means "trying to watch better through the adoption of a slower pace in order to tie an authentic relationship with the things to see" (p. 83); and discovery means "the implementation of an authentic relationship, as opposed to sight-seeing or to 'tourism'" (p. 84). What all interviewees declared enjoying is to mingle with people in order to know their mores: "people, as they are, as they inhabit, as they live, what they are talking about, how they think, things they are doing . . ." (p. 85). These words could be extracted from our interviews of 2010–2011. One can find in the latter, the same contempt for mass tourism and the same primary motivation: "go to the essentials, it is going to meet people, locals, to see how they live, how they are doing, their mentality, . . . It's not mass tourism, going to the hotel and seeing nothing in fact, it's really going to meet the human being" (interview, December 2010).

Conclusion

In conclusion, we can say that although fair tourism is opposed ideologically to mass tourism, on the level of the reciprocal knowledge produced by the encounter that takes place there, its cognitive output hardly differs from that of mass tourism. This finding does not prevent fair tourism from differentiating itself from mass tourism on other levels, that of achieving a fair trade, in particular.

Moreover, one can support the idea that these two forms of tourism are based on the same imaginary: a world composed of two layers, the front one with the things to be seen ("the touristy") and the back one which refers to people's lives ("the authentic"). Sightseeing is based on having a glance at the façades, but while valuing unexpected entries into the backstage; in fair tourism, the backstage represents the main framework of the experience, but with all the ambiguities caused by constituting people's lives as an object of encounter.

Notes

1 We adopt here the adjectives used by the actors themselves. The two tour operators belong to a group called Association pour le Tourisme Equitable et Solidaire (ATES). This text does not intend to discuss the merits of these qualifiers nor to study the effects of the actions of these operators, the ways in which "locals" reappropriate themselves, the developmentalist intervention or the transactions, the agreements constructed and the misunderstandings that arise between the different categories of actors involved in the achievements of this tourism. We have done so elsewhere (Girard and Schéou 2008; Girard and Schéou 2012).

2 When we use the term "imaginary," we mean it as a collective frame of representations that structures the perception of the world and organizes the elements of reality, a frame which tends to remain unchanged when in contact with these elements. Therefore, this collective frame is defined as something instituted, possessing considerable inertia, which structures the touristic experience without being altered in return by this experience. However, even if this imaginary acts as a collective institution giving us direction, it does not determine practices mechanically and uniformly. People structure their experience through different appropriations of the institutions. Those appropriations vary from the ritual accomplishment of what is required in order to respect the institution, to a selective detachment from it. Sometimes, though rarely, it can almost reach subversion.

3 The ATES website is explicit: "No matter the destination and the stay, the tourist is traveling: in small groups, away from major tourist facilities; under privileged conditions to meet and exchange with people, hosted in homestays or in close accommodations (villages, family run lodgings, camps, etc.); by favoring the local economy (guides, food, transportation, crafts . . .); by respecting the people, their culture and their environment" (http://www.tourismesolidaire.org/menusengager/voyager.html, accessed September 2011).

4 For example, the visit to the school, if there must be one during the tour, takes place at a time chosen by the teacher and not unexpectedly, in order to respect the ordinary activities of the school children.

5 What might be called "hot authenticity," using the distinction proposed by Selwyn between authenticity as knowledge ("cool authenticity") and authenticity as feeling ("hot authenticity") (Selwyn 1996).
6 This is only partly realized, not only because it is not the project of the tour operators (to make the tourists aware of other's cultural codes of hospitality) but also because it adds to an offer of typicality to match the tourists expectations about authenticity. The hut where tourists are lodged has not been built like the villagers spontaneously build their own. The tour operator had to ask them to build the camp using "traditional" methods and materials in order to adjust to the tourists' expectations, which are structured by the aesthetic code of what is "typical." The paradox here is that tourists are required to be housed in a sort of habitat typical of the host culture whereas the people no longer use exactly this type of habitat!
7 This symbolic asymmetry in the transaction is identical to that witnessed by Friedl in Niger. He shows how a community of Tuareg uses the tourists to their own advantage by "1) Playing the role of the 'bon sauvage' who seems to be facing 'banishment from paradise' 2) Appealing to Europeans who are looking for the 'bon sauvage' and are willing to 'save' him. 3) Confirming Europeans in their conviction that they can constructively and sustainably support the 'bon sauvage' in their fight for a 'dignified life' and against 'poverty and calamity' 4) Encouraging Europeans to initiate new projects and/or support existing ones and, finally, 5) Confirming their impression, that in return for this mercy, strong bonds of 'true' and 'long-lasting' friendship as well as thankfulness will emerge between them" (Friedl 2004: 48). The Tuareg and the tourists, says Friedl, both play their roles in the "theatre of friendship": in exchange for Western aid, the Tuaregs from Timia offer a service of friendship.
8 This can be illustrated through one tourist's narrative sequence. She has been invited to visit orphans supported by a villager. During her visit, the villager presented her some embroidery work, which proved not at all to match what she, as an expert, considers to be embroidery (she runs an embroidery shop in France). These "embroidery" samples were made from a shipment "of fabrics and cotton skeins of embroidery" sent by a previous tourist. The conclusion of our interviewed tourist: "*it's a waste of time and of money. I did not dare to tell the lady.*"

Bibliography

AUGE Marc, *Non-lieux. Introduction à une anthropologie de la surmodernité*, Paris, Seuil, 1992.
BECK Ulrich, *What Is Globalization?*, Cambridge, Polity Press, 2000.
BURGELIN Olivier, "Le e tourisme jugé," *Communications* 10: 65–95, 1967.
CHABLOZ Nadège, "Le malentendu. Les rencontres paradoxales du 'tourisme solidaire,'" *Actes de la recherche en sciences sociales* 170: 32–47, 2008.
FRIEDL Harald, "Western money for Southern sympathy: how the Tuareg from Timia are instrumentalizing tourists to support their 'exotic' village," in BURNS Peter and NOVELLI Maria (eds), *Tourism Development: Growth, Myths and Inequalities*, pp. 39–51, Cambridge, CABI, 2004.
GIRARD Alain, "L'esprit du voyage dans le nomadisme frugal de N. Bouvier," in CARMIGNANI Paul (ed.), *Bouleversants voyages: itinéraires et transformations*, pp. 223–243, Perpignan, Presses Universitaires de Perpignan, 2000.
GIRARD Alain and SCHÉOU Bernard, "Tourisme et pauvreté: du tourisme comme instrument de réduction de la pauvreté au tourisme comme sortie du réductionnisme utilitariste?," in DECOUDRAS P.-M., LE GALL M., PUYO Jean-Yves, THAI Thi Ngoc Du and VO SANG Xuan Lan (eds), *Le tourisme durable et la lutte contre la pauvreté*, pp. 85–103, Ho Chi Minh Ville, Agence Universitaire de la Francophonie—Université Van Lang, 2008.

——, "Le tourisme solidaire communautaire à l'épreuve des illusions culturaliste et participative, l'exemple d'une expérience au Bénin," *Mondes en Développement* 40(157): 67–80, 2012.

GOFFMAN Erving, *The Presentation of Self in Everyday Life*, New York, Anchor Books, 1959.

MACCANNELL Dean, "Staged authenticity: arrangements of social space in tourist settings," *American Journal of Sociology* 79(3): 589–603, 1973.

——, *The Tourist: A New Theory of the Leisure Class*, New York, Schocken Books, 1976.

SELWYN Tom, "Introduction," in SELWYN Tom (ed.), *The Tourist Image: Myths and Myth Making in Tourism*, pp. 1–32, Chichester, Wiley, 1996.

TODOROV Tzvetan, *Nous et les autres*, Paris, Le Seuil, 1989.

8 Crafting Archaism, Cultural Entrepreneurs, Indigenous Masks and the Political and Touristic Imaginaries of Heritage in Central America

Julien Laverdure

Introduction

Political anthropology is the branch of social anthropology that is, according to Georges Balandier (1967), "An instrument of discovery and study of diverse institutions and practices assuring the government of individuals, as well as the systems of thought and symbols that found them." So, as well as bureaucracies or places of power, instituted social knowledges, like imaginaries when they become part of a society's "common sense," can be considered institutions. In a dynamic view, political anthropology considers social institutions processes, in constant reproduction, more than the durable objects which they often seek to be considered as.

The particularity of political anthropology amongst other social sciences dealing with politics is its attachment to symbolism, significations, and affects in social relations. For the French philosopher and psychoanalyst Cornelius Castoriadis, imaginaries tend to be the base of social reality, as they institutionalize by the process of symbolization. His work in political anthropology is mainly based on his theory of the imaginary of the institution of society. He proposes to define "the human beings" by their "radical imagination" and their societies by the constant possibility of creation. In the study of political institutions, he emphasizes the importance of their creation as instituted social imaginaries. Therefore in Castoriadis' view, society is essentially a process of auto-creation (1975: 10) and radical imagination is fundamental to this process:

> History is essentially *poièsis*, not imitative poetry, but creation and ontological genesis in and through individuals' doing and representing/saying. This doing and this representative/saying are also instituted historically, at a given moment, as thoughtful doing or as thought in the making. (Castoriadis 1975: 8)

This indeterminate magma of figures/forms/images, constantly created and/or recomposed from ancient elements (Castoriadis 1975: 190), takes shape as "something" and is to be called "reality" and "rationality" (ibid.: 7) when it is instituted. This process takes place in the encounter between political discourses and projects and the movement of individuals. At that moment, social imaginaries become a new form of intelligibility, of social-historical doing, representing, and value (ibid: 10).

The process in which these imaginaries inscribe themselves in reality (and as reality) can be connected to classical works, such as Berger and Luckmann's *Social Construction of Reality*, that seek to study the "processes by which any body of 'knowledge' comes to be socially established as 'reality'" (Berger and Luckmann 1966). Or in many works of Michel Foucault, on the link between the production of knowledge, the construction of a social object and its control. In close relation to this institution of (here, hegemonic) imaginaries in discourses, the construction and marking of social spaces, by authorities aiming to institute themselves as transcendent powers, has been described by several social scientists.[1] It appears that the symbolization (of space in particular and matter in general) is a resource in the race for power (conquest or conservation) (Chivallon 2007: 157), by naturalizing arbitrary social positions.

As for the concept of imagined communities, fundamental for political anthropology, Benedict Anderson (1996) describes the diffusion of communal national imaginaries among individuals of the nation-to-be by the state, using diverse well-known technologies, like censuses, maps, and museums. Tourism has also recently been pointed to as a nation-building device, diffusing imaginaries of community, spaces, and identities (Walton 2009). In the contemporary world (Franklin 2009), diverse political unities such as regional institutions seek to develop imaginaries and to diffuse them through tourism or touristic objects (Laverdure 2010: 66), tourist traffic (Cousin 2006: 20), and the distribution of their grey literature.

Tourism is a prevalent force of globalization, and it is manifested in political and identity reconfigurations. According to Naomi Leite and Nelson Graburn, "[Tourism] is a venue for the construction and performance of national, ethnic, gendered, and other identities" as it is "a form of cultural representation and brokerage" (Leite and Graburn 2009: 35). In this chapter, I would like to present my research on *indigenous* handcrafts, particularly on their production, circulation, and interpretation, but also their political and touristic (marketing) usage. This research focuses on the role of *cultural entrepreneurs*, who accompany the indigenous craftsmen and women, and their production, from the designing to the subsequent "shifting valuation, classification, and circulation" of the "tourist arts" (Leite and Graburn 2009: 43). These intermediary actors are still relatively absent in the studies on cultural reinforcement in ethnic tourism contexts, although they may be very present in most of these phenomena.

This chapter examines various interventions in indigenous communities in Costa Rica, by individuals, associations, and institutions, which aim to develop the handcrafts as a viable product for the tourist market, be it national or international. These products can also circulate and be presented for the symbolic values they represent. Indeed, "'ethnic' or 'primitive' tourist arts occupy a special category in anthropological analysis, because a global system of meanings and markets is already in place for them" (Leite and Graburn 2009: 51). We can see that the values attached to these pieces—authenticity, archaism, autochthony—have become deeply anchored in the social *common sense*. Taking "Boruca masks" as a case study, we examine the detailed trajectory of a cultural association, showing how these values can be used in different contexts, as the masks become *heritage* for the Central America region or an *signifier of identity* for its touristic promotion.

Heritage Tourism as the Diffusion of Imaginaries of Locality

In these different contexts, handcrafts are redefined as parts of cultural heritage, and therefore, they acquire a symbolic and eventually political value. In this regard, the touristic system and heritage are used to achieve similar goals in terms of imaginary constitution and institution. Identity politics and tourism, as two separate forces of imaginary production, are thus also interdependent—one seeks to develop a country image (community identity) for internal consumption, the other builds one (a tourist destination) for external consumption. In my fieldwork, the concept of heritage seems also to link tourism and national identity, as the two are increasingly interconnected in contemporary Costa Rica. For example, Costa Rica's natural biodiversity, which is used to represent the country as a "green heaven" on the tourism market, has also become a tool in national debates on development for opponents of megaprojects to argue: "we present ourselves as a green country to the world, but are we really?"[2] Here, the touristic imaginary has intersected with the national imaginary, as the heritage becomes an answer to the question "what do we have that we want to protect?" would it be natural, material or cultural resources.

In analyzing the heritage tourism phenomenon, concepts like the "imagined community," used by historian Benedict Anderson to describe the cultural formation of the modern nations of the Americas and Europe in the eighteenth and nineteenth centuries (Anderson 1996) or "invented traditions," used by Eric Hobsbawm to describe how these nations impose their legitimacy (Hobsbawm 2006), are still very relevant.[3] With regard to modern Latin America, anthropologist Nestor Garcia-Canclini shows that "historical patrimony is a key stage for the production of the value, identity, and distinction of the modern hegemonic sectors" (1990: 186). The heritagization process is here a reconstruction of the past, which becomes a tradition for the present. As John K. Walton writes: "every practitioner of tourism studies, however immediately contemporary their ostensible concerns, needs to come to terms with the ever-moving frontier of the past" (Walton 2009: 115). Thus, just as heritage tourism studies can work with the concepts used in nation building analysis, touristic circulation, as an imaginaries production force, is increasingly being taken into account in more recent studies on modern nations. Thus, as Walton indicates, the contemporary "cultural heritage" aspects of the tourist experience may have been constructed for the purpose as part of systematic projects in the creation of national or regional identity and distinctiveness, through what Hobsbawm and Ranger long ago described as the "invention of tradition" in such forms as folk dancing and "peasant dress." Walton also writes that "Already in late nineteenth-century Brittany or Cornwall 'traditional' festivals were being incorporated into tourist repertoire" so that tourism "engages with the construction and elaboration of national identities by promoting domestic tourism . . . or encouraging tourist mobility to achieve a sense of national belonging by direct appreciation of the best aspects of the nation" (Walton 2009: 123). On the links between nation formation and tourism, Adrian Franklin writes that

> a wide variety of technologies beside travel made this sense of belonging to a wider social formation possible (the development of better printing presses, the publication of national histories, folklore, natures geographies and national education schemes, for example) but it was also galvanized and consolidated by the building of spectacles and monuments of nation that were intended to be visited pilgrim-like. (Franklin 2009: 78)

Finally, the lines between heritage tourism and the construction of national imaginaries are also blurring in the contemporary touristic "invasion of the everyday" (ibid.: 67). In San José, Costa Rica, like in Europe and many other places (especially cities) around the world, cultural festivals are multiplying, giving participants (mostly nationals: university students and *bourgeois bohèmes*) an image of the *cultural traditions* of the country. In the case of Costa Rica, the classic national imagery of "the white state of the Caribbean" (Chacón and Guevara 1992) appears to have been slowly changing over the last two decades, with a more *multicultural* version of the country's self-imaginary coming into being. Thus indigenous and Afro-Costarican cultures are made more visible by the diffusion of the classic folkloric features: food, music, dances, and crafts—again, partly through the influence of international and national tourism. In this way, tourism and heritage contribute to building imaginaries, and sometimes blur the differences between identity representation for internal and external consumption.

Works on nation building reveal that the national identity idea is actually a "transnational paradigm" (Thiesse 2006). Anne-Marie Thiesse shows that a whole social *machinery* developed in European intellectual fields to build national cultural identities in the nineteenth century. She also emphasized the fact that the social actors taking part in the process were themselves very cosmopolitan, in contact with each other, and traveling through Europe to help various localities develop their traditions and folklore, and improve their heritage. At this time European intellectuals and artists were focused on rural populations; their cultures, made visible, were to become the hearts and souls of the modern nations. It is interesting to note that heritage discourses now and then are very similar, with the same aim to institute new traditions. Furthermore the values attached to indigenous peoples and crafts are the same as those that were superimposed on rural peasants in the nineteenth century: authenticity, archaism, autochthony (as a privileged relationship to the territory). In this way, Walton notes, the

> . . . interpretations of tourist development in imperial, colonial, and postcolonial settings, . . . can also be applied to the internal colonialism associated with the relationships between the 'metropolitan' and the 'peripheral' within Western Europe and North America, as tourist mythologies are created around the inhabitants of 'quaint' fishing villages, or 'rustic' country folk or 'primitive' mountain settlements. (Walton 2009: 122)

Nowadays in San José, a network of individuals participates in the heritagization of the indigenous cultures of the country. These actors don't hesitate to *improve* this heritage, either for social visibility and recognition of the country's cultural diversity, or for the tourism market, as an economic and cultural development tool for the communities.

Interventions in the Indigenous Crafts: New Skills and Innovations

In the Costa Rican context, the indigenous peoples were made invisible in the public sphere, and in the national imaginary. From the end of the nineteenth century, and until the end of the twentieth, the typical Costa Rican was portrayed as the *white worker of the central valley.* In 1940, the public education system taught Costa Rican children that the country's population was "96.6% white," of direct European descent (Chacón and Guevara 1992). Since 1999 though, Costa Rica has adopted a multicultural constitution (recognizing the indigenous languages), following the Latin American trend in this decade. As we have seen before, tourism is also a change maker, since Western tourists expect more and more to experience cultural diversity and *otherness* and, if possible, to take it home in the form of material souvenirs. As a leader in the regional tourism market, Costa Rica has been engaged in eco-tourism since the late 1980s, and also responds to niche market trends by developing *rural* and *community* tourism.

In many places in the contemporary world, a country's cultural aspects appear to be more highly valued (economically), for example, "creative industries" are seen "as a vehicle of economic growth" and "emphasizing diversity is now de rigueur for every city hoping to compete in the global market" (Breidenbach and Nyiri 2009: 15). In this way, social scientists (a few years after development agencies) have observed that indigenous people "appear as the 'best positioned' in this market of cultural difference," emphasizing that this process is "not only a moral economy. Also, invisibly hyphenated, a political-economy" (Comaroff and Comaroff 2009: 144).

In the Costa Rican public and touristic space, one particular *ethnic* craft has acquired relatively good visibility. Firstly because of its technical and artistic quality, and secondly because of its connection with tourist demand, the imaginary of the place it evokes, and its good marketing distribution. This craft, the Boruca balsa carved mask, sometimes represents a—psychedelic—devil face, with colorful and often flashy painting, using pointillist techniques reminiscent of Australian Aborigines' artcrafts (see Figure 8.1).

Another model successful on the international tourism market is the "ecological" mask, representing luxurious tropical nature, surrounding a little Indian face (see Figure 8.2).

Originally, the masks were used for a yearly ritual, *La fiesta de los Diablos*, that takes place in the Boruca village, in the Boruca-Terraba-Curré indigenous territory, in the south-west of Costa Rica. In the past, the masks were quite simple, sometimes not even carved, sometimes tinted with natural elements. Every man of the community participating in the ritual used to carve one for himself, only for

Figure 8.1 Diablo mask

this occasion. In 1984, while the masks were partly being replaced by plastic ones, a Costa Rican dancer and choreographer came together with a Boruca teacher who had a passion for crafting to develop the traditional activity. The teacher then organized a painting and creative workshop with a couple of *handicraft designers*, who dedicated themselves to support rural people to make art involving their direct environment. He gathered a group of children from his family, and the little group traveled every month during a whole year to San José to receive painting lessons and create new mask models. According to the Boruca teacher, another organization close to the designers took the group to the zoological garden, to give them the opportunity to study the *savage* animals of the area. This way, the masks were

Figure 8.2 Ecological mask

renewed, and the *ecological* model was developed, by advising the young crafts-men to be more *indigenous* and to represent the nature that was supposedly *around them*. The masks are now art best-sellers in the good souvenir shops of the capital and at the tourist beaches.

One of the main buyers is a couple from Florida. The woman is the curator of the museum of a botanical garden in Sarasota and the husband organizes the logis-tics by going to Boruca three times a year. Each year they buy around 250 masks, to organize an exhibition-sale for the benefit of the garden. Two or three Boruca artists are invited each year, and they share with the public, giving them work-shops. They are also influenced on these occasions, as they are, for example, asked to make masks representing the orchid symbol of the botanical garden. They also received more painting workshops taught by a specialist. A new model of mask, mixing the devil face and the ecological would be, according to the husband, the consequence of a visit to the Salvador Dali museum of St Petersburg, Florida. Such interventions and innovations are, most of the time, passed over in the presentation of the pieces, at the museum or in the shops. The crafts are sold as traditional, and more ethnic, in the sense of a discourse of cultural and spatial isolation.

There is a precedent to the Boruca case, as another successful tourist craft of Costa Rica, Chorotega pottery, seems to have regained interest—and pre-Columbian patterns—since the intervention of U.S Peace Corps in the 1960s (Weil 1997: 29). A large number of craftsmen in the communities now dedicate themselves to making pieces inspired by the ones found in museum catalogues.

More recently, in another part of the country, two of the designers working with the Borucas (for the masks and women's weavings) are now hired by the Costarican National Institute for Women (INAMU) to develop the artcrafts of the Ngöbe (formerly Guaymi) women, who live in remote territories in the frontier zone with Panama. They have been through a whole process to design, attain the skills, and market the new products, entirely in collaboration with the Ngöbe women.

In the north of central valley, the Maleku community has received workshops conducted by a former student of the Boruca project designers. He is working for the National Learning Institute (INA) to give the Maleku craftsmen painting skills so they can paint their traditional crafts which have also been partially reinvented. The Maleku also make masks, inspired by the Boruca ones that they have had the occasion to see during handcraft festivals around the country. The masks represent a warrior face, surrounded by natural elements, like flowers or animals. Living around the very touristic zone of the Arenal volcano, they sell their products in the national parks, at the end of trekking routes. Each mask comes with a story about the animal spirit that inspired it. Nevertheless, according to the INA trainer, those stories are not yet quite part of the Maleku culture. The Malekus have also developed a tribal dance and costumes apparently inspired by African and Hawaiian clichés, and they perform those dances in tour villages, run by U.S. tourism businessmen.

After their production, it is interesting to study the diffusion of the crafts, their presentation outside the communities where they are produced. What strikes one even more, when one knows the production patterns of the crafts, are the discourses that accompany them. Constructed by promoters, sellers, or even some indigenous producers, the representations of the pieces tend toward romanticism and primitivism. In particular, the interventions of the white designers are systematically "removed from the big picture."

The Crafts' Social Imaginaries

The catalogue for the botanical garden exhibition[4] includes some classical images and values attached to the indigenous handicrafts: primitivism—the pieces are described as the "traditional art of the people of Boruca," "carved using simple tools"; the proximity of nature—pieces are named "Rainforest Masks" and contain "colorful flora and fauna of the artists' native forest" being "the tropical setting that inspired them"; and authenticity—"meet the artists" sessions are organized for the public to have an opportunity to "paint an authentic rainforest mask of your own alongside a Borucan artist." Such encounters can be considered "indirect tourism" (Aspelin 1977; Leite and Graburn 2009: 41)—they share the cultural touristic marketing feature of producing "versions of their own histories as distinguishing features and selling points." We also find in the catalogue a new version of the contemporary meaning given to the ritual and the masks, shared by the mask sellers, some local anthropologists, and some of the craftsmen: the *fiesta de los diablos* would be a reenactment of the fight between Borucan people and *conquistadores*. This version of the ritual's history and meaning is a very popular feature in the masks market. Here it is said that the "diablitos" masks were originally created and worn to scare unwelcome invaders back to Spain in the sixteenth century. These explanations of the masks' meaning and use eliminate other features in the ritual, like animal masks and transvestites, such that some of the more *expert* sellers don't know about their existence, or prefer to ignore them in front of someone assumed to be a tourist.

As Leite and Graburn write: "like tourist arts and ethnicity itself, 'heritage' requires the selection of particular traits to be supported and exhibited" (2009: 45). In the case of the exhibition issue, it would be interesting to know how the story was made-up, between the craftsmen used to the romantic touristic discourses, and the interpretation of the entrepreneur. For example, the *ecological* masks are here (correctly) assumed to be a "contemporary" style, and the Indian face, located on the bottom of the masks, has been described to the intermediary by the craftsmen as the local protector of the forest. The intermediary has then transformed this description and put it in terms that he and his public can better relate to, as being "the face of a shaman."

The market's stakeholders therefore valorize the handicrafts for certain features, matching the social imaginaries attached to them. This market is thus also an exchange of symbolic values. The crafts are essentially valued in terms of tradition (archaism) and autochthony. The social acceptance and legitimacy of these values seems part of the social common sense of the majority of the actors: sellers, tourists, promoters, and media. Participation observation of the tourist craft boutiques selling masks at the beaches or in San José reveals that the sellers built a whole discourse around their product. This speech, given to every client, tends to exaggerate the isolation of the community, spatially but also temporally. In some boutiques, Boruca becomes a sort of indigenous island, lost in the deep jungle and almost unreachable (in reality three buses a day travel there). In the sellers' discourses, 15-year-old photos become "antique testimonials." In some other places, references to the local actors' contemporaneity are simply denied. I myself had trouble trying to explain to a seller that the Boruca painter whose work he was showing me, was that of the French teacher at the Boruca high school. The interaction ended in absurdity, as my interlocutor certainly could not or would not hear my references to such a modern context.[5] In the same way, the objects and production techniques are reassigned to an antique past. This way, the classic burdens of anthropology reappear (Fabian 1983); the evolutionist thought, and its distorted representation of the time of the others—denying them contemporaneity—and its expression through primitivism, are part of the ideology of a certain type of tourism. The salesman erases the interventions, to give their *discovery* an untouched cultural wholeness.

In the case of the Boruca masks and the Costa Rican choreographer's association, beyond its commercial value, this cultural entrepreneur seems to use the mask as a symbolic resource. His association's strategy aims towards a recently emergent political level: the Central America region, and its cultural development. The new region offers new opportunities for "cultural management professionals." As the new institution arises, with foreign and domestic funding, part of its budget is dedicated to the development of the *Central American identity* and *a Central American image for the international tourism* market. The strategy of the association was to try to fulfill the institutional demand for heritage and identifying imaginaries, for example with the staging of the masks I would like to present now.

The Craft as Historical Heritage

In the context of global capitalism, small countries, like those of Central America, are forced to seek to formalize and develop as regions, to reach a *critical mass*, to fit into the international markets. This is particularly true with regard to the tourism market, where the "tour" logic makes small countries collaborate together. The new political region is a subjective space, and has, like the modern nation, a reinvented past and a desired future. Its formalization and institutionalization is a new mobilization space for action, with new resources and new actors' strategies. Here, symbolic construction is motivated by the ambition of material and immaterial resources uptake (Smouts 1997), which therefore requires that new imaginaries constitute, and be inscribed as, realities. In this respect, the Central American Integration System (SICA) is an institutional system, put in place in 1991, with the help and the will of international donors like the European Union. It groups together eight countries of the region: Guatemala, Honduras, Salvador, Belize, Nicaragua, Costa Rica, Panama, and Dominican Republic. SICA works on political, economic, educational, cultural, environmental, social, and touristic integration.

The association of the cultural entrepreneur is thus of "regional projection" and "develops a methodology for the multicultural artistic reinforcement and production in the Central American context." It works in the fields of "cultural management and regional integration," and aims to "promote a multicultural regional self-consciousness through the artistic and social dialogue between tradition and modernity."[6] The association has worked with various tourism institutes of countries in the region, and for SICA's Central American Educational and Cultural Coordination (CECC), the Central American Commission of Development and Environment (CCAD), and the Technical Secretary of the Central American Tourism Council (ST-CCT),[7] among others. The work of the association is part of this context of regional integration, and seeks to fulfill the political demand for *cultural integration.*

Indeed, the promoters of institutional integration also believe in a community of values. SICA's founding principles refer to a "Central American identity" and a "Central American solidarity," an expression of its "deep interdependence, common origin and destiny."[8] The discourse of the SICA Secretary-General announces, among others, policies to "raise a sense of belonging to a particular geographical space," and appeals to an "active Central Americanism" as "a project of central Americans" that should "[exist] in every one [of them]" to "face the challenges of a globalized world." This will to build and demonstrate (at the same time, in a performative way) the existence of a "sense of regional consciousness"[9] shows that, like the modern nations of the nineteenth century, the region needs tools to make the regional identity visible and to ensure its diffusion among the population it administers. Within SICA, the Central American Educational and Cultural Coordination (CECC) has the mission to promote and develop "Central American Regional Integration in the fields of Education and Culture," and to "make real the vision defended by the Central American integration process."[10] To give *the region* a common and legitimate value for the citizens of SICA's various countries, the cultural policy of the CECC proposes to "Highlight and celebrate their cultural heritage." Among the projects of the *Regional Cultural Strategy Plan 2005–2009*, are "the writing of the history of the Isthmus" or the "Central American Popular Cultures Series," aiming for the "rescue and diffusion of elements constituting the regional imaginary." Likewise, it states that "museum networks" should be the "immediate instruments of the Heritage knowledge and [its] accessibility to the population." Here, the project of constructing and diffusing an historic patrimony as a tool of imagined community making is made very clear.

This Central American project is shared by the cultural entrepreneur and his association, and it is in this context that he has put in place an exhibition called *Faces, Devils and Animals, the Masks in the Central American Festivals.* The exhibition has staged the Borucas' works among hundreds of pieces from seven of the eight countries participating in SICA (Guatemala, Belize, Honduras, El Salvador, Nicaragua, Costa Rica, and Panama). Shown in the Museums of the Central Bank of Costa Rica, San José, it is a way for the association to build a homogeneous Central American historical heritage, through the staging of cultural elements presented as authentic. The coherence given to the sample helps define a geographical space for the region and a temporal depth, reified as a tradition. These two dimensions aim to legitimate the essence of Central American identity. The circumstanced construction of an historical heritage responds to one of the objectives of the association: to "recognize and respect ourselves in the cultural diversity that characterizes us as a region."[11] This regional culture recognition goes with the diffusion of information about the exhibition. The principle of a legitimate cultural and geographical unity is relayed by the media. A website states: "more than two hundred and fifty authentic masks, from all corners of the Central American Isthmus, form a brilliant exhibition that domestic [people], and tourists can visit." The text then explains that the visitor will experience "Central American cultural diversity" through these pieces, survivors of "the Mesoamerican indigenous cosmovision."[12] For the publication of the exhibition catalogue, the Costa Rican newspaper *La Nación* wrote: "The masks help to know the isthmus better." The museum director explained: "This is the first great publication around the masks and the human cultural and human [sic] wealth contained by the isthmus." The reporter added that the book: "Helps [one] to know better Central America, through the wealth contained in the beautiful and enigmatic masks, used for traditional dances and festivals of the isthmus."[13] In this article, the director of the cultural association is referred to as a "Central American popular cultural expressions expert." In another article, he explains to the journalist that there is "a great danger for the conservation of many people's cultural traditions, being the influence of economic activities, who want to change the forms and the esthetic of these ones, to please commercial interests." In this way, the circulation of information on the masks legitimizes them in the social field through various processes (for example, the *expert* status) and builds the authentic value of these pieces. In the discourse of the entrepreneur, the esthetic must be saved above all (in this museum context), and especially from economic activities and commercial interests, to ensure the survival of the cultural traditions; the Boruca mask must be seen, again, as a pure and untouched cultural production. Interestingly enough, the contemporary definition of the word "authentic" as a synonym of *sincere, natural, unaffected*, dates only from the early nineteenth century, as it gained a romantic perspective. In the classical use, it is the quality of something that makes law. The ancient Greek αυθεντικός even means: "that consists of an absolute power" (Bailly 1950: 308).[14] In the context of the institution of a new political norm, the historical heritage staged by the cultural entrepreneur, and the construction of a value of authenticity for the masks can appear as a circumstanced mechanism of the invention of traditions.

Before the exhibition at the Museums of the Central Bank of Costa Rica, two other versions of the exhibition were staged outside the country and the region. A version called *Jewels of Diversity* was shown at the World Bank buildings of Washington and Paris, at the Berlin Iberoamerican Institute and at the New York University King Juan Carlos of Spain Center. Through the circulation of the pieces, the association claims "the production of communication and museographic products of international standard, for the promotion of the region."[15] As the discourse of purity fades away, we can see that heritagization can give substance, not only to the internal border of an identity boundary but also the external, so that the representation of Central America through its cultural diversity can represent it on the international market.

The Craft and the Imaginaries of Autochthony

Central American countries and the Central America region are confronted by market liberalization and the weakening of the nation state, which impels them to take advantage of the transnational flows that cross their territories, in the international competition context between destinations. In its projected touristic development, the Central America region sees and organizes itself as a unity: "Central America, as an important integrated touristic destination, accessible and attractive to the international markets."[16] The region needs then to give itself an image, or a brand—as Leite and Graburn put it: "In order to be viable as a tourist destination, a locality must develop an identity that will attract visitors. This 'branding' of place is often achieved through the selection of an emblematic ethnic or cultural trait" (Leite and Graburn 2009: 45). In that perspective, the *territorial marketing* strategy takes into account and reconfigures local identity features, to create a meaningful content for this image. In this regard, references to culture in the SICA discourses generally link it to economic development. Similarly, the Cultural and Educational Commission (CECC) celebrates cultural diversity as an "extraordinary source of identity, creation and values," and clearly underlines in its Regional Strategic Plan that: "in terms of communication and identification, cultural contents are the only real unique referent to the image and projection of a territory."[17]

The use and construction of the heritage by the cultural entrepreneur can vary according to the institutional context and the values superimposed on the masks therefore also vary. The primary discourses on the preservation of cultures from negative economic influences may not match, or may even be contradictory, for example in this other context, where the association stresses the "ineluctable and necessary entry of the cultural products on the market" and the "need to assume the interaction between cultural productions and the tourism phenomenon."[18] Indeed, the intervention in the Boruca handcrafts has been presented in a publication of the Spanish Secretary of Industries, Tourism and Trade as "Good practice in cultural tourism management." In the report, titled *Boruca Masks / Central American Masks*, the association defined a strategy of "valorization of the cultural diversity" in which the intervention is assumed, in respect of the handcraft, as "its improvement as an attraction and an identity signal in the tourist industries."[19] From the regional historic heritage, the mask became in the international tourism system, a sign for the *outside*. Consequently, the cultural entrepreneurs mobilizing it have given it a different set of values.

The imaginaries of indigenous cultures as staged on the touristic market are in this case, as in many cases, the expression of a particular relationship with nature. This allows the actors to play on the cultural as well as the natural heritage. These social imaginaries are thus exaggerated by the cultural entrepreneurs to create symbolic values for the use of other institutions. In the Central America region, heritage often mixes nature and culture. It is represented through official texts as something to preserve as a tourist attraction and a symbol for international communication. The CECC suggests they "encourage diverse cultural expressions, particularly the ones favorable to a relationship of harmony with the environment." The two heritages are also mixed in a CCAD operative program, for a tourism "preserving and benefiting of the socio-cultural and ecological values of Central America," values that would constitute "one of the comparative advantages of the region as an international tourist attraction."[20] Among the "natural and cultural elements of great importance and scale that constitute a huge regional touristic potential" are listed "the archeological sites of world importance and the existence of living cultures that preserve pre-Hispanic traditions and customs." Thus, the cultural association can step into this search for a heritage mixing cultural and natural diversity. In this commercial context, the value of archaism is not so important, so the innovations can be valued. In the *good practices* report, the association wrote that "the revalorization of cultural intangible heritage" has been done through "the appropriation in the community of new technique capacities close to the traditional genuine wood carving aptitudes, for its application in the creation of innovative products." This time, cultural purity and historical depth are not claimed. Another value is constructed in the particular relation to heritage that takes place in the tourism market. The report states: "A by-product has been especially developed for the tourism market: the production of masks called "ecological" because they depict decorative themes inspired by the local natural richness." Although this presents the project in a more dynamic way, it also creates (or answers to a preexistent) indigenous imaginary by not mentioning that the *local natural richness* was observed at the zoological garden in San José. Thus, another kind of authenticity has been constructed, spatial or territorial this time more than temporal. At other places in the report, the closeness to nature of the activity, and its sustainability in relation to the natural environment are exaggerated or staged. The new mask model developed by the craftsmen and the designers can respond to a social demand for mixed cultural and natural diversity, with its Indian face surrounded by luxuriant nature. This representation can be staged to legitimate the value of autochthony, a symbol of the relationship of a group to its territory.

The political force of an institution over the territories it administers, particularly in Latin America, goes with its capacity to include them in the production system. In this way cultural tourism, as ecotourism, helps extend market webs into *unproductive lands* and unredeemed communities. The process creates a political opportunity, as much as an economic one, by asserting the regional sovereignty over territories it participates to invent.

Conclusion

In the actual context of exchanges, multiplication, and political reconfiguration, it is interesting to compare the current with the precedent period of dense communication that led to the formalization of new political identities. Classical and recent works on the construction of modern nations have given us tools to study the current constitution of community imaginaries, political traditions, and the need for the heritage that it creates. Tourist circulation also seems to have played an important part in the constitution of national imaginaries, and, thus, nationalism has been a springboard for tourism. These historical studies and the example of Costa Rican handcrafts, and particularly the Boruca mask and its uses by cultural entrepreneurs, reveal that there is a renewed interest in heritage as a political force to create and demonstrate identities and political legitimacy over new formalized communities, territories, and international political units. It also

shows that a certain field of actors engaged in the heritagization process manipu-
lates and plays on the imaginaries attached to indigenous (or, in the nineteenth
century, "peasant") peoples. They reconfigure, as a professional strategy, local
cultural features, in order to use the symbolic values socially linked to them in
white society, as exchangeable social capital in certain political and economic
arenas. These actors also want to promote multiculturalism in their own country,
and their role is effectively changing the national imaginary. But such brokers,
also in response to a social demand, often use romantic references to the past, and
manipulate values of archaism, authenticity, and autochthony. This analysis of
the Boruca masks trajectory shows, therefore, that this is a very dynamic process
with a continually changing system of interdependent meanings and places. It
is thus increasingly difficult to fix clear boundaries between tourism, heritage,
political, and economic imaginaries.

Notes

1　Christine Chivallon has compiled some of these founding works (by Françoise Paul-
Lévy and Marion Ségaud, Henry Lefebvre, Pierre Bourdieu, Michel de Certeau,
Jean-François Bayart and Jean-Pierre Warnier) in a section of her fascinating article:
"Retour sur la 'communauté imaginée' d'Anderson. Essai de clarification théorique
d'une notion restée floue," *Raisons politiques* 27 (August 2007): 131–172.
2　This kind of argument can be found on the opinion pages of the newspaper *La Nacion*
or heard in forums about mega dam projects in indigenous territories.
3　Despite the fact that numerous simplistic references to "invented traditions" made
regardless of the political context (primordial in the original study) seem to have led
some to reject the notion.
4　*Marie Selby Botanical Gardens*, vol. 38, number 1, January–April 2011.
5　Something like: S: "This piece is by an indigenous painter." J: "Oh, yes, O.G., I know
him, the French teacher." S: "No, you must be mistaken, he is an indigenous painter."
J: "Yes I know he his, but he is *also* a professor at the Boruca college." S: "No, this one
is an indigenous painter."
6　http://www.idrc.ca/en/ev-7301-201-1-DO_TOPIC.html (accessed May 15, 2007).
7　http://portal.unesco.org/culture/fr/ev.php-URL_ID=20855&URL_DO=DO_
TOPIC&URL_SECTION=201.html (accessed May 15, 2007).
8　http://www.sica.int/sica/principios.aspx?IdEnt=401 (accessed May 10, 2007).
9　"Dia de la Integracion Centroamericana," brochure, SG-SICA.
10　Plan Estrategico Regional de Cultura 2005–2009. CECC.
11　http://www.idrc.ca/en/ev-7301-201-1-DO_TOPIC.html (accessed May 15, 2007).
12　http://n4-2005.agendadelturismo.com/index.php?　module=ContentExpress&func=
display&ceid=53&POSTNUKESID=eb811f4c81b911bd1946b1104ec5605b
(accessed May 7, 2007).
13　http://www.nacion.com/ln_ee/2006/julio/05/aldea4.html (accessed May 7, 2007).
14　A cognate of the English word "authority."
15　*Buenas practicas de gestion de turismo cultural*, Spanish Secretary of Industries,
Tourism and Trade, 2004.
16　CCAD, *Programa de Accion Régional por el Desarrollo del Turismo*, 1996.
17　CECC, *Plan Estratégico Regional de Cultura 2005–2009*.
18　http://www.oei.es/pensariberoamerica/ric02a07.htm (accessed May 15, 2007).
19　*Buenas practicas de gestion de turismo cultural*, Spanish Secretary of Industries,
Tourism and Trade, 2004.
20　CCAD, *Programa de Accion Régional por el Desarrollo del Turismo*, 1996.

Bibliography

ANDERSON Benedict, *L'imaginaire national, réflexion sur l'origine et l'essor du nationalisme*, La Découverte, Paris, 1996.

ASPELIN Paul, "The anthropological analysis of tourism: indirect tourism and political economy in the case of the Mamainde of Mato Grosso, Brazil," *Annals of Tourism Research* 4 (1977): 135–60.

BAILLY Anatole, *Dictionnaire GREC—FRANÇAIS*, Hachette, Paris, 1950.

BALANDIER Georges, *Anthropologie politique*, Presses universitaires de France, Paris, 1967/2007.

BERGER Peter and LUCKMANN Thomas, *The Social Construction of Reality*, Penguin Books, London, 1966/1991.

BREIDENBACH Joana and NYIRI Pal, *Seeing Culture Everywhere: From Genocide to Consumer Habits*, University of Washington Press, Seattle, WA, 2009.

CASTORIADIS Cornelius, *L'institution imaginaire de la société*, Seuil, Paris, 1975.

CHACON Ruben and GUEVARA Marcos, *Territorios indios en Costa Rica: orígenes, situación actual y perspectivas*, García Hermanos, San José, 1992.

CHIVALLON Christine, "Retour sur la 'communauté imaginée' d'Anderson. Essai de clarification théorique d'une notion restée floue," *Raisons politiques* 27 (August 2007): 131–172.

COMAROFF John L. and COMAROFF Jean, *Ethnicity, Inc.*, The University of Chicago Press, Chicago, IL, 2009.

COUSIN Saskia, "De l'UNESCO aux villages de Touraine: les enjeux politiques, institutionnels et identitaires du tourisme culturel," *Autrepart* 4(40) (2006): 15–30.

FABIAN Johannes, *Time and the Other: How Anthropology Makes Its Object*, Columbia University Press, New York, 1983.

FRANKLIN Adrian, "The sociology of tourism," in ROBINSON Mike and JAMAL Tazim (eds) *The Sage Handbook of Tourism Studies*, pp. 65–82, Sage, London, 2009.

GARCIA-CANCLINI Nestor, *Culturas híbridas. Estrategias para entrar y salir de la modernidad*, Grijalbo, México, 1990.

HOBSBAWM Eric, "Introduction: inventer des traditions," in HOBSBAWM Eric and RANGER Terence (eds) *L'invention de la tradition*, pp. 11–25, Éditions Amsterdam, Paris, 2006.

LAVERDURE Julien, "'Mucho han caminado las mascaras': l'artisanat boruca, les entrepreneurs culturels et la construction d'un patrimoine centraméricain," *Cahiers des Amériques latines* 65 (2010): 53–74.

LEITE Naomi and GRABURN Nelson, "Anthropological interventions in tourism studies," in ROBINSON Mike and JAMAL Tazim (eds) *The Sage Handbook of Tourism Studies*, pp. 35–64, Sage, London, 2009.

SMOUTS Marie-Claude, "La région comme nouvelle communautée imaginée?," in LE GALES Pierre and LEQUESNE Christian (eds) *Les paradoxes des régions en Europe*, pp. 37–46, La Découverte, Paris, 1997.

THIESSE Anne-Marie, "Les identités nationales, un paradigme transnational," in DIECKHOFF Alain and JAFFRELOT Christophe (eds) *Repenser le nationalisme*, pp. 193–226, Presses de Science Po Paris, 2006.

WALTON John K., "Histories of tourism," in ROBINSON Mike and JAMAL Tazim (eds) *The Sage Handbook of Tourism Studies*, pp. 115–129, Sage, London, 2009.

WEIL Jim, "An ecomuseo for San Vicente: ceramic artisans and cultural tourism in Costa Rica," *Museum Anthropology* 21(2) (September 1997): 23–38.

9 Holidaying in Japan, Falling in Love with Japan

From Pop Culture to Tourism Imaginary

Clothilde Sabre

Introduction

In the field of anthropology, "imaginaries" are not defined precisely, and the ideas of "imaginary" and "imagination" have mostly been included in notions like symbolism, myth, collective representations, and worldview. The discipline has established as its central mission the need to understand the way some groups of people comprehend the world, a mission fulfilled through an accurate study of the way those people understand, interpret, and classify what they are confronted with. But the implicit idea of "imaginary" is actually at stake in many anthropological objects, since the studied phenomena imply connections between concrete elements, shared symbols, collective representations, and personal idiosyncrasy.

Some anthropologists have tried to define imaginary more precisely, investigating such questions as its functions and the way contents and symbols are structured. Among them, Gilbert Durand is famous for his book *Structures anthropologiques de l'imaginaire* (1960), in which he explained that imagination answers a fundamental need of the human spirit and that it fills the function of removing the fear of death. He also argued that this imaginary is structured and logically assembled. This part of anthropology is inspired by psychology and psychoanalysis, using references like Freud, Lacan, or Jung.

The notion of "imaginary" can also be presented as a useful tool to enlighten a social phenomenon. In *Modernity at Large* (1996), Arjun Appadurai speaks of the "work of imagination" and he asserts that, with the worldwide development of media and new technologies of communication, this work of imagination has become a collective social fact which plays a large part in the way people understand their relation to the world. Imaginaries, then, are multiple and available to people in order to create their own imagined identities as well as to gather into imagined communities.

Related to exoticism, imagination and imaginary are also highlighted by the anthropology of tourism. Rachid Amirou, in *L'imaginaire touristique* (1995), has defined imaginary as a "universe of meaning," which creates a "third space" of transition between the tourist and the unknown destination. This "third space" is filled with pictures and symbols that compose a fantasy about the place that has been elected as a tourist site. Tourism imaginaries can be then understood as mediation and as a comprehensive model. The tourist experience is shaped by the previous imaginary, which molded the code of perception of a place and the concrete experience of the discovery. In that context, imaginaries are sets of pictures, references, and knowledge which create a dreamy image of a site, an image that is more or less close to reality, but which works as a guide for the tourist experience

> Even if it is the first time I'm coming, a part of me buried in my stomach remembers it . . . I must confess the most incredible, everything is like I imagined, so much that coming here I feel like I am back home.[1]

These lyrics are quoted from a French song, titled *Ebisu rendez-vous*, in which the members of the band TTC described a trip in Tokyo. The whole text mixes their emotions, which swing between astonishment, wonder, and pleasure, with numerous references taken from Japanese popular culture (*manga*, *Mos Burger*, *Asahi Bier*, *Konami* video games, *kogals*) or more classical items (*sake*, *geisha*, gardens, or the word *arigatô*). Finally, the three singers explain that they want to come back, they are afraid to leave, and they feel a sort of sacred love for the city ("I observe you, then I prostrate myself before you, you obsessed me for so long"). In reality, this song could have been written by any of the groups of tourists I met in Tokyo, French travelers who were also feeling a deep love for the place and who were familiar with contemporary Japanese popular culture and more traditional clichés.

Japan has been seen as an exotic country for a long time in the West, especially in France, with changing images that evolved according to successive international contexts. However, Japan was not really associated with tourism, except, of course, for international tourism *from* Japan. Speaking of clichés, Japanese tourists were famous in Paris (and elsewhere in Europe), as highly visible groups of people rushing out of excursions buses to take lots of photos, having a glimpse of the monuments, and leaving as quickly as they came. By contrast, however, very few French people travelled to Japan, as the country was allegedly so far, so different, and so expensive. Moreover, the pictures associated with Japan were either negative ("a nation of ants" as Prime Minister Edith Cresson said publicly in 1991) or positive but so sophisticated and impenetrable that they only spoke to a minority of initiates (as in Roland Barthes' book *Empire of Signs*, 1970).

With the worldwide success of Japanese pop culture at the end of the twentieth century, the exoticism of Japan was renewed with elements drawn from pop culture's contents, such as manga, anime series, and video games. Fandom grew and those who were interested in these forms of leisure developed a specific interest in Japan, creating fantasies about the country which were pictured in the stories they enjoyed. Thus, a tourism imaginary linked to pop cultural content could be used to investigate trips to Japan made by tourists who declared themselves fans of or passionate for Japanese pop culture.

Using ethnographic data, this chapter attempts to show that, in the case of French fans travelling in Japan, the passion is strongly linked to the imaginary that Japan fans developed before their trip, an imaginary which evolves during the stay and which guides the discovery of Japan and the experience of being a tourist. A new model of tourism is therefore created by fans during their stays in Japan, as they experience the mix between the previous imaginary built on pop cultural references and the concrete experience of being a tourist. This experience then fertilizes and enlarges their picture of Japan, favoring a new relation to the country. We will see through the example of a specific community of French travelers how their common experience of being fans of pop culture and spending time together in Japan lead them to share deep emotions and to literally "fall in love" with Japan.

On a conceptual level, this work is guided by the conception of tourism presented by researchers like Rachid Amirou (1995) and Nelson Graburn (1983), themselves inspired by the work of Edmund Leach (1961) on masked festivals and Victor Turner on pilgrimage (1974). To present it briefly, pilgrimages, as well as tourist journeys, are divided into three temporal stages: before the experience, during the experience, and after. This schematic division is drawn from the structure of traditional rites of passage, and the three moments correspond to the three phases of a rite of passage: first, separation from the group and the rupture with everyday life; second, a moment of liminality[2] when the group exists as a communitas and the members live a common experience; and finally, reintegration of the individuals into society, being changed by the whole experience. This pure model has been discussed by Graburn as an efficient scheme to analyze tourism phenomena, as a limited moment and "one of those necessary structured breaks from ordinary life" (1983: 11). The role of imaginary has been emphasized by Amirou (1995), who considered tourism as "a quest of meaning," guided by previous images and symbols built before the stay. We will regularly return to these notions throughout the discussion, to show how French fans I met were attracted to Japan by a specific imaginary linked to pop culture, and to show that through this experience of pop culture tourism, they developed a new tourism imaginary of Japan.

Pop Culture as Tourism Imaginary

First, some ethnographic details are necessary to understand the dynamic of the community of travelers. As an ethnographer, I have been immersed for some years in the French community of fans of manga, animation, video games, pop music, and other productions linked to Japanese cultural industries. These pop cultural productions have been successful worldwide since the end of the twentieth century,[3] a craze exemplified through the global hit of the Pokémon.[4] It is in this context that I heard about Autrement Le Japon, a small travel agency created by a French man and his Japanese wife and exclusively dedicated to Japan.[5] This travel agency was offering a package tour dedicated to manga and I joined the group in August 2007, as a tourist and as a participant observer. Since that moment, I have been closely immersed in the community of Autrement Le Japon (commonly shortened to ALJ). The agency has no office in France (the manager lives in Japan) and all arrangements are conducted through a website[6] and a newsgroup.[7] Consequently, I made participant observations during my stays in Japan with ALJ's travelers (a "package manga tour" in 2007 and the summer of 2008—July and August—in residence with a group of people who were staying one month) but also through regular observation of the newsgroup, complemented by interviews with some of the tourists while in Japan.[8] Thanks to the newsgroup, I had access to the thoughts and exchanges of the future travelers before the trip and also to their comments after coming back home. Moreover, having developed close relationships with some of the travelers and having kept in communication with them after the stay, I was informed of the elements linked to the reintegration of the liminoid experience of the stay. We will see later how tourists who traveled with ALJ formed a community of lovers of Japan, but first we have to consider the role of pop culture tourism in their common interest in Japan.

Based on this specific experience with Autrement Le Japon and fieldwork in France among the fandom,[9] the idea of a trip to Japan as "media pilgrimage" emerged. Nick Couldry, who developed the concept, defines media pilgrimage as "journeys to points with significance in media narratives" (2005: 72). In terms of imaginary, this means that tourists who perform that type of pilgrimage are drawn to specific sites because they enjoy specific contents (television series, animation, film, manga, and so on). The more the visitors are fans, the more the sites are significant to them. In the case of French fans of manga, I have noticed that, as fans, they share common references about the productions and their context, that is, the source of these productions: Japan. As a result, fans develop a specific imaginary of Japan, a dreamy image composed of all the details they have seen in the content they enjoy. Susan Napier calls it the "fantasyscape" (2007: 11), meaning that this imaginary enables the creation of a playful identity and a fantasy world to dream about. I would add that fans use this fantasy world to immerse themselves in a dreamy Japan, creating a kind of "fantasized Japaneseness," to escape from their usual everyday life. This idea, then, is close to what Appadurai described in *Modernity at Large* (1996) as "the work of imagination" (1996: 66). In Appadurai's terms, media contents are appropriated by the viewers who used them to create a specific and imagined identity. The example is linked to deterritorialized communities, as people with foreign origins create their own images of their parents' homeland through media contents that originated in that country. The process can here be used metaphorically: French fans are not far from their homeland, they are far from their dreamland.

The trip is, then, a way to see the places that appear in the various series admired by the community of fans, places that compose a sort of fantasy map of Japan. That map makes sense for initiated people who share the same references about Japanese pop culture. Concretely, French tourists I met visited places or areas because of their relation to certain content—areas such as Akihabara or Harajuku, Ebisu square, a department store in central Tokyo, the Tokyo Tower, and even the Tokyo University campus were considered as highlights, since they are sets for famous manga and anime series. The shops were also favored, as is every place closely associated with pop culture industries.

The process of the media pilgrimage will not be detailed further here but it is important to keep in mind the idea of a common imaginary, shared by the French travelers, which works as a code during their stay. Except for a few, all the tourists I met through Autrement Le Japon were under forty and shared the same fan culture about Japanese pop culture,[10] admittedly with varying degrees of knowledge and involvement, but with a common basis which provides them the same variety of references. These references were at work when the French travelers selected specific sites as "sacred" for their media pilgrimage, but they also provided a broad framework through which to face the experience of spending holiday time in a distant and exotic country. The media pilgrimage was one aspect of the stay, and the liminoid phase that constituted the concrete tourist experience was also a time of amusement and leisure, in a specific group of fellow travelers.

Tokyo as a Holiday Playground

The groups of tourists among whom I conducted fieldwork were spending their whole stay in Tokyo. For the manga tour in 2007, the travelers stayed for eight days in a hotel in Ikebukuro, while the tourists I joined in the summer of 2008 were staying one month in a residence in an inner suburb of Tokyo. In this residence, small rooms were available and facilities (bathroom, kitchen) were shared.[11] The tourists, then, were enjoying urban holidays, staying and living mainly in the city. For Jean-Didier Urbain, cities are significant for visitors: "the tourist is stuck to this first idea: the city condenses the values of a civilization. Its network is a text scattered with immutable symbols. It is marked out with signs" (1991: 145). The city of Tokyo can, in this respect, thus be considered as a complex group of signs and symbols that represent pieces of Japanese culture. Tokyo is a gigantic city, the capital of a rich and industrialized country, where millions of people are concentrated. Hurrying, crowds, malls, and skyscrapers compose the urban landscape, but touches of Japanese cultural tradition are scattered everywhere, like women in *yukata* (a kimono made of cotton) during the summer or the many temples and shrines. The French tourists were fascinated by these signs. The majority of them stayed in the capital the whole month, leaving occasionally for an excursion to Kyoto or to other famous places. It was in that specific urban context that the liminoid experience of the stay was lived by the groups, but it was nevertheless lived as a leisure and holiday experience.

Being on Holiday

The tourists who came with ALJ choose a specific formula: flight and accommodation were booked for them, but the schedule was free. Many activities were offered (free or not) but everybody was free to organize their time (the manga tour was only eight days long, so the activities were more concentrated but the atmosphere was the same). The tourists who stayed one month in a residence had to organize their everyday life, to buy food, to cook, to clean their room. Many of them expressed the feeling of a routine:

"I take the rhythm, I make my own daily routine, I buy some food at the shop, I live here!" (female, 22)

"We actually live one month in Japan, we have to clean our room, to go shopping and we go out so we live here." (male 20)

This idea of "living here" is the expression of the sedentary aspect of tourism: taking time, feeling relaxed, and staying in the same place for a longer period. This state of mind also influenced the way the tourists organized their days and visited the city: many of them got up late in the morning (or later than they planned), and they explored the city slowly, and voluntarily got lost while they went to selected points:

"We leave for a specific area, and we choose some points of interest in this area, and finally we wander around so much that most of the time we don't even arrive at the area! But we are here for that too, strolling about." (female, 35)

"We like to sit on a bench in the street, just to watch people living." (male, 25)

These examples illustrate the tourist attitudes described by Jean-Didier Urbain (1991: 148), from the model of Icarus, who wants to see and to recognize the signs that compose the city, to the model of Theseus, who wants to look at the interstices and to stroll about and to melt in to the life of the city. The tourists who came with ALJ were doing both, with a wide range of mixed behaviors, but they all shared the feeling of being immersed in city life, even if it was just a little and just for a while. Besides, they also felt very relaxed: "I feel good," "I feel unstressed," "Life is relaxed here," were common expressions of well-being among the tourists. We will see later how the French visitors considered this feeling of relaxation as a property of Japan itself, but here we can make the link with the general idea of being on holiday, to reassert that the city of Tokyo is a frame for spending the vacation, no different in that function than hotel resorts on sunny beaches or villas in the countryside of France.

Tourist Behaviors

This was illustrated through the behaviors adopted by the French tourists in Tokyo. As such, they were mixing various attitudes that are attached to travel and leisure trips. They went sightseeing in the city, with a specific interest in the sites of their media pilgrimage, but not only that. Some of them had a huge list of things to do, others were more explorers, but they all crisscrossed the city, thanks to the system of public transportation, which was considered an attraction by itself. The Tokyo metro and trains are, for French visitors, an exotic curiosity and the groups I followed certainly shared that state of mind. Admiring the landscape of the city from the elevated railway lines, trying to find the correct itinerary for crowded stations, observing the sleeping office workers, the manga readers, and the video game players or, late at night, the drunken salarymen, the observation and fascination were intense.

The travelers were also living a life of leisure and entertainment, close to what can be observed in holiday resorts. As in those places, time for entertainment and night life was important, with many nights out spent in bars and clubs, drinking alcohol, and trying to meet Japanese boy- or girlfriends. One bar in the area of Shibuya, the Hub, was especially famous among the tourists, since it had been elected headquarters by former participants of trips with ALJ, who frequently speak of it in the newsgroup. Whether they decided to go or not, all the participants were informed about the Hub and its famous drunken parties.

Photos and Souvenirs

Like all travelers who visit foreign places, the French tourists took lots of photos of nearly everything. Even when it was forbidden (it is common in Japan to ban photography, particularly in shops), some of the tourists tried to avoid the interdiction and to get round it, arguing that it was legitimate to capture those unique moments. Once they were back in France, photos (and videos) played two roles: as proofs and distinctive signs for their family circle and friends, and a way to relive the emotions that were felt during the stay:

> "When I feel really depressed I watch the videos I made during the trip." (female, 22)

> "(When we came back) we put the video on DVDs, I watched them so many times this year! It makes me feel both good and heartbroken." (female, 20)[12]

Another way to collect and fix memories of the stay was to purchase souvenirs or items only available in Japan. Choices and attitudes depended on the taste and budget of each tourist, but everybody tried to keep some material traces of the trip—as one tourist explained: "You know that when you return from Japan, you will need to bring a piece of it with you" (male, 25).

The importance given to the international parcel shipping system is one sign that testifies to that purchasing need. Questions around international shipping are frequently asked in the ALJ newsgroup, and it was one of the first pieces of information given on arrival in Tokyo on every trip I joined. On flights between Paris and Tokyo, the maximum weight allowance for luggage was 20 kilos, so sending the many items bought or collected[13] during the stay was a major preoccupation of the tourists. At the end of the manga tour giant scales were provided in the hotel lobby, while at the residence on the summer 2008 trip the tiny set of scales in the women's bathroom became the source of numerous conflicts when it disappeared for a few days. These details are trivial and seem anecdotal, but they reveal the importance of material media, as well as the photos and videos. The items which were bought in Japan filled various functions, all linked to the importance of the stay for the fans and tourists. They buy manga books, anime DVDs, figurines, CDs, art books, clothes, traditional souvenirs, "typical" Japanese items (like chopsticks, fans, or kimono), and so on. All these items testify that the trip was made, that it was real, and having them can also facilitate a recreation of the experience of being immersed, filling the fantasyscape with objects that are from Japan and that are made sacred by the fact that they were bought during the stay.

Identity on Holiday

Another aspect of the stay is what Rachid Amirou has called "identity on holiday": "travels are working as a laboratory where the tourist dreams, or tries to escape from his mundane life, either making his life different, inventing an acceptable world during his holidays, or making himself different creating an imaginary identity" (1995: 236). Indeed in the example of French fans of pop culture in Japan, both aspects are in evidence: the trip is the concrete experience of a previous and dreamy imaginary world, while the liminoid experience of being a group of tourists influences the behavior of the travelers. The atmosphere is relaxed and festive and the usual norms are not respected.

Coming back to the model of tourism and pilgrimage, this period is related to the formation of a specific sociability between the fellow travelers: the community becoming a communitas. Communitas is defined as the opposite of the usual social structure and it draws the participants to "develop a great spirit of good companionship and egalitarianism" (Turner 1969: 96). This following quote expresses that break with habitual feelings and the strength of the emotion:

> "I hate being obligated to stay in a group, I absolutely don't want to be part of a flock of sheep, I hate that and I was thinking: wait a minute, I am coming to Japan because I want to discover the country, does it mean that I also have to put up with all the other French for 30 days? But ultimately I had a great surprise with regard to the human aspect, and I liked it!" (female, 35)

Amirou calls groups of people bound together as communitas "micro societies of holidays" (1995: 253), communities that are based on a playful sociability. A common and strong feeling of being part of the group is characteristic and the relations are intense and very emotional. My fieldwork led me to witness the creation of that sort of group. During the short manga tour, the 39 participants were not tied together, but some shared a visible closeness and I noticed that one micro group (five people who didn't know each other before the stay) were sticking together, spending the nights talking in their hotel room, and even refusing to be separated during a dinner with some Japanese people. The phenomenon was perhaps more flagrant during July 2008. The number of French tourists in the residence was small (13 arrived on the 1 July, 15 arrived on 12 July) and very strong bonds were formed as a result. Some had been friends beforehand, but almost everybody was integrated into the group, and the feeling of being a part of something important and unique was very strong: once back in France, the members stayed in touch, named themselves the "Japan Summer Team 2008 (or JST08)," exchanged photos and video via social networks like Facebook, and organized gatherings in France. One of its members expressed his feelings during the stay:

"When I arrived at the airport, I directly got into the group, and I thought: this group is awesome! I was expecting maybe fewer common activities, I was not expecting it at all but I really think the group is awesome!" (male, 20)

Another example introduces another aspect of the type of sociability created by the communitas: Christophe and Richard were two men in their thirties, who spent the summer of 2008 at the residence. They were both fond of Japan and, for a few years, they visited Tokyo regularly with Autrement Le Japon. Spending their time together, they seemed to know each other very well and to be close friends. However, Richard explained that actually they only saw each other during their trips, and didn't even call each other on the phone in France. He told me that Christophe was: "one of the people that I call 'the people of Japan' because I only see them in Japan."

   This type of relationship is indeed strongly linked to the structure of Autrement Le Japon. As explained above, ALJ's newsgroup is very important and this is where former participants can relate their experience and exchange advice and opinions with future travelers. ALJ began in 2002 as a tiny structure, at first organizing only two trips per year, with a small number of participants. Being successful, ALJ offered more and more stays, and the number of participants increased, but always with a core of followers who went back to Japan with ALJ and, for some, continued to be very active on the newsgroup. So, the communitas that is formed during the stay continues through the newsgroup and prolongs the feeling that former participants belong to a specific community. They all feel related by the love they feel for Japan, a deep sentiment which is strongly related to the way they live their stay in Japan.

Being in Love with Japan

This idea of "love" may seem outrageous but it reflects the path followed by the tourists: first fans of Japanese pop culture, they go to Japan and literally "fall in love" with the country. This is a story that was told by most of the French tourists I met with Autrement Le Japon; it is also the line promoted by the travel agency. On the agency's website, the idea of "passion" is emphasized as the organization introduces itself as "an alternative to the classical travel agencies."[14] The text speaks explicitly to "the innumerable fans who find themselves in one or another culture of Japan" and the word "passion" is used several times.[15] This echoes the discourse of the founder of the agency during the interview:

"We are looking for people who are passionate about Japan . . . we don't want someone who went to Peru the year before, comes to Japan this year and who is constantly speaking of his next trip in South Africa next year, for example. We are not interested by that kind of people, we are only interested in people that are here for Japan."

This line was constantly reasserted by the founder but also by many of the former participants. They all drew a portrait of the "wrong traveler," an image associated with the pejorative stereotype of the tourist and characterized by the absence of a deep passion for Japan. Considering the country as one more exotic place among others seems unforgivable to them. In a discussion on the newsgroup, one young man wrote: "there are too many French tourists in Tokyo, but the aljistes[16] are most of the time real lovers of the Japanese culture, while many French came here just to follow the latest trend."[17] This summarizes the emotional implication praised by the ALJ community: they feel different from other tourists because they are "real lovers" of Japan. Belonging to the community is then a sign and a demonstration of that strong love. That distinction is very important for the tourists and after a first stay, they generally declare themselves not only fans of manga and anime but fans of Japan. The experience of the stay is in effect the moment when this emotional feeling reaches its climax. This passion for the country is linked to the strong emotions experienced during the stay, not only as a fan and a member of the communitas but also through the discovery of another culture.

The Intercultural Experience

Most of the tourists who travel with ALJ are attracted to Japan by their interest in its pop culture, but this is not the only perspective they have on Japan. Their previous imaginary also creates a large space for an imagined immersion into Japanese culture and everyday life. These pictures are built on the various knowledge collected about Japan, with heterogeneous information unified as personal representations. Drawing from everything they can find (not only pop culture content, but also documentaries, movies, websites, video, books, magazines, and more), the fans enrich their fantasyscape with living images of what they conceive as the "real Japan." During the stay, these images are confronted by the concrete experience. Rachid Amirou considers that, in the tourist experience of the stay, the previous imaginary that guides the travelers is a "transitional space" (1995: 272) which creates mediation between the tourist and the other. Manipulating pictures and fantasies about a far-off country makes it possible to go beyond the difference and to overcome the unknown, as does exoticism. Thus, in our example, the French tourists' encounter with Japan, its culture, and its inhabitants is mediated by the foreign visitors' fantasyscape. Nevertheless, this imaginary is not fixed: adjustments, updates, and widening are made during the stay. The tourists I met in Tokyo all shared a positive and enthusiastic opinion of Japan and many discussions detailed the qualities and good aspects of Japanese life: safety, kindness, hospitality, order, and respect were praised as common values that characterized the Japanese people and their behaviors. The general atmosphere in Japan was judged to be friendly and reassuring, and the tourists declared that they felt confident and relaxed. Interactions with the Japanese were also highly considered and encouraged by ALJ, as the agency organized meetings with French-speaking Japanese. In everyday life, exchanging with the inhabitants is more complicated. In the street, even if passers-by are quick to stop and to help lost visitors, the exchanges are often short and communication is not that easy, the language barrier being a major obstacle. On the contrary, in the frame provided by

ALJ, starting a conversation is easier and comfortable, and the relaxed and party atmosphere helps to develop friendship.

Seduction and Love Affairs

Love stories were also sought by the French tourists. Many of them praised the beauty of the Japanese men and women and dreamt of meeting a boyfriend or a girlfriend, going to bars and discos to increase their chances of finding someone. Holidays are a moment of liminality, the usual norms are loosened, sexual adventures are allowed and, during the stays, some of the men clearly explained that they wanted to find someone so they could tell their friends and to realize their fantasy. The French women were less explicit, but some explained that they "dreamt of meeting a handsome Japanese guy" and also asserted: "you don't know where to look, there's hot guys everywhere!" This aspect of fantasy and desire is not only directed onto the exotic and seductive other, but also onto the ego, such that the game of seduction is then a way to enhance personal identity. The fantasyscape is an intimate space in which personal identity is developed and highlighted, and in the concrete experience of the trip, that magnified identity is at stake. So, if "the dream" comes true, that positive and valuable personality is strengthened and recognized. This is exemplified by the feeling of being more seductive in Japan than in France (one male, 22, told me: "Here, many girls come to see me, while in France I am always rejected! That's great!"). So, the seduction of and a love for idealized Japanese people played a great part in the tourists' desire for immersion, with implications for their personal and fantasized personality. Through these possible love stories, they invented themselves as different and special.

Being a Gaijin

In Japan, the French Caucasian tourists were physically different, and maybe exotic. Tokyo now welcomes more and more foreigners every year, but the obvious physical difference is still perceptible, and the French fans largely insisted on it. Most of them didn't speak Japanese but, among the few words of vocabulary they possessed, "gaijin" was well known. The word means "foreigner" in Japanese, and it can be used neutrally but also pejoratively. Almost everybody reported incidents tainted with alleged racism: they found a seat in a crowded train or subway and nobody sat next to them; they were insulted by some drunken man; they were not served in a restaurant, and so on. These small incidents were not rare but never violent and they were always interpreted as a consequence of the uniqueness of Japanese culture. "Those who are not born Japanese will never be Japanese" explained the tourists, so it is acceptable to be confronted with mistrust and curiosity. Sophie and Linda (aged 20 and 22) were quite passionate about it and reported a number of incidents—mainly looks from men, interpreted as "perverse," or pushing in a crowd. Insisting on the fact that Japanese were "racist," these two girls were paradoxically fond of Japan: it was their second trip and they were both planning to spend at least one year in Tokyo later. One of them was hoping "to marry a Japanese man" and they were inexhaustible when they spoke about their passion for Japan. So, how does one interpret their anger against alleged racism? This attitude had the function of filling the gap between their fantasyscape and what they experienced. They had both created a magnified image of themselves immersed in a dreamy Japan, and if sometimes reality didn't match their conceptions, they used the idea of racism—considered not as a personal attack but as an inevitable consequence of the specificity and isolation of Japan—to justify the gap without having to question their own dream.

We can add the common mistake made by the Japanese, who mistook the Caucasian tourists to be American citizens. Most of the French were disappointed by that error and they wanted to affirm their nationality. Being French was conceived as a source of prestige, as one of them explained:

> "The Japanese love French, they love the French language, France and French people . . . they mistrust white people a lot but at the same time they worship us." (male, 20)

Thus self-identifying as French also becomes a way to resolve the problem of the distance with Japanese people: immersion is limited by the insurmountable cultural difference, so otherness is praised through the supposed high value of being French. This was exemplified in the discourse of two French tourists who were not related but both of whom had Asian origins. They told me they were disappointed by and a bit jealous of the way Japanese people were curious about the French Caucasian tourists, while at first they were not interested by them, supposing that they were Japanese. The differences here, then, become positive and attractive and a way to preserve the fantasy of immersion in an ideal Japan.

Role Play

That perspective can be illustrated with the idea of role play. During the stay, the discovery of and immersion into Japanese culture are the core of the intercultural experience, and the tourists generally felt strong emotions when they experienced what they had earlier imagined. Some were just spectators but others wanted to join in and participate. In July 2008, the group discovered that a small *matsuri* (Japanese festival) was running for two days in the neighborhood of the residence. One young man, named Yannick, took the silk kimono he had just bought in a shop and joined in with the local inhabitants who were dancing around a small tower where a man was playing *taiko* (Japanese traditional drum). He didn't speak Japanese and he wasn't used to these festivals, but he told me after that it was a dream to "do the same as they do." After that, other tourists bought *yukata* (light cotton kimono) and they went back to the festival the following evening to join in the dance and to take photos. The point here is not to estimate if the tourists were really trying to meet Japanese people but to note that they were mainly interested in their own experience of immersion, happy to "play the Japanese,"

Figure 9.1 Manga tour, 2007

whether or not they actually exchanged with the Japanese participants. What was also striking in the incident was the attitude of this young man in the following days: he became silent and spent the last days of the stay at the residence, watching Japanese animation on a computer. This incident reveals another aspect of the superimposition of the fantasyscape onto concrete experience. In that case, we can suppose that Yannick experienced the immersion he desired, feeling strong emotions, and consequently tried to preserve the climax, not attempting further immersion but returning to his earlier and dreamy imaginary.

Providing another illustration, the photo in Figure 9.1 was taken during the Manga tour, in August 2007. Some participants decided to wear the *yukata* that were available in the hotel room and gathered in the hall of their common floor to take the group photo. Compared to the previous example, the role play was more collective and very playful. The members of the group shared the moment, which was more like *cosplay*[18] than a real attempt to immerse themselves in a fantasized Japanese identity, since in this instance they stayed together and didn't try to mingle with Japanese people. Here the communitas seems more important than the personal fantasyscape, but references to such role play were common and the pleasure of playing with costumes was shared by everyone in the specific tourist space of the hotel.

The Fear of Returning to France

Another way the deep love for Japan was expressed was the feelings of sadness and fear associated with the end of the stay and the return to France. Leaving Japan meant the end of the liminoid period, the playful and emotional tourist experience, and then the return to everyday life, in which the fantasyscape is only an exotic dream. During the interviews conducted in Japan,[19] to the question of returning, the answers all had the same tone: "it is going to be horrible," "I prefer not to think about it," "I am going to be depressed," and so on. The reactions were always negative, even if the tourists didn't project themselves into a long-term stay in Japan. Some were quite excessive, such as those who spoke of depression and despair. The solution seemed, then, to elaborate plans to come back and settle in Japan. Some were realistic, planning to take advantage of student exchanges or to save money for a while to try to get a working-holiday visa[20] for a year. Others were in a complete fantasy, speaking of dropping everything to return to work as a baker, a teacher of French, or a waiter, ignoring the facts that a visa is difficult to obtain, that they didn't have any of the skills for these jobs, and that they spoke neither Japanese nor English. The information I collected after the stays confirmed that this latter group of fantasists let their plans of settling vanish, while satisfying themselves with other tourist trips to Japan.

This repetition of visits is another element of the specific type of tourism presented in this chapter. During the first stay, the liminoid experience of tourism is mixed with the emotional immersion into the fantasyscape, and it creates a climax of emotions and enhanced identity. The tourists feel well in Japan, they feel "themselves" and they want to repeat that positive experience, as one of them explained: "I would like to be able to come every two years, to come regularly to Japan because I feel at home here, in this atmosphere" (female, 25). Richard and Christophe, who in 2008 were coming to Japan for the seventh time, both recounted the same path, from a first shock to a real need to come back and to "have a shot of Japan" whenever they could. But at the same time they wished to maintain the barrier that made them tourists and not permanent residents, to avoid the coercive aspects of Japanese society, like the exhausting days of work or the permanent feeling of being a stranger. Remaining a tourist allows one to take only the good aspects of immersion in Japanese life, always maintaining a distance but then allowing oneself to be there just for pleasure. In the community of travelers who evolved around ALJ, this routine of visits is one of the best pieces of evidence for their love for Japan—and the core of the ALJ community comprises those who come regularly. This phenomenon is linked to the agency's beginning: it was so small that the founders met personally with every traveler and kept up exchanges with them after the trips. With the agency getting bigger every year, the relationship between the founders and the tourists is less intimate, but those who invest themselves in the newsgroup and in the meetings that are regularly organized in France continue to strengthen this community of "lovers of Japan."

Conclusion

This ethnographic presentation has revealed that the tourists who came to Japan mainly because they were fond of its pop culture, developed a passion for the country, a passion deep enough to lead them to repeat their visits and to invest themselves in a community of regular travelers to Japan. The "work of imagination" (Appadurai 1996: 66) is here the core element that initiates the first trip and that binds together the various aspects of the tourist experience as it is lived in Japan. The pop culture imaginary guides the media pilgrimage aspect of the trip, while the tourist experience is lived through the communitas and the intercultural encounters. As a consequence the previous fantasy is enriched by the real-life experience of the stay and is fertilized by the aspects of tourism that are inherent to such adventure. The fantasyscape based on a passion for pop cultural contents is mixed with the tourist experience and gives birth to a new tourism imaginary, which leads the tourists to experience a new form of stay, composed of two typical and, at first, different aspects of travel: an exotic trip in a far-off and unknown place, mixed with sedentary and repeated stays in the same place. Japan becomes, then, a new type of tourist destination.

Taken as two opposite models, Japan and France exemplified those two types of stays. Until recently, Japan was not considered as a tourist destination, and, even if the country has actively promoted its tourist sector with some results since the beginning of the twenty-first century,[21] it is still a generally unknown destination, specifically to those from Europe.[22]

On the other hand, the case of France is also remarkable, as the country is regularly ranked first for inbound tourism, with a great appeal also for domestic trips. Compared to Japan, in 2010, France received five times the number of tourists.[23] France is considered the country of tourism *par excellence*, and a numerous variety of experiences and trips can be had there: package tours, hotel resorts, sedentary stays in vacation homes, and so on. The points of interest are numerous, from cultural tours to the three "S"s (sea, sun, and sand, a successful recipe in mass tourism). Moreover the French are familiar with all these types of trips, even if they don't practice all of them.

Seen from a French perspective, travelling in Japan and travelling in France can be taken as examples of two types of trip, symbolized on one hand by the organized tour to a far-off and exotic country, and on the other hand by the sedentary type of tourism known as *villégiature* in French. *Villégiature* is defined by Marc Boyer as a stay in one place, with time dedicated to rest and to various leisure activities, the journey being of little importance (2008: 229). Boyer opposes this form of holiday to the tourism he associates with migration and movements, and—we can add here—hurrying. The ethnographic analysis developed here reveals that the "lovers of Japan" I met with ALJ mix both poles: they travel to a far-off place about which they have often dreamt, while they also stay long enough to take their time and to feel relaxed and not submitted to an imperative schedule. Moreover, by insisting on the *villégiature* aspect, the tourists initiate a routine of stays, travelling regularly to Japan, as if they were going to their own holiday home, but with the additional pleasure of the intercultural context. The cultural imaginary developed through the passion for Japanese pop culture gives birth to a tourism imaginary that makes Japan a place of *villégiature* and a tourism more invested in long-term exchange.

A final point of note is the way that passion for Japan influences the lives of the tourists who declare themselves "lovers of Japan." They feel strong emotions during their trip, occasioned by the superimposition of the prior imaginary and the concrete images collected during the stay. The imaginary is at work not only during the stay but also after, and we can assume that this tourism imaginary is, for these passionate travelers, important enough to have further consequences in their everyday life, between and after their visits. More than an imaginary that operates only during vacation time, this tourism imaginary seems to have an important role in the biography of these travelers. Two questions can be raised in conclusion: is this phenomenon important enough to spread among a larger number of tourists, or is it only for those who hold to the code of the fandom and who want to realize their own media pilgrimage? Moreover, is media pilgrimage still at stake when the travelers make more than one trip to Japan? Tourism linked to pop culture contents has recently been promoted further by the Japanese Tourism sector. However, we saw that this is only one part of the experience and of the imaginary, so it will perhaps not be directed toward the "lovers of Japan" like the members of the ALJ community, but toward their nemeses: "the wrong travelers," those who just came "to see," without that deep feeling of love.

Notes

1   Author's translation from French. All the quotations from books, interviews, or songs which were originally in French have been translated by the author.
2   Turner (1974: 15) explains that he prefers the word "liminoid" to "liminal" to qualify the experiences which are set into the contemporary secular world. We will, then, follow his suggestion in this chapter.
3   To be precise, Japanese anime and manga arrived in France earlier, during the 1980s, and their success rose during the 1990s.
4   A video game media franchise owned by Nintendo, based in fictional *Poke*t *Mon*sters, created in 1996.
5   This was the case when I conducted fieldwork among them, but in 2011 they added two new destinations: New York and Korea, a change probably resulting from the decrease of tourism to Japan after the earthquake and tsunami of March 2011. The company renamed itself Autrement les Voyages. New York failed but another destination, China, was added in 2012. However, Japan is still the main destination of the travel agency, but with some changes: more thematic package tours and private tours.
6   http://www.autrementlejapon.com/fr/index.php.
7   http://autrementlejapon.forumzen.com/. However, due to evolutions of Internet and social networks, the newsgroup is progressively loosing its interactivity, former and future travellers exchanging now on the ALJ Facebook page.
8   Twenty-two tourists were interviewed in the summer of 2008 while they spent their holidays in Tokyo with ALJ. All the interviews were about one hour long; they were conducted at the residence, in the rooms or in the common hall, and were recorded. An interview was also conducted with the founder of Autrement le Japon (August 2008) and with a French employee (a former participant in the trips) who was working for ALJ at the time (August 2008).
9   Before the specific research on tourism in Japan, some observations and interviews were conducted among the French community of fans.
10   Age is significant regarding the history of Japanese pop culture in France. Anime were broadcast in the 1980s and manga began to be translated during the 1990s, so people who were already adults at that time were not really touched by the phenomenon.
11   Commonly named "gaijin house," these types of residences mainly accommodate foreign students.
12   These two interviews were conducted in July 2008, but the interviewees had already travelled to Japan the year before.
13   Some kept every free item they could collect, like the promotional fans or flyers handed out in the street.

14 http://www.autrementlejapon.com/fr/notre-conception-du-voyage-au-japon (accessed September 30, 2012).
15 Ibid.
16 This neologism, commonly used in ALJ groups, is mix of ALJ and *(tour)istes*.
17 http://autrementlejapon.forumzen.com/t1351-depart-groupe-pika-du-10-aout (accessed September 30, 2012).
18 From "*cos*tume" and "*play*," it points to people who dress up as a pop culture character. It is a widely spread phenomenon in Japanese pop culture.
19 Although they are not detailed here, the spontaneous reactions collected during the Manga tour were of the same tone.
20 A working-holiday visa is a type of visa that allows French under 31 to spend one year in Japan and to take a part-time job. Candidates need to prove that they own at least 4,500 euros (around 5,800 US dollars) and they are officially not allowed to work in bars, disco clubs, and the like.
21 An official campaign, promoting pop culture, the "Cool Japan campaign," was launched in 2002.
22 Japan was ranked 30th outbound tourism destination in 2010, with 8,611,175 visitors (http://www.veilleinfotourisme.fr/japon-japan-92214.kjsp, accessed September 30, 2012).
23 77.1 million foreign visitors to France in 2010 (http://www.insee.fr/fr/themes/tableau. asp?reg_id=0&ref_id=NATTEF13532, accessed September 30, 2012).

Bibliography

AMIROU Rachid, *Imaginaire touristique et sociabilité du voyage*, Paris, Presses universitaires de France, 1995.

APPADURAI Arjun, *Modernity at Large*, Minneapolis, MN, University of Minnesota Press, 1996.

BARTHES Roland, *Empire of Signs*, New York, Hill and Wang, 1982 [1970].

BOYER Marc, *Les villégiatures du XVIe au XXIe siècle. Panorama du "tourisme sédentaire,"* Paris, EMS Editions, 2008.

COULDRY Nick, "On the actual street," in David Crouch, Rhona Jackson and Felix Thompson (eds) *The Media and the Tourist Imagination: Converging Culture*, pp. 60–75, New York, Routledge, 2005.

DURAND Gilbert, *Structures anthropologiques de l'imaginaire*, Paris, Dunod, 1960.

GRABURN Nelson, "The anthropology of tourism," *Annals of Tourism Research* 10 (1983): 9–33.

LEACH Edmund R., "Time and false notes," in E.R. Leach (ed.) *Rethinking Anthropology*, pp. 132–136, London, Athlone Press, 1961.

NAPIER Susan, *From Impressionism to Anime: Japan as Fantasy and Fan Cult in the Mind of the West*, New York, Palgrave Macmillan, 2007.

TUNER Victor, *The Ritual Process: Structures and Anti-Structure*, Chicago, IL, Aldine, 1969.

——, *Dramas, Fields and Metaphors: Symbolic Action in Human Society*, Ithaca, NY, Cornell University Press, 1974.

URBAIN Jean-Didier, *L'idiot du voyage*, Paris, Payot et Rivages, 1993 (Plon, 1991).

10 "Like Nowhere Else"

Imagining Provincetown for the Lesbian and Gay Family

Liz Montegary

Introduction

In my contribution to this collection, I place travel and tourism studies in conversation with queer cultural studies, and I employ Foucaultian methods of discourse analysis to think critically about the production of space and, specifically, the construction of tourist imaginaries. This involves mapping the material histories that make possible the conflicting and competing imaginaries circulating within particular tourist sites. That is, what social processes, political practices, and economic structures undergird the imaginaries that tourism operators and tourists themselves create and consume, and in what ways do these discursive formations impact the people (affectively and physically) and the places (the actual land itself) that find themselves entangled with the tourism industry?

Like other queer studies scholars engaging with postcolonial studies and critical ethnic studies, I use the term "queer" not to represent an identity or a population but, instead, to signal a theoretical investment in analyzing the gender, racial, and class politics of space and sexuality. As such, queer critiques of travel and tourism attend to the ways in which dominant tourist imaginaries—imaginaries that tend to reflect nationalist attachments or imperialist longings—are often organized around white middle-class ideals of heteronormativity. The rise of the lesbian and gay tourism industry has thus depended upon the cultivation of new tourist imaginaries and often involves the remapping of spaces previously imagined as heterosexual. But, as queer cultural studies scholars argue, lesbian and gay imaginaries are not inherently resistant to—and are sometimes strategically incorporated into—dominant sociopolitical formations. For instance, lesbian and gay tourist experiences may coincide with nationalist celebrations manufactured through exploitative capitalist practices, and mainstream tourism boards may foster "alternative" imaginaries in order to target the niche market of lesbian and gay travelers. This is not, however, to say that the project of disrupting dominant imaginaries is destined for failure. Queer cultural studies scholarship seeks to understand the complicated stakes involved in remapping (hetero)normative spaces while simultaneously exploring the ways in which clashing imaginaries produce new and unexpected possibilities.

Placing travel and tourism studies in conversation with queer cultural studies, this chapter draws upon Foucaultian methods of discourse analysis to think critically about the production of lesbian and gay tourism imaginaries. Specifically, I map the material histories that make possible the competing imaginaries underlying the nascent lesbian and gay family vacation industry in Provincetown, Massachusetts. What social processes, political practices, and economic structures undergird the imaginaries that tourism operators and tourists themselves create and consume in this small resort town? The term queer, in this context, does not represent an identity or a population but, instead, signals a theoretical investment in analyzing the gender, racial, and class politics of space and sexuality. As such, queer critiques of travel attend to the ways in which tourism imaginaries tend to reflect nationalist attachments or imperialist longings and are often organized around the white, middle-class ideals of heteronormativity. The rise of the lesbian and gay tourism industry has thus depended upon the cultivation of new tourism imaginaries and often involves the remapping of spaces previously imagined as heterosexual. Yet, as queer cultural studies scholars argue, lesbian and gay imaginaries are not inherently resistant to—and are sometimes strategically incorporated within—dominant sociopolitical formations. Lesbian and gay tourist experiences may coincide with nationalist celebrations manufactured through exploitative capitalist practices, and mainstream tourism boards may foster alternative imaginaries to target the seemingly lucrative lesbian and gay niche market. Even still, this chapter does not suggest that the project of disrupting dominant imaginaries is destined for absolute failure. In what follows, I consider the complicated stakes involved in remapping (hetero)normative spaces while simultaneously exploring the ways in which clashing imaginaries produce new and unexpected possibilities.

Located on the eastern-most tip of Cape Cod where the Nauset tribe once thrived, Provincetown has served as a Yankee whaling port, a Portuguese fishing village, a U.S. naval base, an artist colony, a colonial New England town, and a popular gay travel destination. Despite the town's small size, Provincetown is currently home to three different tourist-centered organizations. The Chamber of Commerce's website, established as the Board of Trade in the late nineteenth century and incorporated in its current tourism-focus form in 1957, invites travelers to "an historic town that knows how to have fun."[1] In addition to promising visitors award-winning beaches and rich artistic culture, the Chamber of Commerce is particularly proud of the Pilgrim Monument, a 250-foot granite tower that commemorates the arrival of the Pilgrims (who initially landed in Provincetown before proceeding to Plymouth) and the signing of the Mayflower Compact in 1620. The Provincetown Business Guild, formed in 1978 by gay and gay-friendly business owners in response to what was perceived as the Chamber of Commerce's anti-gay marketing strategies, paints a much different picture of Provincetown. Claiming that "gay life is everywhere," the Guild describes Provincetown as a "place of magic," where "young sweethearts," "seasoned couples," and parents "with their strollers" vacation alongside "leathermen, bears, dykes on bikes, transgender folk, and lots of shirtless hunky boys."[2] In 1997, in what may have been an attempt to ease the tensions between the Chamber of Commerce and the Business Guild, local officials established the Tourism Office and Visitor Services Board. The Tourism Office's website has since branded Provincetown with the conveniently ambiguous tagline "Like Nowhere Else," a place where tourists can choose whether to vacation in an historic city steeped in American pride or to visit a magical resort exuding gay pride.

At first glance, the competing imaginaries appear organized around a question of whether Provincetown should market itself as a charming colonial town or a premier gay destination. I, however, argue that this reductive reading of Provincetown is not helpful in understanding the multiple tourism imaginaries at play within the lesbian and gay family vacation industry. For the past 15 years, Provincetown has been the site of the largest formal gathering of lesbian and gay families in the United States. An event that began as a small backyard barbecue hosted by two gay dads has since exploded into seven days of corporate-sponsored workshops and social gatherings run by the national nonprofit organization Family Equality Council.[3] Each year, during the first week in August, several hundred families descend upon gay-friendly Provincetown to play on the beaches, visit the local historical landmarks, and attend the official Family Week events.[4] Although the Council, according to their website, runs the week in the hopes of helping parents and their children "make the world a better place for all loving families," the annual conference-vacation has also played a role in directing the tourism industry's attention to an untapped niche within the lesbian and gay demographic. Interestingly, however, the historically pro-gay Business Guild has expressed much concern about how the presence of children radically alters the atmosphere of Provincetown and, as a result, hurts the sales at high-end restaurants and boutiques and all-night bars and clubs.[5] What, I ask, might the debates around Family Week tell us about the politics of sexuality organizing the tourism imaginaries of Provincetown?

Through a discursive analysis of scholarly and popular histories of Provincetown, promotional materials from the town's three tourism organizations, and news media coverage of the annual Family Week celebration, I illustrate how the tourism industry in Provincetown—even as different sectors of the industry produce conflicting conceptualizations of the town—has depended upon and continues to reinforce the structures of global capital. Rather than simply concluding that this week-long celebration of family values undoes the radical potential of a destination like Provincetown, I question the assumption that a resort town can ever truly exist outside dominant cultural patterns and that travel—even lesbian and gay travel—is ever a truly liberatory practice. Following the gay marketing moment of the 1990s and the subsequent boom in the lesbian and gay tourism industry, cultural geographers and tourism studies scholars began examining the construction and touristification of gay spaces, the role of travel in sexual identity formation, and the relationship between sex, health, and tourism.[6] Researchers working in this vein tend to focus almost exclusively on the leisure practices of economically privileged and normatively gendered white men and to uncritically celebrate the visibility that lesbian and gay tourists achieve as cosmopolitan consumers.[7] In distinction, I follow the lead of queer cultural studies scholars like M. Jacqui Alexander and Jasbir Puar who bring the insights of postcolonial theory and transnational feminism to bear on their investigations of lesbian and gay travel.[8] This scholarship insists upon an historicized examination of tourism in relation to other forms of travel, migration, and displacement and with respect to the gendered, racialized, and classed relations of power organizing lesbian and gay communities. Likewise, I argue that the study of tourism imaginaries is incomplete without a consideration of how histories and discourses of colonialism, capitalism, and empire-making inform modern practices of travel.

This project shifts the focus of tourism studies away from the international travels of lesbians and gay men with impressive disposable incomes and toward the domestic circuits traversed by lesbian and gay parents with children. My investigation of Provincetown allows for a careful unpacking of the multiple narratives of exceptionalism that constitute a particular location and thus expands our understanding of the relationship between travel, nationalism, and sexual politics. Moreover, I contend that the growing popularity of lesbian and gay family vacations must be understood in relation to the move within U.S. lesbian and gay politics toward what Lisa Duggan describes as homonormativity.[9] Over the past few decades, many lesbian and gay activists have responded to the intensified rise of pro-business liberalism (or neoliberalism) and the rightward shift of U.S. political culture by abandoning progressive calls for a redistribution of wealth and resources and, instead, emphasizing the importance of gaining recognition as citizens and consumers. This chapter extends existing critiques of homonormativity to think critically about the production of lesbian and gay parents as viable political subjects and a profitable market segment. Through an investigation of the tourism imaginaries emerging in relation to family equality activism, I illustrate how the incorporation of children into the lesbian and gay tourism-activism dynamic further aligns homonormative identities and politics with the interests of capital and the state. At the same time, however, I ask whether the multitude of desires and practices enacted within Provincetown might momentarily disrupt the seeming homonormativity of Family Week and might create space for imagining a queer family politics.

Escape to the Cape

In order to understand the spatial and political imaginaries structuring the annual Family Week celebration, it is first necessary to understand the sociopolitical and economic hierarchies on which the Provincetown travel industry depends. To imagine Provincetown as defined by a division between heteronormative and non-heteronormative is to flatten out the complex tensions that currently exist between and among locals and tourists and to ignore the violent processes of displacement and exploitation that have made tourism in this region possible. The Chamber of Commerce and the Business Guild may target different segments of the population, but both organizations—along with the Tourism Office—sell tourists on the promise of escape: the chance to travel back in time to the colonial roots of "American democracy" and/or the opportunity to abandon the reality of homophobia in favor of a gay utopia. These escapist fantasies, however, mask the relations of power that make possible a tourist-activist event like Family Week. For whom is escape possible? And at whose expense?

Popular histories of Provincetown—such as the versions circulated by the tourism organizations and the local museums—reproduce folkloric narratives about New England's "colonial" past and often begin with the arrival of the Mayflower. Although Provincetown, like Hyannis and other areas of Cape Cod, has been promoting itself as a resort area since the nineteenth century, the end of the whaling industry and the Industrial Revolution created the need for more aggressive tourism promotion campaigns. During the first decades of the twentieth century, Provincetown followed other northeastern towns in remaking itself as a vestige of "colonial America" and, in 1910, erected the Pilgrim Monument to mark the birthplace of "American democracy."[10] In 2010, to commemorate the monument's 100th anniversary, the Chamber of Commerce's annual travel guide featured an article on how the massive structure reminds visitors that the "great experiment with American democracy"—which "continues to be the envy of the entire world"—began in Provincetown.[11] This celebration of "freedom" and "equality" deliberately forgets the displacement, enslavement, and deaths of the Nauset people who hunted and fished on the tip of the cape and effectively masks the violences inherent to U.S. settler colonialism and the manufacturing of nationalist tourism imaginaries.[12]

Jumping from the arrival of Pilgrims in the seventeenth century to the establishment of a Yankee whaling industry in the nineteenth century, popular histories of Provincetown describe the circuits of immigrant labor that gave way to a vibrant Portuguese fishing community, but never mention the exploitative conditions these workers faced and the racism directed toward these men and their families. Because early twentieth-century constructions of New England promised tourists an escape from congested urban areas filled with growing immigrant populations, Provincetown's long-standing and expanding Portuguese communities—who were instrumental in the development of recreation and hospitality businesses—required tourism promoters to devise marketing tactics for managing racial and national imaginaries. Through the strategic commodification of ethnic difference, Provincetown sold a neatly packaged version of "Portuguese culture" and thus capitalized on the (white) tourist desire for "authentic" yet safe encounters with the "foreign."[13] Celebratory narratives of the resort town also gloss over the use of Provincetown Harbor as a naval supply base during World War I, an indication not only of the investment in creating a pre-modern colonial historical site but also of the normalization of mobilizing civilian sites in times of war. Instead, popular histories, such as the version told in one of the Business Guild's official guidebooks, remind potential tourists that "ever since the Pilgrims first landed on [Cape Cod], [Provincetown] has been providing the perfect oasis for people in need of escape."[14] The project of reimagining Provincetown during the first half of the twentieth century was an uneven process instigated by the Industrial Revolution and larger shifts in global capital. Yet, according to the version of history presented to tourists, the transition from fishing village to coastal resort / colonial outpost / artist colony was an easy transformation for what had historically been a quintessential site of U.S. exceptionalism.

In her critical look at how the site of the Pilgrims' initial landing morphed into a world-renowned gay resort, historian Karen Christel Krahulik explains that Provincetown is best understood with respect to the postindustrial capitalist projects that inspired the making of ethnic resort towns and identity-based urban enclaves. During the first half of the twentieth century, she explains, Provincetown gained notoriety as an artist colony where non-heteronormative genders and sexualities could thrive.[15] The resort town attracted an eclectic group of artists who, in the wake of World War I, were looking for domestic alternatives to the expatriate lifestyle and whose presence, over the next few decades, attracted tourists in search of (homo)erotic arts and culture. During World War II, when the U.S. Navy docked the North Atlantic Fleet in the Provincetown Harbor, sailors participated in the town's growing gay tourism economy as both tourists and tourist attractions. By the end of the war, Provincetown had already gained a reputation as a vacation destination that not only welcomed but actually needed the gay dollar. Even as the "lavender scare" of the Cold War prompted some entrepreneurs, clergymen, and local government officials to embark on gay purity campaigns, the majority of businesses continued to promise tourists from a variety of racial, sexual, and class backgrounds the chance to encounter and, if desired, to experience sexual transgression. Although the eclectic collection of people who traveled to and through Provincetown for a few hours or a few years during the postwar era cannot all be captured under the sign of "lesbian" or "gay," it is still important to note that the vitality of the local tourist economy came to depend upon the practices of travel and consumption that defined the growing lesbian and gay middle class.

During the latter half of the twentieth century—and especially following the boom in lesbian and gay tourism during the 1990s—Provincetown's tourism imaginaries have targeted an increasingly privileged class of travelers. White gay men, in particular, have constituted the majority of the tourist population and have dominated the tourism economy as entrepreneurs. According to feminist scholar (and former resident of Provincetown) Susan Cayleff, the purchasing power of these tourists and/or business owners has driven real estate prices obscenely high, thus forcing working-class white and Portuguese locals to move either up- or off-Cape.[16] As the process of gentrification has depleted the local labor pool, Provincetown businesses have become dependent on the importation of seasonal workers from Jamaica and, increasingly, Eastern Europe. These migrants might take pleasure in spending the summer in a gay resort town, but are often paid below minimum wage to live and work in questionable conditions. Clearly, privileged forms of leisure travel are made possible by what Mimi Sheller describes as the demobilization and remobilization of racially and economically marginalized populations.[17] The tourism imaginaries that lesbian and gay travelers consume while visiting Provincetown are made possible by the transnational flow of capital, the global circulation of identities, discourses, and histories, and the physical movements of entrepreneurs, migrants, and workers. Built upon histories of dispossession and structures of exploitation, Provincetown has become a gay resort catering to a wealthier and whiter population that tends to adhere to middle-class norms of respectability, consumerism, and property-ownership.

Homonormative Imaginaries

With this history in mind, I understand Family Week as predicated on processes of displacement and circuits of labor migration that—in spite of the event's investment in "making the world a better place for all loving families"—actually threaten to break apart other family and community formations. Furthermore, the project of increasing the visibility of respectable lesbian and gay parents who organize their lives around domesticity and consumption further marginalizes non-homonormative forms of queerness. Family Week assumes a traveler who can afford to vacation in Provincetown, whose family adheres to relatively normative kinship structures, and who wants to show their children where the Pilgrims landed. Unlike the locals and tourists who argue that Provincetown's reputation as a radical sexual playground with no rules (and great shopping) will be ruined by a surge in the number of parents traveling with children, I see the tourism imaginary surrounding Family Equality Council's annual celebration less as a disruption to business as usual and more as a slightly reconfigured continuation of current travel trends. Family Week invites lesbian and gay parents and their children to vacation where the exceptionalism of democracy in the United States becomes defined by the sexual tolerance and multicultural diversity imagined as inherent to Provincetown. Here, I would like to consider the ways in which Family Week has signaled (if not instigated) a shift in the gay tourism industry more broadly and to ask what the new trend tells us about the racial and class politics of U.S. lesbian and gay political culture.

As Jasbir Puar has documented, the appeal of the lesbian and gay niche market has generally focused on the flexibility these tourists are imagined to have with their time and money due to the absence of children. More recently, however, the industry has started targeting lesbians and gay men with children, offering gay family-friendly and gay-friendly family options and even designing family vacation packages.[18] Interestingly, while the lesbian and gay tourism market in the United States continues to be dominated by upwardly mobile white men, the growing number of lesbians with children has led to an increase in the visibility of women as tourists.[19] In addition to Family Week in Provincetown and Family Equality Council's other conference-vacations, it is becoming increasingly common for standard pride celebrations and other special events to designate areas for children and to incorporate family-centered activities.[20] Hotels and other venues catering to gay tourists in cities like Philadelphia and resort towns like Fort Lauderdale now hail lesbian and gay families,[21] and domestic tour operators have expanded their repertoires to offer trips for lesbians and gay men with children.[22] Many tour operators and travel agents credit Rosie O'Donnell with initiating the industry's decision to begin advertising lesbian and gay family packages.[23] Following the launch of her lesbian and gay family cruise company—an idea she apparently conjured up while enjoying Family Week with her children[24]—other cruise operators have followed R Family Vacations' lead and have entered the lesbian and gay family vacation business.[25] According to Harlan Godes, the owner of an upscale Los Angeles-based travel agency catering to the lesbian and gay community, "Family vacations will be the biggest change in [gay travel] in the next ten years."[26]

Gay tourism, in this light, ceases to summon up images of dangerous promiscuity or shameless perversity. By emphasizing "family fun" and a commitment to providing parents and children with a "safe environment," Family Equality Council sheds any association with hedonistic eroticism and, instead, signals a level of maturity, monogamy, and respectability not often connected to non-heteronormative forms of travel and consumption. Within the context of a family vacation, lesbians and gay men spend money not in an attempt to advance a perverse political agenda but, rather, in the name of bettering the lives of their children. Therefore, to increase the visibility of lesbian and gay families on vacation is to announce the end of the lesbian and gay community's unruly adolescence and its ascension into an adulthood invested in familial (and national) futurity. In other words, I view the expansion of Family Week as not simply a response to the growing number of parents within lesbian and gay communities but as a strategy for placing children at the center of lesbian and gay tourism-activism imaginaries. The tactical incorporation of children into the realm of lesbian and gay tourism further depoliticizes and desexualizes homonormative identities and thus advances the activist project of constructing lesbians and gay men as patriotic consumer-citizens deserving of rights and recognition.

In many respects, the arrival of lesbian and gay parents on the cape also aligns with the broader shifts happening in the local tourist economy. Provincetown continues to welcome non-homonormative subjects like bears, leather communities, and trans-identified people, but these groups now represent clearly recognizable and potentially lucrative market segments.[27] For the most part, however, the local tourism boards organize the lesbian and gay vacation experience around high-end boutique capitalism and, since the 2004 legalization of same-sex marriage in Massachusetts, the wedding and honeymoon industry.[28] Over the past 10 years, local elected officials and law enforcement officers have once again identified public sex as a primary concern and have reinvigorated concerted efforts to "clean up" Provincetown's gay scene.[29] Given the ways in which state practices of surveillance interpret gender and sexual deviance through structures of race and class,[30] it is possible to understand the intensified policing of parks and beaches and the increased number of arrests for disorderly conduct and public indecency as an attempt to secure the racialized and classed borders of lesbian and gay respectability. The tourism imaginary championed by the Chamber of Commerce, the Tourism Office, and Family Equality Council coalesces around an investment in slightly modified ideals of respectability and (white) middle-class modes of consumption.

Some locals and tourists, however, fear that attempts to revamp Provincetown's tourism profile are ruining the resort town. Three years ago, the Business Guild expressed their frustration with how the presence of children during Family Week transforms the atmosphere of Provincetown. Interestingly, while a story on the controversy in *The Provincetown Banner* elicited several comments from readers concerned with the destruction of a certain sexual scene,[31] the Business Guild was primarily worried about how a different demographic would hurt sales at boutiques, guesthouses, art galleries, and first-class restaurants. The presence of the child posed a threat to a tourism imaginary defined not by promiscuous encounters but by conspicuous consumption. Consequently, Jennifer Chrisler, the executive director of Family Equality Council, responded to the Business Guild's frustrations by making lesbian and gay families legible as consumers. The Chamber of Commerce confirms that toy stores, ice cream shops, whale-watching boats, and the Pilgrim Monument enjoy an increase in business when children are present, and Chrisler reminds other businesses that Family Week "gives a great introduction to Provincetown for a whole new generation" and should be understood as an investment that promises future returns.[32] The official tourism-activism imaginary produced during Family Week, like the competing imaginaries manufactured by the local tourism organizations, is arranged around consumer culture and indicates the homonormativization of lesbian and gay politics.

With that said, I am not sure that all of the families who participate in Family Week are necessarily looking for a sanitized version of queer culture or would support a crackdown on sexual deviance and the subsequent intensification of police surveillance. Perhaps some parents deliberately decide to schedule their family vacations at the center of what local law enforcement officers have called a "hotbed of public sex for randy exhibitionists."[33] Given the availability of babysitting services during Family Week,[34] it is quite plausible that some lesbian, gay, and queer tourists spend their days with their children and their nights dancing in the clubs or cruising well-known sites for anonymous sex. Some parents might actually take pleasure in exposing their children to a queer space that exceeds the limits of homonormativity, where children can chat with drag queens, encounter a range of gender presentations, and travel through a largely sex-positive environment. It is also possible that parents who are not necessarily seeking out opportunities to expose their children to alternative gender and sexual practices will do so anyway: several alleged incidents involving families who were whale watching or exploring the dunes when they stumbled upon naked men engaged in a variety of group sex acts have raised much anxiety about the safety of children vacationing on the cape.[35] Despite the presence of police and the threat of arrest, the Provincetown imagined as family destination does not exist discursively or materially apart from the Provincetown imagined as sexual playground.

So, while I remain critical of the ways in which Family Equality Council works with the tourism industry to uphold racist, colonialist, and imperialist capitalist structures and caters to an already privileged sector of lesbian and gay communities, I also contend that the multiple desires circulating within and through Provincetown might productively disrupt—if only for a moment—the homonormative imaginaries associated with family equality politics and the family vacation business. This chapter calls for a mode of queer cultural studies critique that refuses a blanket dismissal of all calls for inclusion and normalization and that, instead, illuminates the inconsistencies and ambivalences within U.S. homonormativities. For parents and children looking to create a queerer kind of family, Family Week might actually provide a site for imagining a more innovative, pro-sex family politics. And, if we assume that homonormative tourism-activism imaginaries always fall short in their approximation of (hetero)normativity, then we might also consider the unexpected and potentially transformative effects of those moments when Family Week inevitably fails to deliver properly wholesome family fun. The task of queer scholars and activists, I argue, is to identify and infiltrate the fissures within homonormativities in the hopes of fostering more radically imaginative modes of family formation and political engagement.

Notes

1 The Chamber of Commerce's website no longer features the slogan "Welcome to Provincetown: An Historic Town that Knows How to Have Fun" and, at the moment, displays the less wordy (but, in my opinion, less enticing) heading "Provincetown: Cape Cod's Most Popular Vacation Destination!"

2 The description of Provincetown cited here is no longer available on the Business Guild's main website but still appears on their Facebook page (http://www.facebook.com/ptownbizguild, accessed October 1, 2012).

3 In 1996, Tim Fisher, executive director of Gay and Lesbian Parents Coalition International (now known as Family Equality Council), and his partner Scott Davenport hosted an impromptu barbecue while vacationing in Provincetown. The following summer, the council replaced their annual conference with Family Week, a week-long conference-vacation in Provincetown. Fred A. Bernstein, "For Gay Parents, a Big Week in the Sun," *New York Times*, July 22, 2007.

4 Attendance rates at Family Week grew steadily for the first decade of the event. In 2002, over 400 families registered for Family Week, representing 31 states in the United States and four additional countries (Canada, China, France, and the United Kingdom). Noelle Howey, "Generations of Pride," *The Advocate*, June 10, 2003, p. 40. Recently, however, Family Equality Council has noticed a drop in attendance: numbers dipped from approximately 315 families in 2008 to 215 families in 2009. Although some blame the decrease on Provincetown's inadequacy as a family-friendly destination, Family Equality Council remains confident in the appeal of Family Week and attributes the decline in attendance to the weak economy. Pru Sowers, "Family Week Politics Minimized in Provincetown," *Provincetown Banner*, August 13, 2009.

5 Sowers, "Family Week Politics Minimized in Provincetown."

6 Jon Binnie's 1995 study of Amsterdam and London's Soho neighborhood is one of the first essays on the construction of gay tourist spaces and emerges alongside other cultural geography literature concerned with heteronormativity of sexualized spaces. "Trading Places: Consumption, Sexuality, and the Production of Queer Space," in David Bell and Gill Valentine (eds), *Mapping Desire: Geographies of Sexualities* (New York: Routledge, 1995), pp. 182–199. A few years later, Annette Pritchard et al. published an analysis of the touristification of gay spaces and the resulting "degaying" effect. "Reaching Out to the Gay Tourist: Opportunities and Threats in an Emerging Market Segment," *Tourism Management*, 19/3 (1998): 273–282. Howard L. Hughes began studying the connections between the function of tourism in gay identity formation in the late 1990s and recently published a monograph on how tourism marketing affects the everyday lives of lesbians and gay men. "Holidays and Homosexual Identity," *Tourism Management*, 18/1 (1997): 3–7; *Pink Tourism: Holidays of Gay Men and Lesbians* (Cambridge, MA: CABI, 2006). In 2002, Stephen Clift et al. edited the

first collection specifically focusing on lesbian and gay tourism and included several essays on sex, travel, and HIV prevention. *Gay Tourism: Culture, Identity, and Sex* (London: Continuum, 2002).

7 Gordon Wait and Kevin Markwell's book-length study of gay tourist practices is situated within the field of hospitality and tourism studies but makes a significant break from the tendencies I describe above. In an attempt to understand the place of recreational travel within Western gay cultures, Waitt and Markwell sketch a much broader history of travel and same-sex sexuality and begin to grapple with histories of colonialism and nationalism. Ultimately, however, their research offers only a cursory engagement within postcolonial and transnational studies and feminist and queer theory. *Gay Tourism: Culture and Context* (New York: Haworth Hospitality Press, 2006).

8 See M. Jacqui Alexander, *Pedagogies of Crossing: Mediations of Feminism, Sexual Politics, Memory and the Sacred* (Durham, NC: Duke University Press, 2005) pp. 21–89; Jasbir K. Puar, "Circuits of Queer Mobility: Tourism, Travel, and Globalization," *GLQ*, 8/1–2 (2002): 101–137; Jasbir K. Puar, "A Transnational Feminist Critique of Queer Tourism," *Antipode*, 34/5 (2002): 935–946. See also Inderpal Grewal and Caren Kaplan, "Global Identities: Theorizing Transnational Studies of Sexuality," *GLQ*, 7/4 (2001): 673–674.

9 Lisa Duggan, *The Twilight of Equality?: Neoliberalism, Cultural Politics, and the Attack on Democracy* (Boston, MA: Beacon Press, 2003), p. 50.

10 Karen C. Krahulik, *Provincetown: From Pilgrim Landing to Gay Resort* (New York: New York University Press, 2005), pp. 36–37. For more on the making of "New England" and its "colonial" past, see Dona Brown, *Inventing New England: Regional Tourism in the Nineteenth Century* (Washington, DC: Smithsonian Institution Press, 1995).

11 Provincetown Chamber of Commerce, *Provincetown: 2010 Visitor's Guide* (Provincetown, MA: Provincetown Chamber of Commerce, 2010), p. 3.

12 In his recent work on what he calls "queer settler colonialism," Scott Lauria Morgensen insists upon an understanding of U.S. homonormativities as conditioned by and complicit with white settler colonialism. Scott Lauria Morgensen, *Spaces between Us: Queer Settler Colonialism and Indigenous Decolonization* (Minneapolis, MN: University of Minnesota Press, 2011), pp. 26–27. Gay resort towns and gay-friendly cities are literally built upon stolen land, just as homonormative identities are built upon histories of sexual colonization. Thus, I argue that queer critiques of lesbian and gay tourism remain incomplete without addressing the ways in which leisure travel and other privileged forms of mobility have historically provided a route to settler citizenship for non-Native people in the United States.

13 Krahulik, *Provincetown*, pp. 46–47.

14 Provincetown Business Guild, *The Gay and Lesbian Guidebook* (Provincetown: Provincetown Business Guild, 1999), quoted in Krahulik, *Provincetown*, p. 45.

15 Krahulik, *Provincetown*, pp. 132–134. See also Sandra L. Faiman-Silvan, *The Courage to Connect: Sexuality, Citizenship, and Community in Provincetown* (Urbana, IL: University of Illinois Press, 2004). For more journalistic accounts of Provincetown's rich erotic history, see Michael Cunningham, *Land's End: A Walk in Provincetown* (New York: Crown Journeys, 2002); Peter Manso, *Ptown: Art, Sex, and Money on the Outer Cape* (New York: Scribner, 2002).

16 Susan E. Cayleff, "Review of *The Courage to Connect: Sexuality, Citizenship, and Community in Provincetown*," *Journal of the History of Sexuality*, 16/1 (2007): 118–119.

17 Mimi Sheller, "Demobilizing and Remobilizing Caribbean Paradise," in Mimi Sheller and John Urry (eds), *Tourism Mobilities: Places to Play, Places in Play* (New York: Routledge, 2004), p. 16.

18 In 1999, at the annual Gay and Lesbian World Travel Expo, tourism promoters were already talking about the possibility of running cruises for lesbians and gay men with children. Puar, "Circuits of Queer Mobility," p. 105. Two years later, the Third Annual

Gay and Lesbian Tourism Conference included a panel entitled the "Lesbian and Gay Family Market." Puar, "A Transnational Feminist Critique of Queer Tourism," p. 944n8.

19 According to representatives from Club Skirts Parties for Women and *Damron* travel guides, the rapid growth of lesbian families significantly altered the lesbian tourism industry during the late 1990s and early 2000s. Puar, "A Transnational Feminist Critique of Queer Tourism," p. 939.

20 San Francisco Pride, for instance, now includes a "Family Garden" area in order to provide a child-friendly space for families who wish to participate in the celebration. In 2007, a women's event promoter in South Florida launched "Gay Day Family," which involves three days of family-oriented activities connected to the annual "Gay Days" celebration at Disney World.

21 For example, Philadelphia's "Get Your History Straight and Your Nightlife Gay" campaign offers lesbian and gay parents the opportunity to balance child-friendly attractions during the day with adult-centered activities at night. Similarly, one of the many gay-owned guesthouses in Fort Lauderdale mobilized a fairly successful word-of-mouth campaign to gain recognition as "the family alternative for alternative families." L. Halden, "Gay Family Traveler," *OutTraveler*, June 27, 2007.

22 For example, Out West Adventures has recently offered family options, such as their "Yellowstone: The Classic Family Vacation" package (http://www.outwestadventures. com/). The tour operator Alyson Adventures established a separate division, Alyson Family Adventures, which offers a variety of vacation packages for lesbian and gay parents and their children, including a tour of the Galapagos Islands and a rafting trip in the Grand Canyon (http://www.alysonadventures.com/gay/gay_family.htm).

23 Halden, "Gay Family Traveler."

24 Ann Stockwell, "Ro, Ro, Ro Their Boat," *The Advocate*, March 28, 2006, p. 51.

25 Shortly after Rosie's first cruise, the "vacation planning expert" Cruise One offered tour groups for lesbian and gay families who wanted to vacation together but were comfortable doing so on a "straight" cruise. Over the past five years, Olivia Lesbian Travel has been more consistent in catering to families and has offered a number of cruise and resort packages for parents and their children.

26 Jamie Wetherbe, "Attracting 'Out' Travelers," *Travel Age West*, May 12, 2008.

27 Annual pride celebrations—like Bear Week, Fantasia Fair, Leather Weekend, and Women of Color and Allies Weekend—have resulted in newly identified tourist populations. These niches within a niche must be catered to, if not for the entire summer season, at least during the designated weeks and weekends.

28 The legalization of same-sex marriage boosted lesbian and gay tourism in Provincetown and, more broadly, Massachusetts. Same-sex marriage, as Nan Boyd documents, functions as a travel indicator and a tourist attraction. Nan Alamilla Boyd, "Sex and Tourism: The Economic Implications of the Gay Marriage Movement," *Radical History Review*, 100 (2008): 228. Provincetown capitalizes on the influx of couples traveling to Massachusetts to get married. According to town hall authorities, over 1,800 couples registered to marry in Provincetown between 2004 and 2007. Gary Lee, "For Gay Couples, Bonding in New England," *The Washington Post*, September 16, 2007, p. 6. Today, all three tourism organizations include information on their websites about getting married in Provincetown. Additionally, tourism in Massachusetts is also thought to benefit from the fact that an expansion of rights is read within the travel market as a measure of gay-friendliness.

29 Cayleff, "Review of *The Courage to Connect*," p. 119. Although the question of public sex and the policing of popular cruising sites have structured local Provincetown politics for the better part of the twentieth century, the last decade has been characterized by a decreased tolerance for street-based behavior and a dramatic increase in the number of citations for public sex. See, for example, Mary Ann Bragg, "Park Officials Target Sex in Dunes," *Cape Cod Times*, June 13, 2008; Katy Jordan, "Sex Acts on Provincetown Beaches Prompt Outrage," *Boston Herald*, July 8, 2008. It is

not particularly surprising that an expansion of lesbian and gay rights on some fronts (such as the decriminalization of sodomy, the legalization of marriage in some states, and the repeal of "Don't Ask, Don't Tell") would incite a racist and classist backlash against forms of queerness that cannot be easily normalized.

30 In her analysis of race, gender, and state violence, Joy James writes, "some bodies appear more docile than others because of their conformity in appearance to idealized models of class, color, and sex; their bodies are allowed greater leeway to be self-policed or policed without physical force." Joy James, *Resisting State Violence: Radicalism, Gender, and Race in US Culture* (Minneapolis, MN: University of Minnesota Press, 1996), p. 26. For an insightful discussion on how racialized state surveillance practices target gender-nonconforming bodies, see Toby Beauchamp, "Artful Concealment and Strategic Visibility: Transgender Bodies and US State Surveillance after 9/11," *Surveillance & Society*, 6/4 (2009): 356–366.

31 For instance, one commenter expressed his anger with what he perceived to be the Chamber of Commerce's and the Tourism Office's attempt to "CHANGE [Provincetown] to make it the way they want [it] to be." Kids, he argues, "are not wanted in a WILD GAY PARTY TOWN": "Who the heck wants MORE STROLLERS on the sidewalk, KIDS making noise in nice restaurants, who wants to tuck in [a] bulge, put on a shirt, watch your language, [and] be appropriate in front of the kids[?]" Pru Sowers, "Shop Owners Grouse about Family Week," *Provincetown Banner*, August 9, 2008.

32 Sowers, "Shop Owners Grouse about Family Week."

33 Jordan, "Sex Acts on Provincetown Beaches Prompt Outrage."

34 On the "Family Week FAQS" website, Family Equality Council offers to put parents looking for babysitting services in touch with teens who are interested in "mak[ing] some money" while vacationing with their own lesbian and gay families (http://www.familyequality.org/get_involved/events/family_week/family_week_faqs/>, accessed October 1, 2012).

35 Bragg, "Park Officials Target Sex in Dunes."

Bibliography

ALEXANDER, M. Jacqui, *Pedagogies of Crossing: Mediations of Feminism, Sexual Politics, Memory and the Sacred* (Durham, NC: Duke University Press, 2005).

BEAUCHAMP, Toby, "Artful Concealment and Strategic Visibility: Transgender Bodies and US State Surveillance after 9/11," *Surveillance & Society*, 6/4 (2009): 356–366.

BERNSTEIN, Fred A., "For Gay Parents, a Big Week in the Sun," *The New York Times*, July 22, 2007, http://travel.nytimes.com/2007/07/22/travel/22journeys.html (accessed 2013).

BINNIE, Jon, "Trading Places: Consumption, Sexuality, and the Production of Queer Space," in David BELL and Gill VALENTINE (eds), *Mapping Desire: Geographies of Sexualities* (New York: Routledge, 1995), pp. 182–199.

BOYD, Nan Alamilla, "Sex and Tourism: The Economic Implications of the Gay Marriage Movement," *Radical History Review*, 100 (2008): 223–247.

BRAGG, Mary Ann, "Park Officials Target Sex in Dunes," *Cape Cod Times*, June 13, 2008, http://www.capecodonline.com/apps/pbcs.dll/article?AID=/20080613/NEWS/806130 324 (accessed February 14, 2011).

BROWN, Dona, *Inventing New England: Regional Tourism in the Nineteenth Century* (Washington, DC: Smithsonian Institution Press, 1995).

CAYLEFF, Susan E., "Review of *The Courage to Connect: Sexuality, Citizenship, and Community in Provincetown*, by Sandra L. Faiman-Silva," *Journal of the History of Sexuality*, 16/1 (2007): 114–120.

CLIFT, Stephen, Michael LUONGO, and Carrie CALLISTER, eds, *Gay Tourism: Culture, Identity, and Sex* (London: Continuum, 2002).

CUNNINGHAM, Michael, *Land's End: A Walk in Provincetown* (New York: Crown Journeys, 2002).

DUGGAN, Lisa, *The Twilight of Equality?: Neoliberalism, Cultural Politics, and the Attack on Democracy* (Boston, MA: Beacon Press, 2003).

FAIMAN-SILVAN, Sandra L., *The Courage to Connect: Sexuality, Citizenship, and Community in Provincetown* (Urbana, IL: University of Illinois Press, 2004).

Family Equality Council, "Family Week," 2012, http://www.familyequality.org/get_ involved/ events/family_week (accessed October 1, 2012).

GREWAL, Inderpal and Caren KAPLAN, "Global Identities: Theorizing Transnational Studies of Sexuality," *GLQ: A Journal of Lesbian and Gay Studies*, 7/4 (2001): 663–679.

HALDEN, L., "Gay Family Traveler," *OutTraveler*, June 27, 2007, http://www.outtra veler.com/ exclusives_ detail.asp?did=596 (accessed January 30, 2011).

HOWEY, Noelle, "Generations of Pride," *The Advocate*, June 10, 2003, p. 40.

HUGHES, Howard L., "Holidays and Homosexual Identity," *Tourism Management*, 18/1 (1997): 3–7.

——, *Pink Tourism: Holidays of Gay Men and Lesbians* (Cambridge, MA: CABI, 2006).

JAMES, Joy, *Resisting State Violence: Radicalism, Gender, and Race in US Culture* (Minneapolis, MN: University of Minnesota Press, 1996).

JORDAN, Katy, "Sex Acts on Provincetown Beaches Prompt Outrage," *Boston Herald*, July 8, 2008, http://www.bostonherald.com/news/regional/general/view. bg?articleid=1105329 &srvc=rs (accessed January 30, 2011).

KRAHULIK, Karen C., *Provincetown: From Pilgrim Landing to Gay Resort* (New York: New York University Press, 2005).

LEE, Gary, "For Gay Couples, Bonding in New England," *The Washington Post*, September 16, 2007, p. 6.

MANSO, Peter, *Ptown: Art, Sex, and Money on the Outer Cape* (New York: Scribner, 2002).

MORGENSEN, Scott Lauria, *Spaces between Us: Queer Settler Colonialism and Indigenous Decolonization* (Minneapolis, MN: University of Minnesota Press, 2011).

PRITCHARD, Annette, Nigel J. MORGAN, Diane SEDGELY, and Andrew JENKINS, "Reaching Out to the Gay Tourist: Opportunities and Threats in an Emerging Market Segment," *Tourism Management*, 19/3 (1998): 273–282.

Provincetown Business Guild, *The Gay and Lesbian Guide Book to Provincetown* (Provincetown, MA: Provincetown Business Guild, 1999).

——, "Welcome to Provincetown: Where Gay Life Is Everywhere," 2011, http://ptown. org (accessed March 8, 2011).

Provincetown Chamber of Commerce, *Provincetown: 2010 Visitor's Guide* (Provincetown, MA: Provincetown Chamber of Commerce, 2010), http://www.ptownchamber.com/ wp-uploads/p-chamber-2010guide.pdf (accessed February 2, 2011).

——, "Welcome to Provincetown: An Historic Town that Knows How to Have Fun," 2011, http://ptownchamber.com (accessed February 2, 2011).

PUAR, Jasbir K., "A Transnational Feminist Critique of Queer Tourism," *Antipode*, 34/5 (2002): 935–946.

——, "Circuits of Queer Mobility: Tourism, Travel, and Globalization," *GLQ: A Journal of Lesbian and Gay Studies*, 8/1–2 (2002): 101–137.

SHELLER, Mimi, "Demobilizing and Remobilizing Caribbean Paradise," in Mimi SHELLER and John URRY (eds), *Tourism Mobilities: Places to Play, Places in Play* (New York: Routledge, 2004), pp. 13–21.

SOWERS, Pru, "Shop Owners Grouse about Family Week," *Provincetown Banner*, August 9, 2008, http://www.wickedlocal.com/capecod/news/business/x1005608948/Shop-owners-grouse-about-Family-Week (accessed January 30, 2011).

——, "Family Week Politics Minimized in Provincetown," *Provincetown Banner*, August 13, 2009, http://www.wickedlocal.com/provincetown/news/business/x159136 5648/ Family-Week-politics-minimized-in-Provincetown#axzz1JVUprWa1 (accessed April 1, 2011).

STOCKWELL, Ann, "Ro, Ro, Ro Their Boat," *The Advocate*, March 28, 2006, pp. 51–57.

Tourism Office and Visitor Services Board, "Provincetown: Like Nowhere Else," 2011, http://www.provincetowntourismoffice.org (accessed March 8, 2011).

WAITT, Gordon and Kevin MARKWELL, *Gay Tourism: Culture and Context* (New York: Haworth Hospitality Press, 2006).

WETHERBE, Jamie, "Attracting 'Out' Travelers," *Travel Age West*, May 12, 2008, http://www.travelagewest.com/Tools/Travel-Articles/Attracting--Out--Travelers/ (accessed January 20, 2011).

Part III

Media and Imaginaries, Reflexivity and Performativity

Madina Regnault

Since the temporality of imaginaries is an issue throughout this book, we could not conceptualize tourism imaginary without situating it in the "*longue durée*" of the French historian Fernand Braudel (1958). Since the mid-1950s, Braudel has stressed the need for historians to look beyond social time or "*l'histoire événementielle*" (the history of events) in order to embrace "*la longue durée*," the slower-moving structures and cycles of centuries. Mental representations evolve through these cycles. Georges Duby (1975; 1978), who was also part of the second generation of French historians of the Ecole des Annales, defined the term "*imaginaire*," which he preferred over "*mentalités*," as "the structural, ideational images that societies create" (1975). Jacques Le Goff also used "*l'imaginaire*," which does not have the same signification as "imaginary." In *L'Imaginaire médiéval* (1985), he refers more to "imagination," which included explorations of time and the history of dreams and dreaming. These initial approaches to imaginaries show us how the concept changed over time but also in space, especially because of the dialogues between disciplines in the humanities. One of the transdisciplinary pioneer works that help us to understand how ritual and symbolism are not personal but collective representations, built on socio-political context, is the famous book *The Invention of Tradition*, edited by Eric Hobsbawm and Terence Ranger (1983), which demonstrated that many "traditions" are, in fact, recent inventions. We could think, for instance, of the so-called "traditional" Sirtaki dance that tourists want to see when they visit Greece: it was actually invented in 1964 for the movie "Zorba the Greek."

In this context, tourism imaginary is seen as a moving process engaging various actors. Tourism imaginaries exist because of storytellers and the combination of all types of media through which the stories travel. With mass media, tourism imaginaries are spreading faster and faster, and all over the world. With the explosion of new kinds of social networks, everyone takes part in this production of tourism imaginaries. New types of imaginaries emerge, constructed by new generations of tourists who are more revealing of their journeys and who are also constantly looking for something different to the experiences of older generations of tourists. Based on the notions of the "reflexivity" and "performativity" of tourism imaginaries, the various contributions in this third part of the volume illustrate how the narratives of tourism imaginaries evolve over time. The experienced, sensed, and collectively imagined forms of tourism are displayed through the circulation of texts, images, and a large variety of other data, providing the readers of this volume with numerous possibilities of "terrains" (fields of research).

Bibliography

Braudel, Fernand (1958) "La longue durée." *Annales* 13(4): 725–753.
Duby, Georges (1975) "Histoire, société, imaginaire." *Dialectiques* 10–11: 111–123.
—— (1978) *Les trois ordres ou l'imaginaire du féodalisme.* Paris: Gallimard.
Hobsbawm, Eric and Terence Ranger (1983) *The Invention of Tradition.* Cambridge: Cambridge University Press.
Le Goff, Jacques (1985) *L'Imaginaire médiéval.* Paris: Gallimard.

11 The Marvel of Tropical Waters

The Invention of an Imaginary at the Pace of Technological Advances

Luc Vacher

Introduction

If we reflect on the conditions for the emergence of a tourism imaginary, our thoughts immediately turn to changes in perceptions, the importance of representations, and even the role of tourism marketing, but we rarely tackle the question by taking account of the technical conditions necessary to the creation of this imaginary. It is this dimension which we hope to focus on by means of this chapter on the touristic invention of tropical waters.

In a previous research work (Vacher 2012), we identified three major inventions necessary to the recognition of these tropical waters as an object of desire, namely their delightful warmth, the spellbinding colors of lagoons, and the incomparable richness of the aquatic fauna of coral reefs. We considered the way bathers switched from therapeutic bathing to leisure bathing at the end of the nineteenth century, how, with the development of beach games and swimming, areas to practice these activities moved from the Channel coast to the Atlantic coast in France, and the way that, at the dawn of the twentieth century, Jack London hailed the warmth of the tropical waters of Hawaii as being particularly conducive to the practice of water sports such as surfing. We then saw that as of the 1920s, summer bathing in warm water no longer appeared inappropriate and that from Florida to the French Riviera, a whole host of new summer activities sprang up. This was also the inception of dreams of vacations on tropical shorelines where the water is warm all year round.

In the same research we also gave a rapid overview of the invention of the water's color and the transformation of coral reefs from navigation hazards to symbols of nature threatened by climate disturbance. But we did not elucidate the technological conditions which can play a major part in these discoveries.

How did the turquoise waters dotted with corals and multicolored fish, which are now plastered across the covers of travel agency brochures promoting the merits of insular tropical destinations, find their way into our imaginaries? When, how, and where were they invented? What are the technical conditions making it possible to perceive them and subsequently show them?

We will tackle the questions from three angles. Firstly we will shed light on this notion of tropical water, what precisely do we mean? Then we will turn to the conditions which enabled the color of the lagoon to be perceived, before finally focusing on those having associated it with marvels of marine life.

Tropical Waters? What Are We Talking About?

What do we mean when we talk about tropical waters? Of course, we are not talking about a reality encompassing the distribution of masses of water on the surface of the planet. Similarly, we are not merely in an image-based reality since as Amirou reminds us (1995: 32): "Touristic images are not restricted to those incarnated in iconographic, artistic and advertising production; they extend to the universe of mental images, if not that of myths." We are therefore examining tropical waters as a cultural construct calling on representations and practices.

- Does it therefore represent a touristic realism with a space dimension, a sort of geotype or geo-semantics field? In terms of questioning of touristic imaginaries, we examine the stereotypical character which would make it possible to divide up today's world entirely given over to tourism into big blocks. Jean-François Staszak, in his consideration of exoticism, provides answers to these questions with the notion of the geo-semantics field which is "comprised firstly of a geographic space, considered as coherent, vast and fairly distant, and secondly a fairly uniform series of specific stereotypes which contribute to its definition and possibly its appeal" (Staszak 2008: 20). But as much by the scale as by the importance of cultural interrelations in the definition of these fields, this notion is not particularly suited to our message. Jacques Lévy's notion of a geotype as a "complex spatial arrangement, the composition of several chorotypes" (Lévy and Lussault 2003) is more neutral, Lévy viewing the chorotype as an elementary spatial arrangement comprising a scale, a metric, and a substance. But here again the value of identifying a tropical coastal destination as a geotype and tropical waters as chorotype is undoubtedly limited. Over and above demonstrating the existence of tropical waters in a tourism typology which would bear out its importance in relation to another imaginary form, we will note that its registration is part of the tourism realities/imaginaries with outlines which vary depending on whether we are talking about the "tropical banks and islands" of Dehorne and Saffache (2008), the "pleasure periphery" of Turner and Ash (1975), the "tropical dream" of Löfgren (1999), or the "tropical insular worlds" of Auvray (2009).
- So how did we identify these tropical waters? It was not a question of seeking a biogeographical or ecosystem-related reality since the waters we are concerned with are a reality of the touristic imaginary. They had to be defined by a touristic communication and usage.

Running a query through a search engine such as Google shows that these tropical waters are an omnipresent component with the tropical palms and the tropical beach of the "tropical destination." These tropical waters are systematically the transparent waters of the lagoon on a tropical island or those lapping a (white) sand coral beach.

It therefore seems important for the tropical seashore destination to offer white sand, transparent water, and abundant fauna, elements which are all associated with the presence of a coral reef in a tropical zone. The presence of these reefs which only truly thrive in clear water implies another condition for touristic tropical waters: they must be warm in every season. The optimum water temperature is 26–27°C (79–81°F) and few corals exist in reefs with a water temperature which drops below 18°C (64°F).

The map of tropical waters (see Figure 11.1 in the color plate section) is therefore easy to draw up. It is simply a question of taking a water temperature map according to seasons defining a zone where the reading does not fall below 24°C all year round and then adding in the distribution of coral reefs. The major tropical seashore zones which are well known show up immediately.

The Color of Turquoise Blue in Tropical Waters

Before expanding on this aspect in greater detail, we should point out that this presentation corresponds to a snap-shot of the current state of our research into tourism practices. It is likely that the literary or cinematographic landmarks which offer us points of reference in time will be supplemented in the future.

How and when was the "paradisiacal" color of tropical waters invented? To invent it, it has to be pronounced. It is by saying it that it will start to exist and it constitutes a recent invention in travel writing. There is no description of a turquoise lagoon in the travel logs of James Cook (1768–1779) or Bougainville (1768). Nor do writers such as Jacques-Henri Bernardin de Saint-Pierre in *Paul and Virginia* (1788) or Pierre Loti in *The Marriage of Loti* (1879) dwell on the color of the tropical waters of Mauritius or Tahiti, both preferring instead to tell tales of exotic love at the foot of refreshing waterfalls amid a profusion of vegetation (see Figure 11.2 in the color plate section). The same goes for Mark Twain whose *Roughing It* (1872) recounted his travels in Hawaii in the 1870s.

If we examine the palette of words deployed by an author like Pierre Loti in 1879 when describing Polynesia in *The Marriage of Loti*, it can be seen that the most commonly used tonalities are black and white, followed by blue, red and pink, accompanied by green and yellow. Blue is therefore the most frequently used color, although it only features three times to describe the waters of the lagoon (a word he never uses) and, in remarkably uninspiring ways, "blues which are unpaintable," or "lukewarm, blue water," and "the dark blue sea, crashed onto a beach of broken snow-white coral"; formulations which in no way allow the reader to imagine the turquoise color which would become the sign of touristic recognition of tropical waters. The only time he writes of the color "of turquoise" is in describing the color of a lizard or a gecko. The color of the lagoon simply passed unnoticed.

This lack of attention paid to the colors of the lagoon can only accord more importance to the description of the Englishwoman Isabelle Bird, an intrepid traveler who as early as 1875 was one of the first to write in the following terms: "the sea is blue with the calm, pure blue of turquoise, but crystalline in its purity" in a travelogue on *The Hawaiian Archipelago*. But it is the writings of Jack London, published in the American press, concerning his various travels in the Pacific between 1907 and 1915, which were to impose the description in colors of tropical waters and enable Waikiki to become one of the benchmark locations in the history of tourism. In 1908, London was on the Hawaiian beach of Waikiki, from where he conjured up this color-based perspective of the aquatic richness of the islands:

> As I write these lines I lift my eyes and look seaward. I am on the beach of Waikiki on the island of Oahu. Far, in the azure sky, the trade-wind clouds drift low over the blue-green turquoise of the deep sea. Nearer, the sea is emerald and light olive-green. Then comes the reef, where the water is all slaty purple flecked with red. Still nearer are brighter greens and tans, lying in alternate stripes and showing where sandbeds lie between the living coral banks. (London 1908: 64)

In the same year of 1908, Henry De Vere Stacpoole, an Irishman who had sailed the Pacific as a physician in the merchant navy, published the emblematic *The Blue Lagoon* a novel describing the travails of two young shipwreck survivors on a southern Pacific island lapped by waters which were "calm, almost as a lake, sapphire here, and here with the tints of the aquamarine." He does not deploy the term turquoise like London but instead writes of the "blue of heaven." The Fiji Islands which served as the backdrop therefore appear almost simultaneously with Hawaii on the map of paradisiacal waters (see Figure 11.2 in the color plate section).

Although writers made no reference to the lagoon's color before the early twentieth century, in a somewhat surprising manner painters followed the same approach. Eighteenth-century artists such as the Englishman William Hodges, who in 1773 painted Tahiti during James Cook's second voyage, called on a palette of hues used for the landscapes and lighting of Europe. Had things changed one century later? If we take a painter like Gauguin who stayed in Tahiti as of 1891 and whose palette was decidedly more colorful than the accounts of Loti, it can be seen that he took little interest in the sea in his paintings of Tahiti (1891–1893, then 1895–1901) and the Marquesas (1901–1903). His art frequently depicts Polynesians bathing but generally in streams. Sea water, when it is shown, is most often consigned to the background. Moreover, blue hues only have an extremely discreet presence in his paintings compared to the

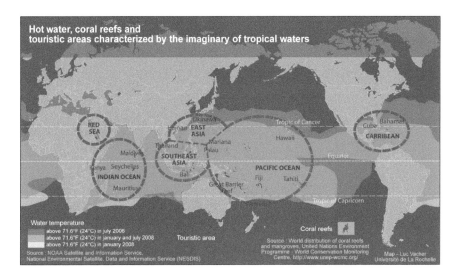

Figure 11.1 Hot water, coral reefs and touristic areas characterized by the imaginary of tropical waters

Fifty most used words clouds* in three «tropical» novels

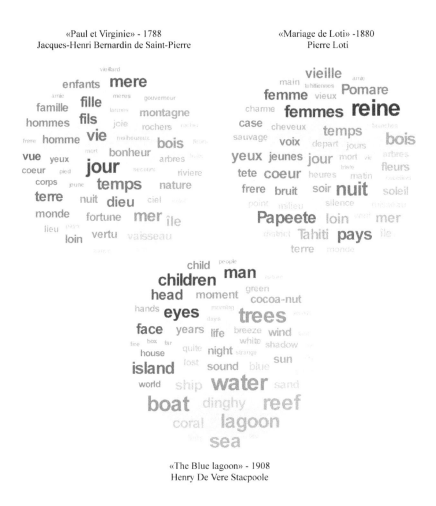

«Paul et Virginie» - 1788
Jacques-Henri Bernardin de Saint-Pierre

«Mariage de Loti» -1880
Pierre Loti

«The Blue lagoon» - 1908
Henry De Vere Stacpoole

* Nouns, place names and character names
if historical figures. Size depending on the frequency

Tag clouds designed by Luc Vacher
with TagCrowd, http://tagcrowd.com/

Figure 11.2 Word clouds for 50 most used words in three "tropical" novels

Chromatic analysis of four Paul Gauguin paintings

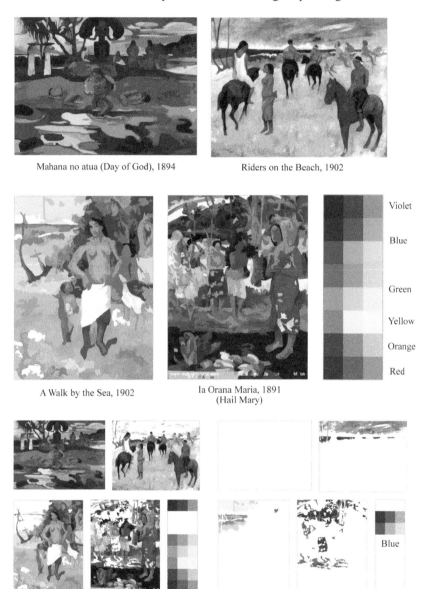

Mahana no atua (Day of God), 1894

Riders on the Beach, 1902

Violet

Blue

Green

Yellow

Orange

Red

A Walk by the Sea, 1902

Ia Orana Maria, 1891
(Hail Mary)

Blue

Figure 11.3 Chromatic analysis of four Paul Gauguin paintings

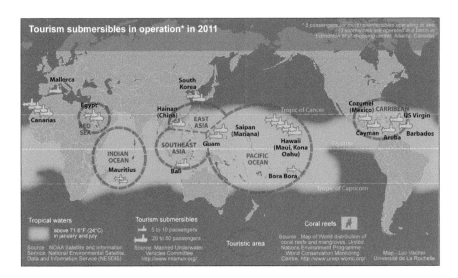

Figure 11.4 Tourism submersibles in operation in 2011

exuberance of his palette. If we examine the role of colors in the few canvases on which he depicts the sea, this aspect is striking (see Figure 11.3 in the color plate section).

However, as explained by Michel Pastoureau (2002), the pigments enabling transcription of aquatic transparencies became readily available with the invention of Prussian blue which was marketed as of the eighteenth century and enabled transparent shading in painting from blue to green.

Although Gauguin did not represent the blues of the lagoon, postcards which began circulating in the late nineteenth and especially the early twentieth centuries brought little progress. These were produced in black and white and even when colored, in general by hand, those depicting lagoons via the faded blue inks are few and far between. The first tourism posters were no more sensitive to turquoise colors which were hard to reproduce on the printer's press. In the first half of the twentieth century, they promoted the luxury of cruises to Hawaii or the elegance of Cuban casinos. The current plethora of replica vintage posters designed by contemporary artists using the graphic codes of the 1920s–1930s but late twentieth-century colors should not blind us to this fact. This provides an opportunity to pay tribute to the talented Californian painter Kerne Erickson who, for the past 10 years, has been a prolific contributor to the market for vintage posters with "between the wars" creations which end up being more common than real ones.

It was not until the appearance of phthalocyanines, pigments originating from the petrochemicals sector introduced to industry in 1938, that printers were able to reproduce lighter blues. But color printing remained a luxury which was not particularly accessible in the 1930s, the first color photo in *Vogue* magazine dating from 1932 (Lemagny and Rouillé 1998). The offset process would not trigger the rise of color printing until the 1950s–1960s.

In fact, the transparency of turquoise lagoons would first be rendered thanks to light rather than pigments. Photographic technologies which would make it possible to popularize color appeared just before World War Two. Kodachrome color films in the United States and Agfacolor in Germany, giving rise to slides and filming in color, were first marketed in 1936. It was on the silver screen that the switch from black and white to color changed the perception of the tropical environment. This can be illustrated by the images presenting Polynesia in two versions of the movie *Mutiny on the Bounty*. In the 1935 movie directed by Frank Lloyd and starring Clarke Gable, the symbolic paradisiacal nature of the South Seas is conveyed by visual codes compatible with black and white, such as the outline of the coconut tree. The 1962 Technicolor remake by Lewis Milestone with Marlon Brando was able to display the transparency and color of tropical waters. This lagoon water would then become for most an essential part of the paradisiacal dimension of the South Seas.

Since then, turquoise blue has colored the bottoms of swimming pools. Harry's New York Bar in Paris claims it was first to create the Blue Lagoon cocktail in 1960 while the Obao Company came up with a turquoise bubble bath in 1963.

The blue of the South Seas became a regular feature of the covers of most travel agencies' catalogues which benefited from the transparency of glossy paper as of the 1970s, when hotel islands first emerged coupled with improved accessibility to the main tropical destinations thanks to falling air fares.

The turquoise color of tropical lagoon waters therefore added to the panoply of the imaginary of the South Seas primarily as of the 1950s and became a key feature of the dream-holiday decor.

The Amazing Richness of Tropical Waters

After discovering the color of lagoons, how was its wonderful fauna invented?

As of the eighteenth century, it was widely realized that tropical seas hosted creatures of extraordinary color and shape. In the second half of the eighteenth century, the *Encyclopedia* of Diderot and D'Alembert presented engravings of corals found in the curiosity cabinets of naturalist scientists. A century later, when Isabella Bird, stayed in Hawaii (1875), she noticed the numerous expat "residents" who owned "cabinets" of minerals, volcanic specimens, shells, and coral alongside collections of arms and other indigenous ornaments. At the market in Honolulu she came across local fisherman willing to sell her magnificent pieces of coral although these had been collected from the reef rather than being the fruit of professional divers. Note that these divers were at work in the late nineteenth century but only in small numbers. They were often Malay and Japanese and fished for mother-of-pearl and pearls in different corners of the world. Their short life expectancy reminds us that, at the time, diving was not a leisure pursuit to contemplate the beauty of the ocean depths but rather a high-risk profession.

In fact, before the early twentieth century, tropical waters were primarily known for the hazards relating to their reefs (Vacher 2008). The descriptions of travelers mainly focused on the danger they represented. In 1836, Charles Darwin, who was one of the first to favor in situ examination of the corals in the lagoon of the Coco Island (Keeling), sailed clear of the treacherous atolls of the Dangerous Isles (Tuamotu). In Tahiti, he marveled not at the color of the lagoon but the contrast between the ocean's choppy water and the mirror-like surface of the veritable "lake" formed behind the reef. Even the redoubtable Captain Nemo, brought to life by Jules Vernes in *20,000 Leagues under the Sea* in 1869, described approaching "the dangerous shores of the coral sea, . . . I had wished to visit the reef, 360 leagues long, against which the sea, always rough, broke with great violence, with a noise like thunder," but he ended up giving them a wide berth.

The desire to contemplate an exceptional environment in situ was considered more important than the value of the specimens of collections after the scientific expedition to Australia's Great Barrier Reef by the British Museum in 1928–1929. Scientists of this era celebrated the discovery of the Great Barrier

Reef as a remarkable monument of nature and alerted the world to the richness of the coral ecosystem. In 1934, the Queensland Government Tourist Bureau in Australia published a *Great Barrier Reef Booklet* which primarily describes the reef as a paradise for fishing while stressing that it is a magnificent site for those who want "to study" the reef. However, the Great Barrier Reef only occupied a secondary role faced with the extraordinary Atherton tablelands waterfalls nearby. It is important to note that images of the underwater world were still thin on the ground at the time.

The first underwater photographs date from the 1920s with *National Geographic* publishing its first underwater photo of a fish taken off the coast of Florida in 1926. Tourists immediately flocked to witness these marvels unveiled by scientists as illustrated by the posters of the Queensland Government Tourist Bureau printed in 1933.

However, methods for observing the underwater environment remained limited. The aquascope, a tube with a glass bottom or the cumbersome diving suit with helmet which Hergé had his characters still using in *The Secret of the Unicorn* in 1944, only permitted arduous exploration of the marine environment.

World War Two played a major role in advancing discovery of the ocean's depths. In the early 1940s, the "Aqualung," the autonomous diving suit enabling users to swim under water without being attached to the surface as was the case with the standard diving suit, was developed by Jacques Yves Cousteau and Emile Gagnan. This revolutionary equipment for underwater exploration soon gained popularity around the world.

The first films on the underwater world were released during World War Two. In 1942, the Austrian diver Hans Hass, presented a film (in black and white) shot on the coral reefs of Curaçao off the coast of Venezuela. It shows the heroic diver repelling sharks with pikes in a scene worthy of Jules Vernes. The sea remained an intimidating environment full of danger. One year later came the release of *Eighteen Meters Deep*, the first film by Cousteau, but the vision of the ocean depths only really changed as of the 1950s.

The success of the film *The Silent World* by Jacques-Yves Cousteau and Louis Malle was another major landmark: shot in the Mediterranean, the Red Sea, and the Indian Ocean, it won the Palme d'or at Cannes in 1956 and the Oscar for best documentary in 1957. The film marked a major break with the public's perception of the underwater world. The imagery of sea monsters gave way to a new world where underwater torch light finally revealed the colors.

In the late 1950s and early 1960s, diving with air bottles began to take hold and national federations were set up. Training courses for divers and monitors were introduced. In 1965, underwater diving became a tourism activity in its own right with the opening of the Freeport City in the Bahamas, the first tourism complex specialized in diving.

Today, the world of the Caribbean is central to this kind of tourism which remains inaccessible for many tourists due to the cost, training, or, quite simply, apprehension. Swimming with a mask and snorkel slowly developed after World War Two as increasing numbers learned to swim in those societies enjoying access to tourism, although many remained reluctant to take to the water.

This is why tourism companies operating in tropical destinations endeavored to meet the demand of tourists with no particular penchant for diving but who were keen to contemplate the marvels of nature—fauna from reefs which in the 1970s acquired the status of a threatened splendor to be seen "Before nature dies" as Jean Dorst put it in 1965. Today, the tourism value of coral reefs, the temple of biodiversity, teetering on the edge of an imminent demise due to global warming, is at its height.

Glass-bottomed boats were no doubt first used in California at the turn of the last century to view fish around the island of Santa Catalina. They have since become essential to all tourism sites lapped by tropical waters. Underwater observatory systems or giant aquariums generally supplement the offering for tourists along the coastlines in question.

The first semi-submersibles, boats disguised as submarines allowing people to look out of portholes dotted along the sides of the hull, no doubt first appeared in the 1930s to view the freshwater site of Rainbow Springs in Florida. In 1983, the first semi-submersible was placed in operation along the Great Barrier Reef by Doug Tarca. It met with immediate success and in the late 1980s became standard equipment for major tourism sites.

The semi-submersible did not pose the problem which can easily be imagined for a real submarine; however, the idea of a tourism submarine which came into being on Lac Léman, during the Swiss National Expo in 1964–1965, became an albeit discreet reality in the 1980s. The first tourism submarines able to hold over 20 people in sea environments were the series of Atlantis submarines, the first of which began operations in 1983 in Grand Cayman, a British overseas territory to the south of Cuba (CAPSS 1990). Since that time, 15 or so major tourism submarines have operated in the world (see Figure 11.4 in the color plate section). Naturally, questions of safety and respect for the environment mean that it is often easier to maneuver this type of vessel around a wreck than close to a fragile coral reef.

However, it is worth asking whether these tourism activities, like diving with new underwater helmets, snuba[1], scuba doo,[2] and such like are not in actual fact all about obtaining an image (photo) of yourself in extreme and therefore flattering conditions. On the Great Barrier Reef, the preparations and supervision of participants in this short adventure to obtain the much sought-after snap are not particularly compatible with peaceful observation of the beauties of the marine world. This no doubt represents another type of tourism experience focused more on the dream of technology than the dream of nature.

Conclusion

To conclude, it can be seen that there undoubtedly exists a certain mismatch between the geography of the imaginary of tropical waters and that of tourism activities in these waters. The Pacific islands have a central place in their invention; the Caribbean has been and still is the testing ground for multiple tourism experimentations. But the logic of embracing tourism meant that, as of the 1970s and the rise of hotel islands, the Indian Ocean came to strongly embody the activities enjoyed in paradisiacal tropical waters. The growing popularity of tourism under the tropics then put Southeast Asia and, in particular, Thailand and Bali on the map for these tourism activities, whereas in southern China hybrid imaginaries are emerging in places like Hainan, mixing the codes to offer a new interpretation of tropical environments.

This mismatch between the space of images and the space of activities is also related to the accessibility of sites. Here we are thinking of the cost and time of transport but also technical conditions for access. The Great Barrier Reef in Australia only truly came into its own with the introduction, in the 1980s, of large, high-speed catamarans which can reach it in a few hours. The reduction in access time also perhaps justifies the creation of reefs with glass bottoms in a shopping mall such as the Dubai Mall in the United Arab Emirates, so helping to change the map of tropical waters and regenerating its imaginary by means of a spectacle which offers the sheer awe of the shark show while flagging the fragility of the emblematic sea turtle.

Notes

1 Lightweight diving equipment bringing air from the surface, as opposed to bottled supplies.
2 Underwater "scooter" with diver's head enclosed in air space supplied from a compressor on the surface.

Bibliography

AMIROU Rachid, *Imaginaire touristique et sociabilités du voyage*, Paris, Presses Universitaires de France, 1995.
AUVRAY Bénédicte, *Entre ailleurs et nulle part: la fiction de l'enclave touristique*, Hyper Article en Ligne—Sciences de l'Homme et de la Société (HAL-SHS), 2009, [Online, May 12, 2010], http://halshs.archives-ouvertes.fr/halshs-00483021.
BERNARDIN DE SAINT PIERRE Henri, *Paul et Virginie*, Paris, Imprimerie de Monsieur, 1789.
BIRD Isabella L., *The Hawaiian Archipelago: Six Months among the Palm Groves, Coral Reefs, and Volcanoes of the Sandwich Islands*, London, John Murray, 1875.
COËFFÉ Vincent, "La plage, fabrique d'une touristi(cité) idéale," *L'information géographique*, 3 (2010): 51–68.
Committee on Assessing Passenger Submersible Safety (CAPSS), National Research Council, *Safety of Tourist Submersibles*, Washington, National Academy Press, 1990.

DEHOORNE Olivier and SAFFACHE Pascal, "Le tourisme dans les îles et littoraux tropi-
    caux: ressources et enjeux de développement," *Études caribéennes*, 9–10 (2008), *Le
    tourisme dans les îles et littoraux tropicaux et subtropicaux*, [Online, September 8,
    2008], http://etudescaribeennes.revues.org/852.
DORST Jean, *Avant que nature meure*, Neuchâtel, Delachaux et Niestlé, 1965.
Équipe MIT, *Tourismes 2, Moments de lieux*, Paris, Belin, Collection Mappemonde, 2005.
——, *Tourismes 3, La révolution durable*, Paris, Belin, Collection Mappemonde, 2011.
GAGE John, *Color and Culture: Practice and Meaning from Antiquity to Abstraction*,
    Boston, MA, Little, Brown, 1993.
——, *Color and Meaning: Art, Science, and Symbolism*, Berkeley and Los Angeles, CA,
    University of California Press, 2000.
JAMES Constantin, *Guide pratique aux eaux minérales et aux bains de mer*, Paris, Masson
    et fils, 1867.
LEEUWEN (van) Thomas A.P., *The Springboard in the Pond: An Intimate History of the
    Swimming Pool*, Cambridge, MA, MIT Press, 1998.
LEMAGNY Jean-Claude and ROUILLÉ André, *Histoire de la photographie*, Paris,
    Larousse-Bordas, 1998.
LÉVY Jacques and LUSSAULT Michel eds, *Dictionnaire de la géographie et de l'espace
    des sociétés*, Paris, Belin, 2003.
LÖFGREN Orvar, *On Holiday: A History of Vacationing*, Berkeley, CA, University of
    California Press, 1999.
LONDON Jack, "Riding the South Sea surf," *Women's Home Companion*, October 1907,
    p. 10, republished under the title "A Royal Sport," chapter 6, *The Cruise of the Snark*,
    New York, Macmillan, 1911.
——, "Finding one's way on the sea," *Harper's Weekly*, August 1, 1908, republished
    under the title "Finding one's way about," chapter 4, *The Cruise of the Snark*, New
    York, Macmillan, 1911.
LOTI Pierre, *Rarahu, idylle polynésienne* (édition 1991 sous le nom *Le mariage de Loti*),
    Paris, Flammarion, 1879.
PASTOUREAU Michel, *Bleu, histoire d'une couleur*, Paris, Editions du seuil, 2002.
ROBERTS Kenneth Lewis, *Sun hunting: adventures and observations among the native
    and migratory tribes of Florida, including the stoical time-killers of Palm Beach, the
    gentle and gregarious tin-canners of the remote interior, and the vivacious and semi-
    violent peoples of Miami and its purlieus*, Indianapolis, IN, Bobbs-Merrill, 1922.
STACPOOLE, Henry de Vere, *The Blue Lagoon*, London, T. Fisher Unwin, 1908.
STASZAK Jean-François, *Géographies de Gauguin*, Paris, Bréal, 2003.
——, "Qu'est-ce que l'exotisme?," *Le Globe, Revue genevoise de géographie*, 148 (2008):
    7–30.
TURNER Louis and ASH John, *The Golden Hordes: International Tourism and the
    Pleasure Periphery*, London, Constable, 1975.
TWAIN Mark, *Roughing It*, Chicago, IL, American Publishing Company, 1872.
URBAIN Jean-Didier, *Sur la plage. Mœurs et coutumes balnéaires (XIXe siècle–XXe
    siècle)*, Paris, Payot, 1994.
VACHER Luc, "La structuration d'un espace touristique littoral: le cas de la Grande
    Barrière de Corail en Australie," in MARROU L. and SACAREAU I. (eds), *Les
    espaces littoraux dans le monde*, pp. 61–82, Gap and Paris, Ophrys, 1999.

——, "La construction de l'espace touristique de la Grande Barrière de Corail: entre protection de l'environnement et modifications de l'accessibilité au récif," *Études caribéennes*, 9–10 (2008), *Le tourisme dans les îles et littoraux tropicaux et subtropicaux*, [Online, September 8, 2008], http://etudescaribeennes.revues.org/1152.

——, "La découverte récréative des eaux tropicales . . . et on inventa l'eau chaude et le blue lagoon," *Les Cahiers d'Outre-Mer*, 260 (October–December), 2012, [Online, October 1, 2012], http://com.revues.org/6749.

12 From the Invention of an Imaginary to the Promotion of Tourism

Greece through the Lens of the Photographer F. Boissonnas (1903–1930)

Estelle Sohier[1]

Introduction

The notion of "imaginary" (*imaginaire*[2]) is often used today in French historiography. Though it remains undertheorized and does not correspond to a specific field, its use reflects historiographical changes since the 1970s, including new ways of questioning past societies, the creation of new research objects, and the mobilization of new kinds of source material.

In France, the notion of imaginary was adopted by historians at the end of the 1970s, arising out of the history of mentalities (*histoire des mentalités*). Georges Duby and Jacques Le Goff, eminent historians of the journal *Les Annales*, authored pioneering works (Duby 1978; Le Goff 1985). The imaginary was defined as a field made up by all the representations that overstep the limits established from experience, and the chains of deduction allowed by them, whose territory covers the whole field of human experience, from the collective to the most intimate (Patlagean 1988: 307). The notion is acknowledged to be fluid (Le Goff 1985), and has proven quite useful in many scholarly investigations.

Jacques Le Goff sought to distinguish the notion from the symbolic, the ideological, and representations: the imaginary is seen as a collective, social and historical phenomenon, that "nourishes and makes humans act" (Le Goff 1985: II and VII). Beyond the history of representations, the aim is to study the way representations act upon the "real." Social imaginaries become an important issue of cultural history (*histoire culturelle*), giving priority to commonly shared values, forms, and symbols, over individual intellectual creations.

One of the characteristics of the approach for most historians is to refuse to search for permanent features of the human mind. They devote special attention to the temporal and spatial contexts, but also to the diversity of possible interpretations and to the polysemy of objects. Discourses are contextualized in their social environment of production, media, and itineraries. Ways of reading and seeing are interrogated, as well as modes of accreditation and veridiction (Chartier 1989). The aim is to better understand the way human beings of each era and social category have interpreted previous schemes and reintegrated them to a coherent body of representations and practices.

The use of the notion by historians of all periods encouraged the inclusion of new kinds of source material such as literature and art. A wide range of documents are mobilized: written, oral, and iconographic (that is, myths, legends, poetry, or popular literature, but also ceramics, statuary, illuminated miniatures, paintings, photographs, and animated images for more recent periods). The contents of the documents are deciphered, but also their functions and uses in permanently changing social, political, ideological and technological contexts.

The imaginary is not generally considered in itself (with some exceptions such as Boia 1998) but connected to other objects, which explains the frequent use of the notion. New objects of history have been built through its use: the body, dreams, feasts, the relation of self and others, a history of sensitivity magnificently developed by Alain Corbin (see Corbin 1988). Its use also allows the revitalization of approaches to belief and religion, social movements, sciences, or political history, including the history of ideas, parties, and collective entities (villages, nations, empire, and so on), as developed in the seminal works of Pierre Nora and Benedict Anderson (Anderson 1981). Geographical imaginaries are also an object of history (Schwartz 1996), approached by both cultural history and geography.

Greece occupies an old and exceptional place in the European geographic imaginary, as well as in the histories of both tourism and photography. Since the Renaissance, the region has been visited by learned individuals who consider it the cradle of Europe. Emblematic places of Greek antiquity, such as Athens, became part of the route of the Grand Tour of European aristocrats and intellectuals at the end of the eighteenth century. Following the foundation of the new state, in 1833, the country attracted ever more, and more varied, visitors. The Parthenon was consequently photographed in October 1839, just two months after the announcement of the invention of the daguerreotype in Paris (Schwartz 1996: 21). The Olympic Games organized in 1896 are considered a pivotal moment in the development of seasonal tourism, hotels, and occupations linked to such activities (Dritsas 2003). And if mass tourism dates only from the 1960s, Greece saw a boom in organized trips already during the 1920s and 1930s, always linked to classical European culture.

The work of Fred Boissonnas was realized in this last period, which also coincided with the growth in mass media and photographic reproduction in various forms. The Genevan photographer's encounter with Greece was fortuitous. He traveled there originally in 1903, at the request of an English aristocrat who wanted a photograph of Mont Parnassus on the model of Boissonnas's prized photograph of Mont Blanc shown at the Universal Exposition of Paris in 1900. During the following three decades, Fred Boissonnas undertook some dozen additional voyages across Greece, taking tens of thousands of photographs.

Many amateur and professional photographers had already been active in Greece, following 1839, yet Fred Boissonnas was able to bring a new gaze to the country, still recognized as such today (Peltre 1997: 298–299).[3] A substantial part of his photographic archive was purchased by the Greek government coincident with the 2004 Olympic Games and deposited in the Thessaloniki Museum of Photography. Various exhibitions were mounted to honor his work, and several of his books were translated and republished, particularly the deluxe volumes realized with Daniel Baud-Bovy (Baud-Bovy and Boissonnas 1910; 1919[4]). According to one advocate of Greek heritage to the outside world, the work of Boissonnas continues to hold currency today not only for its artistic and historic values, but also because his photographs had contributed to the "formation of European public opinion regarding Greece," making him an "ambassador of modern Greece."[5]

In their time, Boissonnas's photographs were disseminated in Greece, and throughout Europe and the United States, via exhibitions, public lectures accompanied by lantern slides, and myriad publications—including art books, international newspapers, illustrated magazines, brochures, and postcards. Though Boissonnas attained international renown through his photographs, he was also in fact a publisher, writer, and businessman. Parts of his photographic work, his private papers, and his correspondence with the Greek government reveal that the photographer was engaged with a wide chain of actors internationally, and that his vast production was put to many ends, yet foremost to the promotion of tourism.

The power of images and their role in the construction of tourism have been amply demonstrated in studies carried out since the 1970s (among recent works, see in particular Crouch, Jackson and Thompson 2005, and Robinson and Picard 2009). If tourists do not necessarily register social and economic realities, they do on the other hand respond strongly to circulating images (Crouch and Lübbren 2003). An integral element of this phenomenon, photography has played a central role in the process of constructing geographical imaginaries in society. If we define the idea of a geographical imaginary as an ensemble of physical and mental images which interact to confer meaning and coherence to a space, for a group of people at a given time (Debarbieux 2003; Sénécal 1992), we can consider that Boissonnas created and promoted a new geographical imaginary regarding Greece.

This case study allows an analysis of the relationship between photography, geographical imaginaries, and tourism in one of its earliest manifestations, that is, the manner in which images were perceived and then disseminated through mass media in the 1920s and 1930s to instill a vision of Greece that would promote tourism, several decades before the rise of mass tourism more broadly. The work and career of Boissonnas can help us understand the manufacture and deployment of this imaginary by inscribing this process in time, deciphering its media, and identifying its actors and their social, political and economic motivations.

Greece in the World, by Way of Image and Text

Fred Boissonnas's work concerning Greece is vast and took form in diverse media during the first three decades of the twentieth century: photographs, heliographs, postcards, art books, illustrated brochures, decorative stickers, and so on, The correspondence exchanged between the photographer and the Greek government between 1918 and 1922, today preserved at the Ministry of Foreign Affairs in

Athens, helps better discern the context of this production, to retrace its diffusion internationally and, above all, to better apprehend the ways this work was perceived and used by different actors. It clarifies the role given to images, and to the imaginary.

Propaganda through Images

A well-known photographer in Switzerland and beyond, the owner of several photographic studios in Europe, Fred Boissonnas at the close of World War I proposed his services to the Greek government, by way of the Greek consul in Geneva. A few months later, in March 1919, a contract was signed between the artist and M. Politis, the Greek Minister of Foreign Affairs. The Greek government made the substantial sum of 600,000 Swiss francs available to Boissonnas, to allow him to establish a publishing house and to "pursue the publication of his illustrated works and the preparation of photographic material needed for exhibitions and lectures about Greece."[6] The correspondence exchanged between the photographer and the Hellenic government leading up to the contract is explicit as to its purposes. It allows us, as well, to retrace the stages in the development of his Greek work. Between 1903 and 1913, Boissonnas traveled on various occasions to Greece with the art historian Daniel Baud-Bovy and other collaborators, assembling some 10,000 images. The photographs were reproduced in various works, most notably *La Grèce par monts et par vaux*, published in 1910 (with an English edition, in 1920: *In Greece: Journeys by Mountain and Valley*). The exceptional quality of this monumental art book was recognized not only in Switzerland, but also in Greece and beyond in Europe. Already by April 1913, Boissonnas was entrusted by the Hellenic government, through M. Romanos, to photograph the newly conquered provinces, especially Epirus, Macedonia, and Crete, "in order to release as quickly as possible popular illustrated books which will make their beauties known."[7] Following a series of military victories, the Greek government wished to ratify through European diplomacy an increase by nearly 70 per cent in its national territory (Clogg 2002: 79).

In 1919, the primary objective was the same, but the project, of longer duration, also had explicitly touristic goals. From 1905 on, Boissonnas had written memoranda to the Greek government on various occasions to demonstrate the potential political, commercial, and touristic usefulness of his photographic work.[8] In 1919, he proposed developing a deliberate, structured, and rapid propaganda campaign:

> this great launch, combining exhibitions, lectures and the distribution, on a large-scale, of our popular photo books and special brochures, not only will have a great political impact but could have incalculable results toward tourism, and it isn't an exaggeration to say that a few hundred thousand francs, invested this way, would bring millions in return to the country of origin.[9]

Dedicating a significant share of its budget to Boissonnas's project, the Greek government shared its objectives.[10] In December of 1918, the Minister of Foreign

Affairs transmitted a brief report on his meeting with Boissonnas together with the Greek head of state, Eleftherios Venizelos: the three explored the foundations for a "far-reaching photographic organization destined from now on to serve our national propaganda and thus to become a permanent publicity organ for development, commerce, industry and tourism in Greece."[11] This propaganda was intended to influence the Peace conference where Greece aspired to win territory. Inscribed within the dominant ideology of the Greek state since the nineteenth century, the "Great Idea" aimed to restore the Byzantine empire by incorporating all the zones of the Near East where significant portions of the population were culturally Greek, with Constantinople as the capital (Clogg 2002: 46–47). In parallel, the government sought to develop and channel tourism in Greece.

The different clauses of the contract were quickly put into effect, but not for long. For political and economic reasons, the Greek government soon lacked the means to pay its bills; the Great Idea fell apart in 1922, after the military defeat against the Ottoman Empire and the massive population transfers that ensued. In the wake, Boissonnas's publishing house filed for bankruptcy, leading to the financial demise of the enterprise. Meanwhile, other means of propaganda through images had been created, and would be exploited again later, even if in a less ambitious framework. This contract was just one moment in the career of Boissonnas, which all the same allowed the establishment of an ambitious and concerted initiative. For us it is an invaluable document in so much as it makes explicit the means, the potential uses, and the goals of image production.

To Make New Spaces Known, to Give Them Signs and Sense

The collaboration between Boissonnas and the Greek government is evidence of a shared belief in the power of images and their potential impact for the country's economy. The photographs of Boissonnas were chosen to lead a pro-Greek propaganda campaign for several reasons. The most obvious is the high formal quality of Boissonnas's photographic work, universally praised and recognized in Greece and in the rest of Europe. The second reason was expressed by Daniel Baud-Bovy in a letter where he defended the economic stakes of their project:

> It involves undertaking for Greece, its industries, its natural products, its waters, etc. an intense and methodical propaganda campaign through images. The majority of men are like St. Thomas. They want to see to believe. So many people have laughed in my face when I've spoken to them of the forests of Greece. Greece, for them, is nothing but an immense Attica. Show them views of the forests of Arcadia, of the Pindus, or of Olympus, and then they are convinced right away. Hence, it is a powerful means, long proven, to solicit the interest of the foreigner, the traveler, the capitalist.[12]

Fred Boissonnas crisscrossed Greece as no other traveling photographer had before him, photographing different regions, both ancient and new, as they became integrated to Greek space. The distribution of these images opened new spaces and new perspectives to the European imaginary, signaling their existence, estheticizing them and giving them meaning.

Fred Boissonnas gave meaning to his images in varying ways. He frequently relied on implicit or explicit references to other iconographic or literary works when composing his shots or when reproducing them in various media. By publishing his photographs alongside different texts, particularly travel narratives or extracts from classical European literature, he turned to culture and collective memory to give sense to his iconographic documents and to "inscribe" their meaning. His work was the vehicle for a new geographic imaginary in that he proposed a new approach to Greek space, as well as time, by juxtaposing, even confounding, ancient and modern Greece. This was explicitly the goal in his collaboration with the renowned French Hellenist Victor Bérard (1864–1931), translator of *The Odyssey*. In 1912 the photographer accompanied the archeologist on a journey around the Mediterranean to document and prove through images Bérard's thesis: Ulysses' journey took place in a real geographic space which can be retraced[13] (Figures 12.1 and 12.2).

Figure 12.1 Victor Bérard, *Dans le sillage d'Ulysse: album odysséen*, 1933: "Les grottes d'Eumée"

118. LES FUREURS D'ÉOLE

ἔρρ' ἐκ νήσου θᾶσσον, ἐλέγχιστε ζωόντων ...
ἔρρ', ἐπεὶ ἀθανάτοισιν ἀπεχθόμενος τόδ' ἱκάνεις.

Décampe de mon île, ô le rebut des êtres!...
Décampe!... tu reviens sous le courroux des dieux!
(X 72, 75).

Figure 12.2 Victor Bérard, *Dans le sillage d'Ulysse: album odysséen*, 1933: "Les
fureurs d'Eole"

The reading of literary works in anticipation of travel, or while moving between sites, was a common practice, one which Boissonnas drew upon to create a body of work that would bring together literary fictions, past and present travel narratives, and images. The search for the locations of the different stages of *The Odyssey* and the association of myths with real places was, beyond its scientific purpose, a way to confer meaning on space. Boissonnas's photographs gave substance to the myths, linking them to the landscape, encouraging in this way travel simultaneously in space and time, two fundamental elements to the geographical imaginary of tourists.

This approach furthermore was propitious for the expression of a collective Greek sentiment in relation to a territory that was still in a process of construction. The imagination is sometimes an "essential key for arriving at the idea of the real," making it possible to face a chaotic, often hostile, environment, devoid of any *a priori* meaning (Sénécal 1992). Through the imaginary that it carries, the work of Boissonnas was used to lend coherence and meaning to a Greek territory that was undergoing great transformation. The work was used for propaganda not only because it arose from a recognized artist, but also because it constituted, more broadly, the synthesis of a collective imaginary: a synthesis of the new Greek territory, a synthesis of its past and its present, but also a synthesis of the myths that underlay it.

His production, however, could not be the vehicle of a new geographical imaginary if it could not be disseminated. Boissonnas wasn't satisfied to imagine, produce, and publish his documents; he endeavored to make them consequential—and profitable—by using as effectively as possible the visual economy of the first decades of the twentieth century. He advocated the systematic distribution of his images throughout European society, and through them, an ideology resting on a new geographic imaginary.

Photography and the Visual Economy of the 1920s–1930s

The distribution of images to targeted publics was an integral part of the initial proposals of Boissonnas to the Greek government. After enumerating the various forms of "material which would allow reaching every walk of life," the photographer advocated setting up exhibition halls in all the important cities.[14] His proposals were inspired by the Swiss touristic model: "there isn't among us a single place, a single business, that doesn't print illustrated publicity. Here in Greece, nothing. Isn't it the moment, then, to begin? I have thousands of photos to illustrate everything that you could want."[15] He suggested as well the opportunity of creating official tourist information bureaus in Athens and Salonika "as we have in Geneva and all the cities of Switzerland,"[16] adorned "with views of the region in paintings and photographs, run by a man knowledgeable about touristic issues, who would offer, as in our case, invaluable services."[17] The rise of a tourism infrastructure offered new channels for the distribution of images destined to tourism promotion. The photographer contacted, for example, maritime companies and railroads to distribute his albums in their branch offices and on their ocean liners.[18]

Boissonnas similarly envisioned a whole series of derived products aiming to reach distinct publics. In addition to his works conceived as fine art, where the photograph and the quality of the impression had as much importance as the text, he published series of postcards, heliographic plates, and stickers, as well as more mass-market books, in ordinary or deluxe versions, in English, French, and German.[19] Beyond these, his images were reproduced in the illustrated press around the world.[20]

The ultimate failure of his publishing house, precipitated by the Greek political crisis and a rise in the exchange rate which hindered the sale of Swiss merchandise in the European market, did not, for all that, bring an end to the photographer's engagement with Greece. In 1930, he published a brochure titled *Tourism in Greece*, with 40,000 copies, disseminated in four languages (French, English, German, and Spanish). This publication stood apart from earlier guides for the number and quality of its illustrations, reproduced by heliograph (Figures 12.3–12.5). Boissonnas again enacted some of the stronger

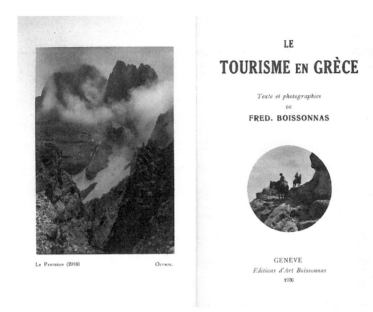

Figure 12.3 Fred Boissonnas, *Le tourisme en Grèce*, Genève, 1930, pp. 2–3

Figure 12.4 Fred Boissonnas, *Le tourisme en Grèce*, Genève, 1930, pp. 68–69

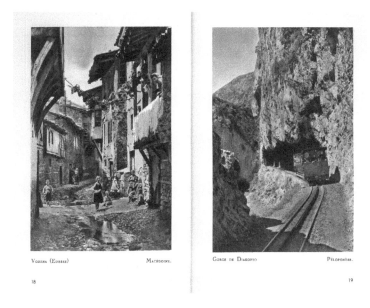

Figure 12.5 Fred Boissonnas, *Le tourisme en Grèce*, Genève, 1930, pp. 18–19

ideas he had developed in the 1919 contract and in his deluxe volumes, such as the juxtaposition of ancient Greece and modern Greece, urbanized and industrialized (Figure 12.5). The rapidly improving means for reproducing photographs in the 1920s and 1930s contributed to this revolutionary tool for creating new geographic imaginaries, destined to ever larger and more diverse publics.

A New Imaginary for New Practices

Greece, up until then, received an elite cultural tourism limited to a few regions which were visited exclusively for their Greek and Byzantine heritage. Through his photographs, Fred Boissonnas promoted simultaneously new destinations and distinct touristic practices.

A Greater Greece, United in Space and Time

Boissonnas's photographs and publications appealed to a new relation to space, in so much as they covered the whole of Greek territory and surrounding lands, even anticipating territorial conquests (for example, Macedonia). The diversity of Greece, furthermore, was highlighted by way of the variety of its landscape (cities and countryside, forests and mountains, sea and coastlines), its people, and things to be seen there (archeology, certainly, but also folklore, agriculture, monastic life, and so on) (Figures 12.6 and 12.7). The photographer invited the viewer to go beyond ruins, to consider also a relationship with the local populations, which he portrayed as warm and welcoming. His convivial scenes allowed viewers to imagine themselves in the spaces photographed, and instilled an interest in travel.

Distinct social groups of the population (city-dwellers, peasants, women, the elderly) were photographed, with particular attention given to signs of folklore (costumes, local celebrations). Viewers are again invited, by way of these encounters, to travel in space and time:

> One of the great appeals of traveling off the beaten path is encountering these ancestral virtues, these customs, this nobleness which extends back to antiquity. . . . This entire people has so much wit, such veneration for their past, such attachment to their age-old customs! They show hospitality with the ease of the heroes of the Odyssey. Mentor and Telemachus were no better received in Pylos than we at Zemenon.[21] (Boissonnas 1930: 25)

Figure 12.6 Daniel Baud-Bovy and Fred Boissonnas, *En Grèce par monts et par vaux*, 1910, p. 45: "Zéménon. Un four"

Figure 12.7 Daniel Baud-Bovy and Fred Boissonnas, *En Grèce par monts et par vaux*, 1910, plate 10, p. 54: "Argos. La citadelle de Larisse"

© Fred Boissonnas/TMP Archive, courtesy of the Thessaloniki Museum of Photography Archive

Beyond the rhetorical effect, at play is a wish to superimpose geographies, epochs, as well as fiction and reality.

This new vision linking the past and the present is reflected in Boissonnas's iconographic approach to ancient ruins, the most striking example of which is the case of the Parthenon, a common object of travel photographs since 1839 (see Yiakoumis 2000). Boissonnas, however, managed to renew the image of the monument both at the formal and symbolic levels, choosing quite an original angle, but also especially in drawing from the elements: the sunlight, the water, the clouds (Figure 12.8). He developed, more generally, a sensitive approach to the ruins, which he photographed much as he photographed the living and dynamic elements of the modern Greek landscape. His photographs invited the viewer to move beyond an intellectual approach alone to the ruins, appealing as well to the senses, opening the way for new notions of tourism in these regions.

A Country for Investors

The relation to time in the work of Boissonnas is paradoxical, given that a significant emphasis is also given to change. Books and sets of postcards

Figure 12.8 Daniel Baud-Bovy and Fred Boissonnas, *En Grèce par monts et par vaux*, 1910, Plate 1, frontispiece: "Le portique Nord de l'Erechtheion"

© Fred Boissonnas/TMP Archive, courtesy of the Thessaloniki Museum of Photography Archive

juxtaposed a timeless Greece, "eternal," and signs of its demographic and economic transformation (Figure12.5):

> in this still new Greece, so interesting for its intense modern activity, the development of its ports, its commerce and industry, the prodigious assimilation of more than a million and a half refugees, each day offers a contrast, an ancient vestige and, not far, a factory or a new city popping up as in America.[22] (Boissonnas 1930: 29)

A land of contrasts is put forward, complicating any vision of the country that merely valued its ancient and Byzantine past.

Diverse audiences were in fact targeted by these documents in order to favor the development of a tourism industry: on the one hand, the potential tourists; on the other, foreign investors, and among them perhaps especially members of the Greek diaspora who were playing a significant role in the country's infrastructure development (Dritsas 2003). In his letter to Greek authorities making the case for the economic stakes of their project, Daniel Baud-Bovy drew up a list of tourism infrastructure and businesses to be established following the Swiss model: beach resorts (for example, at Piraeus), health spas (on the flanks of Olympus), more rail stops, and hotels.[23] The illustrated brochures were conceived to reveal spaces, give birth to notions and desires, and to demonstrate the touristic possibilities of certain regions. The images of a "modern" Greece, endowed with diverse means of transport, normal and ordered city planning and businesses, should have encouraged these investors by allowing them to see the resources that would be available to them, and by inviting them to join a process already under way.

During the 1920s and 1930s, tourism did go through a period of transition in Greece. The end of conflicts, the pacification of various regions, the opening of transportation routes, the increase in automobiles, and the development of rail links at the national level as well as internationally (with the Orient Express) unlocked new geographical horizons, creating new possibilities for exploiting tourism (Dritsas 2003: 188).

Cruises Following Ulysses, Mountaineering on Olympus

During his career, Fred Boissonnas collaborated with various writers and scholars such as Victor Bérard, mentioned above. If the results of that latter partnership were not published until 1933, as *Dans le sillage d'Ulysse* (In the Wake of Ulysses), their undertaking had echoes in Europe well before. Communicating to the Greek government in 1919, Fred Boissonnas explicitly presented this scientific approach as a possible means for developing cruise-ship tourism:

> This last work awaited by all the intellectual elite of the two worlds, is regarded an immense success. It brings Homeric studies to the fore of current events at the same time as it will spark a whole series of Homeric cruises along the coast of Greece.[24]

This new view of the world offered by science, relayed through media such as photography and its derivatives, was seen as a means for promoting new tourist practices. In this way, the photographer wove a connection between intellectual, political and artistic circles in order to propose a political and economic application for the new notions of the world and the past arising from archeology.

The "Homeric cruises" were not the only touristic products envisioned by the photographer. Boissonnas and Baud-Bovy were the first to scale Mount Olympus, in 1913, just after the incorporation of the region to Greece. On the occasion, they took photos which later were widely disseminated in various formats (Figure 12.3). In 1918, the two Genevans suggested to the Greek government the notion of creating a health spa on the "flanks of Olympus."[25] In 1927, Boissonnas again climbed Olympus, but this time as part of a collective ascent, in the company of 25 tourists of various nationalities, and just a few days after the establishment of a Greek Alpine Club, the creation of which he had encouraged. In several writings published during the same period, the photographer proposed the systematic exploitation of the sportive, curative and hunting resources of this mythic place.

> We could thus imagine the extensive trails that this uninterrupted succession of summits, which we were just listing, and which have a mean altitude of 2,700 meters, would offer skiers. Imagine this marvel, to float above the Aegean sea, at the height of the snow fields of the home of the gods! To flutter from peak to peak in the azure ether. But it would still be necessary to get there without too much time or trouble.[26] (Boissonnas 1930: 48)

In the same document, Boissonnas advocated the creation of curative establishments along the Swiss model, all while protecting this zone by giving it the status of National Park.[27] His various writings promoting tourism at Olympus are illustrated with emblematic and suggestive photographs. Two photographs, of the highest peaks of Olympus, were especially used in conference series, invitation cards, magazine illustrations, books, and brochures. The captured elements (clouds and snow, abrupt and polished cliffs), the range of light (from the most bright to the most dark), as well as the captions ("Tarpeian Rock," "Victory Peak," "Throne of Zeus") demonstrated all at once the beauty of this geographic site, its accessibility, and its touristic possibilities (skiing, climbing), all while retaining its mythological aura. The recurrent use of these same images inscribed these sites in the collective imagination, and prepared their staging for tourism.

In making visible the Greek territories now united within one state, though distinct and often unknown, yet laden with meaning for classical European culture, the photographs of Boissonnas permitted the creation of a realm between the Greek state, still in formation, and potential travelers, both Greek and foreign. Disseminated through lectures, exhibitions, postcards, and sundry publications, the photographs functioned as lures, all the more effective in that their interpretation was not closed, but open, and accessible to diverse publics. Lending themselves to multiple readings, the photographs furthermore were used by a variety of actors.

One Imaginary, Multiple Uses

Elefthérios Venizélos was the first Greek statesman to request the editorial and photographic services of Fred Boissonnas as part of his program of government, briefly initially during his first mandate as Prime Minister in 1910–1915, and later, on a more ambitious scale, in 1919 with the signing of the contract alluded to earlier (see Boudouri 2003). Communication is one of the greatest political qualities attributed to Venizélos (Kitromilides 2008: 5), considered the founder of modern Greece. Recourse to the work of Boissonnas and the geographic imaginary that it conveyed was one of the means used by Venizélos to defend Greece on the international stage, and to promote an independent Greek territory within expanded borders. The photographs were also conceived as instruments for the development of the tourist sector, the importance of which the statesman had already recognized prior to World War I (Dritsas 2003).

The development of an imaginary through texts and images to promote tourism carried dimensions that went beyond commercial and economic interests alone. It was a tool as well for developing the national identity of the young state, for claiming recognition and rights on the international stage, and for furthering the consolidation of a still-unstable national territory.

After 1922, the terms of the contract between Fred Boissonnas and the Greek government were no longer applicable, and the involvement of the photographer in promoting Greek tourism took other forms.

Tourism, a New Bridge between Greece and Europe after 1922

Following the considerable difficulties which Greece confronted at the beginning of the 1920s, the time of the "Great Catastrophe," various actors within Greek society and its diaspora sought to draw attention again to tourism (see especially Peltre 1997: 295–301). Internal and external tourism was then promoted toward several ends: in addition to its economic interest, it was intended to create a popular touristic consciousness (Boudouri 2006: 61) but also, with regard to a foreign public, to counterbalance the mishellenism resulting from the war against the Ottoman Empire. Some Greek politicians considered ways of developing propaganda using text and images, especially photography (Boudouri 2006: 60), even if not under an explicit program. In 1929, Venizélos established the Hellenic Tourism Organization to better organize this new sector, counting especially on images, which were sought and used immediately. The tourism organization in Greece today indeed still relies on glossy photo albums (Dritsas 2003: 203, note 8).

Businessmen were also involved in tourism promotion. Magazines were published toward this end during the 1920s and 1930s, where photography was granted an important place. Several of them used images by Boissonnas. *Le Voyage en Grèce*, the most sumptuous of these publications, has been the object of several recent studies and one book. Published between 1934 and 1939 and directed to cruise passengers, this periodical had been established to "create a tie between Greece and its visitors by way of writers, artists and contemporary scholars" (Basch and Farnoux 2006: 1). Boissonnas had a direct and indirect influence on this editorial project, at several levels. The attention given to the layout of the magazine echoed the two art books about Greece published by Boissonnas and Baud-Bovy. Additionally, various issues included photos by Boissonnas, conferring through their quality and layout a unique status to the magazine (Védrine 2006: 119). Far from serving as simple illustrations, these images demonstrated Greece as "frozen within an eternal present" (Védrine 2006: 126).

Boissonnas's influence is also discernible at another level. The magazine was published under the direction of Hercule Joannidès, a Greek national with ties to Venizélos, exiled in France, and also director of the Neptos company which organized cruises to Greece. The 1930s saw a boom in organized voyages and cultural tourism, paralleling the rise of a leisure society and paid vacations in certain European countries. The goal of *Le voyage en Grèce* was to promote archeological cruises organized under the sponsorship of French national museums and the School of the Louvre (Basch and Farnoux 2006: 1–2). The company notably proposed a cruise following the path of Ulysses, for which renown figures, including writers, poets and academics, were invited along for free. Boissonnas and Bérard's approach was explicitly followed (Boudouri 2006: 59). Though it is impossible to know exactly the role played by Boissonnas in this phenomenon, the photographer formed part of the network of businessmen, politicians, and artists involved in the process. It was in connection with Hercule Joannidès, for example, that Boissonnas returned to the summits of Olympus in 1927.

The touristic cruise industry in part grew out of the ideas and imaginaries developed earlier by Boissonnas and his collaborators. The creation of a geographic imaginary by way of diverse iconographic and textual documents, therefore, preceded the development of infrastructure or the establishment of corresponding touristic practices. Boissonnas's role demonstrates that the boom in the tourism industry was owed to a diverse network of actors, among them the artists who constructed images of certain destinations prior to their becoming objects of tourism.

The Metaxas Dictatorship and the Imaginary Promoted by Boissonnas

Further along in the 1930s, Greek political power found new uses for tourism and the imaginary which underlay it, renewing interest in the sector. Coming to power in 1936, General Metaxas installed a dictatorial and retrograde regime, with a manner of communicating based in a nearly fascistic style and rhetoric (Clogg 2002: 115). Following the model of contemporary fascistic regimes in Europe, he promoted, for example, the idea of a "third Hellenic civilization," combining the (contradictory) values and prestige of both ancient and Byzantium Greece (Clogg 2002: 116). Starting in 1936, a post was created for a Subsecretary of State for the press and tourism, under the Ministry of Foreign Affairs, having among its duties the organization of tourism in Greece and the development of propaganda abroad (Dritsas 2003: 190–191). Tourism promotion was made an integral part of propaganda efforts more generally. One magazine, *In Greece*, appeared between 1936 and 1939 and was directed to foreign travelers in order to project the image sought by the Greek government. Photographs by Fred Boissonnas were published in the magazine, but beyond being mere pictures, their gaze of Greece was taken to advance an idea of the racial and cultural continuity of the Greek people since antiquity.

In 1938, Boissonnas was decorated by the Metaxas regime.[28] Beyond the convenient image of Greek geographic and historical unity promoted in his work, it was without doubt the rural, traditional and folkloric Greece highlighted in his photographs that caught the interest of this ultra-conservative regime. The attention brought to tourism by the Metaxas regime did not respond to political and economic interests alone, but also to social goals, the Greek government seeing it as an instrument for mobilizing all sectors of the population, especially women and rural-dwellers (Dritsas 2003: 191).

A geographic imaginary used for tourism promotion is a semantic reduction useful as well for reifying the image of a country. It doesn't just engender tourism and help accumulate foreign reserves; it is also a potential tool for varied political ends, to be deployed toward distinct publics. Fred Boissonnas was just one gear in a chain of actors who used the imaginary he helped create for diverse, even opposing ends.

The Twenty-first Century: Reactivation of an Imaginary?

In recent years, various of Fred Boissonnas's works have been republished in Greece, where the government also acquired, on the eve of the 2004 Olympic Games in Athens, a large portion of Boissonnas's photographic archive. Since the 1990s, several traveling exhibitions have been organized, including one dedicated to Mount Athos. And many of Boissonnas's photographs are also available now on the Internet. This (re)appearance of images by Fred Boissonnas in Greek public space is undeniably linked to the renewed interest that photography has held in our societies since the 1980s–1990s. But it also corresponds to shifting conceptions of tourism in Greece: after several decades of developing mass tourism, government policy since the 1990s has changed owing to several factors, particularly environmental degradation and deindustrialization. Efforts have since been made to diversify touristic offerings by developing, for example, cultural tourism, agrotourism, and health-related tourism. This phenomenon corresponds not only to a growing concern with environmental preservation in Greece, but also with highlighting and enacting heritage for cultural and educational purposes (Dritsas 2003: 199). Tourism has been increasingly seen as a means to balance regional development by mobilizing communities hitherto excluded, particularly in rural areas, so as to bring them into the market and generate employment.

The purchase and development of Boissonnas's Greek photographic archive reflects, above all, its heritage value.[29] This renewed interest is perhaps consistent with a wish to again enrich tourist practices by emphasizing new aspects of Greek culture. We might ask if the utilization of these photographs is not equally a way of reviving the imaginary that had been fashioned by the photographer, just as Greece again needs to renegotiate its identity in the face of internal and external challenges. The philhellenists Fred Boissonnas and Daniel Baud-Bovy saw in the promotion of beach, cultural, health or rural tourism several interests for Greece:

> There would be a double action: on the one hand, to develop that which we call the 'foreigner industry,' and on the other, to work in order that the results of this campaign contribute to embellish Greece, so that it prospers with regard to its natural beauties, its local architecture . . . Once again, the experience gained in Switzerland would be so useful, be it in the one sense, be it in the other.

Their optimistic conception regarding the role of a tourist industry is still meaningful, nearly a century later.

Conclusion

The photographer Fred Boissonnas played a pioneering role in the establishment of tourism in Greece by creating an imaginary linked to the promotion of novel touristic practices. His work found echoes in Greece as well as abroad because it was the product of both a hybrid and collective imagination, arising out of both Greek and European culture. The association of images and texts is an effective tool for establishing an imaginary: the iconography gives force and attractiveness to the message, while texts give meaning and depth to the images, linking them to additional referents. By putting literature and photographs side-by-side, by disseminating the same spectacular images across an entire range of documents, such as in the case of views of Olympus, Boissonnas created "markers" (MacCannell 1976, and Crouch and Lübbren: 2003: 8)—making places known, showing their beauty and accessibility, and changing their meaning. He thus prepared them for investment by the tourist industry. The case of this photographer illustrates the importance of the 1920s and 1930s for the creation of geographic imaginaries for tourism, the history of such imaginaries being inseparable from the media that served as their vehicles. This period was fundamental in the spread of geographical imaginaries, all the more evident given that many images produced during this time are reentering circulation today, still functioning as markers.

The various reutilizations of the work of Boissonnas for different political ends illustrate the manner in which a single geographic imaginary can be exploited, both inside and outside a country. The stakes are not economic alone, but also social and political. They raise the question of the links between a geographic imaginary directed toward tourists and the policies of the receiving nations, for whom the control of the imaginary may be inscribed in relations of power with foreign states. Boissonnas's career equally shows how the media sought to construct and promote a tourist imaginary from an array of actors. Through his images, the photographer linked the scientific world, the political sphere, and investors with a broader public.

Notes

1 The author warmly thanks Daniel Hoffman for the translation of the article, and Vangelis Ioakimidis, Irène Boudouri, Hercules Papaioannou and Nina Kassianou for their help and advises in Greece.
2 The translation of the word *imaginaire* is difficult, as in French it serves both as a noun and as an adjective, and as a noun it is different from the term *imagination*. In the context here, however, it may lay close to the English term "collective imagination."
3 For the author, Fred Boissonnas may even have contributed to the renewal in the way painters looked at Greece during the interwar period.
4 The two deluxe, large-format books realized by Daniel Baud-Bovy and Fred Boissonnas were recently reissued in facsimile: *En Grèce par monts et par vaux*, Athens, Militos, Eleftheroudakis, 2007 [1910]; *Des Cyclades en Crète au gré du vent*, Athens and Militos; Eleftheroudakis, 2007 [1919]. See also Boissonnas (2001), published to accompany an exhibition held in Thessaloniki and London (Hellenic Centre) during 2002–2003.
5 Published interview with the director of the Foundation for Hellenic Culture, Sofia, Bulgaria, November 2009. (http://www.grreporter.info/en/trip_mount_athos_through_eyes_fr%C3%A9d%C3%A9ric_boissonnas/1237, accessed December 1, 2012).

6 Archives of the Greek Foreign Ministry, Athens. Archives of the central service, 1922, folder 98, sub-folder 4-2-2. Contract signed March 27, 1919 between M. Politis and M. Boissonnas in Paris.

7 Archives of the Greek Foreign Ministry, Athens. Archives of the central service, 1922, folder 98, sub-folder 4-2-2. Letter of F. Boissonnas to M. Kapsambélis, general consul in Geneva, August 21, 1918, p. 4.

8 "Je préconisais alors des voyages méthodiquement organisés non seulement à travers les contrées de la Grèce de 1905, mais aussi à travers les terres qui devaient revenir à la mère-patrie." (I recommended then methodically organized trips not only across the Greek regions as of 1905, but also across the lands that should return to the mother-land.) Archives of the Greek Foreign Ministry, Athens. Archives of the central service, 1922, folder 98, sub-folder 4-2-2. Letter of F. Boissonnas to M. Kapsambélis, general consul of Geneva, August 21, 1918, p. 5.

9 Archives of the Greek Foreign Ministry, Athens. Archives of the central service, 1922, folder 98, sub-folder 4-2-2. Letter of F. Boissonnas to M. Kapsambélis, general consul of Geneva, August 21, 1918, p. 9.

10 This study, until now, has been based only on the French-language correspondence.

11 Archives of the Greek Foreign Ministry, Athens. Archives of the central service, 1922, folder 98, sub-folder 4-2-2. Confidential telegram of M. Politis to the Foreign Minister in Athens, December 14, 1918 from Paris.

12 Archives of the Greek Foreign Ministry, Athens. Archives of the central service, 1922, folder 98, sub-folder 4-2-2. Copy of a letter from Daniel Baud-Bovy to Fred Boissonnas, October 29, 1918, p. 1.

13 The expression "Victor Bérard's complex" is now used by literary critics to describe the way some travelers believe that, in the course of their journeys, they have found places cited in works of fiction. See Montalbetti (1997). For a brand new version of a photographer's traveling around the Mediterranean along the path of Ulysses, see photographer Stefano De Luigi's 2012 *iDyssey*. Jessie Wender, "Stefano de Luigi's idyssey, *The New Yorker*, September 24, 2012. http://www.newyorker.com/online/blogs/photobooth/2012/09/stefano-de-luigis-idyssey.html. I thank Daniel Hoffman for this reference.

14 Archives of the Greek Foreign Ministry, Athens. Archives of the central service, 1922, folder 98, sub-folder 4-2-1. Letter of Fred Boissonnas to the consul in Geneva, October 28, 1918, from Geneva.

15 Archives of the Greek Foreign Ministry, Athens. Archives of the central service, 1922, folder 98, sub-folder 4-2-1. Report written by Fred Boissonnas to the Minister, M. Politis, July 1, 1920, from Athens.

16 Ibid., p. 11.

17 Ibid., p. 12.

18 Archives of the Greek Foreign Ministry, Athens. Archives of the central service, 1922, folder 98, sub-folder 4-2-1. Copy of a letter from the General Office of the French railways and navigation administrations and companies in Switzerland ["office général pour la Suisse des Administrations et Compagnies Françaises de Chemin de Fer et de Navigation"] to Fred Boissonnas, July 25, 1921, from Bern.

19 The list of the books published in the early 1920s was sent to the Greek government together with a report in 1921. Archives of the Greek Foreign Ministry, Athens. Archives of the central service, 1922, folder 98, sub-folder 4–2-1. Letter of Fred Boissonnas to the Greek government, November 17, 1921.

20 The Centre d'Iconographie, of the Genevan public library, and the Photographic Museum of Thessaloniki, in Greece, maintain folders of press clippings featuring photos by Boissonnas, gathered from newspapers from around the world between 1900 and the late 1930s.

21 "Un des grands charmes du voyage en dehors des voies ordinaires est de retrouver ces vertus ancestrales, ces usages, cette noblesse qui reportent à l'antiquité. . . . Tout ce

peuple a tant d'esprit, un tel culte de son passé, un tel attachement aux antiques usages! Il exerce l'hospitalité avec la simplicité des héros de l'Odyssée. Mentor et Télémaque ne furent pas mieux accueillis à Pylos, que nous à Zéménon."

22 "dans cette Grèce toujours nouvelle, si intéressante par l'intense activité moderne, par le développement de ses ports, de son commerce et de son industrie, par la prodigieuse assimilation de plus d'un million et demi de réfugiés, chaque jour offre un contraste, un vestige antique et non loin de là, une usine ou une ville nouvelle sortie de terre à l'américaine."

23 Archives of the Greek Foreign Ministry, Athens. Archives of the central service, 1922, folder 98, sub-folder 4-2-2. Copy of a letter from Daniel Baud-Bovy to Fred Boissonnas, October 29, 1918.

24 "Ce dernier ouvrage attendu par toute l'élite intellectuelle des deux mondes, est appelé à un immense succès. Il mettra les études homériques au premier plan de l'actualité en même temps qu'il déclenchera toute une série de croisières homériques sur les côtes de Grèce." Archives of the Greek Foreign Ministry, Athens. Archives of the central service, 1922, folder 98, sub-folder 4-2-2. Letter of Fred Boissonnas to M. Kapsambélis, general consul in Geneva, August 21, 1918.

25 Archives of the Greek Foreign Ministry, Athens. Archives of the central service, 1922, folder 98, sub-folder 4-2-2. Copy of a letter from Daniel Baud-Bovy to Fred Boissonnas, October 29, 1918, p. 8.

26 "Nous pûmes ainsi nous figurer les immenses champs de course qu'offrirait au skieur cette suite interrompue de sommités que nous énumérions tout à l'heure et dont l'altitude moyenne est de 2 700 mètres. Imaginez cette merveille, planer sur la mer Egée du haut des champs de neige de la demeure des dieux! Voltiger de cime en cime dans l'azur éthéré. Mais encore faudrait-il y parvenir sans trop de peine et de temps."

27 Boissonnas (1928) and Boissonnas (1930: 52).

28 Personal communication from M. Hercules Papaioannou, September 2010, curator at the Thessaloniki Museum of Photography.

29 Personal communication from Irène Boudouri, May 2011, Athens.

Bibliography

ANDERSON Benedict, *Imagined Communities: Reflections on the Origin and Spread of Nationalism*, London, Verso, 1983.

BASCH Sophie and FARNOUX Alexandre (eds), *Le voyage en Grèce (1934–1939). Du périodique de tourisme à la revue artistique*, Athènes, École Française d'Athènes, 2006.

BOIA Lucian, *Pour une histoire de l'imaginaire*, Paris, Les Belles Lettres, 1998.

BOUDOURI Irène, "Photographie et politique extérieure. L'apport de la famille Boissonnas (1905–1922)," in *Actes du colloque sur l'histoire de la photographie grecque, Cythère, 2002*, Thessaloniki Museum of Photography, 2003, pp. 47–59 (in Greek).

——, "*En Grèce* et *Le voyage en Grèce*: deux revues touristiques de l'entre-deux-guerres," in BASCH Sophie and FARNOUX Alexandre (eds), *Le voyage en Grèce (1934–1939). Du périodique de tourisme à la revue artistique*, Athènes, École Française d'Athènes, 2006, pp. 55–67.

BURGUIÈRE André, *L'école des Annales. Une histoire intellectuelle*, Paris, Odile Jabob, 2006.

CHARTIER Roger, "Le monde comme représentation," *Annales. Économies, Sociétés, Civilisations*, 44–6 (1989): 1505–1520.

CLOGG Richard, *A Concise History of Greece*, Cambridge, Cambridge University Press, 2002 [1992].

CORBIN Alain, *Le territoire du vide*, Paris, Aubier, 1988.

CROUCH David, JACKSON Rhona and THOMPSON Felix, *The Media and the Tourist Imagination*, London and New York, Routledge, 2005.

CROUCH David and LÜBBREN Nina (eds), *Visual Culture and Tourism*, Oxford, Berg, 2003.

DEBARBIEUX Bernard, "Imaginaire géographique," in LÉVY Jacques and LUSSAULT Michel (eds), *Dictionnaire de la géographie et de l'espace des sociétés*, Paris, Belin, 2003, pp. 489–491.

DRITSAS Margarita, "Tourism in Greece: A Way to What Sort of Development?," in TISSOT Laurent (ed.), *Construction d'une industrie touristique aux 19e et 20e siècles: perspectives internationales*, Neuchâtel, Alphil, 2003, pp. 187–210.

DUBY Georges, *Les trois ordres ou l'imaginaire du féodalisme*, Paris, Gallimard, 1978.

GALANI-MOUTAFI Vasiliki, "Tourism Research on Greece: A Critical Overview," *Annals of Tourism Research*, 31(1) (2004): 157–179.

KITROMILIDES Paschalis (ed.), *Eleftherios Venizelos: The Trials of Statemanship*, Edinburgh, Edinburgh University Press, 2008.

LALIOTI Vassiliki, "Ancient Greek Theatres as Visual Images of Greekness," in ROBINSON Mike and PICARD David (ed.), *The Framed World: Tourism, Tourists and Photography*, Farnham and Burlington, VT: Ashgate, 2009.

LE GOFF Jacques, *L'imaginaire médiéval*, Paris, Gallimard, 1985.

LE GOFF Jacques et al., *Histoire et imaginaire*, Paris, Payot, 1986.

MACCANNELL Dean, *The Tourist: A New Theory of the Leisure Class*, New York: Schocken Books, 1976.

MONTALBETTI Christine, *Le Voyage, le monde, la bibliothèque*, Paris, PUF, 1997.

ORY Pascal, "Qu'est-ce que l'histoire culturelle," *L'histoire, la sociologie et l'anthropologie*, Paris, Odile Jacob, 2002, pp. 93–106.

PAPAIOANNOU Hercules and TSOUKA Anetta, "Travel between Sky and Land," in *Fred Boissonnas. Travel to Mount Athos (1928–1930)*, Athonit Center (Mount Athos), in collaboration with the Thessaloniki Museum of Photography and the Hellenic Culture Organisation SA, Athens, Thessaloniki, 2006, pp. 19–23 (in Greek).

PATLAGEAN Evelyne, "L'histoire de l'imaginaire," in LE GOFF Jacques (ed.), *La nouvelle histoire*, Brussels, Complexe, 1988, pp. 307–334.

PELTRE Christine, *Retour en Arcadie: le voyage des artistes français en Grèce au XIXe siècle*, Paris, Klincksieck, 1997.

RIOUX Jean-Pierre and SIRINELLI Jean-François (eds), *Pour une histoire culturelle*, Paris, Seuil, 1997.

ROBINSON Mike and PICARD David, *The Framed World: Tourism, Tourists and Photography*, Farnham and Burlington, VT: Ashgate, 2009.

SCHWARTZ Joan, "The Geography Lesson: Photographs and the Construction of Imaginative Geographies," *Journal of Historical Geography*, 22(1) (1996): 16–45.

SCHWARTZ Joan and RYAN James, *Picturing Place: Photography and the Geographical Imagination*, London, I.B. Tauris, 2003.

SÉNÉCAL Guy, "Aspects de l'imaginaire spatial: identité ou fin des territoires ?," *Annales de Géographie*, 101(563) (1992): 28–42.

VÉDRINE Hélène, "La substance des spectres: les textes d'E. Tériade autour des photographies de Fred Boissonnas et d'Eli Lotar," in BASCH Sophie and FARNOUX Alexandre (eds), *Le voyage en Grèce (1934–1939). Du périodique de tourisme à la revue artistique*, Athènes, École Française d'Athènes, 2006, pp. 119–134.

WALTER François, *Les figures paysagères de la nation. Territoire et paysage en Europe (16e–20e siècle)*, Paris, EHESS, 2004.

WICKENS Eugenia, "The Sacred and the Profane: A Tourist Typology," *Annals of Tourism Research*, 29(3) (July 2002): 834–851.

YALOURI Eleana, *The Acropolis: Global Fame, Local Claim*, Oxford and New York: Berg, 2001.

YIAKOUMIS Haris, *L'Acropole d'Athènes. Photographies 1839–1959*, Paris, Picard, and Athens, Potamos, 2000.

Primary Sources

HOMER, *L'Odyssée*, trad. Victor Bérard, Paris, Librairie Armand Colin, 1942.

BAUD-BOVY Daniel and BOISSONNAS Fred, *En Grèce par monts et par vaux*, Genève, ed. Boissonnas; Athènes, C. Eleftheroudakis, 1910.

——, *Des Cyclades en Crète au gré du vent*, Genève, ed. Boissonnas, 1919.

BÉRARD Victor, *Dans le sillage d'Ulysse: album odysséen*, Paris, A. Colin, 1933.

BOISSONNAS Fred, "*L'Olympe, parc national de la Grèce*," *L'Acropole*: *Revue du Monde Hellénique*, Paris, January–June 1928.

——, *Le tourisme en Grèce*, Genève, ed. Paul Trembley, 1930.

——, *Images of Greece*, Athens, Rizarios Foundation, 2001.

BOUVIER Bertrand, *Fred Boissonnas to Agion Oros En Etei 1930/ Fred Boissonnas, le Mont Athos en 1930*, Athènes, Ammos, 1994.

Fred Boissonnas. Travel to Mount Athos (1928–1930), Athonit Center (Mount Athos), in collaboration with the Thessaloniki Museum of Photography and the Hellenic Culture Organisation SA, Athens, Thessaloniki, 2006 (in Greek).

Archives of the Greek Foreign Ministry, Athens

Archives of the central service, 1922, folder 98, sub-folders 4–2–1 and 4–2–2.

13 Beyond Imaginary of Place

Performing, Imagining, and Deceiving Self through Online Tourist Photography

Iris Sheungting Lo and Bob McKercher

Introduction

Imaginary involves imagination but it is not precisely imagination. More than imagination, the term "imaginary" entails the process through which reality is constantly produced and mediated (Salazar 2012). In the context of tourism, such a process shapes and is shaped by how distant places and otherness are represented and transformed into attractions through material and intangible images (Graburn and Gravari-Barbas 2011; Gravari-Barbas and Graburn 2012). This chapter aims to articulate how tourist photography as staged performance facilitates the imaginary of the tourist self. By revealing the how and why of online travel image inclusion and exclusion by Hong Kong Chinese tourists, existing conceptualizations of tourist imaginaries are extended.

Travel photography is said to be simultaneously a producer and a product of the tourist gaze. Within a hermeneutic circle, tourist imaginaries are produced through photographic images diffused by tourism practitioners and mass media (Urry 2002). These collective imaginaries are said to be powerful in determining where tourists travel and what tourists do on site (Gravari-Barbas and Graburn 2012). Tourists are motivated to search for projected images and to capture these images through their cameras. They then show these mediated imaginaries to others as proof of their travel (Urry 2002). Underpinned by Urry's (2002) gaze theory, a number of studies (Caton and Santos 2008; Garrod 2009; Jenkins 2003) compare tourist photographs with mass-produced images to confirm the impact collective imaginaries have on tourist behaviors. Tourist photographs are suggested to be replicas of these widely circulated images, as they seem identical to each other.

Nonetheless, Scarles (2009) argues that existing studies on tourist photography do not tell us how tourists subjectify the collective imaginaries into their own imaginations. It is almost impossible to mark a beginning and an end to the meaning of tourist photographic practices in a very straightforward and circular manner as tourists have the ability to reflect, relate, and transform the collective imaginaries into their own imagination and experience of the place based on their sense of self and others, past experience, and personal interests. Tourists can reject and be skeptical about the imaginaries which commercial photography offers at their anticipatory stage. When tourists encounter the place and photograph the iconic images as suggested by the hermeneutic circle, they do not aim to capture only the image. Rather, it is the feeling, sensations, and moods they have towards a place that they want to capture. Not only do collective imaginaries transform over time, individual imaginaries and memories of travel can also transform in time. The meaning of photographs and tourist photographic acts vary from moment to moment. Photography is not exactly a replacement for memories. Rather, it is the fractured, frozen moment that helps create and revise memories to suit our needs and identities. Hence, the seemingly identical image does not automatically imply identical imaginary.

Very often, existing conceptualizations of tourist imaginaries are largely built upon the ways places and the general others are shaped and represented through and for tourism (Salazar 2012). Greater effort is made on the analysis of the macro level of formation of travel image and imaginaries as a means to shed light on the shaping of tourism and its practices. How the tourist subjectifies imaginaries is not researched in depth. Nonetheless, Gravari-Barbas and Graburn (2012: 2) argue that the analysis of tourist imaginary should not be limited to the collective shaping of place. It should also include "the imagination of tourists, both as producers of imaginaries and as imagined entities themselves." And as Salazar (2012) suggests, after all "the agents who imagine are individuals, not societies."

Lately, there seems to be a performative turn in tourism studies and an urgent call for recognizing tourists' sense of self in photographic practices (Belk and Yeh 2011; Urry and Larsen 2011). More and more, tourists are seen as active producers of collective imaginaries than passive receivers of norms. Along with this turn, tourist photographic practices are increasingly studied as "performed" rather than "preformed" (Larsen 2006). In his new book with Larsen, Urry also starts to move away from only highlighting the visual aspects of the tourist gaze to also acknowledge the performative nature of tourist photography (Urry and Larsen 2011). Based on Goffman's conception of performance (1959), Urry and Larsen (2011) suggest that picturing is an enactment of impression management besides being a form of consumption of the visuals. Hence, more than producing and consuming places, tourist photography is also a producer and a product of an ideal self. Yeh (2009) argues that tourist photography portrays more than a physical presence of self in a particular place at a particular time. Through a study of Taiwanese university students' photographs and their travel narratives, she finds that photography indeed allows tourists to "create a more heroic romanticized self" and to situate themselves in the world. Leung (2010), building upon Bourdieu's theory, considers tourist photographs and their narratives as markers of class distinction. By analyzing middle-class Chinese backpackers' photographs on a travel-themed photoblog of Shangri-la, she finds that these tourists distinguish themselves through showcasing their cosmopolitan values—not through wealth, not through place, but through the ways they photograph and experience the sites, by framing out "undesirables" to exhibit their view of a place and of others. Hence, photography is "a (re)presentation of how they want to be seen and show how they see the world" (Leung 2010: 101). Therefore, the framing and not framing of travel memories do not merely reflect the collective imaginary of place but the imaginary of the tourist self as well.

Online Tourist Photography and the Formation of Self

A discussion on the imaginary of the tourist self would be incomplete without referencing Lacan's articulation of the imaginary. Lacan proposes a framework of three registers that explains the formation of the sense of self, otherness, and the world. These three registers are the real, the symbolic, and the imaginary. In particular, both the symbolic and the imaginary are developed from the mirror stage. The "mirror stage" is when a realization of self as an object takes place for the very first time (Bailly 2009). It is the moment in which self learns to translate the fragmented images into an ideal, a wholeness of ego (Bailly 2009; Loos 2002). The illusionary unity of self-image provided by the mirror stage is thus a vital step for the self to develop ego stability (Markham 1999). Indeed this mirror stage continues beyond childhood. Other's reactions are in fact an invisible mirror to us in our everyday life (Cooley 1972). The formation of self as an object is thus a two-way flow: the internalization and the externalization of image. The imaginary is where the internalization and the formation of the wholeness of self takes place, and the symbolic is where self learns to make this ideal, wholeness of ego accessible to the external world (Loos 2002).

Why in particular is online tourist photography chosen as the context for a study of tourist performance and imaginaries of self? Online tourist photography offers a unique kind of performance and imaginary of self. Three components foster the nature of this performance into a more illusionary and deceptive than everyday,

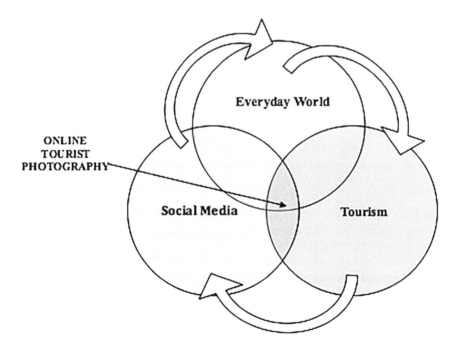

Figure 13.1 Performing and imagining self through double-liminality

face-to-face one: tourism, photography, and social media. Unlike face-to-face or other kinds of immediate interaction, social media can provide the tourists with a secured backstage area and more time to prepare for their presentation of self to others. Furthermore, online performance can be consumed by a larger sphere of audiences regardless of time and geographical locations and is carried out continuously without the physical presence of the performer until the photographs are deleted from posts. Most importantly, travel experience can be easily concealed or (re)presented as it is not accessible to others if it is not shared. Therefore, one can enjoy higher flexibility to perform an ideal self to others through the two liminal spaces (see Herman 2005 for the definition of liminality): tourism and social media. At the same time, these two liminal spaces are largely visual-oriented. Photographic images are still, fragmented, selected, and editable. Hence, it is particularly powerful in highlighting the partial realities of ourselves we wish others to see, freeze the moments, and turn them into the only, whole, eternal truth. In that case, photography can blend very well into these spaces and help deliver these partial realities of self to our everyday life world in a very convincing manner (see Figure 13.1). It is believed that an analysis of online tourist photography can illuminate the performing, imagining, and deceiving character of the tourist self.

Method

A reflexive, dramaturgical, and ethnographic approach was adopted to examine online tourist photographic practices. Fieldwork took place between the beginning of 2009 and mid-2011, meaning that the first author had been a producer and an audience of online performances during the said period for the purpose of this study (Wittel 2000). Based on a population study of Hong Kong Chinese photography dissemination (see Lo, McKercher, Lo, Cheung, and Law 2011), fields of study and four sample criteria were defined to select participants. A total of 13 Hong Kong Chinese tourists who posted travel photographs on Facebook and/or blogs were recruited through purposive and snowball sampling. The participants ranged from close friends of, to complete strangers to the first author. Semi-structured interviews of approximately 80 to 160 minutes each were conducted to obtain participants' accounts of their images, their photographic practices, their travel experience, and their online-sharing experience. An ethnographic visual analysis and a dramaturgical analysis were carried out to interpret the interview and visual data. Each case was analyzed holistically and was then cross-compared with other cases to identify common patterns and differences. To highlight the performative nature of their photographic practices, the informants are all labeled as the "performers" in this chapter. Their names have been changed to ensure anonymity.

The ideas and concepts discussed here were developed gradually from the first author's PhD studies at The Hong Kong Polytechnic University. The initial ideas were then expanded and modified largely through ongoing discussions with the second author, feedback from participants at the Tourism Imaginary Conference hosted in February 2011 and from participants in Professor Graburn's Anthropology seminar "Tourism, Art and Modernity," both at the University of California Berkeley, as well as invaluable suggestions from Prof. Dean MacCannell. Relevant literature and concepts were drawn upon to help interpret the oral and visual data because of these ongoing, fruitful discussions.

The Performing Self

> While celebrated for producing visions and memory, tourist photography's 'small world' of positive extraordinariness produces invisibility and forgetting. Tourist images produce 'calculated memory,' the way one would like to be remembered and to remember places. They conceal as they reveal. They represent a reality that is a projection of their maker's desires. (Bærenholdt, Haldrup, Larsen, and Urry 2004)

Travel Self in Performance

In order to stage an ideal self to their distant audiences, tourists have to dramatize their expression and to maintain expressive control. One has to put in a lot of effort to do this but without the audiences' noticing the effort (Goffman 1959). The camera offers a stage on which posing, freezing one's movement, smiling, being physically close to others in front of an attraction seem all so natural and normal. The camera, in that sense, magically turns the travel moment into a performance for memories, which will be shared with the tourist's future self and others.

Online travel images that included the 13 performers or their travel companions often captured the least "natural" moments of their travel as there was always a lot of posing involved in images posted on line. However, when locals were photographed, quite often they did not pose for the camera and were not even aware of the camera (see Figure 13.2).

The poses also did not fully represent the level of enjoyment experienced by the performers while traveling. Sometimes, the travel albums in which the performers and their travel companions performed different types of poses as well as closeness among them were indeed the trips which the performers did not find most enjoyable or memorable. For example, "Billy" posted photographs of his trips to Taiwan and Beijing. He went to Taiwan with his male friends and thus he felt he was able to act and speak freely and truly enjoy himself. There were also serendipitous moments in Taiwan, unlike during his Beijing trip in which everything was within his expectations. He also did not seem to get along very well with his two female travel companions on his Beijing trip. He explicitly complained about how these female travel companions restricted the guys from having fun and that he had to adjust his behavior accordingly to accommodate everyone's wish. Nonetheless, his photographs seemed to tell very different stories. In his album of Taiwan, there were not many group photographs. This could be due to the fact that one of his travel companions did not want his photographs to be posted on Facebook. In any case, there was a lot of distance between the travel companions whenever they were photographed together. They also did not look very excited in their

Figure 13.2 An example of online photography of locals shared by one of the
participants on Facebook

photographs. Instead their smiles were very tense and limited. In contrast, there were many group photographs in his album of Beijing. A lot more poses, closeness, and playfulness among the travel companions were in evidence.

A similar pattern was also found in "Ria's" case. Her photographs of her trip to Beijing with her parents and her younger sister involved a lot of playfulness and humor. They captured "Ria" and her parents as "always in action." In contrast, photographs of her trip to Lijiang (in western China) with her mother displayed less variety of poses, which were also still and restricted. Smiles seemed stiff and the photographs captured her "motionlessness." However, she told me that the Lijiang trip was her most unforgettable trip so far as she was able to explore areas where tourists could not visit. There were many serendipitous moments during her visit to Lijiang, unlike during her Beijing trip in which everything was so well planned.

The performative nature of tourist photography seems to reject the notion that the authentic self of the tourist, if it ever exists, can be experienced through escaping from the social norm of one's origin of place, at least this is the case with those who carry a camera with them or are photographed while traveling. In front of the lens, another social norm is being enacted. In front of the lens, another reality is being created and authenticated (Barthes 1980).

The Different Forms of the Ideal Self

Once the images were framed, the tourists had to decide whether the images should be saved, deleted, or shared. Some people adopted a more proactive role in the selection of images for online performance, while others were more passive, deleting repetitive and/or out of focus images or images that did not reflect an ideal self. To some performers, their online postings were more about the presence of self and/or travel companions than the place itself. Sometimes, the places were not as important as how the performers appeared in the photographs. To some tourists performance of self through online travel images could be more about the aesthetics of self than the far-off places they toured. For example, "Disney" played with her travel photographs and turned herself into a model through editing software. She was not particularly concerned whether her friends could recognize the places she had traveled to. Instead, she had to look pretty in the photographs. As she stated:

> "Actually you can't really tell where I am. Look at this picture! It looks as if I am at the Great Wall [in fact she was in Portugal] haha! I didn't write any captions at all so many of my friends have no clue where these places are, how funny!"

Yet, performers can be quite strategic in terms of including or excluding their physical selves in their online performances. Their perceptions of what kept their audiences' interest and what kind of impressions their online photographs could give off had a great impact on their image selection process. For example, "Ria" had a mixture of self and non-human photographs. She said that posting too many photographs of herself might lead others to see her as narcissistic. Hence, a good mixture of self, travel companions, and pure scenic photographs is important in controlling impressions. "Vivian" strategically did not include too many photographs of herself, as she believed that her physical self was not the selling point of her online performance. Instead it was through showcasing aesthetic places and her helpful travel advice that an ideal self could be produced. As she noted "I don't think that's what attracts the audience to the blog. It's not about my face. I'm not a celebrity."

Another reason why some performers did not include themselves in photographs was the lack of confidence in their physical appearance. Some performers simply disliked seeing themselves in photographs. Instead, some preferred to perform their ideal selves through their photographic senses and skills than showcasing their physical selves. For example, "Kit" got involved in photography so that she could avoid being photographed by others by having a camera in her hands. "Fung" enjoyed photographing others but rarely included himself in the pictures. He thought he looked too "weird" for photographs. Whenever he was in photographs, he was with a group of friends and with a very reserved smile. At times, he pulled funny faces as well.

Some did not mind including themselves in the photographs but also preferred to polish their photographic skills and senses for better online performances. For example, "Yang" reflected on the changes in his behavior since he started to perform online. He started to learn more about photography and buy expensive photographic equipment so that he could produce more ideal images and a happier self. He commented "well after using Facebook, I'd want to enhance my photographic skill. I'd buy a nicer camera to take better photos. I can be happier and the viewers are happier too."

Hence, whether it be a photograph of oneself or a place, the sense of one's self performing is always involved to a greater or lesser degree (see Figure 13.2). These images of others and places represent the skills, experience, capability, and the worldview of the performers. For this reason, quite a few performers enjoyed spending time and effort in enhancing the attractiveness of the place as a means to perform their ideal selves and to differentiate self from others. "JC's" thoughts are common. He stated

> "I enjoy taking photographs. The more I take photos, the more I focus on the quality. Everyone knows how to take a photograph. Everyone has his or her own interesting angle of seeing a place. But how can you make it pretty and powerful to make others feel like 'wow, so nice!' How can you emphasize the effect of something you want to express?"

The photograph in Figure 13.3 was shared by one of the participants on Facebook in 2009. The performer received compliments from the audience such as "This is absolutely beautiful. You are a very talented photographer." This compliment has remained on the performer's Facebook profile since February 2009.

Sometimes images of the performer's significant other could be what helped them to perform their ideal selves. For example, "Yang" enjoyed sharing photographs of his girlfriend who posed like a model. "Yang" received compliments from his friends for his photographic skill and for his dreamlike girlfriend. "Tracey" preferred sharing photographs of her family instead of the place to differentiate her performance from the mass-produced images. She explained her reasons thus:

> "Well, if I travel, I rarely take photos without people in them. We are not photographers. Why don't you simply buy postcards if you want pure landscape picture? Even if there's scenery I want to take photos of, I still need a person in the photo. My husband took most of the landscape photos. And I don't think they are something special. I want to share with others that, well

this is my travel trip. Or it's our family's travel trip. So that's why I don't post many landscape photos."

Sometimes, the performers chose different social media to perform their ideal selves in different forms. For example, "Kit" tended to present a more positive, happy self on Facebook where she was connected to a larger sphere of audiences including her boss. She felt relieved to present a more negative self on her blog, as the target audience was mainly her close friends. Hence, a more sincere, reflective self could be seen as ideal in this context.

The Imagining Self

> "I see only from one point, but in my existence I am looked at from all sides." (Lacan 1998: 72)

What is most interesting about online sharing is that there is no guarantee that there will be any audience for one's performance. This type of performance is what strikes Silverstone (1999) the most when he expresses that he could not grasp the nature of a performance without an audience. Indeed, through the selection process of posting and sharing photographs online, tourists produce and consume their travel photographs at the same time. They are the first audience of their own performance.

The performers had to view their own photographs at least twice before they were allowed to be on stage. Usually they took a look at the photographs to decide whether another shot should be taken. It was not unusual for the performers to take more than 100 shots on the same scene to ensure that at least one photograph was good enough for sharing. Some chose to delete photographs that were not up to their satisfaction right away. Some chose to wait until they could have a better look at the photographs again on their computer screen before any deletions were made. "Billy" noted:

> "With pure scenic photos, I need to view them carefully before I post them. For example, some of them looked quite ok on site, but then when I came back I realized, 'what? This angle of the site is quite ordinary.' To post it online seems to be a bit awkward. Or perhaps no matter how I tried to modify I still could not express the image I had in my mind at that moment. But no, I don't delete photos on-site. You never know if you can save the photo or not, so I usually wait until I can see the photos on the computer screen. It's really hard to view them on the small [camera] screen. I always try my best to rescue the photos whenever possible."

Hence, the production of online images requires previewing one's own performance from the back stage. If that is the case, then how can self be an audience and a performer at the same time? Goffman (1959) argues that self-illusion or self-alienation can become necessary if self is also the audience. Through photography, tourists are then able to gaze at themselves as an object, as another person,

(Barthes 1980) who is both familiar and unfamiliar to them. Photography is able to give the tourists a visual experience of their own bodies, of the moments, of their travel companions, and of the place that they might not be able to experience without the use of this technology (Pocock 2009). It provides the tourist a new way of conceiving self. Not only can tourists learn about others and themselves by viewing their own photographs, they can also get to view their physical travel self, their extended self (for example, girlfriends and family members) and their travel experiences through the eyes of others. Marie-Francoise Lanfant (2009) called this phenomenon "the imagined gaze." There is always a sense of being gazed at whether they were actually being gazed at or not. For example, "Pak" told the first author that photographs were taken to satisfy his girlfriend's request despite his unwillingness to be in them. Although he disliked pictures of himself, he posted them to his Facebook profile anyway. When asked why, he indicated others might think about him wrongly, as if he intentionally selected photographs of him and his girlfriend. He also mentioned that after viewing his travel photographs again during the interview, he regretted posting some in which he thought he looked terrible. He felt like deleting them but could not do so as others might notice he'd deleted them.

The performers were found to be very conscious of the "gaze of the others" on them. They felt like others were always there to judge what they did, posted, or did not post online, although they often stressed that they did not care how others thought about them. Even performers who were less selective in image-sharing had certain criteria of what not to post. The bottom line was drawn according to what they imagined others' perceptions of them through their photographs might be. "Pak," who insisted he did not care what others thought of him, said "What will people think about me if I keep posting all these repetitive photographs online? They will think that this guy is really weird! He must have some issues."

The subject of seeing becomes the object of being seen. However, it is not the panoptic type of gaze proposed by Foucault (1975). Tourists do not behave only according to the expectations of others. They simply work to improve their performances through the eyes of others. Since the performers were very concerned with producing well-received performances through which to project their ideal selves, the "imagined gaze" became the most powerful gaze in determining what they shared online. Such an imaginary of self could sometimes consume a lot of time when it involved heavy thinking, as noted by "Sandy," who stated

> "Most people don't write captions but I love to write captions. Because I am not like others who simply click 'all' and boom here you go. I did have to choose carefully what to share because there are some that cannot be seen by others, some of them also are very terrible, and some of them are *mo liu* [pointless, meaningless in Cantonese]. I think those who view my photos, I mean I am also one of those who view others' photos as well, so I think some people just share everything and they are so boring, I won't click each photo for viewing but only viewing as a whole album or as a set of photos instead. And so I took my time, I had to choose photos, view each of them slowly, and

then write captions, so I can waste two to three hours for each album I post. So each day I could only post one to two albums."

The performers could also reflect on their previous viewing experience of others' performances as a reference point for their own performances. For example, "Sandy" found those performances that presented every single detail of the trips very "boring." Hence, she preferred to spend a lot of time and effort to "carefully" view her own photographs one by one before sharing, in spite of the fact she found the process tedious. "Lily" also learned from her sister's performance that the quantity of images could sometimes get in the way of the quality of images. She noted "my sister takes a lot of nice photos. Her photos are amazing. But she posts too many! Look at hers, people are starting to get bored of her photos even though they are nice!"

At times, comparing others' performances to their own could result in a sense of pride. For example, "Ria," "Sandy," and "JC" took pride in their online photographs and often saw themselves as being different from typical Hong Kong tourists because of the types of images they captured.

Alternately, it could leave the performers with a sense of shame. During the interview, "Fung" said that he rarely viewed his photographs of Japan again because he disliked seeing them. When asked why, he explained "they look like they are taken with a common (or inexpensive) digital camera. Why can't I take nice photos like others? Even though those who do not know anything about photography can take better photos than me . . . ." He further explained that he often looked at others' photos online, be it on Flickr or Facebook. Whenever he viewed others' photographs on these social media, he wished he could take photographs as nice as theirs. He felt like he had all this photography knowledge and equipment but sadly lacked artistic sense and creativity. He continued: "It's such a shame that they are here (on Facebook and Flickr)." When asked why he posted them online if they were that bad, he replied "they looked kind of okay to me when I first posted them but now when I look at them, they are really terrible."

He did not receive many "likes" for his travel photos and suspected that the quality of his photographs could be the reason why. Therefore, not only a constant comparison of his photographs with others' photographs shaped the way he looked at his travel photos, but the reactions from the audience also played a part in his "imagined gaze." More than that, such an imagined gaze also impacted the way he looked at himself as an amateur photographer. He felt like he did not have the talent to be a good photographer and questioned whether actually he could be one.

Yet, some performers chose to interpret their audience reactions differently. Instead of seeing themselves or the quality of the photographs as the reasons why the performances was not well received, they chose to relate audiences' viewing experiences to the posting strategy. For example, "Lily" explained how she came to understand the viewing experience of her audience through their pattern of reactions. "See . . . this place [posted in her album "Day One" of India] is not my favorite and the photos are not that nice but these people just 'like' them, and then the one I like better [album of her last day in India] only two people 'like' just because I posted too many albums and this happens to be the last one."

Learning from audience reaction to better one's own performance was never an easy task. Especially on Facebook, the performers could not see the facial expressions of their audiences. The "like" function is even more ambiguous to a participant like "JC" as he complained "I don't really know what you like. Did you like the place, the girl in the photo, or what? And I can't even see your facial expression. I can't tell what you really think about my photos."

To the performers, the audiences can easily hide their real feelings about the photographs behind the computer screen. Positive reactions could merely be a form of face giving rather than an indicator of enjoyment or appreciation. The performers were aware of the fact that their audiences were also tactical beings. After all, the performers were also the audiences to many other performances.

The Deceiving Self

> The imaginary is the realm of image and imagination, deception and lure. The principal illusions of the imaginary are those of wholeness, synthesis, autonomy, duality and, above all, similarity. The imaginary is thus the order of surface appearances which are deceptive . . . . (Evans 1996: 82–83)

Both the internalization and the externalization of images require deception. Deception naturalizes the process of internalizing and externalizing ideal selves and helps make the ideal self the only reality of self. The performers had to ensure that the audiences did not view the photographs as performance but that the images simply reflected the characters of their experience and self. If the photographs were seen as a form of performance, then the ideal self would not be success-fully projected. Sometimes, the performers even had to deceive themselves in order for the performance to take place successfully, especially if a sincere self is considered an ideal self to be performed. Hence, the performers had to deny the performative nature of their practices by offering various justifications for sharing the selected, edited images online.

By showcasing their ideal selves online, the performers deceived their audi-ences by framing and sharing only the desirable ones in order to reflect the wholeness of self and experience. "Billy" commented on the process he used by noting "but now, I will be like, oh this photo is great, but if it is for sharing online, then I will need to enhance its quality before I post it. So that means, I have to do this type of editing work now, I can take many photographs but you only get to view a few."

By performing in front of the lens for their future selves to view, they deceive themselves into believing that the images captured "natural moments" of their travel. Yet, by excluding images of an unattractive self, a particular gaze of the self was shaped in time to set the standard of what "normal" self should be. Kit's comment on the self-selection process is typical of what others also said: "yes, I'd still post as long as I am not too ugly in them hahahahah. At least it has to be my normal self."

Sometimes, the performers believed that by changing the front, the back could also be changed. Successful online performances could become a remedy for some of the performers when they encountered sadness or boredom in their everyday life. They went back to their Facebook pages to view their own performances as a means to lift themselves up. Online performance could also become what caused pain when the meaning in photographs was no longer the same. During the first interview, "Fung" rarely talked about his experience in Japan. When asked if there were any moments that he found unforgettable, he said that the trip was good but there was nothing special. There was no particular moment that he could recall as very special or exciting. Rather, he often talked about the quality of his travel photographs. Whenever he thought about the trip, he felt like it was such a pity that he had not been able to take many nice photographs given that the scenery was spectacular. Half a year after the first interview, he deleted all his photographs of Japan as his partner had broken up with him and was with another person. He admitted that the deletion was due to the quality of his photographs as well as the break-up. When asked why his travel photographs had to be the first to go, he replied, "well, the memory is too intense—it's the two of us you know."

Yet, he still kept photographs of his former girlfriend in his other online albums. When asked why he did not delete those photographs as well, he asked, with a very curious tone, "what other photographs?" It seemed like he had not realized there were still photographs of her online. To "Fung," the deletion of his photographs in Japan symbolized the deletion of his most intense moments with his ex-girlfriend despite the fact that he rarely looked back at his travel photographs. "Fung" deceived himself into believing that by deleting the photographs that he rarely viewed, the hurtful memories would no longer be there to haunt him back stage.

Conclusion

Photography provides a stage on which tourists can naturally perform for future audiences. They pose for, they frame, they select, and they edit images to prepare for a performance of an ideal self. When they produce these front-stage memories, they are conscious of the potential gaze of others. This imagined gaze induces a learning process of image formation through ongoing observation, self-reflection, and imagination. Whenever tourists view their online photographs, they desire to travel again, as they see and thus remember the "positive extraordinariness" of travel, of place, and of self (Bærenholdt, Haldrup, Larsen, and Urry 2004). Front-stage memories can bring changes to the back stage as the process of producing an imaginary simultaneously "helps produce our sense of reality" (Salazar 2010). When their front-stage memories can no longer bring them happiness, the photographs are removed from public display. The removal of photographs can be a symbol of forgetting the past to ease the intense pain that the memories can bring. Online photo sharing therefore involves a certain degree of self-deception, which necessitates the act of lying to oneself of the possibility and impossibility of remembering and forgetting travel moments. Through the reactions of the audiences, tourists can also convince themselves of the desired images they project to others (Rosenberg 1986).

Tourist photographs do not merely exhibit tourist imaginaries of place, others, travel, and fantasy. What is absent from and present in their photographs is indeed shaped by tourist imaginary of self. Such an imaginary of self is facilitated through performances that take place at both the front stage and the back stage. The production and consumption of online tourist photography is a complex, long, continuous learning process of framing, selecting, editing, performing, viewing, imagining, reflecting, observing, and deceiving the tourist's self. Online tourist photography is a performance of self through which an imaginary of self through the eyes of others is possible.

Bibliography

BÆRENHOLDT Jørgen Ole, HALDRUP Michael, LARSEN Jonas, and URRY John, *Performing Tourist Places*, Ashgate, Aldershot, 2004.

BAILLY Lionel, *Lacan: A Beginners Guides*, Oneworld Publication, Oxford, 2009.

BARTHES Roland, *Camera Lucida: Reflections on Photography* [1980], translated by HOWARD Richard, Vintage, London, 2000.

BELK Russell and YEH Joyce Hsiu-Yen, "Tourist photographs: signs of self," *International Journal of Culture, Tourism and Hospitality Research*, 5(4): 345–353, 2011.

CATON Kellee and SANTOS Carla Almeida, "Closing the hermeneutic circle: photographic encounters with the other," *Annals of Tourism Research*, 35(1): 7–26, 2008.

COOLEY Charles Horton, "Looking-glass self," in *Symbolic Interaction: A Reader in Social Psychology*, MANIS J.G. and MELTZER, B.N. (eds), Allyn and Bacon, Boston, MA, pp. 231–233, 1972.

EVANS Dylan, *An Introductory Dictionary of Lacanian Psychoanalysis*, Routledge, New York, 1996.

FOUCAULT Michel. *Discipline and Punish: The Birth of the Prison*, Random House, New York, 1975.

GARROD Brian, "Understanding the relationship between tourism destination imagery and tourist photography," *Journal of Travel Research*, 47(3): 346–358, 2009.

GOFFMAN Erving, *The Presentation of Self in Everyday Life*, Doubleday, New York, 1959.

GRABURN Nelson and GRAVARI-BARBAS Maria, "Introduction: imagined landscapes of tourism," Special issue of *Journal of Tourism and Cultural Change*, 9(3): 159–166, 2011.

GRAVARI-BARBAS Maria and GRABURN Nelson, "Tourist imaginaries," *Via@, Tourist Imaginaries*, no. 1, http://www.viatourismreview.net/Editorial1_EN.php, 2012.

HERMAN Lisa, "Researching the images of evil events: an arts-based methodology in liminal space," *Qualitative Inquiry*, 11(3): 468–480, 2005.

JENKINS Olivia, "Photography and travel brochures: the circle of representation," *Tourism Geographies*, 5(3): 305–328, 2003.

LACAN Jacque, *The Four Fundamental Concepts of Psycho-analysis*, Penguin, Harmondsworth, 1998.

LANFANT Marie Francoise, "The purloined eye: revisiting the tourist gaze from a phenomenological perspective," in *The Framed World: Tourism, Tourists and Photography*, ROBINSON Mike and PICARD David (eds), Ashgate, Farnham, pp. 239–256, 2009.

LARSEN Jonas, "Geographies of tourism photography: choreographies and performances," in *Geographies of Communication: The Spatial Turn in Media Studies*, FALKHEIMER Jesper and JANSSON Andre (eds), Nordicom, Gøteborg, pp. 243–261, 2006.

LEUNG H.Y., "Chinese bloggers on backpacking: donkey friends tourism, travel writing, and photography in contemporary china," M.A. Thesis in Asian Studies, University of California at Berkeley, 2010.

LO Iris Sheungting, MCKERCHER Bob, LO Ada, CHEUNG Catherine, and LAW Rob, "Tourism and online photography," *Tourism Management*, 32(4): 725–731, 2011.

LOOS Amanda, "Symbolic, real, imaginary," *Theories of Media: Keywords Glossary*. http://csmt.uchicago.edu/glossary2004/symbolicrealimaginary.htm, 2002.

MARKHAM Mick, "Through the looking glass: reflective teaching through a Lacanian lens," *Curriculum Inquiry*, 29(1): 55–76, 1999.

POCOCK Celmara, "Entwined histories: photography and tourism at the Great Barrier Reef," in *The Framed World: Tourism, Tourists and Photography*, ROBINSON Mike and PICARD David (eds), Ashgate, Farnham, pp. 185–197, 2009.

ROSENBURG Morris, *Conceiving the Self,*, Basic Books, New York, 1986.

SALAZAR Noel, *Envisioning Eden: Mobilizing Imaginaries in Tourism and Beyond*, Berghahn, Oxford, 2010.

——, "Tourism imaginaries: a conceptual approach," *Annals of Tourism Research*, 39(2): 863–882, 2012.

SCARLES Caroline, "Becoming tourist: renegotiating the visual in tourist experience," *Environment and Planning D: Society and Space*, 27(3): 465–488, 2009.

SILVERSTONE Roger, *Why Study the Media?*, Sage, London, 1999.

URRY John, *The Tourist Gaze: Leisure and Travel in Contemporary Societies*, Sage, London, 2002.

URRY John and LARSEN Jonas, *The Tourist Gaze 3.0*, Sage, London, 2011.

WITTEL Andreas, "Ethnography on the move: from field to net to Internet," *Forum Qualitative Sozialforshung/Forum*, 1(1): Art. 21, http://nbn-resolving.de/urn:nbn:de:0114-fqs0001213, 2000.

YEH Joyce Hsiu-Yen, "The embodiment of sociability through the tourist camera," in *The Framed World: Tourism, Tourists and Photography*, ROBINSON Mike and PICARD David (eds), Ashgate, Farnham, pp. 199–216, 2009.

14 The Tourism Websites of Metropolitan Areas

Between the Image and the Imaginary

Philippe Viallon

Introduction

Communication is highly valuable tool for the study of tourism as a social phenomenon. The communications approach is two-fold. First, it examines all types of messages linked to tourism, including word-of-mouth, the Internet, the postcard, and so on. Second, it looks at the array of organizations directly and indirectly involved in tourism and at individuals who are potential tourists.

Since Aristotle, we regard communication as a method to influence and convince others to accept new ideas or to change behaviors, including, in this case, the acquisition of tourist goods. The important economic and social aspects of tourism have led to an ever-greater refinement of the techniques used to persuade people to become tourists, and the arrival of the digital revolution has further enhanced those methods. But tourist choice, which is linked to going elsewhere and usually to an expenditure of money, cannot be explained simply by conditions of supply and demand, as a strictly market approach would dictate. Research in the field of tourism communications has highlighted the complexity of the decision-making process, and especially the role of the imaginary, of potential tourists.

An analysis of the current status of tourism communications thus allows us to look at the new strategies that go beyond simple facts to influence the imaginaries of potential tourists. New forms of communication include those that, rather than immediately encouraging the message recipient to action, instead work to instill broader, lasting impressions through language and images. Images in particular are considered very valuable in this approach because of the tight link between the two concepts of image and imaginary. Using tools from other disciplines, including linguistics and semiotics for analysis, and psychology and sociology, the science of communications provides an original approach to the tourism phenomenon.

Among all of the promotional tools currently used by urban tourist destinations, websites have become indispensable (Gravari-Barbas 2006). In the planning of a trip, the first of the three elements of a vacation (Boyer and Viallon 1994) the Web is now the most important medium both for procuring information as well as for paying for plane tickets, hotels, and so on (UNWTO 2010). The Web's structure of "one to many" allows a site's single message to reach thousands or millions of viewers. These are viewers, however, whose backgrounds and perspectives vary enormously. Two categories of website readers can be defined. First are those who have a common culture with the desired destination, usually defined as a common language. In this case, any cultural differences between the potential tourist and the destination manifest themselves at the individual level. The issue then becomes one of how to respond to the variety of individual imaginaries in order to convince potential visitors. Relevant personal variables have been previously defined by tourism anthropologists as age, social milieu, gender, birthplace, and so on (Graburn 1983; Cousin and Réau 2009; Leite and Graburn 2009). However, no single study to date has comprehensively examined them all. The second type of potential tourist is one whose native language and culture is different to those of the destination (Laplante 1988). The characteristics of the individual remain important, but are overlaid by intercultural imaginaries, often created in part by stereotypes. In this case the question becomes one of how to manage interculturality in Web communications (Bédard 1999; Morand and Mollard 2008).

Cultural differences are not a new element in leisure travel. Indeed, many would regard them as one of the motors of tourism (Cohen 1979). For tourism communication, the most common current strategy for dealing with cultural, that is, language, differences is simply translation. But a host of questions arise about this seemingly straightforward approach. Is it simply text that is translated, or images as well? Do all urban tourist destinations use the translation strategy in the same way to attract potential visitors? How does this cultural adaptation actually work (Singh and Baack 2004; Hillier 2004)? Do websites try to impose their own imaginaries or are they merely acting as mirrors for their viewers? What is the role of images (Crouch and Lübbren 2003; Pink, Kürti and Afonso 2004)? And finally, despite the diversity of destinations and the cultural origins of potential visitors, are there common elements in the translation approach? To respond to these questions, we have analyzed the websites of 19 large urban tourist destinations.

The selection of sites was based on French tourists' interests. Thus we opted for a classification system established by a French tourism enterprise called hotel. com, which sells hotel stays through the Internet. On its site, it publishes a semi-annual survey of hotel prices, and as a by-product it has developed a list of those foreign cities most visited by the French based on hotel reservations made on its site between January and June 2010. It is possible that another similar site would show different results, because it is difficult to believe that more French go to Tokyo than to Venice or Marrakech. However, our objective is not to establish a list of most preferred destinations, but rather simply to have a list of cities likely to interest French tourists. To this group of foreign destinations, we have added the three most visited cities in France in order to examine how, in reversing the cultural perspective, these three manage their websites. The cities selected are: New York, London, Las Vegas, San Francisco, Barcelona, Los Angeles, Rome, Tokyo, Amsterdam, Miami, Brussels, Marrakech, Venice, Madrid, Montreal, Prague, Paris, Lyons, and Nice.

The tourist websites of these 19 cities will be studied using already developed tools for analyzing websites (Nielsen 2001; Robbins-Stylianou 2003; Greffe and Sonnac 2008; Rouquette 2009) as well as those for understanding images

(Joly 1996; Viallon 1996; De Bonville 2000). More than the website content itself, it is the differences between the different linguistic versions that will be examined. The responses to the questions posed above will be derived from a combination of the existing literature on the subject and the analysis of the sites themselves.

Theory/State of the Art

Three concepts are essential here: (1) destination theory; (2) the image and the imaginary; and (3) communication and interculturality (Gudykunst 2003; Ang and Van Dyne 2008).

Destination Theory

Destinations have been widely studied, especially in the English-language literature. As Fakeye and Crompton (1991) remind us, the subject is a complex one. Promotion of a destination involves three steps: informing people, persuading them, and drawing upon their existing notions of a place. As Nadeau et al. (2008) recommend with regard to country destinations, it is in a country's self-interest to expand the approach to this concept because the image of a nation and its attractiveness as a tourist destination go hand-in-hand. Other criteria such as the environment, health, or political stability, to cite a few, are equally important. Baloglu and McCleary (1999) have defined 17 variables in several categories: the range of information sources such as professional advice, word-of-mouth advice, advertising, books, and movies; the characteristics of the traveler such as age and level of education; and the goals of the traveler in terms of relaxation, adventure, knowledge, sociability, prestige, price/value relationship, and image or attractiveness of the destination.

However, in all of these studies, cultural differences are generally ignored. Why is this the case?

The Relationship between the Image and the Imaginary

The relationship between the image and the imaginary is not solely linguistic. The common etymology of these two words, in English as in French, can be deceiving. How is it possible for someone to evoke his or her own imaginary without first describing visual images? Serge Tisseron (2002) has defined three elements in this relationship:

- The reality, which exists independently of the individual, but which is perceived through each person's own subjectivity. There are thus as many realities as there are individuals apprehending them.
- The image reproduced on paper, television, computer, and so on. Except in the case of synthesized images (which requires another level of analysis and will not be dealt with here), all images pass through and are the product of everyone involved in transmitting it: most obviously the photographer, but also the person

responsible for the site, the webmaster, and all others with a role in the development of the website. And the number of images grows continuously. Even before the Internet, drawings, film, and television had increased the number of images seen by people, and the Internet has enlarged this number exponentially.

- The mental images, those in our heads that populate our imaginary. These mental images come from three sources. Level 1: the reality seen with our own eyes, filtered through the subjectivity of the moment. Level 2: the images we have seen in photographs, film, television or on the Internet. Level 3: images that we ourselves have produced, whether in dreaming or imagining them while listening to a friend recount the details of a trip, reading a travel guidebook, a novel, and so on.

Whatever the origin of these mental images, they have certain characteristics in common.

- They evolve over time. Our brains function in such a manner that often less important stored information either completely disappears or is relegated to a place in the brain where it is more difficult to recall. This process is as much quantitative as qualitative. In addition, mental images are often idealized over time. In general, in adults, before the aging process sets in, the last images received are the most vivid, but emotional factors can affect this situation.
- the source of the image may be forgotten. People are not always capable of recalling the precise origin of their mental images (Kosslin 1980). Do these images come from my own photographs or from those in a guidebook? Have I been to a place or simply seen a photograph of it? The response to such questions often is based on what one knows. For example, "I have never been in Antarctica, thus the images I have of that place must be based on other sources." On the other hand, "On my last trip to San Francisco more than 30 years ago, did I see the Golden Gate Bridge emerging from the fog or is it the image that I saw on the Internet or in the guidebook I bought that stays with me?"

Communication and Interculturality

The well-known expression of Watzlawick (1967)—"one cannot not communicate"—applies also to tourism communications. All individuals are potential or virtual tourists and all information, visual and non-visual, can be used to imagine a place as a tourist destination. Conversely, paraphrasing Bateson (1972)—"no mere words exist"—no uniquely tourist place exists. Moviemakers have benefited from this understanding by getting financing to film in certain locations. This was the case when producing *The Lord of the Rings*. Tourism professionals also recognize the potential of post-film tourism, as was also the case for the film location of *The Lord of the Rings* (Hudson and Ritchie 2006; Singh and Best 2004). And it is not simply tourism communication that feeds our imaginary. Every news broadcast, every misconception, every mental image derived from a verbal narrative can also contribute to our imaginary of a place.

The communications environment will influence and give value to these images at two levels. On the first level, our national culture will strongly mark our image of a country or a city. Stereotypes (Gudykunst 2003) play an important role here, regardless of their veracity, and the collective imaginary also plays a critical role. Therefore, it is essential to know the cultural origins of the Internet users in order to adapt the tourism communication strategy appropriately. The second level is that of the individual and her own culture. Here it is much more difficult to manage public communications, since it takes the form of "one to many." Although it is impossible to provide a unique message for everyone, it is feasible to envisage individualized messages for categories of people by age, sex, social or professional status, and so on (Robbins-Stylianou 2003). For example, within certain websites there are pages directed at specific groups such as children or the gays, but it is difficult to go much farther in individualizing public communication. How is it possible to learn if I as tourist would prefer to visit Silicon Valley rather than Napa Valley, or would I like to visit both?

Given these three elements—the image of the destination, the image and the imaginary, and intercultural communication at both the individual and group level—it becomes a complicated challenge for metropolitan areas to manage their websites in an era of growing competition for tourists.

Findings

For this chapter, three criteria have been used: (1) translation of websites into foreign languages; (2) use and manipulation of images; and (3) influence of the translation on the choice of image. Although it may seem paradoxical to examine text before image, when images are our fundamental concern, we have done so because websites cannot survive on images alone. Text and image both appear, allowing the Internet user to construct his or her own interpretation based on the redundancy, understanding, complementarities, contrast, or absence or presence of a relationship between text and image. As Thierry Lancien (2000) has shown, these interpretations are manifold.

Language Strategies

The strategies concerning languages and translation of sites vary widely. Brussels' site has 11 languages, the most we found. Miami's site is in English alone, and so is New York's, but it offers 52 other languages, including Haitian Creole and Filipino, through the use of Google's translation program. This solution, which tries to provide functionality at minimum cost, proves in fact to be quite unhelpful. The resulting text often is incomprehensible. The Google translation pages can also result in problems with the images.

The choice of English as the most common language is not surprising, given its double function as the international language of both communication and global culture. The frequent use of French can also be explained by the group of sites examined. It would seem that the choice of language is a function of the native tongues of either the current or anticipated tourists. However, the analysis reveals some unexpected findings. Marrakech does not have a page in Arabic, and Miami does not have one in Spanish despite having one of the largest Spanish-speaking populations in the United States.

A comparison between the origins of the largest contingents of tourists and the languages of tourist websites shows a certain logic. The languages of the 10 countries which provide the largest number of tourists are those most often found on websites. The only significant exception to this finding is German. The explanation may derive from the fact that many Germans travel with tour-operators to sunny destinations rather than to cities.

The first conclusion is that there are great differences in the number of languages. This comes either from a desire to flatter certain groups by showing them the importance of their language and culture and easing communication, or from a strategic decision to have only one language like Miami or New York, where communication in English is a common element of the American Dream.

Beyond just the number of languages, it is also important to look at how they are handled, especially in relation to other tongues. Several cities vary the number of website pages translated into foreign languages. If the original language version is considered as the long version of the site, some sites have full-length foreign language text as well, while others have shortened versions of various lengths. Of the 16 cities studied that have a foreign language version of their website, 11 have completely translated their text, while five have resorted to long versions and/or medium and/or short ones.

It is not possible to discern clear patterns. Among the sites with many translations, Prague has its entire text fully translated into 10 languages. Brussels' site is in 11 languages, and it makes a special effort to provide different information to French-speaking Belgians and Quebecois than is provided to the French. On the other hand, Paris, London, and San Francisco, which also have at least partial translations in many languages, bring Internet users back to French or English for the full text. For sites with fewer languages, again there is no clear pattern. Barcelona, Los Angeles, Rome, Marrakech, and Madrid translate the entire text, while Las Vegas and Amsterdam have no translations. The French sites are equally varied.

So what can we conclude on this subject? Each city develops its own strategy based on the costs of translation and the importance that it gives to each potential group of tourists. In the end, the value of the site depends on the Internet user and the value placed on learning about tourist destinations in one's own language. However, it is worth pointing out that, of the cities listed as most frequently visited by the French by the site hotel.com, the five cities of New York, Las Vegas, Los Angeles, Miami, and Venice do not have French versions of their websites. So much for the idea that the French place great importance on using their language and have weak competence in others!

Images of Tourist Destinations on Websites

In order to deal with a manageable quantity of information, we have restricted our analysis to images on home pages only.

The size of the home page of the sites analyzed varies in length. The entirety of some home pages can be seen only with the aid of the scrolling function. This variation in size of the homepage is related both to the number and size of photos contained on it. Our analysis will be presented in terms of percentage of the homepage occupied by photos.

In the visual analysis, photographs, all pictorial images and maps are considered as images. Logos and graphic chips have not been included. The rest of the homepage consists of the text and background color. All video material has been considered as a photo, taken at the time of the recording, even though the video may significantly modify the reader's overall perception of the page.

When looking at the results, the diversity of strategies is striking. At the low end, the Rome website uses 10 percent of its homepage for images, while at the other end of the scale Marrakech uses 67 percent. The difference among the sites can be lessened by the use of color tints, but if this device is eliminated it becomes very clear how large a place is given over to imagery.

To do the quantitative analysis, it was necessary to save homepage after homepage and that revealed one of the surprising findings of this work. With the exception of London and Los Angeles, the beginning of a homepage, that is, what the viewer sees on the screen when the homepage comes up, has much more imagery than the portion of the homepage reached by scrolling. We will return to the question of why more importance is given to images at the beginning and to text thereafter in the conclusion.

What do these images represent? People, animals, nature, monuments, important objects, and other things In the case of multiple images presented in several of the categories, it is the most important image that has been selected. This image was defined as either the one in the center of the screen or the one that occupied the most space. We used a typology with four categories of images: People, Nature, Buildings, and Objects. With this typology, the two categories of Buildings and People stand out clearly from the others. Buildings appear in eight of the 18 cases, while People appear in seven of the 18. Using buildings as images seems logical on the websites of cities that are substantially defined by their built environment. However, for Amsterdam, Los Angeles, and Tokyo, Nature is the dominant characteristic based on our method. The people shown on websites appear to be residents rather than tourists. The image of the city presented to the Internet user is thus more suggestive of what there is to see rather than what there is to do (Martinec and Salway 2005). The difference is important, because in the first case, it is as if the viewer is truly in the realm of fiction that agrees with the imaginary. In the second case, the user is in a state of reflection, often accompanied by a look to camera which subverts the fiction. It must be noted that the Brussels website has not been analyzed because practically all the imagery is in the form of either slide shows or film.

We have been unable to discern any relationship between the imagery on webpages and the characteristics of the destination such as location (New World or Old), spoken language (French or English), or size of the metropolitan area.

How are these images presented? As our last criterion, we have analyzed how many pages have images with special effects. These include blurred images, photos with shadow effects, strong contrasts of light and dark, or taken at night, or iconic images such as the Golden Gate Bridge rising above the fog. In effect, we looked at any iconic or plastic part of the image that strives to influence a potential visitor's mental image of a place rather than its reality. The results range from zero percent for Amsterdam to 100 percent for Montreal. In other words, Amsterdam is offering its reality to the tourist, while Montreal is presenting dreams. All four of Montreal's photos are taken at night, suggesting a city at play and its attendant fantasies. Marrakech and Las Vegas are also notable for their substantial use of special effect images. One could theorize that Marrakech is playing on the Western image of the Orient, as Said has shown, while Las Vegas, the gambling city par excellence, suggests dreams of great gain to Web users. The low frequency of use of these types of images in the other websites does not allow for any further hypotheses about strategies.

Translating Images

Finally, we examined the images and text of several different linguistic versions of websites. It appears that there are essentially no or very few differences in the various languages presented. For most sites, the translation is strictly linguistic and does not take account of cultural differences. Only London, the most visited city in the world, does otherwise. Is this simply chance? Is London's attraction the cause or the consequence of these linguistic changes that speak more directly to different cultures? It is difficult to say, but it is the case that the French version of the site has more information about restaurants, while the German version concentrates more on shopping, and the English version emphasizes bargains.

Conclusion

Our work confirms a certain number of observations that have been previously made in other studies (Viallon 2004; 2008). They are as follows:

- There are no common strategies using intercultural and iconic approaches for the websites of the metropolitan areas examined here (Singh and Boughton 2002; Giessen and Viallon 2009). Some cities, like New York or Miami, rely solely on their own unique character. If tourists are interested in New York or Miami, it is because of they are *sui generis* and any attempt that they would make to adapt their website to the culture of their visitors would make them less so. This reasoning has the double advantage of both simplicity and cost-effectiveness (Cunliffe 2004). However, virtually all the other cities have several linguistic versions of their websites, even though in some cases the choice of languages may be limited. Montreal's website is in only English and French, perhaps justified by the origins of its tourists. The number of languages may be wider based on knowing where tourists come from. The most visited cities (London and Paris) have the greatest linguistic offerings, although this apparent range of languages proves to be a bit misleading. After one or two clicks away from the homepage, the number of languages may abruptly drop and the viewer may find certain information in a much more restricted number of tongues, often only English.

• regarding images and the imaginary, which are closely linked, it would appear from our analysis that website creators regard both as universal languages, an idea which we believe is false. With the exception of London, which modifies its images and text according to the language of the site, the images and text of the other sites are unchanged in the various linguistic versions. Why? Because of a false idea of the capacity of images to express universal meaning, or simply because it is easier? Surely for both reasons. The French city websites are no different. As a medium of communication, the Internet is still in its infancy. The urban tourist destinations, which compete aggressively for tourists, must learn to take into account an element as essential as the representations of their potential visitors. Currently, it appears that their sites focus more on providing information and explanations rather than on playing on potential visitors' emotions (Kim and Yoon 2003). The cultural differential, whose elements are invisible, remains a hidden dimension (Hall 1969) largely neglected by tourism professionals.

Bibliography

ANG, Soon and VAN DYNE, Linn (2008), *Handbook of Cultural Intelligence*, New York: Sharpe.

BALOGLU, Seyhmus, MCCLEARY, Ken (1999), "A model of destination image formation," *Annals of Tourism Research*, 26: 868–897.

BATESON, G. (1972), *Steps to an Ecology of Mind*, Chicago, IL: University of Chicago Press.

BEDARD, François (1999), "Adaptation aux nouvelles technologies dans l'industrie du tourisme," *Téoros*, 18(3) (autumn): 33–39.

BOYER, Marc and VIALLON, Philippe (1994), *La communication touristique*, Paris: Presses universitaires de France.

COHEN, Erik (1979), "Rethinking the sociology of tourism," *Annals of Tourism Research*, 6(1): 6–11.

COUSIN, Saskia and REAU, Bertrand (2009), *Sociologie du tourisme*, Paris: Editions la Découverte.

CROUCH, David and LÜBBREN, Nina (2003), *Visual Culture and Tourism*, New York and Oxford: Berg.

CUNLIFFE, Daniel (2004), "Promoting minority language use on bilingual websites," *Mercator Media Forum*, http://www.aber.ac.uk/mercator/images/cunliffefinal.pdf, accessed March 5, 2010.

DE BONVILLE, Jean (2000), *L'analyse de contenu des médias: de la problématique au traitement statistique*, Bruxelles: De Boeck Université.

FAKEYE, P.C. and CROMPTON, John L. (1991), "Image differences between prospective, first-time and repeat visitors to the Lower Rio Grande Valley," *Journal of Travel Research*, 30(2): 10–16.

GIESSEN, Hans and VIALLON, Virginie (2009), "L'élaboration des sites Internet dans des pays différents: prédominance culturelle ou contrainte du média?," *Proceedings International Conference: New Medias, Convergences and Divergences*, Athens.

GRABURN, Nelson (1983), "The anthropology of tourism," *Annals of Tourism Research*, 10(1): 9–33.

GRAVARI-BARBAS, Maria (2006), "La ville à l'ère de la globalisation des loisirs," *Espaces*, 234: 48–56.

GREFFE, Xavier and SONNAC, Nathalie (2008), *Culture Web*, Paris: Dalloz.

GUDYKUNST, William B. (2003), "Intercultural communication theories," in GUDYKUNST, William B (ed.), *Cross-Cultural and Intercultural Communication*, Thousand Oaks, CA: Sage, pp. 167–189.

HALL, Edward T. (1969), *The Hidden Dimension*, New York: Doubleday, Anchor Books.

HILLIER, Mathew (2004), "The role of cultural context in multilingual website usability," *Electronic Commerce Research and Applications*, 2(1): 2–14.

HUDSON, S. and RITCHIE, J. Brent (2006), "Promoting destinations via film tourism: an empirical identification of supporting marketing initiatives." *Journal of Travel Research*, 44(4): 387–396.

JOLY, Martine (1996), *Introduction à l'analyse de l'image*, Paris: Nathan.

KIM, Seehyung and YOON, Yoohik (2003), "The hierarchical effects of affective and cognitive components on tourism destination image," *Journal of Travel and Tourism Marketing*, 14(2): 1–22.

KOSSLIN, S.M. (1980), *Image and Mind*, Cambridge, MA: Harvard University Press.

LANCIEN, Thierry (ed.) (2000), *Multimédia: les mutations du texte*, Fontenay-Saint-Cloud: ENS Editions.

LAPLANTE, Marc (1988), "Culture vécue et représentation touristique," *Téoros*, 7(1): 25–27.

LEITE, Naomi and GRABURN, Nelson (2009), "Anthropological Interventions In Tourism Studies," in JAMAL, Tazim and ROBINSON, Mike, *The Sage Handbook of Tourism Studies*, Thousand Oaks, CA: Sage, pp. 35–64.

MARTINEC, Radan and SALWAY, Andrew (2005), "A system for image–text relations in new (and old) media," *Visuel Communication*, 4: 337–371.

MASSOU, Luc and MORELLI, Pierre (2009), "Sites Web et blogs africains: modèles de publication en ligne," in KIYINDOU, Alain et al. (eds), *Communication et dynamiques de globalisation culturelle*, Paris: Editions l'Harmattan, pp. 157–172.

MIT (2005), *Tourismes 2, Moments de lieux*, Paris: Belin.

MORAND, Jean-Claude and MOLLARD, Brice (2008), *Tourisme 2.0. Préparer son voyage / Préparer son offre de tourisme*, Paris: M21 Editions.

NADEAU, J., HESLOP, L., O'REILLY, N., and LUK, P. (2008), "Destination in a country image context," *Annals of Tourism Research*, 35(1): 84–106.

NIELSEN, Jacob (2001), *Designing Web Usability: The Practice of Simplicity*, München: Markt + Technik.

PINK, Sarah, KÜRTI, Laszlo and AFONSO, Ana Isabel (2004), *Working Images: Visual Research and Representation in Ethnography*, London: Routledge.

ROBBINS, Stephanie and STYLIANOU, Antonis (2003), "Global corporate web sites: an empirical investigation of content and design," *Information & Management*, 40: 205–212.

ROUQUETTE, Sébastien (2009), *L'analyse des sites Internet: une radiographie du cyper-esp@ce*, Bruxelles: Editions de Boeck Université.

SINGH, Kamal and BEST, Gary (2004), "Film-induced tourism: motivations of visitors to the Hobbiton movie set as featured in *The Lord Of The Rings*," in FROST, Warwick, CROY, Glen and BEETON, Sue (eds), *International Tourism and Media Conference Proceedings*, 24–26 November, Melbourne: Tourism Research Unit, Monash University, pp. 98–111.

SINGH, Nitisch and BAACK, Daniel (2004), "Web site adaptation: a cross-cultural comparison of U.S. and Mexican web sites," http://jcmc.indiana.edu/vol9/issue4/singh_baack.html, accessed March 3, 2010.

SINGH, Nitisch and BOUGHTON, Paul (2002), "Measuring web site globalization: a cross-sectional country and industry level analysis," *American Marketing Association Conference Proceedings*, 13: 302–303.

TISSERON, Serge (2002), *Les bienfaits des images*, Paris: Odile Jacob.

UNWTO (2010), *Tourism Highlights*, Madrid.

UNWTO / OMT (2006), http://www.unwto.org/facts/eng/pdf/historical/ITA_1950_2005.pdf, accessed March 1, 2010.

VIALLON, Philippe (1996), *Analyse du discours de la télévision*, Paris: Presses Universitaires de France, QSJ no. 3111.

—— (2004), "La Méditerranée au risque de la communication touristique," in BAIDER, Fabienne, BURGER, Marcel and GOUTSOS, Dyonisos, *La communication touristique / Tourist Communication*, Paris: L'Harmattan, pp. 191–214.

—— (2008), "Immigration et tourisme: prolégomènes à une approche interculturelle de ces phénomènes," in CHOUIKHA, Larbi, MEYER, Vincent and GOOURA, Wahid, *Interagir et transmettre, informer et communiquer: quelles valeurs, quelle valorisation?*, Tunis: ISD, IPSI, SFSIC, pp. 59–68.

VIALLON, Philippe and HENNEKE-LANGE, Sandrine (2011), "L'excellence des sites web touristiques: l'interculturalité en ligne de mire," *Téoros*, 30(1): 62–70.

WATZLAWICK, P., BEAVIN, J.H., and JACKSON, D.D. (1967), "Some tentative axioms of communication," in *Pragmatics of Human Communication: A Study of Interactional Patterns, Pathologies, and Paradoxes*, New York: W.W. Norton, pp. 48–71.

15 Transportation Catastrophes and Travel Imaginaries in the French Mass Illustrated Press, 1890–1914

H. Hazel Hahn

Introduction

Le Petit Journal, founded in 1863 by Moïse Polydore Millaud, was the first truly mass French newspaper. In the 1890–1914 period it focused foremost on domestic and foreign affairs, crime, colonial wars, and disasters. Its circulation was a million in the 1890s and declined to 800,000 in 1900, mainly due to its anti-Dreyfus stance, although it was generally known for its "apoliticism" (Wolgensinger 1989: 78–9; Avenel 1900: 854). It was famed for the sensationalistic full-color front and back engraved images of its weekly supplement, *Le Petit Journal supplément illustré* (hereafter *PJSI*), that began appearing in November 1890. From 1897 to 1901 each supplement included three full-page color images, quite remarkable given its low price of one sou (five centimes). The images depicted events that had happened two to three weeks earlier, given the long process of image production. *PJSI*'s images had a fairly diverse content. A large portion of the images was on non-violent topics like political debates, portraits of politicians and military heroes, celebration of French achievements in colonies, exhibitions, news of royalty and celebrities, and scenes of everyday life. The images also often graphically represented scenes of violence like catastrophes of all variety, crimes, and people being killed by animals in zoos, with expressions of horror on people's faces and lots of blood splashing about. The images, some of which were based on photographs, were in a style recalling illustrations of juvenile adventure novels and somewhat cartoonish. Conveying a sense of innocence, this style was curiously suited for depicting scenes of a wide variety of violence.

As Table 15.1 shows, between 1891 and 1913 the percentage of violent cover images in *PJSI* ranged from 10 to 60 per cent. In 1906, a record 31 (out of 52) violent cover images included five on crimes, five on animals harming humans, five involving ships, aerostats, or bicycles, five on other disasters (fire, mine crash, explosion, hiking accident, and so on), four set in French colonies, and seven on social conflicts (riots and protests), political violence, or social violence (lynching and so on) in France and abroad. One typically sensationalistic image managed to depict both the act of a young woman accidentally shooting her younger sister—with fire flashing from a rifle—*and* the reaction of the victim—falling with an expression of shock and pain on her blood-stained face

(*PJSI*, Dec. 30, 1906, cover). The ebb and flow in topics reflected current events. China was the setting of four violent covers in 1900, and the Russo-Japanese war of nine in 1904, while French colonial wars in Africa were featured throughout the period. Some violent covers were on sensational personal violence, such as duels fought with unusual means like axes or whips (*PJSI*, Jan. 8, 1911, cover; Apr. 17, 1910, cover). Wars could also be the justification for publishing intriguing images of female warriors called the "Jeanne d'Arc" of Macedonia or Albania respectively (*PJSI*, July 26, 1903, cover; May 21, 1911, cover).

Scholars have theorized that the depoliticized and moralizing character of journalism under the French Second Empire seems to have led to the sensationalism of *Le Petit Journal* (Cragin 2006: 237). This interpretation only partly explains the appeal of the sensational. The ubiquitous popularity of sensationalist news today is not explained through previous censorship and the release of repressed demand for censored topics. Dominique Kalifa in *L'Encre et le sang* has provided a much more nuanced argument, underlining the modern and urban—especially Parisian—nature of crime as seen from the popular milieux (Kalifa 1995). According to Kalifa over-representation in the sensationalist mass press about violent crimes such as murder and rape, often traced to uncontrollable passions or alcoholism, resulted in a void in the social imagination that did not correlate well to social reality. Kalifa also underlined interconnections to popular stories of crime and revenge, debates on public security, and theories of social psychology.

In addition to these issues, sensationalism should be situated in the expansion of the marketplace of the media and fiction, taking into account public taste for often spectacular representations of violence of all variety. When we focus on the violent images published in *PJSI*—as opposed to the mostly textual content of the daily paper—as Table 15.1 shows, we see that covers on sensational catastrophes, including transportation accidents, fires, explosions, and natural disasters, or images of war as well as political and social conflicts, were just as frequent as images on crimes, in part because visual depiction of certain crimes like rape was taboo.[1] The paper was often explicitly political in its enthusiastic support of the French empire, its nationalism—and anti-German feelings—, its anti-Dreyfus

Table 15.1 Violent cover images in *PJSI*, 1891–1913

	Number of violent cover images	Crimes	Modern transportation disasters and accidents	Animals harming humans	Other disasters and accidents	War, political and social conflicts
1891–1894	6–16 out of 52	0–4 per year	1–4 per year	0–1 per year	1 per year	4–8 per year
1895–1898	5–14	1	0–2	0–2	0–4	2–5
1899–1902	10–15	0–3	0–1	0–2	1–3	7–8
1903–1906	17–31	3–10	4–7	0–5	1–5	7–11
1907–1910	19–27	6–10	4–8	0–3	2–5	3–6
1911–1913	10–16	0–6	0–4	0–1	0–4	2–6

stance, and its sympathetic portrayal of the French military and the police as duty-bound and heroic in colonial battles, disasters, or fighting crimes. In reporting on such situations, *PJSI* was far from apolitical. However, I will argue that reports on transportation catastrophes in *PJSI* were not foremost concerned with the aim of raising awareness about social issues or morality. On closer inspection, the images turn out to have a range of styles and to contain a variety of cultural references, including narratives and imaginaries about travel and tourism, both domestic and foreign. In addition to existential catharsis, social issues, and imperial rivalry, as well as the notions of progress, civilizing, and entropy, I highlight a voyeuristic desire for vicarious experience as well as the pleasure of looking at images about violence.

Modes of Transportation: Trains

Modern modes of transportation were of considerable interest to the public, as they enabled travel and leisure and were also crucial for military activities and colonial battles. One of the very first images of trains that appeared in *PJSI* depicted a crime scene, deftly combining two of the favorite themes of the paper: crime and modern transportation (*PJSI*, May 16, 1891, cover). In a train cabin a man has just shot a man and a woman. The gun is emitting a flash of fire, and smoke is filling the cabin. Blood is trickling down the woman's neck, and from the shot man's temple. A woman's hat, a purse, and an open book are visible in the foreground, signs of a typical train journey and a moment of relaxation brutally interrupted. An explanatory text noted that a French nobleman, during a train journey from Madrid to France, suddenly shot his wife and a friend, injuring them slightly, and claimed that he saw them in a posture indicating their betrayal of him.[2] The victims' friends claimed that the perpetrator was a morphine addict living away from his wife, after the death of a child had broken the last link between the two (*PJSI*, May 16, 1891, p. 7). The text tied conflicting interpretations about the incident to an ethical issue—whether the man was justified in shooting the victims. However, more than the ethical issue, it was the visual drama that was to appeal to the viewer as the caption, "A drama on the railroad," underlined. The composition of the image was aimed at maximum dramatic effect. The image does not indicate the severity of the injuries; it only becomes clear through the text that the injuries were slight. If the ethical issue was the key, there was no need to depict the very moment of the crime, which was imagined, as if happening in the present. As with the aforementioned image of a hunting accident, the image managed to depict both the act and the result of shooting, so it was actually a composite image. It was meant to transport the reader into the cabin, who would feel vicarious horror. Thus the image was meant to dramatize much more than inform. Another cover, depicting a train robbery, was composed of three sequential images forming an unfolding drama about robbers stealthily getting onto the moving train, shooting a man, and then escaping (*PJSI*, Dec. 8, 1907, cover). Such images partook in the culture of spectacular representation of everyday realities in a period of intense popularity of fictional and nonfictional stories about crime.[3]

LE BRIGANDAGE EN ORIENT
(Arrestation d'un train)

LA COLLISION DE VILLEPREUX
Scènes d'épouvante et d'horreur pendant l'incendie des wagons

UN DRAME DANS LES AIRS
Trois aéronautes précipités dans la mer

UN PICK-POCKET QUI SE SAUVE EN BALLON

TRAGIQUE RENCONTRE DE DEUX AÉROPLANES

An image (see Figure 15.1) with the caption "Robbery in the Orient (Seizure of a Train)" (1891) was something that might well have inspired Jules Verne's novel *Claudius Bombarnac* (1892), set on a train along a fictional Grand Transasiatic line that is attacked by bandits (*PJSI*, June 20, 1891, cover). In the image Europeans are being taken away by armed robbers, one of whom is firing a pistol. The accompanying text began with a sarcastic observation, that "[w]e live in an era of progress" compared to earlier times when victims of robbery were taken to distant forests, and reported that the robbers abducted a group of European men to extort ransom, sparing Greeks and women. "Progress" here conveyed the idea that development in modern transportation was accompanied by development of new methods of violence; the robbers were equipped with the latest models of weapons (*PJSI*, June 20, 1891, p. 7). The text conveyed the idea that the Orient is a wild destination, where European travelers can encounter unexpected adventure, that they cannot take a secure journey for granted, and that the train, as an agent of progress, is countered by modernized violence.

Images of robberies set in France differed from ones set in "exotic" lands. Looking at one cover depicting a French postman robbed and bound to railroad tracks, the viewer was meant to focus on the desperate struggle of the victim trying to free himself in time—which he did (*PJSI*, Sept. 12, 1909, cover). The clear expression of intense will and terror on the man's face is meant to elicit sympathy and admiration, for the viewer to see him as an everyday hero. The captions and related texts affected the intended reception of the images. While the report on the train robbery in the Orient was about a dangerous adventure for Europeans in a less advanced civilization, the one about the postman is about a scary experience of one Frenchman, without a commentary on the state of French civilization.

While train robbery was a relatively rare theme in *PJSI*, that of train accidents was more common. In one cover a train is gruesomely mangled along with a metal bridge in Münchenstein, Switzerland (*PJSI*, June 27, 1891, cover). Victims are swept into a river; some people are desperately dangling from the wreckage; some are falling from the train; while others are shrieking and struggling in horror. The text noted that the iron bridge, built by a French company with German iron, was a failure. The reporters of *Le Petit Journal*, the text proclaimed, "with their zeal, activity, and conscience," owed to the readers this image of a "terrible accident that plunges so many families into despair" (*PJSI*, June 27, 1891, p. 8). In spite of this moral tenor of the text highlighting the mission for informing the public, the graphic image points to sensationalism, and the exploitation of a tragic event. In such a case the image was only secondarily a "hook" to attract the reader in order to inform, given the brevity of the text. Rather, the moral expressed in the text was a pretext for the image, which was the central attraction; it was what sold the paper. In a similar scene of a train fallen off a bridge in France, men in boats rescue bloodied survivors from the river below, while corpses float by. The wreckage of the train is half submerged in the river (*PJSI*, Aug. 18, 1907, p. 264). The panoramic composition of the image was presumably aimed at depicting as much of the disaster as possible. In another scene of a train wreck with a partially submerged train, in Dorpat, Russia, some of the victims are falling into the water, while many are desperately struggling in the water (*PJSI*, May 30, 1897, p. 316). Composed like a landscape painting and in subdued colors typical of such paintings, yet depicting a content utterly different from them, this image would have elicited a jarring sensation. It was about a "real" event presented as if happening in front of the viewer's eyes. However, it could, taken out of context, easily be taken for a strange painting or an illustration for an adventure novel. The fact that it was an imagined, painterly reconstruction of what happened, rather than a photograph—or an image based on one—mitigated the sense of reality. The image thus referred to other popular and high-cultural images circulating in this period. Rather than one definitive response, a range of responses would be the result; the creator of the image, or the "author," disappeared, while the image created a chain of reactions and intertextual connections.

In another catastrophic scene, about a double derailing caused by "a criminal assault," the themes of crime and train accident were combined, while a scene of a collision between a train and an elephant, as happened in Siam, inserted an element of the exotic (*PJSI*, May 31, 1908, cover). A collision (see Figure 15.2) between an express train and another train also yielded a "scene of horror," a sensational catastrophe which, again, would have repulsed and appealed simultaneously (*PJSI*, July 3, 1910, cover, p. 210). "Horrible accidents" of people being hit by trains or trams were portrayed, as in a scene of a woman and a girl hit by a tram, and two women and two girls about to be hit by an express train (*PJSI*, May 28, 1905, p. 170; June 16, 1912, p. 8). A caption, "Catastrophe of the Metropolitan," announced that the new underground system also produced disasters (*PJSI*, Aug. 23, 1903, cover). A rare image of the train as an agent of civilization depicted the inauguration of a railroad in Algeria (*PJSI*, Feb. 18, 1900, p. 56).

Modes of Transportation: Aerostats and Dirigibles

Much more than trains, which were familiar sights since the 1840s, aerostats and dirigibles[4] were ultimate objects of curiosity and celebration symbolic of technology, adventure, daring, and freedom, "illustrious invention[s]" that only few people actually used (*PJSI*, Jan. 20, 1901, p. 21). A dirigible named "Republic," floating in the air over a tranquil countryside and watched by farmers, was portrayed as an iconic symbol (*PJSI*, Sept. 20, 1908). The landing of *Le Petit Journal*'s own dirigible provided an occasion for celebration and self-publicity (*PJSI*, Jan. 3, 1909, p. 8). However, aerostat accidents were also depicted a dozen times between 1891 and 1909. "A drama in the air" (see Figure 15.3) with "three aeronauts precipitated into the sea" depicted three men, with horror expressed on their faces, tumbling out of an aerostat in the air, the tranquil sea with sail boats floating marking a cruel contrast to their fate (*PJSI*, June 17, 1906, p. 192). What was the moral of such a story? Why such a detailed depiction of men in the act of dying? The text noted: "again a painful page is to be added to the history of tragic ascensions." The accident happened during a festival in Milan, when two aerostats were launched for crossing the Alps but were pushed by wind into different directions, one of them ending in the accident (*PJSI*, June 17, 1906, p. 186). So there was no moral to the story; the text was not advocating any position or making any suggestions to make dirigible journeys safer. The image was simply a graphic portrayal of a sensational, tragic event. Nor were there morals conveyed in reports about aerostat accidents caused by lightening, or a crash (see Figure 15.4) that took place over the English Channel (*PJSI*, July 25, 1891, p. 8; June 16, 1907, p. 192; Apr. 18, 1909, cover). The latter image depicted, as usual, a moment of great drama. A drowned woman is floating; two male aeronauts are in grave danger; their condition of being trapped and entangled by the balloon's ropes denotes not only their struggle for survival but also their despair in being unable to get to the woman floating just out of arm's reach. Despair is also highlighted by one of the men's intent look towards the woman even as he precariously holds on to the balloon. The scene captured a moment of much movement; the viewer cannot tell how the aerostat would move and in turn determine the men's fate, which is only made clear by the caption. The presence, in the background, of a boat indicates that help is on the way but is too late for at least one of the victims, adding to the senses of drama and tragedy, while the barely visible lighthouse further heightens the sense of tragedy by indicating that the shore is tantalizingly close. Muted colors also emphasize this sense. The tricolor flag underlines patriotism while also informing as to the provenance of the aerostat or the nationality of the aeronauts—but, typically, stops short of clarifying precisely which information it is conveying. The artful composition manages to pack a great deal of visual clues that serve to narrate an unfolding drama rather than to inform precisely. The image invited the viewer to imagine the subsequent scenes. The very gap between the highly detailed image and the brief and sober text encouraged this process.

Some reports on accidents did have morals. Military victims of the crash of the dirigible "Republic" were eulogized as "heroes who died for science and the fatherland"; Marianne, symbolizing France, covers the victims with the tricolor flag (*PJSI*, Oct. 10, 1909, cover). The eulogizing of military heroes was a pronounced theme of the paper. The back page of the above issue depicted the crash itself, the moment when the men realized that things were going horribly wrong (*PJSI*, Oct. 10, 1909, p. 328). Such scenes of catastrophic denouement conveyed the idea that the victims were brave, daring people who sacrificed themselves for a cause, rather than people who foolishly endangered themselves and others. The images and texts also highlighted the idea of the aerostat as a unique and symbolic mode of travel which, in theory, frees people, but in reality often entails danger. The images and texts repeatedly relayed the message that modern technology can fail, but that trying, daring, and sacrifices are necessary. However, while the reports unquestioningly upheld the notion of progress and the view that modern transportation symbolized the superiority of European civilization, the repeated images of catastrophes and failures likely collectively undermined a sense of confidence and assurance about linear progress.

An image particularly arresting for its bizarreness and drama, of two women dangling in the air, one of them holding onto the hair of the other, was reported as "a really extraordinary fact," of an American gymnastic aeronaut who saved, 300 meters in the air, an unfortunate woman who had accidentally lifted off (*PJSI*, Sept. 16, 1906, cover). There was no moral to the story; the gymnast was simply a hardy young woman, and the event an extraordinary happening. A particularly intriguing image (see Figure 15.5), of a pickpocket escaping in an aerostat, combined two of *PJSI*'s favorite themes: aerostat and crime. The balloon, a spectacular object, is used for a daring escape by a criminal inches away from the grasp of policemen (*PJSI*, July 23, 1911, p. 240). The criminal is aiming a gun at his victim, all the while mocking him. The image comes close to depicting the criminal as a brilliant hero although stops short by depicting his cunning and un-heroic facial expression. Although this image went against the grain of *PJSI* which portrayed military officers and police officers as duty-bound heroes, it must have resonated widely with the broad public, when fictional thieves like Arsène Lupin, a suave and charming gentleman-burglar modeled on English equivalents, were widely popular and seen, as anarchists often were, as popular heroes facing down the state police apparatus. Another image meant to amuse was that of two men in an aerostat running from the grasp of German peasants, by cutting the rope that the peasants are pulling, causing them to fall in a heap and thus "punishing the greedy peasants" demanding money (*PJSI*, Apr. 4, 1909, pp. 112, 106). This was a typical anti-German image frequently found in *PJSI* since the Franco-Prussian War and the loss of Alsace and Lorraine. In a cover on a French aerostat that crashed in Alsace, children are joyfully taking away French earth from the aerostat; the image combined the themes of aerostat accident and patriotism (*PJSI*, Nov. 12, 1911, cover).

Modes of Transportation: Automobiles

PJSI depicted the automobile as a sign of progress, mobility, speed, and leisure. As an open-air vehicle, it also stood for sportsmanship. An image of a lion enjoying a ride next to a human driver in the countryside, passing by frightened peasants, was an example highlighting the automobile as a symbol of individual leisure and freedom, in this case taken to an excessive measure (*PJSI*, June 20, 1909, p. 200). In an image with the caption "The parade of the locomotion through the ages. The Present looking at the procession of the Past," about an exhibition in Paris, men and women in fashionable and luxurious coats, hats and furs are enjoying themselves watching the "Past," comprising various forms of transportation, including carriages, an ox-pulled cart, and so on (*PJSI*, Dec. 22, 1907, p. 408). Some of the past modes of transportation are clearly foreign, set in Asia for example. The linear sense of the past and the future connected through progress was also conveyed in an image titled "The effects of new civilization in Tripoli," in which a man on a camel looks at an automobile leaving a trail of sand dust. The caption, "An encounter of the locomotion of the past and the future in the desert," made it clear that the automobile, seen as a dynamic agent of development, was a harbinger of the future (*PJSI*, Nov. 5, 1911, p. 360). Other positive images of automobiles set in colonies included one of Hubert Lyautey, the Resident-General of Morocco, arriving in Marrakesh in a car with a mounted machine gun, and one of an all-terrain vehicle transporting a French general across Algeria (*PJSI*, Oct. 13, 1912, cover; Jan. 5, 1913, cover). A cover on Russian officers being rescued in a car in Manchuria during the Russo-Japanese War was more complicated (*PJSI*, Oct. 2, 1904, cover). Gunfire is exchanged; an injured Russian officer, managing to shoot a Japanese man, is depicted as heroic. The car, seen as a beneficial mode of technology, fit into *Le Petit Journal*'s extensive reporting on the war that was much more sympathetic to the Russians than to the Japanese. However, the paper throughout the war made it clear that this was a brutal war with a great human toll, fought in harsh conditions; thus there was much more contextual depth provided for this image than usual. Unlike for French colonial wars, the paper's reporting on this war was marked by a sense of ambivalence. Reporting that some Japanese soldiers were found frozen to death in Manchuria, a text noted that in the terrible cold half a million men had the "terrible courage to cut each other's throats," and that the winter would "add more horrors to the horrors of the war" (*PJSI*, Feb. 12, 1905, cover, p. 50).

As with trains or aerostats, images of catastrophes involving automobiles far outnumbered celebratory ones. Cars' mobility was often depicted as challenged by obstacles and even severely limited due to the absence of infrastructure like roads, as in a scene of a car being pulled out of a swamp by a large group of horses in Mongolia. In another scene based on a photograph, "the first car that penetrated into a Korean city" causes havoc, scattering people in a panic, throwing one man off a bull—loaded with logs—into the air upside-down, and generally creating a mess (*PJSI*, July 14, 1907, p. 224; March 7, 1909, p. 80). Contrasting the panic on Korean faces are the facial expressions of four Europeans—two men and two women—in the car. The driver looks determined, and the man next to him looks blasé and impassive, while one woman looks amused. The text explained that

> Koreans are apathetic people, lazy, routine-bound, little curious of mani-festations of progress. The laziness of Koreans is legendary. While women accomplish the hardest work, one sees men sitting around from morning to night in the streets, one enormous pipe in the mouth. . . . Koreans imagine that the devil incarnate arrived in this diabolical vehicle. (*PJSI*, March 7, 1909, p. 74)

Thus the car is an agent of European civilization penetrating even the sleepiest corners of the world, and the travelers, agents of modernization.

However, in Europe, too, cars encountered a wide variety of obstacles, whether the police issuing fines for excessive speed, or ostriches harassing a car and its passengers (*PJSI*, June 26, 1904, p. 208; Jan. 10, 1904, cover). Some of the images conjured ideas of class conflict and tensions between urban, bourgeois sophisticates and rural villagers, as well as tensions between the ideals of freedom and speed on the one hand, and the societal reality full of rules, restrictions, and hazards, on the other. Drivers were often seen as careless, even reckless, and the appearance of automobiles as sudden intrusions as conveyed by the caption: "The surprises of automobilism: unexpected guests." In the image in question, onto a group of picnic-goers, two men and a woman are falling, as their car precariously dangles from a small bridge (*PJSI*, Sept. 23, 1906, p. 304). People look alarmed and dumbfounded. Plates are overturned; an umbrella, hats, and wine bottles have fallen into the water; and a dog is barking amidst the picnic meal. Rather than affirming a moral about the need to drive carefully, this image was meant to distract and amuse. Another cover depicted an inverted scenario, a "singular misadventure happening to automobilists," a "lunch on the grass interrupted by shells," when "tourists" having a picnic found themselves unintended targets of military exercises nearby (*PJSI*, Sept. 8, 1907, cover, p. 282). Another cover, showing a chaotic scene of people in exotic costumes escaping from a burning float at a parade, combined the themes of exoticism, disaster, and technology (*PJSI*, Apr. 8, 1906, cover).

However, the majority of images about car accidents, including collisions between cars, between cars and trains, or between cars and motorcycles, were anything but funny (*PJSI*, May 15, 1904; Dec. 18, 1910; May 6, 1900, cover). An image about a collision of a car with an express train graphically depicted victims covered in blood, a woman falling out of the burning automobile, and a man being burned (*PJSI*, Nov. 6, 1904, cover; May 15, 1904, cover). In one scene bodies as well as mechanical pieces from mangled cars, as well as a car itself, are flying in the air, with victims' faces and broken limbs covered in blood (*PJSI*, Aug. 18, 1907, cover). Post office vans, one of which was shown as having crashed into a shop, were declared to be the "terror of Paris," and a collision between an autobus and a fiacre in Paris, depicted with the latter crushed and a fallen aristocratic woman being helped, was judged to be the result of the "wrongdoings of the autobus" (*PJSI*, July 18, 1909, cover; June 2, 1907, cover). The freedom afforded by cars also meant they could be used for willfully lethal purposes, as shown in a scene of "a dramatic suicide" of two lovers in a car having gone off a cliff in San Diego (*PJSI*, Oct. 6, 1912, pp. 320, 314).

Modes of Transportation: Airplanes

Aviation elicited widespread fascination, as can be perceived through images of air shows, or through an image about a "[s]ensational experiment of aviation" taking place above a stadium full of spectators (*PJSI*, Sept. 5, 1909, cover; Nov. 26, 1906, p. 280). People flying airplanes were true individualists, as flying was not subject to the constraints of space that challenged automobilists, and moreover flying was, in this nascent period of aviation, very dangerous, in part because the pilots and passengers were often entirely exposed in the air. In the image with the caption "marriage on an airplane" a pilot, the wedding couple, and a priest fly over a tranquil countryside, while people cheer from below (*PJSI*, Aug. 27, 1911, p. 280). In one image *Le Petit Journal*'s plane, arriving in Morocco, is enthusiastically greeted by Moroccans and the French military alike (*PJSI*, Oct. 1, 1911, p. 320).

Some images about inconvenient encounters, such as a bull running into a plane, were comic (*PJSI*, Sept. 25, 1910, p. 312). However, many images showed how aviation was fraught with grave danger, as can be seen in a scene (see Figure 15.6) of an air collision during an air show (*PJSI*, July 6, 1913, p. 216). The cover of the same issue showed two children plunging to their deaths while boating at Niagara Falls; thus the issue packed a one-two punch by reporting on sensational accidents (*PJSI*, July 6, 1913, cover). Another image with the caption "A catastrophe in the air" pushed the limits of the representable, in depicting a dead man with gray skin and much of his clothes burned off, falling out of an airplane in flames (*PJSI*, May 25, 1902, p. 168).[5] The popular French aviator Pierre Védrines, while attempting an emergency landing, ended up getting injured when telegraph wires caused the plane to be suspended in the air vertically, and the "heroic but imprudent" pilot, without a helmet, to fall out. He landed on railroad tracks and was nearly run over by an express train, which was stopped in time (*PJSI*, May 12, 1912, cover, p. 146). This incident, not only about a potential collision between a train and an airplane but also about obstacles in the way of airplanes such as telegraph lines—another sign of technological progress—likely reminded the public about the complications of modern life and the potential dangers of aviation seen as a heroic, daredevil feat.

Modes of Transportation: Ships and Underwater Vessels

Ships were depicted as not only the most established, and often glamorous, mode of transportation for long-distance travel, but also as crucial for colonial expansion and defense, as can be seen in scenes of launchings of battleships or luxury liners, or in an image of the Suez Canal full of luxury liners, military ships, and boats (*PJSI*, Jan. 3, 1904, cover; Jan. 17, 1904, p. 24). The modernity of the canal and the ships contrast to camels along the bank. Submarines elicited much fascination; in one scene a huge crowd admires a submarine (*PJSI*, July 28, 1901, p. 240). However, again, catastrophic events caused by war, storms, or human errors were much more frequent. Both an image about the "catastrophe of *Victoria*," an English battleship that sank, costing 358 lives, subsequent to a collision with a battleship, and one about the Russian ship *Petropavlosk*, torpedoed by the Japanese resulting in 600 deaths, were panoramic views of the ships being destroyed, bodies falling into water or being blown into the air, and so forth (*PJSI*, July 8, 1893, cover, p. 215; Apr. 24, 1904, cover).

Reports about simply bizarre events included one about a jaguar appearing on a ship's deck and one about a woman who picked up and threw overboard a little girl (*PJSI*, Dec. 5, 1909, p. 384; Dec. 2, 1906, cover). Such reports were foremost meant again to intrigue or shock, but informing the viewer about potential dangers of ship travel occurred as a secondary effect. Underwater disasters and accidents were also depicted. Scenes of diving accidents included one of a diver struggling with a giant octopus whose tentacles are wrapped around his limbs, neck, and shoulders and squeezing, reminiscent of an illustration from Verne's *Twenty-Thousand Leagues Under the Sea* (1869) (*PJSI*, June 16, 1912, p. 192; May 20, 1906, cover).

One would imagine the sinking of the *Titanic* in April 1912 to have yielded graphic images. Actually, this was not the case. The vast scale of the disaster and loss of life—reported then as nearly 1,400—seem to cause the paper's usual rules of reporting to be suspended. Following much coverage in the daily paper, the first engraved image about the event, which appeared 14 days later with the caption "The loss of the largest liner in the world. The 'Titanic' sank after a collision with an iceberg," simply depicted the moment of the liner hitting the iceberg and a chunk of the iceberg breaking off (*PJSI*, 28 April, 1912, p. 136). This non-violent image was no doubt sensationalistic, but only because the public already knew a great deal about the disaster. In addition to the usual brief note, a long article detailed the Anglo-German battle for supremacy in the search for the fastest, largest and most comfortable Transatlantic liner, and described the *Titanic*, "a true floating palace," in which, among other things, a large variety of sports including horse riding were available (*PJSI*, 28 April, 1912, p. 130). Only two other images related to the event appeared in the next two months, one about a religious ceremony for the victims held at the disaster site, and one about drills for liner passengers for getting onto lifeboats (*PJSI*, 5 May, 1912, p. 144; 2 June, 1912, p. 171). The text for the latter noted that while passengers should not be frightened, it was "more dangerous to hide potential danger than to show it without exaggeration . . . ." This reassuring message was highly ironic. It just happens that two weeks before the sinking of the *Titanic PJSI* published an image of a chaotic and frightening scene of a lifeboat full of women—most of them in nightgowns—men, and children overturning, causing people to be thrown into the water and drown, even as people come down a rope onto the lifeboat from a stricken steamship, *Oceana*, which sank following a collision (*PJSI*, March, 31 1912, p. 104). This image, about people going suddenly from enjoying travel in a luxury steamship to fighting for survival on a lifeboat in the middle of the night, and dying, must have—just a short time later—been seen as a sinister foreboding of a much greater disaster. The contrast between the reports on *Oceana* and the *Titanic* yields valuable insight. Both the magnitude of tragedy and the intensity of interest about the latter affected reporting, so that a simple image about the moment of impact for a ship deemed unsinkable *was* the most iconic and comprehensible image possible, while at the same time being in good taste. The scale of the disaster made the public self-conscious about enjoying graphic images about it.

Unintended Moments of Travel, and Other Types of Disasters

There were also unintended moments of travel, such as a scene of an eagle abducting a child while the mother and others run after them helplessly (*PJSI*, Sept. 23, 1906, cover). Another fluke incident was a "tragi-comic misadventure during a wedding," narrated through an image of wedding guests and the bride falling through the roof of a barn and onto cows, and another image of the cow carrying away the bride on its back. The bride tries to hold onto a tree branch, while wedding guests attempt to stop the cow (*PJSI*, Jan. 12, 1908, p. 10).

Other kinds of disasters such as explosions, fire, and bombings merit a brief discussion here, as two portrayals of such catastrophes, a fire at a theater in Chicago that caused "terrible panic" and 587 deaths, and a fire at a charity ball in Paris, are useful for getting at both the cultural imaginaries such images elicited and their psychological effects. In the image about the fire in Chicago, as the theater burns and fills with smoke, people in evening attire are struggling to get out, falling on top of one another and are choking to death (*PJSI*, Jan. 17, 1904, cover). One man, in attempting to get out, has placed his hand on the neck of a woman, inadvertently causing her to choke more. The text noted the vulnerability of theaters in Europe and the United States to fire, and described other disastrous fires in theaters. The image again provokes the question as to why this scene was depicted. This disaster was not about a crime, recklessness, moral failings, or social issues. It could be said to raise alarm about the vulnerability of theaters to fires, but the text was not urging for measures to be taken. The image, in graphically depicting a scene of catastrophe, provided something akin to an existential relief through vicarious experience. The details of the scene were meant to transport the viewer to the scene of the catastrophe, make the viewer feel, simultaneously, horror, fear, sympathy, and guilt at being interested in this image, but also relief that the viewer was not there. At the same time, like all of the paper's images, the image is very much about a moment happening, a drama unfolding before the viewer's eyes. In this image this sense is particularly heightened, because the perspective of the viewer is from inside the theater, where the victims are trapped and struggling to get out. Therefore the image functions similar to a scene in a film; the image *appeals* to the viewer, by repulsing and attracting simultaneously, by causing horror, fright, and sympathy, but also the sheer thrill of consuming a sensational piece of news while being safe.

An earlier cover, on a fire at the Bazar de la Charité in Paris organized by aristocratic women which claimed 126 victims, was similar to the above in some respects but different in others (*PJSI*, May 16, 1897, cover). Here the overriding emphasis was the sense of tragedy. The accompanying text underlined the reasons: "All these women, young girls, even children, for the most part titled, rich, happy, meeting there for the cause of charity and who die suddenly in sufferings more atrocious than the victims of the barbaric Middle Ages did!" (*PJSI*, May 16, 1897, p. 159). In the center of the image is a beautiful young woman, barely conscious as she is being propped up by a man. With her eyes closed, her face is pointed upwards; one arm is raised, and one of her shoulders is exposed. The figure recalls scenes from tragic operas, plays, or melodramatic novels; she is a heroine in a drama who embodies the tragedy of the occasion. In front of her another beautiful young woman has fallen in a faint next to a boy, and on the left the face of a woman, holding a girl, expresses horror. This image contrasts to the one about the fire in Chicago, in that unlike in the latter in which everyone seems to be for oneself, trampling on one another, here people are helping one another. The central figure is being gallantly helped by a man. The back page of the issue depicted a somber scene of the aftermath, of corpses being collected (*PJSI*, 16 May, 1897, p. 160). The image set in Chicago was much more voyeuristic than the one set in Paris represented like a tragic drama on stage. The two images reveal the paper's distinctive views of American and French upper classes; much more respect and sympathy were accorded to the latter.

Theories of Photography

For Roland Barthes still photography showed "an illogical conjunction of here and then" with a quality of "real unreality," due to an earlier temporal position. According to Rudolf Arnheim photography lacks "the dimensions of time and volume" and thus produces a weaker impression of reality than cinema does thanks to its depths in time and space (Metz 1991: 12). Film "produces a strong impression of reality because it corresponds to a vacuum, which dreams readily fill" (Metz 1991: 10). What about the visions of catastrophes of *PJSI*, of actual events, rendered in style far from photographic but rather somewhat cartoonish? Do such images, through the lack of the sense of reality, turn the real into the unreal? Do they inhibit the production of dreams or to the contrary encourage more? I would suggest that the stylized depictions enabled the viewer to suspend reality to an extent, turning the real into the unreal, allowing the viewer to enjoy the consumption of the image that often depicted extremely violent, graphic situations, most of the time just before the moment of death. The minimal texts, which often simply did lip service to ethical or social issues, played minor secondary roles and much of the time hardly directed the viewer's interpretation, as the interpretation was meant to be done through the intense, colorful, and large images. The images, in their graphic detail, were transgressive in many ways, but also stayed within bounds, following the unwritten rule against the depiction of nakedness, mangled bodies, or body parts. At the same time, the choice of the medium allowed for much more graphicness of depiction than photographs which were not yet good for details. Moreover, as we have seen, the medium also allowed for the most sensational possible rendering of any given scene of violence, by juxtaposing segments of an act and its aftermath—both of which were frequently imagined in the absence of photographs—seamlessly into one scene. Along with a partial suspension of the sense of reality, then, the images further encouraged imagined scenes of horror.

Zoo Violence and Other Scenes of Wild Animals

Among *Le Petit Journal*'s images of accidents was a subtheme of zoo violence. Some scenes depicted ferocious animals such as lions, pumas, tigers, and boas attacking and even devouring circus performers, some of whom had accidentally fallen into cages (*PJSI*, Apr. 25, 1891, cover; Jan. 24, 1904, cover; May 19, 1907, p. 160; Apr. 13, 1908, cover; March 3, 1912, p. 72). One depicted a bear attacking a horse and a man in the street, while another pushed the limits of the representable by depicting an "extraordinary suicide," a man whose neck is seemingly severed by a lion (*PJSI*, July 29, 1906, cover; Sept. 27, 1908, p. 312). In another case a man, who entered a cage of a lion in order to have his photograph taken with the lion, is "devoured" by it (*PJSI*, Sept. 29, 1895, cover). A photographer outside the cage is watching; next to him is the camera. The presence of the camera makes the gruesome image doubly troubling, as it reminds the viewer of the voyeuristic position the viewer is in, inside the cage, viewing this grotesque scene with eyes that function like the camera. The fact that the photographer is not taking a photograph reminds the reader that this incident may not be fit to be seen, that it might be inappropriate to watch this. The themes of accidents at zoos and violent encounters with animals seem to reveal, to an extent, the irrationality of the human will to dominate animals—in itself a subtheme of the human will to dominate nature—but also fascination with that will as well as with the perceived revenge of the animals exposing human vulnerability. Humans being attacked and killed by ferocious animals inside cages perhaps produced a peculiarly fascinating sensation, in that it was about the reverse travel of the human, going into a claustrophobic cage, the reverse of what much of the fantasies of travel were producing in this period: traveling long distance and seeing exotic lands—where the animals come from—and being free, mobile, victorious, and admired. These images, more than scenes of wild animals killing humans during hunting or other similar scenarios which were also depicted in *PJSI*, likely elicited particular sensations.

Conclusion

Modern modes of transportation in the 1890–1914 period were associated with modernity, mobility, progress, speed, individuality, patriotism, colonial expansion, heroism, leisure, luxury, and sportsmanship. Yet the fascination with catastrophes and violence, as seen through *PJSI*'s representations, reveals a darker side. Such representations constructed contradictory narratives, oscillating between the ideas of technological progress and technological failure, freedom, and danger, the domination of nature and that of defeat by nature, and so on. Moreover, the sense of linear progress, frequently expressed vis-à-vis lands seen as under-developed, was undermined by the sense that progress was frequently blocked and limited. This should not be so surprising. The belief in progress and civilization widespread among intellectuals and the educated in France, of the second half of the nineteenth century through the years before the outbreak of the Great War, was not incompatible with the sense that there is not always necessarily linear progress, that things are always meant to get better. This sense had multiple sources. The historical dramas of the French Revolution with its phases of intensive political experimentation and the radical phase ending in a great deal of violence, as well as subsequent revolutions, undermined a sense of historical linear evolution that certain Enlightenment philosophers emphasized, notably Marquis de Condorcet in *Esquisse d'un tableau historique des progrès de l'esprit humain* (1793–1794). Furthermore, a

272 H. Hazel Hahn

sense of entropy was quite widespread among the elite, and was not incompatible with a conviction that scientific development would lead to universal progress (Serres 2003). In addition, acute senses of national and imperial rivalry against Germany, Britain, the United States, Russia, and other empires and potential empires, also undermined a sense of national confidence and further provided justification for colonial expansion (Hahn 2012). Thus images of technological marvels deployed in North Africa in the years leading up to the Great War would have often provided a subtext of relief against anxiety rather than full-blown confidence.

The construction of contradictory narratives about modern transportation was somewhat mitigated by the confidence with which people believed the idea that modern modes of transportation ultimately stood for progress. Yet, catastrophes and accidents were frequently seen as results not only of limits of human will confronted by nature's powers, but also tragic human errors, conflicts in human intentions leading to social and political conflicts, skirmishes and wars, recklessness, irrationality, or sheer craziness. The at-times hysterical scenes of violent denouement and deaths underlined the sense of unpredictability in life, human fragility, and the impermanence of technological achievement. This was the case even for the most fortunate and endowed—as the news of the fire at the Bazar de Charité underscored—or the most heroic and talented—as in the case of the aviator Védrines who, through a series of unfortunate circumstances, plus his own negligence in failing to wear a helmet, ended up gravely injured. Such images delivered existential angst as well as relief, and vicarious and voyeuristic thrill and guilty pleasure as well as repulsion.

Representations of modes of transportation show a relative range. Some were celebratory, and usually linked with national pride, respect for the authorities, and the civilizing mission. Some, episodes of sheer bizarre, fluke happenings, were simply meant to amuse and distract. The images, depicting disasters and accidents, varied in depictions in respect to the notoriety and severity of incidents, settings, the classes of the victims, and other criteria. We have seen that the images varied in style, composition, and coloring. An event could be depicted as a modern, latest news based on a photograph or an imagined photograph. Or it could emulate a painting, book illustration, poster, or a drama on stage. An image could be a caricature, or feature symbolic figures, most frequent of which was Marianne which appeared whenever the editors of *Le Petit Journal* felt compelled to get across a message of patriotism. All the images were carefully and artfully designed and rendered for maximum impact; rather than speed, striking effect was desired. They were rich in contexts, full of visual references to popular and high cultures that created further intertextual connections and also, due to that similarity, helped sanction the violence of the images. Certain images—about the Russo-Japanese War, for instance—had particular contextual depths.

Above all, the artfully designed images were meant to dramatize, shock, provide vicarious thrills, and be voyeuristic, rather than inform. In producing images that were spectacles of the "real," the extraordinary out of everyday life, the images depicted the imagined moment of the present, right after the impact of a collision or, in the case of large ships, some time after the impact, whichever produced the most sensational imagery of mangled wreckages and other terror-inducing details—situating the viewer extremely close or farther away depending on the desired effect. Often a single image was meant to convey both the act and the result of violence simultaneously and therefore be the most sensational possible. However, by deploying certain styles and colors or characterizations that mitigated the sense of the real, the sense of the filmic present could be muted, so to the viewer it could seem like one is dreaming. The visual was central, and the textual relegated to a minor role of often providing pretexts for the sensationalism of the visual through allusions to moral or social issues. *PJSI*'s *modus operandi* was upended once, after the sinking of the *Titanic*, an event that proved not to be representable in the usual ways and thus revealed unresolved tensions. At the same time, the image of the ship hitting an iceberg foreshadowed effective moments of filmic trailers about such iconic events. The drive to foremost dramatize had the effect of often preventing the construction of a coherent narrative. The gap between the graphic visual drama and the sober, brief text left a residual sense that the collective narrative was incomplete. This lack of correspondence between the image and the text was deliberate. The text was only meant to encourage visual imagination—since the visual was meant to be associative with other imagery and cultural references—and also was a way out for the viewer enjoying the violent image; somehow articulating the appeal of the violence of the image would have violated this complicity.

Notes

1 The daily paper included some small photographs starting in the mid-1900s.
2 Each text on an image was a short notice published under the heading "EXPLANATIONS OF OUR ENGRAVINGS." All translations are the author's.
3 On spectacular representations of the "real" see Schwartz (1999). On Lupin and Leroux see in particular Vareille (1980).
4 Lighter than air vehicles: aerostats are usually (tethered) balloons and dirigibles have motors and are steerable.
5 Another image pushing the limits of the representable depicted the moment of a child's legs being "mutilated" by an agricultural machine (*PJSI*, Aug. 23, 1908, cover).

Bibliography

AVENEL Henri, *Histoire de la Presse française depuis 1789 jusqu'à nos jours*, Paris: Flammarion, 1900.

BELLEFQIH Anissa, *La Lecture des aventures d'Arsène Lupin. Du jeu au "Je,"* Paris: L'Harmattan, 2010.

CRAGIN Thomas, *Murder in Parisian Streets: Manufacturing Crime and Justice in the Popular Press, 1830–1900*, Lewisburg: Bucknell University Press, 2006.

HAHN H. Hazel, "Heroism, exoticism and violence: representing the self, the 'other' and rival empires in French and British illustrated press, 1880–1905," *Historical Reflections/Réflexions Historiques*, 38(3): 62–83, 2012.

KALIFA Dominique, *L'Encre et le sang: récits de crimes et société à la Belle Époque*, Paris: Fayard, 1995.

METZ Christian, *Film Language: A Semiotics of the Cinema*, trans. Michael Taylor, Chicago, IL: University of Chicago Press, 1991.

SCHWARTZ Vanessa, *Spectacular Realities: Early Mass Culture in Fin-de-Siècle Paris*, Berkeley, CA: University of California Press, 1999.

SERRES Michel, *Jules Verne, la science et l'homme contemporain. Conversations avec Jean-Paul Dekiss*, Paris: Editions Le Pommier, 2003.

VAREILLE Jean-Claude, *Filatures: itinéraire à travers les cycles de Lupin et Rouletabille*, Grenoble: Presse universitaire de Grenoble, 1980.

WOLGENSINGER Jacques, *Histoire à la une: la grande aventure de la presse*, Paris: Gallimard, 1989.

Conclusions

At the Crossroads

Nelson Graburn

In Chapter 1 of this volume, Saskia Cousin offers a brief review of some of the more well-known French approaches to the imaginary before examining how, after decades of being excluded by academics, the very exile of the concept of the imaginary has allowed the notion to find favor. With the notable exception of sociology and anthropology, where the term has been persistently denied any scientific value, French thought has been very interested in questions of the imaginary in philosophy, semiotics, linguistics, psychoanalysis, and literature, especially in the work of Sartre, Bachelard, Caillois, Ricoeur, Durand, Deleuze, Derrida, Lyotard, Castoriadis, Jung, Lacan, and others. Cousin then shows how the introduction of the imaginary into ethnographic research provoked new ideas for the anthropology of tourism and more generally for tourism imaginaries.

The 14 case studies presented in this volume are written by 17 authors from 10 different disciplines;[1] however, none of the chapters is restricted to a single disciplinary research model. All draw on multiple disciplines though obviously some have a primary role and others a secondary one; for instance, history is a component wherever there is temporality—for example, in cases of development—and geography is germane wherever place or region are important. Most of the contributors combine at least two primary disciplinary approaches, for example Raghuraman S. Trichur's account of Goan political and touristic history (Chapter 2), and Iris Sheungting Lo and Bob McKercher's analysis of online tourist photography (Chapter 13), which usefully combines sociology, performance theory, psychology, and anthropology.

Not surprisingly cultural studies—an umbrella term covering a number of approaches to the analysis of contemporary complex, stratified, media-driven societies—is a prime method adopted in the various contributions.[2] Furthermore, here visual/media studies is the most frequently adopted discipline within cultural studies, reflecting our topic—imaginaries—which depends so much on mental and physical images and the contemporary world where such images are circulated by print—for example, Pascale Nédélec's examination of the creation of tourist imaginaries of Las Vegas in advertising and mass media (Chapter 4)—photography—for example, Estelle Sohier's account of how Boissonnas' powerful photography was used to reconstruct Greece's tourist imaginary (Chapter 12)—film—for example, Clothilde Sabre's study of French tourists' consumption of Japanese manga and anime films (Chapter 9)—and Internet media—Philippe Viallon's examination of the creation of imaginaries in metropolitan city websites (Chapter 14). A parallel may be posited between these visual studies of media and the analyses of text, using methods long established in cultural studies by pioneers such as Barthes and Foucault. Two of the above-mentioned cases, Pascale Nédélec on Las Vegas and Philippe Viallon's study of websites examining the uses of multiple languages, combine visual and textual analyses, as does H. Hazel Hahn's discussion of French journal articles on transportation catastrophes (Chapter 15). Though it is not central to our case studies, music is also a key medium for creating and sustaining imaginaries and conveying key messages about tourism and travel. For instance, the appeal of Caribbean culture depends on reggae, jazz, rumba, steel drums, and so on, and the pop music of the 1960–1980s, for example the Beatles, was central to supplying encouraging imaginaries enabling and directing overseas youth travel (Powell 1988).

Other important forms of cultural studies include critical cultural studies,[3] such as Liz Montegary's focus on lesbian and gay family holidays in the United States (Chapter 10), and Orientalism (Said 1978), which is a component of Raghuraman S. Trichur's analysis of postcolonial Goa (Chapter 2) and Alain Girard and Bernard Schéou's finding that, in so-called "Fair tourism" Europeans visiting contemporary West Africa insinuate that rural African people stand outside of time and history (Chapter 7).

Anthropology focuses on culture as an ever-adapting, flexible, collective set of beliefs, ideals, and embodied (learned) habits, among which tourism imaginaries are a growing component; furthermore anthropology arrives at a knowledge and understanding of culture through the method of ethnography, ideally long-term intensive field research and participant observation among the peoples being studied. In our case studies this approach is used not only by anthropologists (Trichur, Regnault, Laverdure, Sabre) but also by sociologist Alain Girard and social economist Bernard Schéou in their West African field research. However, our cases studies go well beyond classical descriptive ethnographies (Malinowski 1922; Dumont 1976) in their focus on the creativity of culture and the emergence and manipulation of tourist imaginaries, for example, Madina Regnault's study of visitors' creation—where previously none existed—of the imaginary of the French off-shore Département of Mayotte (Chapter 6) and Julien Laverdure's discussion of the purposive creation of "ethnic" crafts in Costa Rica by well-meaning intermediaries or cultural entrepreneurs (Chapter 8). These research cases show how anthropology is very capable of adding to our understanding of the contemporary changing, globalizing world, and the recent focus on tourist imaginaries may well be improving and "stretching" anthropology's research methods and analyses.

History consists of narratives (cultural, media, material) and documentation (print, media, archives, mental) that can be both oral history—those narratives carried by people in a community[4]—and written or other forms of communicative media written by someone authorized to set out a narrative for others[5] often in "opposition" to oral history and memory (Nora 1984). Estelle Sohier's account of changes in the twentieth-century Greek tourist imaginary (Chapter 12) and

Hahn's study of French periodical accounts (Chapter 15) rely mainly on written and archival history, whereas Josep-Maria Garcia-Fuentes' examination of the changing meaning of Gaudí sculptures in Barcelona (Chapter 3) uses both official and oral histories. Of course most studies of the development of change, such as Rita Ross's on the complex fictional imaginary of Canadian Acadians (Chapter 5) and Luc Vacher's demonstration of how a chemical innovation enabled photography to depict a particular "turquoise" blue of tropical waters (Chapter 11), rely heavily on recorded (print and visual) history.

Geography is important as a central component of place, distinctive special places, and hence tourist destinations in our studies.[6] But the unique contribution of geography is the conception of such physical imaginaries as the Tropics, central to Luc Vacher's work (Chapter 11), as well the equator, the poles, oceanic currents, and so on, and political imaginaries such as the nation, central to Estelle Sohier's work on Greece (Chapter 12). At least 10 of the chapters in this volume use geographical notions of place and identity to some degree.

Folklore is closely related to anthropology as the study of verbal stories, beliefs, stereotypes, anecdotes and myths which "belong" to define communities. It overlaps extensively with oral history and, as shown above, the modern world of movement and hybridity (Appadurai 1991; Clifford 1997) has enlarged and distorted the concept of a culture-owning community and has multiplied the number and types of channels for the transmission of folklore. Rita Ross's examination (Chapter 5) of a literary folkloric imaginary of the Arcadians of the Canadian Maritimes reveals how agents of the tourism industry and the descendants of the cultural enclave have used the fictional narrative poem *Evangeline: A Tale of Acadia*, by the American poet Henry Wadsworth Longfellow (1847), to build up tourism and to preserve their ethnic identity. Pascale Nédélec's (Chapter 4) examination of the creation of the tourist imaginary of Las Vegas is broadcast through advertising, mass media, and academic publications rather than face-to-face, orally.

Sociology, a discipline whose imaginaries include key ideas such as class, corporation, demographic groupings, friendships, and temporary groups, and whose research methods rely on face-to-face interviews, surveys, social and demographic statistics, and library and archival works, is not central to most or our analyses. However, many of those research cases falling under the rubric of cultural studies, using sociological concepts and many forms of circulated data, could be said to overlap with contemporary sociology. Liz Montegary's study (Chapter 10), for example, focusing on lesbian and gay family holidaymakers in Rhode Island and in relation to commercial and official policies and actions, is heavily sociological (as well drawing on cultural studies). Iris Sheungting Lo and Bob McKercher (Chapter 13) rely on Goffman's notion of performance theory, with individuals playing on-stage roles and working creatively off-stage, a core part of modern sociology which also underlies MacCannell's key works (1973; 1976).

Looking at other disciplines, psychology is a primary discipline in Lo and McKercher's analysis—which draws on Lacan's tripartite development of self—of the strategies of posting tourist photos on social media (Chapter 13), and architecture (and the history of architecture) is of course central to Garcia-Fuentes' delineation of the changing meanings of features of Gaudí's fantasy buildings in Barcelona (Chapter 3). Political science and economics are not, however, primary sources of models for the treatment of imaginaries in spite of Anderson's pioneer work on instruments of modernity and political identity, and also in spite of the key role of economics in such important imaginaries as Marxism or the French Revolution.

Having looked at the role of individual disciplines, we can illuminate the "intersections" where pairs of (or more) disciplines appear together. Again cultural studies is the leader, co-occurring in seven cases. This is to be expected as cultural studies has a legitimate pedigree leading back to political and sociological—even philosophical—analyses, cognate with most of the other social sciences. It often supplies insightful ideational or even ideological frameworks which are supplemented by the in-depth holistic data of anthropology or the spatial scientific facts of geography or the large-scale empirical and quantitative data gathered by sociology. Furthermore, in its contemporary, perhaps less critical form, cultural studies underlies much of the analyses of visual and communicative phenomena so central to tourist imaginaries. In three of our contributions it supplements or works with anthropology: in Chapters 2 and 7 the contribution of Orientalism to the anthropology of colonialism and postcolonial imaginaries, and in Chapter 9, visual/media studies in the anthropological creation of the tourist imagination of Japan.

Textual and visual analyses also work with the closely related discipline of folklore. Visual/media cultural studies[7] also work with geography in Chapter 12 on the development of the Greek nationalist tourist imaginary, and to a lesser extent in Chapter 11 on the Tropics. Visual and discourse cultural analyses combine with geographical identities and imaginaries in Chapter 14 on city websites. Critical cultural studies supplies an important edge to Chapter 10, a sociological discussion of gay vacationers, and to a lesser extent to Chapter 15, an historical analysis of French accounts of transportation disasters. Anthropology, the second most common primary discipline found in the contributions to the volume, quite appropriately uses historical methods and mental constructions in its diachronic analyses.

In summary cross- and multidisciplinary research has gone further in studies of tourist imaginaries than has tourism research in general, as examined by Graburn and Jafari (1990). At that time we noted that "adjacent" disciplines, sharing some concepts, cited and used each other when focusing on similar topics, for example resort life cycles, and that common problem areas in the globalizing world of tourism made this easier by presenting similar problems all over the world, for example the harmful demonstration effect or seasonal labor migration. Our case studies here show that authors using the frameworks and methods of the more "traditional" disciplines are no longer afraid to draw upon the more specialized yet, perhaps, less closely researched segments of the "umbrella" that is cultural studies with its very insightful focus on verbal and visual (and oral) communications and its legacy of critical attention to power gradients and exploitation. Globalization has indeed produced massive homogenization in spite of the backlash of nostalgia and heritage studies, which are also global phenomena and major contributors to tourist imaginaries. Truly marginal socio-cultural situations are much more rare and the near universality of cross-cultural mediascapes (Appadurai 1996) will continue to bring research methods and analytical frameworks and strategies to the crossroads of disciplines.

Notes

1 Anthropology (five authors), geography (three), sociology (two), and architecture, communications and media studies, cultural studies, economics, folklore, history, tourism studies (one each).
2 Cultural studies is a prime approach in nine cases, followed by anthropology (six), history (four), geography (three), folklore (two) and political sciences, psychology, and architecture (one each).
3 Prominently concerned with power relations and exploitation, for example class, gender, disabilities, LGBT studies (see Butler 1990), and New Social Movements (Escobar and Alvarez 1992).
4 A community could be a village of neighbors but today it may consist of a work group, members of an organization, an urban region, the readership of a journal, viewers of TV shows or films, or participants in social media.
5 The line between "official historians" and self-appointed raconteurs, for example bloggers, has been blurred by the many features of the Internet, especially for tourist accounts and imaginaries (see Dann 2007).
6 Not all places are "equally unique." Tourist imaginaries exist for atolls, tropical beaches, ski resorts, wildlife reserves, many of which are in competition and interchangeable in the minds of tourists and hence for the industry. The competition will then depend on price, accessibility, cultural affiliation (language, nationality), and so on.
7 This awkward name might be reduced to "visual studies," which became a PhD Program within the academic department Visual Culture/History of Art at the University of California, Santa Cruz in 1999, closely related to the departments of History of Consciousness and of Anthropology.

Bibliography

Appadurai, A. (1991) "Global ethnoscapes: notes and queries for a transnational anthropology," in Richard G. Fox (ed.) *Recapturing Anthropology: Working in the Present*. Santa Fe, NM: School of American Research Press, pp. 191–210.
—— (1996) *Modernity at Large: Cultural Dimensions of Globalization*. Minneapolis, MN: University of Minnesota Press.
Butler, Judith (1990) *Gender Trouble: Feminism and the Subversion of Identity*. New York: Routledge.
Clifford, James (1997) *Routes: Travel and Translation in the Late Twentieth Century*. Cambridge, MA: Harvard University Press.
Dann, Graham (2007) "From travelogue to travelblog: (re)negotiating tourist identity." *Acta Turistica* 19(1): 7–29.
Dumont, Jean-Paul (1976) *Under the Rainbow: Nature and Supernature among the Panare Indians*. Austin, TX: University of Texas Press.
Escobar, Arturo and Sonia Alvarez (eds) (1992) *The Making of Social Movements in Latin America: Identity, Strategy, and Democracy*. Boulder, CO: Westview Press.

Graburn, Nelson and Jafar Jafari (1990) "Tourism social sciences: introduction." *Tourism Social Sciences*, Special issue of *Annals of Tourism Research* 19(1): 1–11.

Longfellow, Henry Wadsworth ([1847] 1951) *Evangeline, a tale of Acadie*, Halifax: Nimbus.

MacCannell, Dean (1973) "Staged authenticity: arrangements of social space in tourist settings." *American Journal of Sociology* 79(3): 589–603.

—— (1976) *The Tourist: A New Theory of the Leisure Class*. New York: Schocken.

Malinowski, Bronisław (1922) *Argonauts of the Western Pacific: An Account of Native Enterprise and Adventure in the Archipelagoes*. London: E.P. Dutton.

Nora, Pierre (ed.) (1984) *Les lieux de mémoires*. Paris: Gallimard.

Powell, Alison (1988) "Like a Rolling Stone: notions of youth travel and tourism in pop music of the sixties, seventies, and eighties." *Anthropological Research on Contemporary Tourism: Student Papers from Berkeley*, Special issue of *Kroeber Anthropological Society Papers*, 78–79.

Said, Edward (1978) *Orientalism*. New York: Pantheon.

Index